EASTERN ISLANDS

Accessible Islands of the East Coast

David Laskin

Facts On File
New York • Oxford • Sydney

Eastern Islands: Accessible Islands of the East Coast

Facts On File, Inc.
460 Park Avenue South
New York NY 10016
USA

Facts On File Limited
Collins Street
Oxford OX4 1XJ
United Kingdom

Facts On File Pty Ltd
Talavera & Khartoum Rds
North Ryde NSW 2113
Australia

Library of Congress Cataloging-in-Publication Data

Laskin, David, 1953-
  Eastern islands: accessible islands of the East Coast
David Laskin.
    p. cm.
  Includes bibliographical references.
  ISBN 0-8160-1799-9
    1. Atlantic coast (US)—Description and travel. 2. Islands—
Atlantic Coast (U.S.)—Description and travel.   I. Title.
F106.L24 1990
917-404'43'09142—dc20   89-39390

British and Australian CIP data available on request from Facts On File.

Facts On File books are available at special discounts when purchased in bulk quantities for businesses, associations, institutions or sales promotion. Please contact the Special Sales Department of our New York office at 212/683-2244 (dial 800/322- 8755 except in NY, AK or HI).

Text design by Ron Monteleone
Jacket design by Levavi & Levavi
Composition by Facts On File, Inc.
Manufactured by R.R. Donnelley & Sons
Printed in the United States of America

10 9 8 7 6 5 4 3 2 1

This book is printed on acid-free paper.

TABLE OF CONTENTS

DEDICATION

To the memory of my grandmother,
Gladys Cohen Etra,
whose love of travel inspired my own

ACKNOWLEDGMENTS

My first and biggest debt of gratitude goes to all the islanders, island-lovers and members of various organizations who shared their knowledge, stories, memories, opinions, books and photographs with me. In particular I'd like to thank:

In Maine: On the Cranberry Isles, Louise Strandberg on Great Cranberry and Irene Bartlett on Little Cranberry. On Swans Island, Myron Sprague Jr., first selectman, Gwen May, tax collector, Alberta Buswell and Maili Bailey. On Frenchboro, Vivian Lunt. On Isle au Haut, Jeff and Judy Burke. On Vinalhaven, Roy Heisler of the Vinalhaven Historical Society, Henry Gross, Joel Morton, Gerry Dowdy, manager of the Vinalhaven Fisherman's Cooperative, and Spencer Fuller, plant manager with Penobscot Bay Fish and Cold Storage. On North Haven, Jerry T. White, school principal, and Lewis Haskell. On Islesboro, Scot Seabury, town manager, and Kay Gray. On Matinicus, Gladys and Nan Mitchell, Richard Moody, Emory Philbrook. On Monhegan, Willard J. Boynton, first assessor. Gretchen Hall on Peaks Island. Mrs. William Swann and Jean Dyer on Chebeague Island. Johanna von Tiling on Cliff Island. Louise Bennett on Long Island. Irving Fisher on Great Diamond Island. At the Island Institute: Philip Conkling, director, and Julie Levett, project director/Islands School Project.

In the southern New England states: On the Boston Harbor Islands, Greg Chanis with the Metropolitan District Commission and Ellenor Yahrmarkt with the Department of Environmental Management. On Nantucket, Gayl Michael, assistant curator of research materials at the Nantucket Historical Association, Pat Butler of the Historic District Commission, Roger Young, C. Marshall Beal of the Nantucket Conservation Foundation and Dorothy Bartlett. On Martha's Vineyard, Martha Vanderhoop, Charles Vanderhoop, Brendan O'Neill, executive director of the Vineyard Conservation Society, Ann Allen of the Dukes Country Historical Society and John Hough. Ginger Cooper on Cuttyhunk. William and Natalie Bacon on Prudence Island. On Block Island: Pam Littlefield of the Block Island Historical Society, Barbara Burak of the Planning Board and Constance LaRue of the Chamber of Commerce.

In New York state: On Liberty Island, Diana Pardue, chief of the Museum Services Division. On Shelter Island, Dr. Alex Garcia, Sonny Edwards, Michael Laspia, refuge manage of the Mashomack Preserve, Vera and William Anderson, Louise Green of the Shelter Island Historical Society, Gregory Price, Kathleen and Lawrence O'Neill. On Fire Island, Donald Weir with the National Park Service and Robert Abrams with the Great Neck Public Schools. On Fishers Island, Ray Edwards.

In the mid-Atlantic states: Edward Jones, Elmer L. Evans, and Tom Horton on Smith Island. Frankie Pruitt on Tangier Island. Barry Truitt, manager of the Virginia Coast Reserve.

On the Outer Banks: Dorri O'Neil, with the Dare County Tourist Bureau; Bebe Woody and Marcia Lyons, with the Cape Hatteras National Seashore. On Ocracoke, Phil Howard of the Village Craftsmen Store and Henry Ballance. On the Cape Lookout National Seashore, Bob Patton, interpretive specialist, and Chuck Harris, chief of park operations.

On the Sea Islands of South Carolina and Georgia: George Garris, refuge manager of the Cape Romain National Wildlife Refuge. Betsy Stevens at the Fort Sumter

National Monument. Cornelia Bailey on Sapelo. Buddy Sullivan, with the *Darien News*, for help with Sapelo. On Daufuskie, Billie Burn and Lillie Simmons. On Cumberland, Ken Morgan, superintendent of the Cumberland Island National Seashore.

On the Florida Keys: On Indian Key and Lignumvitae Key, Jeanne Parks and Melba Nezbed, park rangers of the Florida Department of Natural Resources. On Key West, Wright Langley, director of the Historic Florida Keys Preservation Board, and Sylvia Knight, with the Monroe County Library.

In addition, I owe a huge debt of gratitude to Felice Nudelman for her exceptional generosity with her time and talent in contributing her photographs to this book.

Staff members of the National Park Service, some mentioned by name above, were a tremendous help in my research on islands that are parts of National Seashores or National Monuments. I'd like to thank them all for their kindness and courtesy.

I want to mention my friends Karen Pennar and Phil Patton for passing along books, maps and information, and Joyce Hartsfield, Regis Obijiski, Paul Farrell and Sue Bryson for sharing their impressions of various islands.

I'd like to thank John Thornton and Doug Schulkind for signing the book up and my editor Deborah Brody for seeing it through.

And last, but by no means least, I'd like to thank my wife, Kathleen O'Neill, for her companionship (and fortitude) on island journeys, for her shrewd comments and her patience in the last, long haul; and our daughters Emily, Sarah and Alice for being such delightful traveling companions.

INTRODUCTION

What is it about a piece of land surrounded by water that appeals so deeply to the human spirit? Go down to the shore and gaze at an island rising from the sea, and you will feel its tug. The allure of its separateness. The promise of escape from the ordinary ticking by of time. The beckoning to cross the water and take up life anew—*out there*. An island is a world shrunk down to a size that makes sense, a realm one can wholly possess and easily defend. Islands preserve a sense of innocence and mystery on an increasingly cramped and bulldozed planet. The very confinement of space on an island is paradoxically liberating: Here, isolated from the common mainland world, you are as free as the eternal elements that surround you.

The allure of islands runs deep in the mythology and literature of Western culture. The ancient Greeks believed that at the end of the world chosen spirits lived in perpetual ease and beauty on the Isles of the Blessed. In Celtic mythology Avalon was the mystical island in the western sea to which King Arthur was taken after death. Sir Thomas More situated his *Utopia* (1516) on an imaginary island. The island setting of Shakespeare's *Tempest* (1611) (thought by some to be drawn from descriptions of Cuttyhunk off the coast of Cape Cod) heightens the power of magic to bewilder and transform. In our imaginations, all islands retain a shred of this magical radiance. Islands are still the location of paradise, even if our idea of paradise is now a vacation that costs a fortune and lasts a week.

Here in America, paradise is near at hand—much nearer than many of us realize. Just off the East Coast, from Maine to Florida, lies one of the world's most impressive collections of islands. Unrivaled in the United States for abundance and variety, these Eastern islands shade from the rocky outcrops off the coast of Maine to the long, narrow barrier islands that parallel the mainland from New York to Virginia; from the vast seaward arc of North Carolina's Outer Banks to the fertile, low-lying Sea Islands of South Carolina and Georgia; from the citrus-bearing islands of central Florida to the brilliant coralline chain of the Florida Keys. Our Eastern islands support cities and wilderness, spruce forests and palmetto groves, puffins and alligators, the Statue of Liberty and the resorts of the leisured rich, forts and sea bird rookeries, Yankee lobstermen and black shrimpers descended from slaves, celebrity writers and struggling farmers, families who have been in possession since Colonial times and families who have moved out yesterday. There are islands on which bustling ports have turned into ghost towns and islands on which ghost towns have come to life again as tourist centers. There are new islands created as storms breach the land and old islands that are sinking beneath the rising sea.

In every state and along every section of the East Coast, there are islands that are remarkable for their beauty—the beauty of Martha's Vineyard's rolling hills, Cumberland's live oak forests, Monhegan's cliffs, Fire Island's barrier beach, Sapelo's salt marsh. Although these Eastern islands have been discovered repeatedly by explorers, fishermen, vacationers, military engineers, many of them retain the old-fashioned charm of places passed over by time. On Prudence Island in Narragansett Bay, on Peddock's Island in Boston Harbor, on Indian Key in Florida, you can see civilization looming across the water with its skyscrapers, highways and motels, but you are blessedly set apart from it. Even in the shadow of major cities, many of the Eastern islands are silent, empty, pristine.

Geography has assigned the Eastern islands a place in history out of all proportion to their size. To the explorers who sailed across the Atlantic from Spain, England, France and Italy in the 16th and 17th centuries, the islands were the first landfall of the New World, and here they planted the first colonies and trading posts. Tiny, obscure Cuttyhunk was the site of the first, failed English settlement in New England in 1602. Roanoke Island in North Carolina had an even earlier English settlement, the famous Lost Colony sponsored by Sir Walter Raleigh in 1587 that disappeared without a trace. Norse mariners may have visited Monhegan in Maine in the 11th century, and European fisherman surely knew and used the island well before the Pilgrims landed at Plymouth Rock. The Isles of Shoals off New Hampshire and southern Maine had a fishing and trading community that was larger and more important that Boston in the mid-17th century.

It may seem strange today that our forefathers chose these inconvenient specks of land for their first North American homes—but we must remember that an island could be defended much more easily than a mainland settlement, that an offshore location was an advantage in an age when the sea was the highway and the mainland was covered by a vast, seemingly impenetrable forest. The islands, though in many cases abandoned as settlements, remained important as forts. Portland, Boston, New York, Charleston, Key West—all have been guarded for much of their history by forts built on their harbor islands.

Having received the first wave of European settlements and suffered the first rounds of European conflict in the New World, the Eastern islands slipped rather quickly from prominence as the centers of power and population moved to the mainland. The American Revolution took a serious toll on many of the Eastern island settlements, but after the war ended, the islanders were left alone to farm the land and fish the vast ocean. Islands that showed early signs of greatness drifted into oblivion. Islanders lost touch with the mainstream of American society. Their culture, their accents, their customs and practices remained frozen in time or, if they developed, they diverged markedly from practices of the mainland. Nantucket Quakers, bound together by family ties and by their odd religion, made their gray-shingled island town the capital of a whaling empire that encompassed "the watery world," in Melville's phrase. The black slaves of the South Carolina and Georgia Sea Islands, imported by the thousands from West Africa to work the indigo and cotton plantations, evolved a culture and language distinct not only from that of their white owners but also from that of black slaves in other, less isolated regions. On Smith and Tangier Islands in Chesapeake Bay and on Ocracoke Island in North Carolina's Outer Banks, the isolated white settlers retained the accents and some of the diction that their ancestors brought over from 17th-century England. Isolation has inevitably given rise to inbreeding on some of the Eastern islands; medical researchers have identified an abnormality of the fatty tissue among Tangier Islanders and a much higher incidence of diabetes than the national average among the old stock of Maine's Vinalhaven.

Isolation, for good or ill, has carried the Eastern islands from the past into the present—but it is doubtful whether that isolation will continue into the future. The islands today have entered another age of discovery, this time by tourists, vacationers and second-home owners. All of a sudden, Americans have gone mad for these quaint little worlds that slumbered so peacefully for centuries just offshore of the Eastern corridor. Here is escape from our dull, drab, congested highway culture; here are fishing villages where boats outnumber cars, landscapes free of shopping centers and motels, beaches unspoiled by parking lots and high-rise condos. The more the islands differ from our mainland, the more we love them; and the more we love them, the more we are making them over in the image of the mainland we were seeking to escape.

The magnitude and the pace of development on many Eastern islands is truly alarming. In the six years from 1980 to 1986, the summertime population of Martha's Vineyard jumped from 55,313 to 94,708; fishermen's houses on Swans Island, Maine, that sold for $3,500 in the early 1960s now go on the market at $100,000; South Carolina's Daufuskie Island, until 1980 the home of a small community of Sea Island blacks, has suddenly sprouted sleek and expensive "residential country clubs" similar to those on neighboring Hilton Head Island. The Conchs (native residents of the Florida Keys) are complaining that they can't afford to buy a house on the islands or pay the taxes if they already own one, and you hear the exact same thing from the Sea Islanders, the Maine lobstermen, the natives of Martha's Vineyard and Nantucket. Our enthusiasm for vacationing on the Eastern islands is not only transforming the once-rural landscapes and crowding up the working harbors with pleasure craft, but also forcing out the island communities. It is yet another sad case of people killing the thing they love.

The tidal wave of development hasn't hit all the islands yet, and some islands have been providently snatched from its reach. The federal government protects a number of important Eastern islands as National Seashores, including Cumberland, Fire Island, Ocracoke and the Core Banks, and other islands have been set aside as wildlife refuges, state nature sanctuaries or parkland. Still other islands are guarded by the wealth of their private owners. The rich have long prized the seclusion and intrinsic exclusiveness of islands, and they have made a number of Eastern islands into their private vacation retreats.

Numerous as they are, the Eastern islands are a precious and fragile resource—just how fragile we are only now beginning to learn. Already development has threatened the existence of some of the animal species that depend on the islands for habitat and nesting grounds, including Atlantic loggerhead turtles, piping plovers, brown pelicans, roseate spoonbills and manatees. On barrier islands, oceanfront building has imperiled the very existence of the islands by flattening the protective dune system. The human communities of the islands are just as fragile and just as imperiled as the plants and animals and landforms—but even more difficult to protect. The islands in the late 20th century may well be undergoing a population shift comparable to the displacement of the Indians by European settlers in the 17th and 18th centuries.

Bridged versus Unbridged Islands

Eastern Islands is organized geographically, from north to south, with a separate entry for every Atlantic East Coast island (or island group) that has no bridge to the mainland and that the public can travel to by regularly scheduled ferry. For reasons of space, however, a number of unbridged islands, including Maine's North Haven and Islesboro and New York's Fishers Island were omitted: Though visitors *may* make the crossing, most islanders and summer folk would prefer they didn't. The bridged islands—and there are some awfully impressive ones, including Maine's Mount Desert, New York's Manhattan and Long Island, South Carolina's Hilton Head, Florida's Miami Beach—are treated much more briefly in the regional introductions. (The one exception to this rule is Key West, an island linked to mainland Florida by the 106 miles and 42 bridges of the Overseas Highway. Key West, at the end of the road, *feels* more like an island out at sea than Miami Beach or Absecon, site of New Jersey's Atlantic City. And anyway, its history, literature and general atmosphere are so compelling it seemed a shame to pass it over.)

The decision to relegate bridged islands to the status of second-class citizens may strike some readers as arbitrary—but in fact, as all island dwellers know and travelers quickly learn, an island connected to the mainland by bridge or causeway has ceased in some fundamental way to be an island. A bridge breaches the isolation that is at the very heart of an island's uniqueness. It reduces the surrounding water from treacherous element to scenery. It annexes the island both physically and spiritually to the mainland.

Of course, again as islanders know all too well and travelers discover sometimes at their peril, the lack of a bridge has its drawbacks. Ferries are a charming and quaint way of arriving at and departing from an island, except when you're stuck in your car for hours (or days) waiting in a ferry line, or when you've broken your leg on the island and need immediate medical attention, or when the wind is howling out of the northeast and you don't have your sea legs. Depending on your circumstances, the sight of the last ferry of the day pulling away from the island dock can fill you with bliss or horror.

Life without bridges does funny things to islanders. Notorious for their clannishness and pride, their distrust of outsiders and their extreme devotion to their privacy and independence, islanders also make the best of neighbors. Islanders are self-reliant because they have to be, but when self-reliance is not enough—when the well runs dry, the baby gets sick, the fishing boat breaks up in a storm—islanders are *there* for each other, and for their seasonal visitors too. I discovered these facts of island life myself when my car got stuck in the mud on Vinalhaven, Maine: The man at the towing service on the mainland laughed when I telephoned for help (it would mean killing an entire day, or more, on the ferry line), but my island neighbors, whom I'd never met before, called around until they found someone who could tow me out. Islanders on all the Eastern islands showed the same generous spirit in sharing with me their time, their stories, their photographs, their memories.

Islanders, I learned, are obsessed with their status as islanders. "You're not an islander unless you were born here and your parents were born here," they told me on Nantucket. "Once an islander, always an islander," they said on Swans Island. "We stick together—we're all one big family," they said on Smith Island. "Even if you've married an islander, even if you've lived here for 50 years, you're still considered a stranger" they insisted on Key West. Islanders often joke about seceding—and there is a kernel of seriousness inside the humor. They are islanders first and Americans second. When the summer crowds go home and the ocean turns gray and rough, America might as well be the moon. A couple of miles of unspanned salt waters makes a difference that only an islander can truly fathom.

INTRODUCTION

Eastern Islands considers the changes of the present in the context of the past, not only the human past, but the far more ancient past of the elemental forces—the glaciers, the winds and tides, the ceaseless pounding of the ocean on the land—that created the islands. The book recounts the history of the islands' discovery and settlement, explores their geology, resources and natural features, and discusses their distinctive wildlife, particularly the astonishing variety of birds that dwell on the islands and stop off on their twice yearly migrations. *Eastern Islands* also takes a look at what man has created on the islands—the villages he has built, the industries he has pursued and abandoned, the monuments he has erected, the cultures he has evolved. It documents the shifts in the islands' populations and economies, the peculiar institutions that islanders have developed to make their offshore lives feasible, and the attempts that are being made to preserve both the island communities and the resources they depend on.

Eastern Islands is above all a book of information. Collected here are facts about the islands' areas and residents, schools and governments, beaches and churches, parks and architecture, zoning and cooking, waste disposal and resource management. It is a book for travelers and armchair travelers, for those who live on (or near) the islands and for those who have glimpsed them from the shore, from the deck of a boat, from an airplane, and have wondered what they are like. *Eastern Islands* is not a tourist guidebook, since it does not contain listings of hotels or restaurants, but tourists can certainly use it in planning their trips, researching their destinations and remembering the sights they saw.

Though I have reported the facts about the Eastern islands as accurately as I could, I do have my prejudices, and these have inevitably influenced how I report the facts. To me, the most interesting islands are the ones on which the native communities remain most in control—the islands that are most insular. Thus I have given more attention to Maine's Matinicus and Smith Island in Chesapeake Bay, where small communities of fishermen and their families are struggling to hold on to their traditional way of life, than to islands that have become primarily summer resorts, such as Shelter Island in New York state or Block Island off the coast of Rhode Island.

The works of literature that have been written on or about the islands also have swayed me, as I'm sure they sway all readers who visit the islands. Melville's thundering description of Nantucket in *Moby Dick* rang in my ears when I visited the island and became part of my experience of the place. Similarly, Emma Lazarus's poem "The New Colossus" has become part of the way we perceive the Statue of Liberty, part of the statue's symbolic meaning. Wallace Stevens's "The Idea of Order at Key West" sets before us one very vivid image of that tropical island city—"bronze shadows heaped/On high horizons, mountainous atmospheres/Of sky and sea ..." And Hemingway's *To Have and Have Not* conjures up an entirely different image of Key West—bar fights, rum-running, fishing and death. These poems and novels were not intended as travel writing. But even more than travel books, they make us see and feel the islands in ways we could not have imagined by ourselves. The Eastern islands have a rich literary tradition that began with the journals and logs of the first European explorers and that continues today in the works of the many writers who live or vacation on the islands.

Finally, the beauty of certain islands has moved me to linger over them. The grinding of the sea on the cobble beaches of Maine's Isle au Haut, the great sweeping sand bars off the west end of Nantucket, the green-gold salt marsh fanning out around Smith Island, the immense flocks of waterfowl on Bulls Island, the flickering virgin forest of Lignumvitae Key in Florida—these are scenes that I feel lucky to have visited, that I relished to recall when writing about them, and to which I hope to return.

The beauty of the islands is something we experience both in space and time. As we ferry across the water, we feel ourselves slipping away and slipping back—away from the continent and back into the past. These bits of offshore land really are worlds apart, worlds of silence and slow time where the elements still govern the lives of men. To their visitors, the islands grant escape and respite from the ordinariness of mainland life; to the islanders, they afford the freedom to carry on the traditions of their ancestors. Of course, the remoteness that we all feel on the islands is to some extend illusory, dwelling as much in our imaginations as the works of literature we read—for even without bridges the islands are linked to the mainland by planes, phone, television, laws, money. But even the illusion of separateness is precious. My hope is that *Eastern Islands* will lead readers to appreciate the preciousness of the islands, real and imagined, and help them to preserve it.

(Courtesy of Joel Greenberg)

Islands of the Northeastern Seaboard

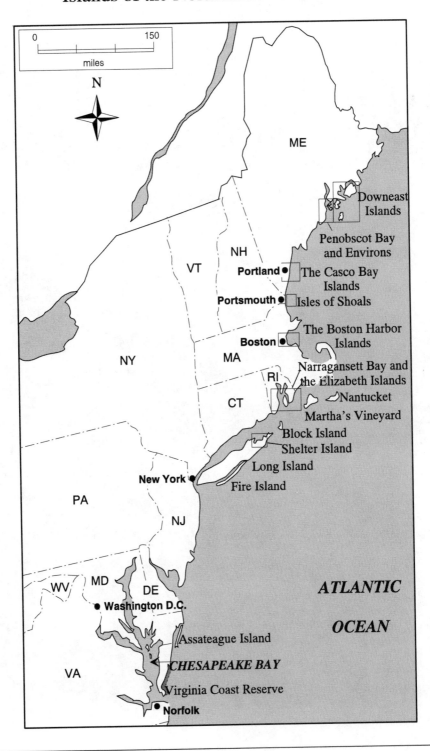

Islands of the Southeastern Seaboard

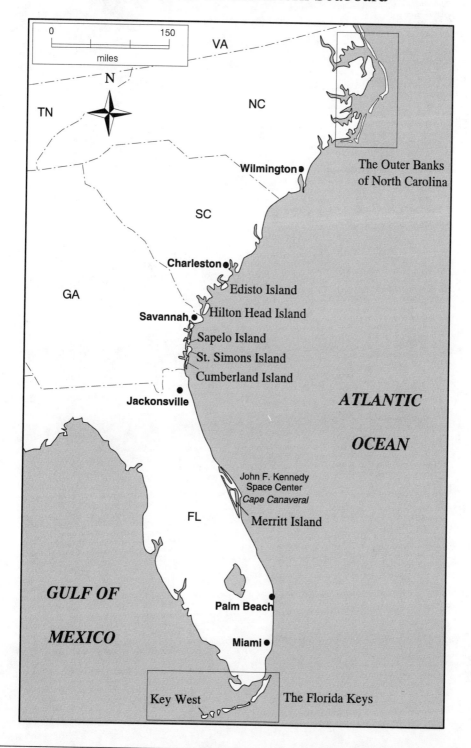

0   150
miles

N

VA

TN

NC

Wilmington ●

The Outer Banks
of North Carolina

SC

GA

Charleston ●

Edisto Island

Hilton Head Island

Savannah ●

Sapelo Island

St. Simons Island

Cumberland Island

● Jackonsville

ATLANTIC

OCEAN

John F. Kennedy
Space Center
Cape Canaveral

FL

Merritt Island

GULF OF

MEXICO

Palm Beach ●

Miami ●

Key West

The Florida Keys

THE ISLANDS OF MAINE

INTRODUCTION

From just about any point along the famous rockbound coast, you are likely to see them. Islands punctuating the horizon line like long, blue beads. Island groups that march like stepping stones across the jagged-edge bays. Distant islands that rear their backs from the sea like great green whales. Islands that line up in vast parallel ranks, like ships at anchor in a steady wind. Islands that seem to grow out of or merge with other islands, so that from shore the prospect is an immensely complicated pattern of arms of land and sea embracing. The islands of Maine are almost too numerous to count. The best we can do is estimate their number at around 3,600, far more than any other East Coast state—unless, perhaps, one counts the mangrove islands of the Florida Everglades, but these are not really *terra firma* as the hard, fast Maine islands are. Together, the Maine islands comprise some 200,000 acres of land and some 1,500 miles of coastline. Islands are such a dominant feature of the Maine coast, that the state's name itself originated to distinguish the mainland—the main—from the offshore islands.

Unlike the East Coast states from New York south, Maine does not feature barrier islands, those narrow strips of sand backed by saltmarsh that unwind like ribbons just a few miles from the mainland. Rather, most Maine islands look like chunks of the mainland that were pried loose and hurled helter-skelter out to sea. In fact, the islands *were* once part of the mainland: These granite hills of the ancient coastal plain became islands when the last glacier melted some 12,000 to 14,000 years ago. It is likely that the swollen ocean waters covered nearly all the islands, and that they emerged only when the land recovered from the crushing weight of glacial ice over a period of several thousand years. Geologists call Maine a "drowned coastline" and the islands are the survivors, the hilltops that have managed to thrust their heads above water.

The Maine islanders—the native inhabitants of these offshore hilltops—are also survivors. There are 14 permanent, year-round communities on the 3,600 Maine islands, and the core populations of all of these communities are the descendants of settlers who came out to the islands in the late 18th and early 19th centuries. In their 200-odd years on the islands, these families have farmed and fished for a living—catching cod, haddock, mackerel, herring and, of course, lobster as the market and the numbers of fish have dictated. Granite quarrying was a major industry on Vinalhaven from the mid-19th century until the early 20th century, and there also were quarries on Hurricane Island, Swans Island, Deer Isle and some of the smaller islands off Deer Isle. But the granite industry is largely a thing of the past, and so is farming. For the core communities of the islands, fishing—mostly lobster fishing—remains.

It has never been easy to live off these stern, rocky islands or to harvest these northern waters that are too cold for swimming even on the hottest summer days, but you seldom hear a Maine islander complain about the islands or the sea or the hardships of isolation. Rather, what they're talking about and complaining about nowadays is the hardship attending the *end* of their isolation. Change is coming to the islands of Maine—more vacationers, more second home owners, more tourists and day-trippers—and change has the islanders on the run. Land on Swans Island has already been priced out of the reach of island fishermen, and they're worrying about the same thing on the Cranberries, on Vinalhaven and Monhegan. On Frenchboro and Matinicus, the year-round communities have dwindled down so low there is concern that they might vanish altogether, leaving the islands entirely in the hands of the summer folk. Peaks Island in Casco Bay is little more than a suburb of Portland, to which island workers commute each day by ferry. On North Haven and Islesboro the islanders have all but given up fishing: There is more than enough work for the natives in caring for the rich summer folk who own most of the land and who are staying on well beyond summer.

This is not the first time that the Maine islanders have seen their off-shore outposts invaded by seasonal residents and visitors. Seaside vacations became all the rage in this country after the Civil War, and from then until the First World War, thousands of well-heeled city dwellers descended on the Maine islands and coastal villages during the summer. Several of the Casco Bay islands sprouted boarding houses and amusement parks for Portland pleasure-seekers. Associations of socially prominent business and professional people bought up large sections of North Haven, Islesboro and Isle au Haut for their summer retreats. Artists came out to paint the rugged splendors of Monhegan, many bought or built cottages and several moved permanently to the island. After the resort boom subsided, some of the islands returned to their previous obscurity; but on North Haven, Islesboro and Isle au Haut the summer colonies proved to be permanent institutions that have transformed the characters of the islands. Monhegan's artists have also endured for well over a hundred years and have become an essential part of that island's life and character.

The current generation of Maine islanders are complaining about the threats to their way of life, but they're not just complaining. On many islands the residents are taking matters into their own hands and trying to solve their problems. Frenchboro made national headlines when it invited "homesteaders" to join the shrinking year-round community. The Swans Island lobstermen have imposed a trap limit on themselves to try to preserve the lobster fishery. Monhegan islanders have protected a good deal of their island from any sort of development. The Maine islanders are also lucky to have the Island Institute, a nonprofit organization dedicated to the preservation of the islanders' resources, culture and institutions. The Island Institute has helped Frenchboro develop its affordable housing project, Vinalhaven to preserve its working waterfront, Islesboro to study its water supply, along with many other projects. The institute's Island Schools Project is helping the 14 island schools find teachers, prepare students for the adjustments to mainland high schools (only three island schools offer instruction beyond the eighth grade) and share ideas, resources and curricula. Seven of the islands have one-room schoolhouses, and the Island Schools Project is helping island teachers and parents deal with the special challenges of this situation. The schools are the lifeline of the smaller, year-round island communities, for without them it would be impossible for young families to remain. Despite the tax burden of running a one-room schoolhouse for four or five students, islanders are committed to keeping their schools going, and the Island Institute is committed to helping them.

The inconvenience of being out to sea and the vagaries of ferry travel have helped the unbridged Maine islands resist development; the bridged islands, predictably, are easier targets. The most famous of the bridged Maine islands is Mount Desert, the site of Acadia National Park, which attracted some 4.5 million visitors in 1988. (By contrast, unbridged Isle au Haut, which contains another section of Acadia National Park, had only about 4,000 visitors arrive by ferry during the same period.) Geologically and scenically, Mount Desert is one of the most spectacular islands on the East Coast, but the crowds and traffic jams of summer can make the natural wonders difficult to enjoy. Back before the National Park lured tourists here, Mount Desert had one of Maine's first (and wealthiest) summer colonies at Bar Harbor, and the summer rich donated much of the land for the National Park.

Deer Isle and Little Deer Isle, a jump west of Mount Desert, are also bridged to the mainland across Eggemoggin Reach. These two islands, though increasingly popular with summer folk, retain much of the rustic "downeast" charm (and calm) that Mount Desert has lost. Stonington at the southern tip of Deer Isle has the gritty atmosphere of a real working town (in the summer lots of artists and craftspeople work alongside the fishermen). Stonington is the point of departure for Isle au Haut.

A number of other Maine islands not covered in the entries below merit notice. Hurricane Island, which like neighboring Vinalhaven was extensively quarried for granite in the late 19th and early 20th centuries, has been the site of the Hurricane Island Outward Bound School since 1948. Those who have their own boats are welcome to visit. For more information, write the Hurricane Island Outward Bound School, P.O. Box 429, Rockland, Maine 04841; outside of Maine call toll-free at 800-341-1744. The Nature Conservancy owns the very lovely Damariscove Island south of Boothbay Harbor, and there are occasional field trips out here. For more information, contact The Nature Conservancy, Maine Chapter, 20 Federal Street, Brunswick, Maine 04011.

Those who have their own boats might want to contact the Maine Department of Conservation for a copy of a free pamphlet about visiting some of the hundreds of small islands owned by the state of Maine. The pamphlet entitled "Your Islands on the Coast" lists 42 islands, from Cobscook Bay in the far northeast down to Casco Bay, that boat owners can reach easily. Write to the Bureau of Public Lands, Maine Department of Conservation, Station 22, Augusta, Maine 04333, or call 207-289-3061.

In the entries below I have omitted four islands—North Haven and Islesboro in Penobscot Bay, Bustins Island in Casco Bay and Squirrel Island off Boothbay Harbor—that are accessible by public ferry but that are privately owned and offer little for the uninvited visitor or day-tripper to do.

North Haven, the sister island of Vinalhaven just across the Fox Islands Thorofare, harbors a year-round community of some 400 carpenters, contractors, boat-builders and fishermen, and 900 additional, very wealthy, blue-blooded "rusticators" in the summer. There is an inn at Pulpit Harbor, one of the finest deepwater harbors in Maine, splendid views of the Camden hills to the west and quiet roads winding past the compounds and cottages of the wealthy. An important archaeological site on North Haven has yielded the earliest Indian artifacts yet discovered on the Gulf of Maine. The islanders were renowned in the 19th century for their skill as boat-builders, and the tradition continues today at Brown's Boatyard. The island's school, with some 66 students, runs from kindergarten to 12th grade. The Maine State Ferry Service (207-594-5543) provides access via car and passenger service from Rockland.

Islesboro, like North Haven, is largely owned by old, wealthy families who have been coming for generations to vacation at their large estates overlooking the bay. In recent years, more and more day-trippers have been coming out to bicycle on the scenic narrow roads, but the islanders and summer folk wish they wouldn't. As on other wealthy summer islands, the indigenous community is dwindling, and the summer folk and year-round retirees are having a hard time finding people to tend the dump and plow the roads. About 550 people live on the island all year, and on peak summer weekends as many as 2,500 people may be vacationing and day-tripping on Islesboro. The 6,000-acre island is 11 miles long with 50 miles of shoreline. There is no real village and few public amenities, but the Dark Harbor area, where many of the big summer compounds are located, has a couple of very nice inns. The Sailor's Memorial Museum at the Grindle Point lighthouse has exhibits of local artifacts and maritime history. The Maine State Ferry Service (207-789-5611) runs frequent car and passenger ferry service from Lincolnville Beach, only three miles across the bay near the popular resort of Camden.

Squirrel Island claims to be the oldest summer colony in Maine, and the island has been owned by an association of summer people since 1870. The Victorian-style cottages, many of them held by the same families for generations, are linked by networks of little paths. For information about the passenger ferry from Boothbay Harbor, call 207-633-2284.

Bustins Island, accessible by passenger boat from Harraseeket Harbor (near South Freeport), harbors a summer colony of rugged individualists who have chosen to make do without telephones, electricity, stores, restaurants or hotels. For those who own its cottages, Bustins Island preserves the real, old-fashioned Maine island experience.

THE CRANBERRY ISLES

GREAT CRANBERRY

Area: 490 acres.

Population: 90 year-round, about 300 in peak summer season.

Location: At the entrance to Mount Desert Island's Somes Sound, 1.75 miles south of Northeast Harbor.

Access: By passenger ferry by Beal & Bunker (207-244-3575) from Northeast Harbor on Mount Desert Island.

LITTLE CRANBERRY (Islesford)

Area: 350 acres.

Population: 90 year-round, about 300 in peak summer season.

Location: At the entrance to Mount Desert Island's Somes Sound, 2.5 miles south of Northeast Harbor.

Access: By passenger ferry by Beal & Bunker (207-244-3575) from Northeast Harbor on Mount Desert Island and in summer by the Islesford Ferry Company (207-276-3717).

The village of Islesford on Little Cranberry Island in the early 20th century. Mount Desert Island rises across the water. (Courtesy of Irene M. Bartlett.)

Downeast Islands

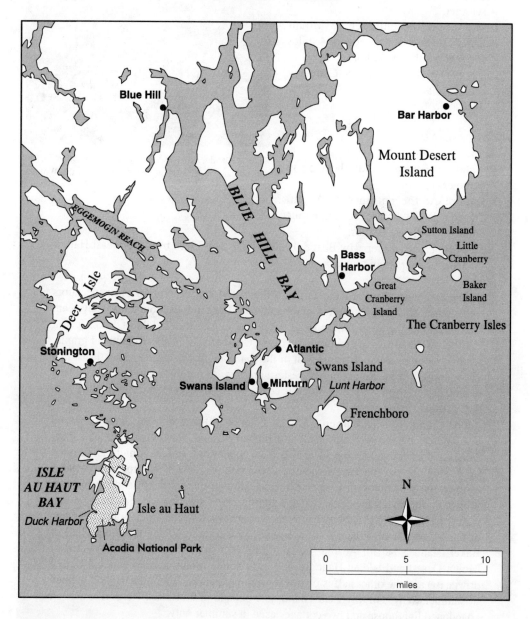

Blue Hill

Bar Harbor

Mount Desert
Island

EGGEMOGIN REACH

BLUE HILL BAY

Sutton Island

Little
Cranberry

Bass
Harbor

Great
Cranberry
Island

Baker
Island

Deer Isle

The Cranberry Isles

Stonington

Atlantic

Swans Island

Swans Island

Minturn

Lunt Harbor

Frenchboro

*ISLE
AU HAUT
BAY*

N

Isle au Haut

Duck Harbor

Acadia National Park

0		5		10

miles

THE ISLANDS OF MAINE

BAKER ISLAND

Area: 123 acres.

Population: 0 year-round; 2 families in summer.

Location: At the entrance to Mount Desert Island's Somes Sound, 4 miles south of Northeast Harbor.

Access: The Islesford Ferry Company cruise boats in summer (207-276-3717).

SUTTON ISLAND

Area: 174 acres.

Population: 0 year round; about 50 in summer.

Location: At the entrance to Mount Desert Island's Somes Sound, 1 mile south of Northeast Harbor.

Access: By passenger ferry by Beal & Bunker (207-244-3575) from Northeast Harbor on Mount Desert Island.

Baker's Island *(1921) by the American artist Allen Tucker.* (Oil on canvas, 25 x 34 inches; collection of the Whitney Museum of American Art.)

The Cranberry Isles sit off the southeast shore of Mount Desert Island like spectators to its tremendous display of coastal mountains. "Tremendous mountains" may seem like a vast exaggeration for a coastal range that climbs to a height of 1,532 feet at Cadillac Mountain, but from the shore of the Cranberry Isles, these humps of granite really do look massive. They rise out of the flat sea with the same sudden thrust that Wyoming's Tetons rise out of the western prairies. And they are, in fact, the highest mountains on North America's Atlantic coast. The Cranberry Isles are spectators with the best seats in the house.

The Cranberry island group was named for a 200-acre bog that once produced quantities of the tart red fruit on Great Cranberry island. However, around 50 years ago, islanders drained the bog in an attempt to control mosquitoes, which can be quite fierce all along the coast of Maine during the summer. The mosquitoes are as fierce as ever, but the cranberries became scarcer, though there are still enough of them growing wild so that the name remains appropriate. Only two of the islands—Great Cranberry and Little Cranberry (officially known as Islesford, which is also the name of the island's small village)—now support year-round populations. About half of Baker Island is part of Acadia National Park (which also occupies a good deal of Mount Desert and Isle au Haut, as well as Schoodic Point on the mainland farther downeast) and the other half is owned by summer people. Sutton Island is inhabited in summers only. On tiny Bear Island, just outside of Northeast Harbor, stands an abandoned lighthouse and two cottages used in summer only.

The Cranberry Isles are so small, the sea presses so close even to the most interior regions, that you never forget you're on an island. That is part of their magic. These are little worlds of spruce and granite, rocky shore and dark forest. Even in summer, when all the homes are occupied and tourists from Mount Desert come over on the ferries and in private boats for the day, the islands maintain their deep stillness. Small as they are, they never feel crowded. These are islands where you can imagine children living their most enchanting dreams and adults remembering theirs. The dreams of winter are more somber. Life on a small island can get awfully tight and confined in the cold dark months—but if you ask them, most islanders say it's when they like their islands best. The little worlds are theirs again, and unlike the outer Maine islands, the Cranberries are close enough to the mainland so that getting off-island is not that hard.

The islanders welcome what isolation their islands still afford. But they wonder how much longer they will be able to afford their islands. Real estate prices here, as on all Eastern islands, are climbing far faster than the incomes of native islanders. The old-timers grumble that in another generation summer people and people "from away" will have bought up all the homes. They may be right. The year-round communities on Sutton and Baker have disappeared. Already there have been more changes on Great and Little Cranberry that the old-timers feel comfortable with. As one island resident put it, "The old complexion of the islands—the charm of them—is having a hard time hanging on." For now, when the summer people pack up and go, the people left on Great and Little Cranberry hang on with lobstering, caretaking and repairing the empty summer homes, boat building and storage, and some construction work.

For islands so small and so close together, the Cranberries are surprisingly varied. Great Cranberry, the largest of the group, is shaped a bit like a big crab whose curving claws nearly enclose a protected harbor known at the Great Cranberry pool. This is where the island's boatbuilding operations used to be, and there is still a boatyard located here. The island's shoreline is broken up in hooks and points defining little coves. At the large meaty central portion of the crab there is a sizable heath (the locals say "hayth") of open, boggy land that used to have a lot of mink and beaver on it. Deer are still commonly seen here, and just about everywhere else on the island too. Great Cranberry has a little cluster of buildings by the ferry landing, but the homes of the islanders are spread out around the island.

On Little Cranberry, the residents live closer together in a cluster of houses and commercial buildings known as Islesford Village, though calling it a village is a bit of an exaggeration. Islesford is all there before you as you step off the ferry: the restaurant, the fishermen's co-op, the church, the museum (see below), the market, the post office, the gift shops. Away from the village on the north shore of the island stand the grandest summer houses, huge old places that command stunning views across to Seal Harbor on Mount Desert. This is the one touch of grandeur on the islands. For the most part, the Cranberries attract a much more modest summer crowd than the wealthy and socially exclusive communities on Mount Desert and other Maine islands. Most of the summer people here are artists, artisans and teachers—not the bankers, businessmen and lawyers who have staked out Northeast Harbor, Islesboro, North Haven and other posh retreats.

On Sutton Island, both Harvard and Princeton own houses for the use of faculty members in the summer, and there are perhaps 18 other summer homes on the island. The roads here are mowed paths, and the woods are thick. Unless you are invited as a guest, there is very little to do and very little reason for you to be on Sutton Island. Baker Island is thickly wooded and at the center of the island stands a lighthouse (originally built in 1828, replaced in 1855 and now automated). There used to be a little settlement here, but the houses have been abandoned. Though you can visit Baker Island in the summer, it's not an easy island to get to. There is no natural harbor or even a pier, so the ferryboat moors offshore and passengers are rowed to shore in fishing dories. Half national parkland, Baker Island feels wilder, more remote and more out in the open ocean than the other islands in the group.

History

The early history of the Cranberry Isles is linked to the history of Mount Desert. The French explorer Samuel de Champlain, who discovered and named Mount Desert during his North American voyage of 1604, is known to have sailed by the Cranberry island group. For a brief period during 1613, a group of French Jesuits led by Father Biard ran a mission at the present site of Mt. Desert's Southwest Harbor, and it is possible that Farther Biard crossed the short span of water to explore the Cranberries at this time. But England also laid claim to this territory as part of the Virginia Company, and when the English settlers in Jamestown learned of the French mission, they immediately sent out Captain Samuel Argall to destroy it. Father Biard was taken prisoner, several Jesuit lay brothers and novitiates were killed and the log buildings put to the torch. Thus began a century and a half of conflict between the English and the French for control of North America.

In the course of the 17th and 18th centuries, Mount Desert and the Cranberries passed back and forth between England and France. The Cranberries were probably used as fishing stations during this period, but they harbored no permanent settlement until after the English finally defeated the French forces outside Quebec in 1759 and took control of the entire Atlantic coast. Settlers lost no time in moving out to the islands: Job Stanwood came to Little Cranberry in 1760 (but departed two years later). Ben Bunker came out in 1762 and stayed, and he was followed shortly by John Stanley, Sam Hadlock and Benjamin Spurling. The core communities on the Cranberry Isles today are still made up of the descendants of the Stanleys, Bunkers, Spurlings and Hadlocks.

The Cranberries occupy a strategic position at the entrance to Somes Sound, which used to be the principal harbor of Mount Desert: Any ship that sails into Somes Sound must pass through one of the sea passages known as the Eastern and Western Ways that the islands define. (Interestingly, Somes Sound is actually a fjord, the only such formation on the Atlantic coast.) Philip Conkling writes in his book *Islands in Time* that soon after settlement, the Cranberries "became important fishing and shipping stations because of their many small, protected harbors." Because of their location, the communities were vulnerable to British naval harassment during the Revolution and again during the War of 1812. During the latter conflict, the islanders, roused by Benjamin Spurling, the founder of the Spurling clan on Great Cranberry, offered some resistance. The British sailors on the sloop *Tenedos* learned that Spurling was hiding two boats in Somes Sound and threatened to burn the boats unless he paid them $350. Spurling was taken prisoner, but not before he had dispatched his five sons to call up the local militia. In the battle that ensued, seven British sailors were killed, but only one Mainer was wounded. The British released Spurling and the *Tenedos* left the Cranberry islanders alone.

Baker Island also has an odd and colorful history dating from this period. It was during the War of 1812 that William and Hannah Gilley moved out to the island and proceeded to raise a family of 12 children. Baker Island, with no natural harbor and no pier even today, cannot have been an easy place in which to thrive, but the Gilleys managed nonetheless. They had oxen, cows, hogs and 50 sheep on the island, and through farming and fishing they were nearly self-sufficient. To raise cash for the things they couldn't grow or fish for, they sold butter, eggs, smoked herring and the feathers of seabirds that they shot in the winter. William Gilley also acquired an income of $350 per year when he was appointed keeper of the Baker Island lighthouse in 1828.

John Gilley, one of William and Hannah's sons, set up on Sutton Island and farmed there successfully for many years. When the summer people began coming to Mount Desert after the Civil War, John supplied the Northeast Harbor community with fresh vegetables, butter, milk and eggs, rowing over in his dory each morning. It was on such a trip in 1896 that 71-year-old John Gilley, still rowing over in October because one child in Northeast Harbor drank his milk, died at sea when the wind capsized his boat. His body was never found. Charles W. Eliot, the president of Harvard University for 40 years and a prominent member of the Northeast Harbor summer community, commemorated the Gilley family in his moving book, *John Gilley, Maine Farmer and Fisherman*. Eliot describes how William and Hannah Gilley came to live on Baker Island and how they dealt with the "formidable isolation which was absolute for considerable periods in the year." Eliot reports that in 1886, John Gilley, who had struggled all his life to farm the hard island soil, sold part of his land to summer people for "forty or fifty times any price which had ever been put on his farm by the acre." It's surprising how quickly the islands stepped from the pioneer period to the resort era, and how long this sort of thing has been happening on the coast of Maine.

Fishing was more important than farming for most of the islanders during the 19th century. Herring was the most lucrative local fishery in the second half of that century, and Conkling notes that Little Cranberry had eight herring smokehouses in 1886. Today, the fishing off the islands is pretty much limited to lobster, with some scalloping in the winter months. There are now six lobstermen working on Great Cranberry and 18 on Little Cranberry, where the Cranberry Isles Fishermen's Co-op is located. The three boatyards on Great Cranberry provide employment for a few more islanders, and there is always lots of work to be done looking after, repairing and renovating the old summer houses. Construction of new houses—perhaps two per year on Great and Little Cranberry—also makes work for island residents. And during the summer months, tourists spend money at island shops and restaurants, and at the bed and breakfast in Islesford.

The Cranberry Isles were initially part of Mount Desert, but in 1830 the five islands petitioned the Maine state legislature to incorporate them as a separate town. The reason the islanders gave was that they had "nearly all their trade business and common connections among themselves" and that they found it burdensome to cross the water to attend public meetings. Since that time they have continued to govern themselves. Islanders on Great and Little Cranberry elect one board of three selectmen and a single board of education oversees the island schools. Each island has a one-room school-house for grades K-8, with 14 pupils currently attending on Great Cranberry and five on Little. Islanders point to the health of the schools as their great hope for the survival of their year-round communities. Both islands have a Congregational church, and there is also a Catholic church on Little Cranberry. Despite the close ties of town politics, families, history and geography, the Cranberries have maintained their independence from each other. "The islands are not as close as you might think," said a town official who lives on Great Cranberry. "There is a definite distinction between the two. They each have their pride, and the people don't travel back and forth that much between the two." There seems to be something about living on an island that breeds pride in place and insularity.

Visiting the Islands

Each summer Islesford draws as many as 20,000 visitors who come for its very nice dockside restaurant and for its museum, the Islesford Historical Museum, located near the ferry landing and currently owned and run by Acadia National Park. Established in 1927 by William Otis Sawtelle, a Haverford College professor who spent his summers on the island, the museum has exhibits of old tools, documents relating to the island's history, objects that have washed up from shipwrecks, household items and a display about lobstering. The museum also has the books and manuscripts of the writer Rachel Field (1894-1942), who summered for many years on Sutton Island. Her books *God's Pocket* and *Time Out of Mind* portray aspects of life on the Cranberries. Next to the museum is the Blue Duck Ships' Store, built in 1850 and run for 25 years thereafter as a ship's chandlery. Like the museum, it is currently owned by the National Park. Islesford has a bed and breakfast for visitors, the only overnight accommodations on the islands.

Aside from the museum, the Cranberries offer little in the way of organized activities or official attractions. Great and Little Cranberry have a couple of summertime gift shops between them, a grocery store each, lots of rocky shoreline and the celebrated views of Mount Desert. Visitors may walk along the islands' roads and beaches, but they should keep in mind that Great and Little Cranberry islands are private land and the privacy of the homes along roads and beaches should be respected. There is no camping on the islands. Islanders complain about the amount of garbage visitors leave behind: They have enough trouble with their own trash, particularly their old cars, which must be barged off the island. For such small islands, the Cranberries have a surprising number of cars (one and a half per household according to one estimate), and in the summer months these unmuffled ancient vehicles compete with walkers, bikers and moped riders on the islands' few miles of paved roads.

The islands are well known for their nesting osprey, and the ferry affords a good view of the nests off the shore of Sutton Island. Probably the best way to view the wildlife of the region is aboard the Baker Island cruise conducted in summer months by an Acadia National Park naturalist. On the way out to Baker, the naturalist points out the Sutton Island osprey nests as well as harbor seals hauled out on East Bunker Ledge and discusses the geology of the region. One striking feature off the west shore of Baker Island is the so-called Dance Floor, a large slab of granite flat and smooth enough to dance on.

The Cranberry Isles really make you stop and think about what it is that people love so much about islands. If they didn't love islands there would certainly be no reason for them to have moved out here and stayed so long, for the Cranberries are not large enough to support much farming nor far enough out to sea to have much of an advantage in fishing and lobstering. It seems likely that the Cranberries were settled *because* they are islands—because they offer that special sense of separateness and completeness unique to islands. Not everyone can live with it, though there are many who dream about it. New families do move out to Great and Little Cranberry from time to time in search of the island life. Some remain, but others move on after a few years. Life on a small island is a wonderful idyll in summer, but in winter it's not for everyone. The land gets to seeming too small, the water too big and alien, and the people too familiar. This is the life the Cranberry islanders are born to; they're used to it and they want to hold onto it. The Cranberry Isles don't seem to offer much, unless you happen to love them. Then, small and limited as they are, they seem to offer everything.

SWANS ISLAND

Area: 5875 acres.

Population: 337 year-round; about 800 in peak summer season.

Location: 5 miles southwest of Mount Desert, 7 miles east of Isle au Haut at the meeting of Blue Hill and Jericho Bays.

Access: from Bass Harbor on Mount Desert by the Maine State Ferry Service (207-244-3254); ferry runs daily, all year; trip is 6 miles and lasts 40 minutes; reservations necessary for cars.

An old view of Burntcoat Harbor, one of the finest natural harbors on the Maine islands. (Courtesy of Alex Munsell and the Swans Island Educational Society.)

On every accessible Maine island talk of development is in the air. On Swans Island, a hilly, largely wooded, irregularly shaped Maine island ringed by other Maine islands large and small, there is more than talk. Development is here. Development on Swans Island has been gathering steam for some time; in the last five years it has exploded. There are more houses being built, more plots of land being sold, more day-trippers, more summer people with more money than ever before. "We're advertised as a nice quiet island," First Selectman Sonny Sprague told me, "but now the island seems crowded in the summer. Last summer a day-tripper who had come here to bike told me, 'You know, for a quiet island you certainly have a lot of traffic.' The island natives are getting to be quite concerned about the growth. It's getting so we look forward to the fall."

Back before regular ferry service from Mt. Desert commenced in 1960, Swans Island was a good deal quieter than it is today. The island supported three small fishing villages with a stable, year-round population, and each year during the warm months a sprinkling of summer people settled in to enjoy the island's many coves, its Burntcoat

Harbor, among the best natural harbors in Maine, its pink granite shores (nearly 300 miles in all), its fields and "mountains" (the highest is Goose Pond Mountain at 240 feet) with views across the water to the more commanding heights of Mt. Desert to the northeast and Isle au Haut to the west. When the ferry started up, more summer people came and with them, inevitably, came day-trippers, their numbers swelling during the sixties and seventies as Acadia National Park on Mt. Desert grew in popularity. Swans Island became one of those off-the-beaten-path travel "secrets," a side-trip that attracted the more knowledgeable, more adventurous tourists who wanted to escape the crowds around Bar Harbor and get a taste of "real" island life. Many of those who came to visit obviously fell in love with the island— it was easy to love—and dreamed of owning homes there.

The first landing of the Maine State Ferry Service boat on Swans Island, March 13, 1960. Regular ferry service has helped open Swans Island to development in the past three decades. (Courtesy of Bernice Carlson and the Swans Island Educational Society.)

History

Swans Island's current development boom actually has some historical precedent, for the initial settlement of the island came about as a result of a grandiose land speculation scheme. The prime mover in the scheme was an 18th-century Scottish-born adventurer named Colonel James Swan, a man whose life could easily supply the plots for several romance novels. Soldier, politician, writer, merchant, Swan was one of the Sons of Liberty responsible for the Boston Tea Party; he fought in the American Revolution; befriended Henry Knox, Washington's secretary of war, and Lafayette; made a considerable fortune by buying up land confiscated from Tories; lived grandly; lost his money; made another fortune in France; became entangled in the French Revolution; was accused of stealing two million francs, denied it and, though he had the money, refused to pay, and spent the next 22 years in a Paris debtor's prison, where he died in 1830.

In 1786, after his American Revolutionary escapades but before his French dealings, Swan decided to set himself up as an American feudal lord. He was 30 years old at the time. Swan chose as his demesne the island that would later bear his name, along with 24 neighboring islands, a total of about 9,000 acres, which he purchased from the Commonwealth of Massachusetts for £18,000. To be a feudal lord one needs serfs, so Swan set about recruiting them, offering 100 acres free to any who would settle on the island with their families and remain seven years. Swan found a number of takers and his island realm took shape: Settlers began clearing off the superb stands of timber on the island, a sawmill and gristmill went up on Burntcoat Harbor, and Swan's manor house—an elaborate mansion with porticoes, colonnades and ballrooms—rose at the edge of the virgin forest. It was a bizarre, fantastic dream, and it failed even before the lord could take possession of his manor. By 1788 Swan was in financial difficulties and he decamped to France and other wild pursuits.

Though Swan gave his name to the island (it had previously been called Burnt Coat, a rough translation of *Brule-cote*, the name the French used for the place) and brought over the first settlers[*], the real patriarch of the island community was a man called David Smith, known on the island as "King David." Smith settled here in 1791, squatted for a time in the ruins of Swan's mansion, had three wives, 24 children and vast numbers of grandchildren. There are quite a few of Smith's descendants living on the island today.

One enduring legacy of the Swan era was a terrific legal tangle over mortgages and land titles. Several men including Daniel Webster acted as Swan's agents, but none succeeded in straightening things out. Ultimately, the settlers acted on their own. Since few of them had paid up on their mortgages, they took squatters' rights and in 1834 organized the island as a plantation with a local government, tax list, school and roads. Swan Islanders settled in to earning their livings, mostly from the sea, though there were also some farms during the 19th century. The island fishermen did exceptionally well with mackerel in the 1870s; in fact, their fleet netted more mackerel than any other in New England and brought a taste of prosperity to the island. But the fat days didn't last long: The mackerel were fished out by the late 1880s and the Swans Islanders, after a period of hard times, tried their hands at herring and then lobster, which continues to be the mainstay of the island's economy, as it is on all working Maine islands. The island's population peaked at the turn of the century with about 800 people, and at this time the island had three fish processing plants, which provided many jobs. In addition, granite was quarried on Swans Island from the early years of

---

[*] Actually Thomas Kench, a deserter from Swan's artillery outfit, was technically the first settler for he came in 1776 and lived as a hermit on Harbor Island in Burntcoat Harbor for some 20 years.

this century until the mid-1920s. (Island lore has it that half the streets in New York were paved with Swans Island granite.) The abandoned quarry at Minturn on the island's south shore has filled with spring water and is now a popular summer swimming spot.

Swans Island's economy and population declined steadily as the 20th century advanced. The quarry shut down, the fish plants closed and the island lost its steamboat to wartime service in 1942. The thirties and forties were hard times indeed on the island, and the community was isolated as it had never been before. Life brightened up after the war when the island gained electric power, and 10 years later, in 1960, regular ferry service commenced between Swans Island and Bass Harbor. With the ferry came the changes, first slowly and then with increasing velocity, that are directing the island's course today.

Exploring the Island

Since getting a car off the island is such an ordeal in the summer, a bicycle is the preferred mode of transport for the visitor to Swans ("people from the mainland come here to learn how to ride bikes," one islander joked). The island has 27 miles of road (12 of them paved), lots of hills but no sharp inclines, and even with the crowds of day-trippers and summer folk relatively little in the way of traffic. It's small enough so that a determined day-tripper with a bike can get around most of it in a day but big enough to require some exertion to do so. The ferry docks on the north shore at the village of Atlantic, the focus of a good deal of the recent development. Aside from the new houses going up, the main attraction here is the island museum and library. Open during the summer months, the museum displays re-creations of an old island school room, a kitchen and post office facade, as well as implements from the quarrying years and an old lobster wharf. All of the objects and furnishings come from the island, mostly from people's attics. Minturn, the village on the east side of Burntcoat Harbor, has the island general store (and motel); Swans Island Village, on the west side, has some pretty Victorian houses, the island's school, the Methodist chapel (one of four island churches), the two working lobster wharves, and views out to the harbor and Harbor Island. Each village has its own post office. For the best view of the harbor and the surrounding small islands, including Harbor Island, Gooseberry and Marshall, pass through Swans Island Village to the lighthouse perched on the steep cliffs at Hockamock Head. This is an excellent spot for a picnic.

If you head north from Swans Island Village and bear left at the fork, you'll come to the Carrying Place, another picturesque spot. This short, narrow neck of land (a mere 20 yards across at high water) connects the larger eastern section of the island with the smaller and less settled part known as "the North." Indians supposedly portaged their canoes here from Toothacher Cove over to Back Cove—hence the name. In the summer the wild roses bloom and whenever it's clear the views northeast and southwest are exceptional. Cross the Carrying Place, proceed left along a dirt road and follow it until it ends at a small turnaround, pick up a path here and walk along it through the woods and eventually you will arrive at Swans Island's hidden gem, the Fine Sand Beach. Really just a pocket of sand that interrupts the island's jagged granite shore, the Fine Sand Beach is barely a speck compared with the vast sandy reaches of Atlantic barrier islands farther south. But on the rocky downeast Maine islands, sandy shores are scarcer than clear summer days, and the sand of Swans Island's sand beach is especially prized for the whiteness and smallness of its grains. Adding to the beauty of this spot are the thick growths of spruce and fir rising right behind the beach. When you are through relaxing on the Fine Sand Beach, there are a couple more scenic spots to poke into. Unlike Isle au Haut with its national park or Vinalhaven with its patches of public land scattered about the island, Swans Island has no organized parkland and no clearly marked hiking trails, but there are paths leading to Goose Pond and from there up Big Mountain (210 feet), which affords a fine view of the island and the sea. Ask an islander for help finding the start of the trail.

These are the sights to see and activities to pursue on Swans Island, but perhaps the main attraction here is the island itself—its back roads, more traveled on than they used to be but still quiet enough by mainland standards, its forests and wildflowers, its fat blackberries that ripen in abandoned fields and along roadsides in August, its coves and headlands, its Burntcoat Harbor, busy in the fair weather months with pleasure craft and active all year round with the sturdy working boats of the island lobstermen. Even with the recent development and changes, Swans Island is still a fine place to wander around, to escape from mainland noise and commerce, to soak up that special aura of the Maine islands—a funny blend of the roughness of life out in the elements and the smoothness that comes to a place when the same families have lived there for generations and worked for generations at the same pursuits.

Island Life: Present and Future

Swans Island families recognize full well that their future will be far briefer than their past unless they do something about what's happening to the island. To their credit, Swans Islanders *are* acting, and have been acting for some time, to preserve what they can of the character of the island and to protect the future of the lobster fishery, their major source of income. True, development is rampant on the island, but it would have been even more rampant had islanders not passed a strict zoning ordinance in 1971 that requires a two-acre minimum for any subdivision. Since then the zoning laws have been amended and strengthened several times, and today the regulations governing shorefront property are especially tough, with limits not only on lot size but also on the number of trees and bushes that can be cleared away. Zoning alone cannot save an island: A Swans Island completely chopped up into two-acre house parcels would be little more than a suburban seaside resort, but it has a long way to go before things get that bad. Meanwhile, at least the zoning provides *some* control.

The island's zoning laws, the first such laws on a Maine island, were passed under the pressure of crisis, for there were rumors at the time that a "Florida-style" developer was going to sell off 234 lots for houses. Islanders succeeded in blocking at least that kind of wholesale land grab. Swans Island also leads the way in taking action on another crisis that threatens the Maine islands—the overfishing of lobsters. In 1984, the island's 40 or so lobstermen got together and petitioned Maine's Department of Marine Resources to set a limit on the number of traps that lobstermen fishing within the officially designated Swans Island waters could use. The six-year trap limit project, the first of its kind in Maine, is to extend until 1990, at which time the fishermen will decide whether they wish to extend it for another six years. When the trap limit went into effect in the spring of 1984, a one-man boat could carry a maximum of 500 traps and a two-man boat was limited to 600 traps. For the following four years, the number of traps was cut by 50 per year so that in 1988 a one-man boat is entitled to 300 traps and a two-man boat to 400.

Burntcoat Harbor Light about 1885. Situated on Hockamock Head on the west side of the harbor, the lighthouse affords good views of the harbor islands. (Courtesy of Alice Burns and the Swans Island Educational Society.)

Lobstermen, by the very nature of their profession, tend to be independent types, and getting 40 of them to agree on anything, especially anything that tells them how to go about their business, is not easy. But the really difficult part of getting the trap limit enacted, said First Selectman Sonny Sprague, was not organizing the lobstermen but persuading the state Department of Marine Resources to agree to it. Full credit for the idea and for its implementation goes to Swans Islanders. It's a good idea and really a very simple one. Due to improvements in the technology of lobster fishing, the lobstermen had really become too good at what they do. Lobster boats equipped with loran, radar, hydraulic haulers and the new-style wire traps, which began to replace old wooden traps on Swans in the late 1970s, were giving the fishermen too many advantages. As they fished more traps and fished them more efficiently, the number of lobsters declined. The more traps they hauled, the fewer lobsters per trap they got. With the trap limit in effect, the lobsters should have a chance to replenish themselves to the point where lobstermen can catch as many (or more) lobsters with 400 traps as they used to catch with 800.

Yes, it's a good idea, but is it working? "It's hard to say," one island lobsterman replied. "Let's just say we're doing as well as anyone and we seem to be doing it with less traps." Some say that the trap limit is too little too late—that the waters have been too intensively fished for too many years to recover in the near future, if ever. But so far, at least, the trap limit has not brought serious hardship to any island fishermen: None have gone out of business and for some the recent seasons have been good. A few Swans Island lobstermen are also supplementing their income by branching out into fin fish, particularly cod and pollack, and scallops in the winters; and there are now three boats going out for shrimp. The trap limit is not going to return Swans Island to that golden age of the turn of the century when lobsters could be picked out of the rockweed at low tide, but it just may allow the island's working community to continue working on the island. "What hope we have is if we can retain the fishing," Sonny Sprague said when I asked him about the future of the community. "If we don't, we'll be a caretaker economy. We have better lives and our economy is better if we're fishing than if we're raking leaves. With the trap limit, we're trying to make sure that the young people can get involved in fishing and have some chance to make a living without having to work like a dog."

Hope and chance: The islanders, having done what they can through the practical measures of zoning and trap limits, entrust their future to these less substantial supports. The contest—Swans Island versus the world of real estate developers and wealthy urban vacationers—is hardly even; but Swans Islanders, though they may not have lots of money, do have determination. As for the outcome, the score is not in yet. We'll have to wait and see.

FRENCHBORO

Area: 2,500 acres.

Population: 65 year-round; 100 in summer.

Location: At the entrance to Maine's Blue Hill Bay, 8 miles southeast of Bass Harbor on Mount Desert Island and 3 miles east of Swans Island.

Access: Car and passenger ferry operated by the Maine State Ferry Service from Bass Harbor (call 207-594-5543 or 207-244-3254). Mail boat service out of Swans Island Village.

Frenchboro's church, schoolhouse and parsonage at the head of Lunt Harbor. (Courtesy of Vivian Lunt.)

As young people move away and the old sell off their homes to summer folk, the dwindling communities on a number of Maine islands worry about how much longer they can hang on. Frenchboro's tiny community of fishermen is not just worrying—

they're taking action. In 1986, when the population was down to 50 people, most of them elderly, with no prospect of new children being born, the residents devised a scheme to save Frenchboro as a year-round working island. The scheme was to offer low-cost housing on free 1.5-acre lots to 10 families who would come to settle here, and the islanders made national news when they revealed it. Homesteading is not a new idea in our nation of sod-busting pioneers, but it is a novel approach to solving the current problems of the Maine islands. So far it's working out well. Over 300 people responded to the island's offer, and about 50 families completed the 10-page application. To date, seven homes have been constructed, including one for the island's schoolteacher. The new families, who were exhaustively screened before being selected (one big catch was that they had to prove they could support themselves on an island that offers just about no employment), began moving out during the summer of 1988. Four of the men will join the island's fishermen in catching lobsters and scallops. Among the homesteaders there is also a writer, a weaver and a boat-builder. One island native admitted that "in the back of our minds we were concerned about something going wrong, but so far we're all getting along pretty well. They're getting used to us and we to them." Already, the island's population has jumped from 51 to 65, and it will probably rise to about 70 when everyone is in place. Most of the new families have pre-school children, so in a few years the student body in Frenchboro's two-room schoolhouse will start to increase (currently there are seven students in grades K-8). It looks like Frenchboro will make it.

The affordable housing project is run by the Frenchboro Future Development Corporation with the assistance of the Island Institute, a nonprofit organization established to help preserve the people and the resources of the Maine islands. The land for the new houses was donated by David Rockefeller's daughter Margaret Delaney who owns 1,000 undeveloped acres on the island. A $336,000 grant from the federal government paid for roads, septic tanks and wells; under the terms of the grant, six of the 10 lots must go to families with low to moderate incomes. Federal grant money also went to building a fire station and a recreation area on the island and to refurbishing island homes.

Frenchboro takes some getting used to for people accustomed to life on the mainland. The island has no year-round stores or restaurants, no doctor, no resident minister, except during the summer, and the ferryboat out of Bass Harbor comes but twice a week on successive days, which means that residents must stay overnight on the mainland when they do their shopping. It also means that Frenchboro is quite difficult to visit for the day. If you're really enterprising you can take the ferry over in the morning, catch the mailboat which runs back and forth from Swans Island four times a week, and then return to Bass Harbor from Swans—but for all this ferry travel, you get but a couple of hours on Frenchboro. Islanders are not too eager to have day-trippers poking around, though they have always welcomed the yachtsmen who visit them in the summer.

Frenchboro is obviously not a place to live (or even visit) if you crave convenience, but there are some undeniable advantages to the rugged, offshore isolation. Frenchboro has virtually no crime. (The startling exception is the disappearance of the town treasurer with $10,000-15,000 of town money in 1988, a case that remains unsolved.) Its spruce and fir forests, hilly terrain, open fields and shoreline are virtually unspoiled; and the views of the mountains of Mount Desert rising out of the sea are spectacular. Many of the homestead applicants said they were looking for a safe, sheltered place to raise their children: Frenchboro is about as far as you can get from the hazards of American urban and suburban life.

The focal point of island life is Lunt Harbor, a U-shaped dip in the northwest coast of the island whose entrance is protected by the small Harbor Island. Lunt Harbor is where the lobstermen moor their boats and pile their traps and gear on rickety little docks. At the head of the harbor cove stands the island's collection of civic institutions: the schoolhouse, the church, the parsonage and the historical society, built in 1986. A single paved road swings around the harbor, a few paths and logging roads branch out into the woods, and that's about all there is to the island. For those who love the stern lonely beauty of the Maine islands, Frenchboro is a gem.

History

Frenchboro (or Long Island, as it was originally called), though long known to Indians and used by them in the summers for fishing, supported no permanent white settlement during America's Colonial period. Colonel James Swan (see Swans Island entry) acquired the island in 1786 as part of his offshore Maine empire, but he concentrated his energies on the island that bears his name and left neighboring Long Island pretty much alone, except to sell it and buy it back in the course of a decade.

The first white settler is believed to have been a William Davis, who sailed the three miles over from Swans Island in 1797. Sometime during the 1820, the Lunt brothers, Amos and Abner, arrived on the island and more or less took over. The Lunts multiplied rapidly and by 1850 there were 13 Lunt households on what was commonly known as Lunt's Long Island. To this day Lunt remains by far the most common family name on the island. Amos's son Israel was the prime mover of the clan: He opened a store at the harbor, sold supplies and gear to fishing boats, helped establish both a school and a Baptist church in 1843, and purchased over 1,000 acres, nearly half the island, for $600 (this is believed to be the same tract that David Rockefeller bought and passed on to his daughter). According to Charles B. McLane's informative book *Islands of the Mid-Maine Coast*, other early families on the island included the Riches, the Walls and the Osiers, but with the exception of a few remaining Osiers, these families are now gone. Then as now the harbor was the focus of community life, and the early photos show quite a few houses standing close together on both sides of the harbor, as well as a number of wharves and warehouses. The federal census of 1870 lists a total of 178 residents and 37 families; fishing and shipping were the primary occupations.

Long Island acquired the name Frenchboro in 1859 as part of a political deal: A lawyer named E. Webster French told the islanders that he'd get them a post office if they renamed their island after him. They agreed, lawyer French delivered, and Frenchboro became the name of the village on Lunt's Harbor and the island's post office address, though the old name continues to be used as well, especially to refer to the island as a whole. In 1890 a Congregational church rose on the island, and in the first decade of the 20th century the increasing student population (60 pupils in 1907) made it necessary to build a new school, which still stands and continues to serve the seven students who attend today. Frenchboro's peak year was 1910, when

197 people lived on the island. Fishing was the basis of the island's economy then as now, and the islanders also made money by cutting the island's timber, building a few boats at the harbor and raising sheep.

Frenchboro's population declined suddenly during the Second World War, when many men joined the armed forces and families moved off the island. Though many residents returned after the war, the island never fully recovered. By 1964 there were only two school-age children left, and to keep the school open the islanders requested that the State Division of Child Welfare place foster children with some of their families. The children lived on the island until they reached high school age, when they had to move back to the mainland; a few have returned to settle here. The Yankee ingenuity that kept the school open then and that is keeping the community alive now was also brought to bear in obtaining telephone service. In 1970 an electronic wiz from Bangor set up a two-digit dial system on the island and later, with the help of a benefactor from California, the islanders raised the money to hook up via microwave to the mainland.

Island Sights and Events

The big event of the year on Frenchboro is the lobster festival held on homecoming day, August 12. The date commemorates the 1941 signing of the Atlantic Charter by Franklin Roosevelt and Winston Churchill on board the S.S. *Missouri* just east of Long Island Head. Profits from the sale of lobster lunches to upwards of 400 hungry visitors and former residents go to the island's church, which usually nets 90% of its yearly budget in this way, and to the historical society, which was established in 1979.

The historical society, housed in its own building since 1986, has exhibits relating to all aspects of island life and history, and a craft shop. It is open from May to October.

Botany enthusiasts may want to make the trip in late July or early August, when hundreds of rare pogonia orchids bloom on a bog in the woods. On the east side of the island there is a cobble beach with smooth round stones, and paths lead through the Delaney holdings to gravel beaches at Eastern Cove and Deep Cove. Unlike Swans Island, Mt. Desert and Matinicus, Frenchboro has no sandy beaches.

In summer, about 50 cottagers join the year-round community, and over the years, the summer people have contributed a good deal to the island. "They are generous and a great help," said one islander, "and they fit in well with the working community." Unlike more accessible islands, Frenchboro is in little danger of being bought up and developed by seasonal residents. It is just too difficult to get there and live here, even in the summer months.

The islanders on Frenchboro are getting a bit tired of the glare of media attention (they've been written up in *People* magazine and the *New York Times* and have appeared on television numerous times). But after all, they did make themselves newsworthy. Their homesteading plan shows a kind of visionary boldness that harks back to the youth of the Republic. These islanders have captured our imaginations by following in the footsteps of our forefathers: They are like the pioneers and immigrants, but in reverse, embracing the unknown not by moving but by summoning it to them. Ten families moving to a new suburban subdivision or a city building just converted to apartments would make hardly a ripple in the life of the community; but on a small island where the same families have been in possession for generations, where the residents know each other with an intimacy unimaginable to off-islanders, the newcomers will set off a social earthquake. Islanders not just in Maine but on all small islands are notorious for their clannishness, their suspicion of outsiders, their pride in a long history of being different and apart from other people. On Frenchboro, the islanders have thrown all that to the wind in their desire to see their community continue. "It's a gamble," one island native said, "but sometimes if you don't take chances, you lose everything." Frenchboro residents new and old are to be congratulated for taking chances in such a brave and original way.

ISLE AU HAUT

Area: 5,500 acres; 6 miles long, 2.5 wide.
Population: 45 year round; about 300 in summer.
Location: Penobscot Bay, 7 miles from Stonington on Deer Isle, Maine.
Access: Passenger ferry from Stonington; contact Isle au Haut Ferry Company, 207-367-5193.

Isle au Haut, as its name makes clear, is a lofty island. Its spine rises in a ridge with five peaks, the highest, Mt. Champlain, reaching 556 feet above sea level. Although hardly a dizzying elevation, it is high enough to make the island a distinct landmark from far across Penobscot Bay. From islands as distant as Vinalhaven and Matinicus, from the shore at Stonington on Deer Isle (the point of embarkation for Isle au Haut), from the decks of boats out on the bay, Isle au Haut looks magnificent: A dark green eminence, ascending from the water in long smooth slopes, it beckons on the horizon like a final shore not yet touched by exploration. In fact, Isle au Haut *is* magnificent. The 45-minute ferry ride through the archipelago of small islands known as Merchants Row is perhaps the most scenic Maine offers, and the island itself is graced with every natural beauty for which Maine islands are celebrated: sculpted granite shores, thick healthy spruce forests, high-prowed headlands demarcating crescent coves, and glorious blue vistas out to the islands, the bay and the ocean. Perhaps best of all from the point of view of the visitor, this beauty and splendor is protected and accessible: More than half of the island is part of Acadia National Park, which also includes much of Mount Desert Island and Schoodic Point farther downeast on the mainland.

The National Park on Isle au Haut occupies most of the island's southern territory, about half its west coast and nearly all of the steep, jagged southern shore. The remainder of the island—the north, the west shore around Moore's Harbor and Isle au Haut Thorofare (a protected strip of water between this island and the smaller Kimball Island) and nearly the entire east side—is private. And though the park and private land share the same island, the same topography, the same beauty, they are sharply distinct. Unlike other national parks where the village stands to service the park and its visitors, on Isle au Haut the village stands deliberately apart. Actually "village" might be too broad a term for the year-round settlement here: In fact, it's more the rudiments of a village. Along the Isle au Haut Thorofare, which has ever been the center of island life, there is a town dock, a church, a store/post office, a town hall/library, a school and a firehouse; and scattered about these buildings and along the island's east shore are the houses where the members of the small but stubborn year-round community (now about 45) live. Elsewhere on the island, most notably at Point Lookout at the northwest tip, there are clusters of summer houses, some dating back more than a century and vacationed in by five generations of the same family.

In a sense there are two—or even three—Isle au Hauts: the National Park, the year-round community, the summer colonies. The division between "summercator" (a local, Maine term for summer rusticators, also known as "those people from away") and year-round resident is common to all Maine islands; what's unusual on Isle au Haut is that there should be an even deeper division between the park and the privately held land. The division goes deeper than geography. It's a division drawn and enforced by the Hautians, summer and year-round residents alike.

The Hautians have fought to maintain their separateness. Fifteen years ago the federal government had plans to expand the national park facilities, extend park lands by condemning abandoned houses, increase the number of day visitors, and generally widen the park's influence and impact on the island. Islanders protested: they already objected to the way some park visitors were straying onto their part of the island, trampling on their yards and on their privacy, scrutinizing them and their village as if they were living displays in an exhibit of "ye quaint olde" island town complete with salty inhabitants. The last thing they wanted was more snooping tourists. So they waged a battle with the National Park Service and after 10 years the islanders, with the support of the summer people, won. Today things are set up so that island people and park visitors pretty much keep to their separate sectors. As a recent article on Isle au Haut in *New England Monthly* put it, the island is "balkanized." The town landing and the park landing are a good five-mile walk apart. (Walking or boating are the only ways for visitors to traverse the distance; islanders alone can drive the roads in the ancient, rickety machines they call cars.)

Day-trippers who want to visit the park (a maximum of 50 was set as part of the agreement between park and islanders) get off the boat at the park dock at Duck Harbor and, unless they're really determined and energetic, never come near the village. Those who want to stay overnight are restricted to five lean-to campsites with a total capacity of 30 people at Duck Harbor (open only during mid-May to mid-October and usually booked well in advance). Thus a visitor to the island would really have to make an effort to snoop on the village—and few bother, since the park has so many lovely places to explore (see below).

Recently, this situation shifted a bit. As of July 1986, a tiny crack opened in the wall separating islander and visitor: An inn opened on Isle au Haut. It's now possible from Memorial Day to Halloween for up to 10 guests with enough money (the cost is $195 per day for two, which includes meals) to stay over on the island. The inn is not actually in the village but a bit of a walk (about 30 minutes) away at the Robinson Point Lighthouse. It's called the Keeper's House and that's exactly what it is: the restored keeper's house to the 1905 lighthouse, which has been automated since 1937. Whether this crack in the wall will grow wide enough for overnight tourists to come pouring onto Isle au Haut remains to be seen. Right now it seems unlikely. From all reports, the residents don't want it and summer people *never* want it.

The inn owners, Jeff and Judi Burke, understand and respect the islanders' aversion to tourism and development. Their inn, with only five rooms in the Keeper's house and an adjoining cottage, is too small to bring in much traffic and it has its own boat landing, so that guests may go right from the inn to the park's hiking trails without ever setting foot in the village. By being sensitive to the feelings of the islanders, the Burkes have won the support of the community. In fact, they have joined the community: They live on the island year-round and their 12-year-old son attends the island school. Their inn seems likely to remain *the* inn, at least for the foreseeable future.

The park, the village and the summer colonies on Isle au Haut continue to revolve in their separate spheres. Even with the inn open to paying guests, it's only a shade less difficult for visitors to breach the village fastness. And that's fine with most everyone who belongs on Isle au Haut.

The Park

It's a bit ironic that summer people joined the fight to restrict the park's expansion on Isle au Haut since summer people were responsible for creating the park in the first place. The donors of the 2,860 acres of parkland were the descendants of Ernest Bowditch, the Boston gentleman who founded the summer colony at Point Lookout back in 1880. Bowditch and his friends originally established the colony as a bachelors' retreat (no women, children or even dogs were allowed); but in time the footloose members of the Isle au Haut Company, as the summercators termed their club, married, their families started accompanying them to the Point, and their cottages grew in number, size and comfort. These are cottages in the upscale sense of the word: rambling, rustic summer retreats bedecked with porches, turrets, gingerbread and lots of rooms for large families and long-staying guests. By 1916 the Point Lookout summer colony was a bustling place, with the clubhouse connected to some 25 cottages by a network of boardwalks. As many as 300 summer folk disembarked on the island each summer for a busy two months of rustic leisure. The summercators, led by Bowditch, had also been busy buying up the island's outlying lands. Bowditch himself owned half of Isle au Haut. In 1943 his heirs donated most of the family's holdings on the island to the federal government to become part of Acadia National Park. And that's how the park came to be on the island.

Unlike the main section of Acadia National Park on Mt. Desert, which is crowded, excessively organized and distinctly oriented to cars, the park on Isle au Haut is quite wild, free of all but official park traffic and relatively empty: In 1988 around 4.5 million people visited the park at Mt. Desert, while only 4,000 disembarked at the National Park landing on Isle au Haut. A park ranger meets the boat at Duck Harbor and explains regulations, offers advice on hikes and how long they'll take, answers questions, distributes maps and reminds day-trippers of the all-important ferry schedule. That schedule gives you a maximum of six hours on the island—time enough to walk over a good deal of the park's fairly rugged terrain if you're in shape and want to move. Sometimes the ranger leads nature walks. But if you choose to be alone, you're on your own. The 17.5 miles of trails that follow the shore and traverse the island's central ridge are well-marked; there are 8.5 miles of dirt road that loop through the parkland and hook up with the five-mile stretch of paved road that passes through the village; there are the lean-tos near Duck Harbor. And that's about it in the way of facilities. The park at Isle au Haut has no interpretive markers, no self-guiding nature loops, no designated "scenic view" turnouts, no refreshment stands or gift shops, no parking lots because there are no cars allowed (aside from the occasional park department vehicle). There is really nothing to do but walk and observe nature. For those who enjoy these activities, Isle au Haut is a paradise.

The shore and the interior of Isle au Haut are strikingly different environments, and the park's trail system is set up so that you can spend time in both in the course of a single day's visit. Perhaps the most impressive stretches of coast are those outlining Western Head in the island's southwest corner and the south shore from Western Head to Head Harbor, which has steep cliffs dropping as much as 100 feet down to a series of small coves. At various points along the shoreline one comes upon cobble beaches—crescent-shaped beaches paved with smooth round stones. The raw material for these beaches was scraped up and deposited here by the glaciers, and then the ocean went to work on the rocks, rolling them against one another over thousands of years until they lost all jagged edges and became round. During the 18th and early 19th centuries, stones from similar cobble beaches on other Maine islands were used as convenient ballast on sailing ships, and later they were laid down as cobblestones (sometimes called popplestones) on the muddy streets of East Coast cities.

To visit the scenic stretch of coast at the west and south of Isle au Haut, take the Western Head Road from Duck Harbor to the Western Head Trail (1.3 miles), Cliff Trail (.7) and Goat Trail (1.8 miles). Then, if you'd like to get a taste of the island's mountainous terrain, you can take the .9-mile Duck Harbor Mountain Trail back to the park ferry landing. One other coastal attraction is the Thunder Gulch at Eastern Head on the island's southeast corner. This is a crevice in the cliffs and ledges that traps incoming waves and shoots them up in the air like geysers. Eastern Head may be reached by a path that turns off from the road that circles the island.

Those who wish to explore the island's mountains more thoroughly should take the three-mile Median Ridge Trail up the central ridge and then from the top of Bowditch Mountain hook up with the 1.1-mile Bowditch Trail that leads over Jerusalem Mountain and down to the park road. The walk is rugged, the spruce trees are tall and draped with lichen, the forest floor is padded with soft emerald moss, the air is clean and bracing, but the views from the central ridge are disappointing: The lower and more accessible Duck Harbor Mountain commands a more panoramic vista of the bay. Part of the east boundary of the park runs alongside the shore of Long Pond, a 1.5-mile-long, narrow freshwater lake good for swimming (try the small sandy beach at its south end). The Long Pond Trail (2.5 miles) leads there and also loops around through the mountains.

The park on Isle au Haut is small and rather intimate for a national park. Day-trippers become acquainted on the boat over from Stonington and run into each other often during the course of their hikes. The park campground at Duck Harbor is like a small, temporary, ever-changing community (there is a three-night maximum stay during the summer season). Though the park is wild and interior trails silent except for bird calls and perhaps the distant hum of a lobster boat, there is not enough acreage to produce the remote, lost-to-the-world feeling that true wilderness gives off. Rather Isle au Haut conjures up a timeless, isolated, world-unto-itself aura, the aura peculiar to islands. The island world is closely bounded: From the top of Duck Harbor Mountain the masts of the sailboats moored below seem close enough to grab and the crash of waves on the south shore cliffs almost sounds in one's ears. But the mainland, though well within sight to the north and west, seems years away. The fact that the park is and will be preserved in its natural state contributes to this feeling of island separateness. When one returns on the boat to Stonington after a day in the park, one has the sense of crossing through time even more than through space. Island time, particularly on an island protected by parks, feels like time before history. To return is to resume the time of defined epochs, decades, daily schedules.

History

But of course there has been history on Isle au Haut—not a lot of it, but enough to have marked out and shaped the settled part of the island. Isle au Haut, like all Maine islands, became an island after the glaciers retreated and melted and the rising ocean waters drowned the coastline. The island's mountains are actually the peaks of mountains whose bases are under water. Of events on Isle au Haut between its birth as an island and the arrival of white settlers we know very little. Indians probably did not live on the island year-round, but they paddled out to it in the summer for its shellfish and birds' eggs, and they drove ducks into long, narrow Duck Harbor (now the spot where visitors to the park disembark) and then caught them in nets. (The shores of Isle au Haut are today one of the only wintering grounds in this region for Harlequin ducks.) There were heaps of clamshells dating from Indian times on the shores of Isle au Haut, as on Vinalhaven and North Haven. As recently as 75 years ago Indians still came over to the island in the summer from mainland reservations to gather grasses and to hunt gulls (now no longer legal).

The island was among the first sighted and named by the European explorers of the New World. According to Samuel Eliot Morrison, Giovanni da Verrazano sailed through Penobscot Bay in 1524 and named three outer bay islands—today's Isle au Haut, Monhegan and Mount Desert—for the princesses Anne, Isabeau and Catherine, the daughters of his patron Henry of Navarre. Late in the summer of 1604, Samuel de Champlain "discovered " the island all over again and he renamed it Isle Haulte, "high island," for its mountain ridge. Later English-speaking settlers had trouble with the French name and supposedly corrupted it in 12 different ways before agreeing on Isle au Haut, which islanders pronounce "aisle a hoe."

The island was not settled by whites until the end of the 18th century. Kimball Island, a jump across the Thorofare, had a white man living on it in 1772 and in 1785 five settlers were noted as inhabiting "Isle of Holt." Three Barter brothers— Peletiah, Henry and William—came here from Boothbay in 1792 and Peletiah sired 10 children. Other early island families bore the names Turner, Robinson, Kimball, Sawyer, Smith, Kempton and Leland; some of these names endure on the island and others can be found carved on the headstones of island cemeteries. In 1802, 24 Hautians petitioned the Commonwealth of Massachusetts for title to the land they lived on. The increasing number of islanders (there were around 180 by 1824) supported themselves by fishing and sheepraising (supposedly, the island's sheep population hit 1,000 by the turn of the century). To make grazing lands they cut down most of the island's trees during the 19th century.

But fishing, more than farming or livestock, was the core of the island's economy. During the 1850s, the islanders turned more and more to lobstering, and in 1860 a

Boston company opened up a lobster cannery on the Thorofare where two dozen women and children worked. Isle au Haut lobsters made their way as far as London's elegant Crosse and Blackwell. On Saturday nights the factory's second floor doubled as a dance hall, and the renown of these dances spread all the way to Deer Isle (islanders remain fond of dancing). In 1874, Isle au Haut split off from Deer Isle and became an independent township. This period also marked the peak of the island's population—at around 274 people (350 including the inhabitants of the nearby islands). From this high point, Isle au Haut's population declined gradually but steadily over the years: 206 in 1890, 178 in 1900, 75 during the winter of 1935 and by the late 1960s as few as two dozen year-round residents.

In his book Islands of the Mid-Maine Coast historian Charles B. McLane attributes the decline of lobstering and of the year-round community on Isle au Haut to three factors: The lack of a good protected harbor near the main settlement on the Thorofare; the advent of the gasoline engine early in this century, which made the island's proximity to prime lobstering and fishing grounds less significant; and the growth of the summer community on the island, which, in McLane's words, "inhibited the continued development of an indigenous economy." With money to be made building and taking care of the summer cottages (and for a time the boarding houses, in one of which Chief Justice Harlan Stone spent his summers for a time), there was less need for the men to go lobstering or for the women to work in the canning factory. Islanders patched together livings by caretaking, fishing and making-do—but with the passing years fewer and fewer of them stayed on. Even the exclusive summer colony at Point Lookout fell on a genteel version of hard times: The cottages were all shut up during World War II and by the time the war ended many of the old members had died. During the 1950s the club was reduced to advertising for paying guests (discreet ads appeared in the Junior League Magazine and, at the club's lowest ebb, in Vogue).

As the year-round population declined, the summertime population grew a bit bigger and more heterogeneous. Some of the little pockets of houses on the island, including the dozen or so houses at Head Harbor, lost all of their year-round residents and became ghost communities, returning to life only during the summer months. In the sixties, when the permanent population dipped below 20, it looked as if Isle au Haut might not survive as a year-round settlement. But the islanders have managed to hang on, with some recent infusions of new blood. These days, after the September exodus of the summer people (among whom there are still some of the old families on the Point as well as a scattering of more recently arrived doctors, lawyers, academics and public officials), about 45 permanent residents remain on the island, many of them relative newcomers who have chosen to make a go of rugged island living. Come November, the deer herd, which park officials estimate at between 300 and 500, far outnumbers the people on Isle au Haut. The deer, who have grown tame because they may not be hunted, are likely to survive. The future of the island human community is not so certain.

The Island Today

The ecology of an island's human community is in many ways just as fragile as that of its plants, trees, fish and game. Too many day-trippers can trample the soul out of a place, as they threaten to do on Monhegan; too many summer houses can tip the balance from working island to resort island, as Swans Island residents fear. When the year-round population drops below a certain point, the human community ceases to be a vital, ongoing social unit and unravels into a collection of survivors. The community on Matinicus seems to have reached that point. The community on Frenchboro is fighting hard to keep its head above water. The community on Isle au Haut is digging in its heels. Whatever pressures and uncertainties they face, the Hautians seem likely to meet them head on. As they demonstrated in their fight with the National Park Service (see above), the community on this island has a determined spirit.

To support that spirit, they have just enough of the essential institutions of community life but no more. There is a store, owned cooperatively by the islanders, that carries everything from groceries to gasoline. There is a town government with three elected selectmen, a school board, a fire warden, a tax collector. There is a post office. (For 60 years the post office had been the domain of Elizabeth Rich—fondly known as Miss Lizzie—surely the island's most celebrated and best loved citizen; sadly, Miss Lizzie, for whom the island mailboat is named, recently left Isle au Haut to live in an old-age home on the mainland.) There is a school with one teacher, at present, and 10 students who attend until they reach the eighth grade, after which they must go to the mainland for high school. There is the Revere Memorial Library. The church, a graceful structure built in 1857 with a pure white spire that dominates the village, has a Congregational minister in residence during the summer months. A cable from the mainland laid in 1983 supplies the island with electricity (before that, islanders provided their own electricity through a central generator that they set up and ran by themselves). Only in 1988 did Isle au Haut receive telephone service (an event that received coverage in the *New York Times*). School, store, ferry, church, post office: It's just enough to keep Isle au Haut chugging along.

The human community on Isle au Haut is a very private and isolated little world, even by island standards; but its privacy, though extreme, is not inviolable. In 1974 a clear, wide window opened on this world in the form of a book called *Here on the Island*, a sensitive and thorough account of the island's character, history and people. The author is Charles Pratt, a New York-based photographer who fell in love with Isle au Haut during his summers there and fulfilled a fantasy of many summer islanders by staying on during the winter months to see what life was *really* like.

Pratt's book, illustrated with his own superb color and black and white photographs, includes portraits of the island's leading citizens, descriptions of lobstering and scalloping, brief essays on the island institutions, its history and future. (Pratt never calls Isle au Haut by its name in the book, identifying it only as "the island," but anyone who has visited will recognize it instantly from the descriptions, place names and photographs.) Together Pratt's pictures and words convey the texture of life on the island: the spirit of community, the sense of the past, the network of communication and kinship that keeps residents together, the social hierarchy of year-round resident, longtime summercator and day-tripper, the struggle the islanders wage (with stoic reserve) to keep their small community going and the pride they take in their self-sufficiency.

From Pratt's book we learn about the islanders' love of dancing, their talent for engine repair, and how they keep themselves occupied and amused during the winters (they play volleyball in the town hall and get together for a complex card game called "83"). Pratt has ferreted out such historic events as the great fire that blueberry pickers set in the 1870s that burned until the snow fell and the chance discovery by island children of a pair of German spies who had holed up in a deserted summer cottage during the Second World War. *Here on the Island* is now a bit dated (the population has increased, the number of schoolchildren has jumped from four to 10, Miss Lizzie is no longer living on the island), but it's still unmatched for its sympathy and its detail. *Here on the Island* not only evokes the "feel" of Isle au Haut, it also captures something of the essential quality of life on all the outer Maine islands.

To keep a year-round community alive there must be a year-round economy. Isle au Haut has one—just. There are a few full-time jobs on the island: one park ranger (there are two summer rangers as well), one schoolteacher, one postmistress and one store manager; and a few part-time jobs, including roadworker and school bus driver. It's not uncommon for islanders to work at a variety of jobs, depending on the season, the availability of work and the mood that seizes them. A number of the men go out for lobsters from March until the end of December, but the Isle au Haut commercial fishing fleet is small compared with that on Vinalhaven or Swans Island. There is some seasonal work for caretakers, carpenters and staff at the inn, but the islanders have never really let themselves become servants for the summer folk. Smallness—in the size of the fishing fleet, in the number of jobs, in the number of people who live all year on the island—is a real concern here.

Though islanders have little desire to see more day-trippers and summer people, they are eager to bolster the year-round community. Keeping the school going is, as Pratt points out, absolutely vital to the survival of the community, for without a school families could not live here. Keeping the school means attracting young couples with children to the island. The town is offering several lots at reasonable prices to any who wish to take up permanent residence on the island (to date only one house has gone up), and for $75 a month a family can rent an old schoolhouse to live in, so long as they remain on the island through the year. The problem, of course, is that there just isn't that much to do or earn during the long island winters. "You have money in summer and in winter you don't—it's the Maine way," one new year-round resident put it.

It's not an easy life, but few Hautians would trade it or see it change. The people do not consider themselves poor, and no one starves or freezes to death on the island. They don't need as much money to live here because there isn't as much to spend money on: no malls, no fast food joints, no home appliance stores. They have their island and they have their lives, and they like both pretty much the way they are.

"Their" island is not strictly speaking theirs alone, for they have shared it with outsiders for a long time now. Isle au Haut has rather a long history of being a hybrid and it has managed to keep its balance throughout that history. The year-round community has lived side by side and in harmony with the summer community for over 100 years; the national park, though it has occupied more than half the island for over 40 years, has neither swallowed up the other half nor transformed it into a tourist corral (though not for lack of trying). Despite having been discovered, invaded, intruded upon and bought up by the outside world, islanders have kept at least some of their land and the village most of its soul. The half of Isle au Haut that is national park is safe—safe, that is, for the enjoyment of us off-islanders. This in itself is a tremendous gift for anyone who cares for the coast of Maine. As for the other half of the island—the populated half—we might be tempted to care less about its survival for we're much less likely to see it and we're certainly made much less welcome there.

Yet in a sense the island community is just as important as the park to the continued health and beauty of Maine's coast. Without this community and others like it, something vital would be missing from the coast: Call it real life. The Hautians have kept the real life of their community going one way and another for 200 years now and they seem determined to hold onto it. As Charles Pratt puts it, "Most of them have not sold out, and they are still there as the true caretakers of an environment where man is not excluded but where nature — a hard manifestation of nature — dominates. They like it that way, and they stay." Perhaps, by dint of luck, mettle, tradition, money and support from summer people, the resources of the sea and their own sheer stubbornness, the islanders will continue to stay on Isle au Haut.

VINALHAVEN

Area: 10,000 acres.

Population: 1,211; about 6,000 in summer.

Location: Penobscot Bay, 12 miles from Rockland.

Access: From Rockland by the Maine State Ferry Service, 207-594-5543 at Rockland or 207-863-4421 on Vinalhaven (takes cars and foot-passengers; reservations necessary for cars in season; trip lasts 1 hour and 18 minutes).

Granite eagles quarried and carved on Vinalhaven in the late 19th century and then shipped to the U.S. Post Office in Buffalo, New York. Many of the Vinalhaven stone carvers were Italian immigrants who moved to the island during the granite boom years and left when the granite industry collapsed during the 1920s. (Courtesy of the Vinalhaven Historical Society.)

Vinalhaven, the largest of Maine's unbridged islands (and third largest island after Mt. Desert and Deer Isle), is a rough and ready kind of place, a jagged-coasted mass of granite that the sea has worked into innumerable coves. People call it a "real working" island, to set it apart from other islands, such as Islesboro, where "real work" has largely given way to the summer home industry. Real work is something of a tradition on Vinalhaven: In the second half of the 19th century and into the first decades of the 20th, the high-quality granite of which this island is made supported an important business in quarrying and carving. With the collapse of the granite industry in the 1920s, the island lost its economy and a good part of its population, and the few who remained turned from the land to the sea to earn their living (or more accurately returned, since the sea has supported islanders since Indians came here in their canoes). Today, a good-sized fishing fleet of some 200 boats goes out from Vinalhaven to work the sea for lobster, as well as herring, cod, pollack, scallop, shrimp and crab; the island's fish-processing plant, a producers' cooperative that went into operation in

Penobscot Bay and Environs

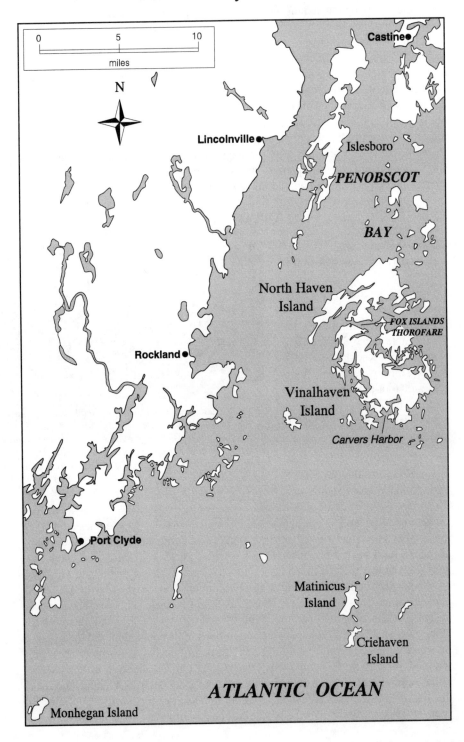

1980, employs from 30 to 75 people (the numbers fluctuate with the seasons) to freeze, process and pack not only the local catch, but seafood brought in from other East Coast locations as well.

As befits a working community, Vinalhaven is well-equipped with services and public institutions (at least by Maine island standards). There is one of just about everything: post office, library, school (elementary and high school classes taught), museum (at the historical society), bank and the only medical center on an unbridged Maine island. The island supports four churches, electric power comes by cable from the mainland, there has been telephone service on the island since 1898, and there is even a year-round dentist. Yes, these are unremarkable, standard features of mainland communities of any size—but Vinalhaven is lucky to have them. If you break your arm on Isle au Haut, need groceries on Frenchboro, or if you're high school age on Matinicus, you have to get off the island for your cast, your bread or your education.

Though Vinalhaven is a working island, it is not intolerlant of—or unprepared for—those who come to play, to rest, to recover or retreat from work. For the visitor Vinalhaven offers the beauty of sea, about 100 miles of Maine's famous rocky coast, several splendid harbors and silent tracts of dark spruce woods, parks, beaches, overnight accommodations and even gift shops. Unlike the noisy, dirty, disfiguring granite industry of yesteryear, the fishing business detracts not at all from the island's physical beauty. On the contrary, most of us find the sight of a squat, white lobster boat rumbling out of a harbor worth pausing for, photographing or even painting, if we have the talent.

Beauty abounds on Vinalhaven—beauty of a rugged, austere, weathered sort. The quaint, cute, pretty and precious have not taken root here. Despite the amenities of civilization and the catering to tourists, there remains something of the frontier settlement about Vinalhaven. Quarrying and fishing have given the island a rough, makeshift look; Vinalhaven never had the soil to support much farming and so never acquired the well-tended, deep-rooted aura of a farming community. Main Street is dominated by odd, gawky high-Victorian structures, somehow Wild West in feeling; and the town itself is unplanned and unmanicured, hemmed on the water side by a hodgepodge of docks, fish plant and lobster co-ops and pitted deeper inland with abandoned quarries (now much prized summer swimming holes). Beyond town, out on the North Haven Road or the Round the Island Road, there are a few houses, a few fields, spruce and pine woods—and, around every bend and from the top of every rise, the water. Vinalhaven's coast is so jagged and twisting that, though the island measures about seven miles long by five miles wide, one is never more than a mile from salt water.

Vinalhaven has its famous artists (most famous is Robert Indiana, the Pop artist best known for piling the first two letters of LOVE on top of the second two and tilting the O to the right), but it is not, like Monhegan, an artist's island. It has its blue-blooded yachting summer residents, but it is not, like neighboring North Haven or Islesboro, primarily an upper-class social colony. It has its tourist facilities, including a small motel right on the harbor, a couple of inns, and a few restaurants serving excellent lobster and seafood, but it is not, like Mt. Desert, a summer resort. Vinalhaven has not gone out of its way for its transient population. It remains proudly its own place and goes about its own business. On Vinalhaven, you take the island on its own terms.

History: Sea and Rock

Vinalhaven, though composed of ancient rock, has only been an island for a mere wink of an eye in geological time. Like its sister islands in Penobscot Bay and farther downeast, it is a product of two enormous natural forces: volcano and glacier. Hundreds of millions of years ago, volcanic action melted rock deep beneath the earth's crust, and when this molten rock froze it became hard, enduring granite. Volcano made the rock, but glacier made the island. The advance of the glaciers tilted the land toward the sea, the retreat of the glaciers scoured out valleys, and the melting of the glaciers drowned Maine's coast. As the released glacial ice swelled the ocean, only the ancient granite volcanic domes and crumpled worn mountaintops remained above sea level. These are today's islands. This final event happened perhaps 12,000 years ago.

As for what transpired on the island between the retreat of the glacier and the "discovery" of Vinalhaven by English explorer Martin Pring in 1603, we know very little. Recent archaeological digs on neighboring North Haven show signs of an Indian village there some 4,500 years ago, and remains of shell heaps on the shores of both North Haven and Vinalhaven are evidence that Indians came to these islands to fish as early as 3300 B.C. Some believe that the Indians were the original summer folk (or summercators, at they're known in Maine), paddling out to the islands for the summer catch, celebrating it with big clambakes on the shore and then returning to the mainland before the big storms of autumn churned up the bay.

Pring, who journeyed out of Bristol, England, sailed the Fox Islands Thorofare (still a favorite cruising ground) between North Haven and Vinalhaven in June of 1603. He probably came on shore on one of the two islands and dubbed them the Fox Islands because of the many silver gray foxes he spotted. More than a century passed before white men tried to settle on Vinalhaven, but the Indians drove them off their traditional fishing grounds. Whites did not succeed in establishing permanent settlements on Vinalhaven until 1766, when Thaddeus Carver came and bought 700 acres, including a sawmill that had been built by Francis Cogswell for summer use. Though the island was named in 1789 for John Vinal, the agent who represented the island's interests in Boston (his son William settled here), Carver gave his name to the harbor on which Vinalhaven's town is built and to his many descendants who still live on the island today. Originally the name Vinalhaven designated a town that encompassed a number of islands including nearby North Haven (once known as the North Fox Island, with today's Vinalhaven called the South Fox Island), Hurricane Island (where an Outward Bound school is located today) and distant Matinicus. Eventually both Matinicus and North Haven broke away to form their own local governments—Matinicus in 1840, North Haven in 1846.

Once Carver had planted himself on the island, many others followed and by 1790 there were 855 people in the incorporated town of Vinalhaven.

Nineteenth-century Vinalhaven was supporting itself adequately from the sea, but if it hadn't been for granite, the island probably would have remained a fairly quiet, sparsely populated fishing community, much as it is today. But there *was* granite— seemingly inexhaustible supplies of beautiful stone, gray and bluish gray, fine and coarse-grained, stone that lay close to the surface of the land and sank deep down into it in unbroken deposits—and the industry that it spawned in the mid-19th century literally changed the face of Vinalhaven.

Commercial granite quarrying began on Vinalhaven in 1826 when a New Hampshire man named Tuck cut out the stone for a jail in Massachusetts. Twenty years were to pass before the business took off: In 1846 a quarry went into operation on Leadbetter's Island off Vinalhaven's west side; three years later the East Boston Quarry opened; by 1860 three others had started up and seven more were opened up between 1860 and 1880. Vinalhaven's island location was not a drawback, since transportation by water was cheaper and easier at the time than hauling the stone overland. Chebeague Island (see Casco Bay Islands below) down the coast in Casco Bay supplied the boats to carry Vinalhaven granite to where it was wanted—and it was wanted first for breakwaters, forts and lighthouses and later for grand public buildings in the nation's major cities.

The first federal contract came in the 1850s with an order for 3,000 cubic feet of stone for Fort Richmond on Staten Island, and after the Civil War business really exploded. In the post-Civil War federal building boom of grand civic structures, granite—somber, august, powerful, enduring—was the material of choice. These years were known as "government times" on Vinalhaven, and the money, the work and the stone seemed endlessly plentiful. The island's population swelled with immigrants from Scotland, Ireland, Scandinavia, Italy, and by 1880 at the peak of the granite years there were 3,380 people here, more than twice as many as today.

It was a noisy, dangerous, dirty business: The din of sledgehammers and, after 1900, steam-driven machinery was supposed to have been fierce. But from the racket, sweat, mangled hands and lost lives on Vinalhaven came hundreds of thousands of tons of magnificent stone to sheathe the State, War and Navy Department buildings in Washington, the Cincinnati Post Office and the Brooklyn Bridge, among many other humbler structures. The most celebrated stones of Vinalhaven are the eight columns that stand in the apse of the world's second largest church (after St. Peter's in Rome), the Cathedral of Saint John the Divine in upper Manhattan. Quarried in 1899, each column was a monolith measuring 64 feet long and weighing over 300 tons—the largest stones ever cut from the living rock. A special lathe was constructed to round and polish the columns and the first was nearly finished when it cracked in two and fell to the ground. The second and third columns also broke on the lathe, and so the Bodwell Granite Company, the island's largest, was forced to make the columns in two sections of 40 and 20 feet. Bodwell received $20,000 for each column, though the breaking of the first three slabs cost the company dearly. Press coverage was considerable when lighters towed the massive column sections from the island of Vinalhaven to the island of Manhattan. The columns stand today in the still unfinished cathedral; if you didn't know they were in two pieces you'd never guess.

A more down-to-earth island specialty was the paving stones that were in demand for city streets in the late 19th century. These were the bread and butter of the granite business. Talented, brawny workers could cut them by the score and they were shipped in loads of 60,000 to the burgeoning metropolises of New York, Boston and New Orleans. Hurricane Island, an important granite island just a jump to the southwest of Vinalhaven, once shipped out 320,465 paving stones in a 12-day period.

The boom years on Vinalhaven were rather few in number. By the turn of the century, granite paving blocks had fallen out of favor because they made carriage and automobile rides too bumpy. Government contracts became harder and harder to come by, and the demand for granite tapered off as cheaper and more versatile building materials, particularly concrete, came into widespread use. The Bodwell Company closed in 1919, and most of the other island outfits followed during the teens and twenties. By the end of the 1930s the granite era had ended.

Nowadays the blasting is over and the islanders have gone back to the sea to earn their livelihood. (Quarrying resumed for a short spell in 1972 when a dozen men cut out 500 granite slabs for new corporate buildings in Delaware and Michigan, and today, with granite coming back into style as more architects choose it over steel and glass for post-modernist skyscrapers, there are rumors afoot that some of the quarries may be reopened.) One can visit the remains of quarries and the smaller granite sites called "motions" at Armbrust Hill, a public park and picnic area on the outskirts of town (see below) and at Lawson's and Booth quarries, each about a mile from town, the former on the North Haven Road the latter on the road that continues on from East Main Street. Underground springs have filled these abandoned quarries with clear, fresh water; their sheltered waters, a good deal warmer than the frigid Maine ocean in summer, make them popular swimming holes (no pets, soap or shampoo permitted). The image of the inheritors of Vinalhaven playing on the ruins of their ancestors' toils puts one in mind of the frailty and transience of even the most rock-hard human pursuits. "Look on my work, ye Mighty, and despair!"

Seeing the Sights: Man's and Nature's

Vinalhaven, though rather small and certainly undeveloped by mainland standards, is still big enough to get lost on. Getting lost is that much easier because the island's 39 miles of public roads bear no street signs. There is no tourist information center, but you can acquire from several shops on Main Street a useful map of the town and island that lists points of interest and includes a telephone directory of public services, hotels and restaurants. Once you're acquainted with Vinalhaven, you won't miss the street signs—anyway, people give directions by landmark, not road name—but getting the lay of the land can be tricky at first. Where you expect unbroken land, there's yet another cove jutting in; roads wind around the inlets, creeks and harbors so that you're never quite sure what direction you're traveling. The cove that was brimming with water when you went by in the morning has been reduced by the action of Maine's considerable tides to a mud flat when you return in the afternoon. It all takes some getting used to. A bicycle is probably the ideal way of getting your bearings in good weather, but, since not all the island's roads are paved, some of the going can be pretty rough. The island is not much of a challenge for the serious biker, but it has hills enough to get the heart pumping. A couple of hours suffice to explore its length and breadth.

Just as Vinalhaven's roads carry no street signs, so its parks and beaches have little in the way of "interpretive markers," trail guides or formal paths, and there are certainly no park rangers or lifeguards. Sightseeing and exploring is strictly informal—even haphazard—and you're on your own as far as what to look at, where to step or how to interpret what you're seeing. But this is fine with most of the people who come here. National park-style nature loops, such as one finds at Acadia National Park on Mt. Desert, would spoil something of the innocence, the roughness of Vinalhaven.

The Town

Unless you fly, you'll arrive in Vinalhaven by ferry, which deposits you at the ferry landing on the outskirts of town. The town of Vinalhaven is the logical place to begin your exploration of the island. From the ferry terminal near Smith Point (site of Grimes Park, a nice spot for picnicking) it's a short walk past the lobster coop, the fish plant and the fire department to Main Street and the heart of town. If you're never more than a mile from salt water on the island of Vinalhaven, you're never more than a stone's throw away from it in the center of town, for Vinalhaven's Main Street is built on a narrow strip of land between two bodies of water—Carvers Harbor and Carvers Pond, a tidal basin that opens out into the harbor through a millrace (there is no mill today, but there is a Millrace restaurant with a view of the channel). On this strip of land sit most of the town's commercial buildings: the restaurants, gift shops, the Tidewater Motel (the only motel on an unbridged Maine island), food stores, gas station. Perhaps the most imposing building on Main Street is the Odd Fellows Hall, an ornate, mansard-roofed, cupola-crowned Victorian pile built in 1885 by the fraternal order known as the International Order of Odd Fellows.

Fifield's hardware store occupies the ground floor of another bedecked turn-of-the-century structure, but even more important than its architecture is its function as the center of island genealogy and lore. Storekeeper Bruce Grindle is an extraordinarily cordial man who spends a good deal of time chatting with the old-timers, collecting photographs of every Vinalhavener, dispensing candy from his famous cast-iron skillet, and answering visitors' questions.

One guide book calls Vinalhaven's Main Street a "tourist's delight," and though the pickings are rather lean compared with such tourist meccas as Newport or Nantucket, they're opulent for offshore Maine. Here are enough craft stores, art galleries, snack bars, restaurants and T-shirt shops to occupy most of a day-tripper's day. You can picnic right in town on the waterfront of Carvers Harbor or stroll to one of the public parks a bit out of town (see below).

Parks and Beaches

Vinalhaven's jagged granite coastline, its scattering of satellite islands (50 or so altogether), its views to narrow bands of water and glimpses to the wide bay beyond is like a scaled-down model of Maine's own famous rockbound coast. Much of the island's shore is in private hands, but thanks to the foresight of generous islanders and summer folk, there are some fine pieces of it set aside for public use. Vinalhaven's parks, though rather small, are plentiful. My favorite is the Lane's Island Preserve, 45 acres of open fields, moorland, marsh and beach (including a small, pocket sand beach, rare and thus prized in Maine) that was purchased by Vinalhaveners and given to the Nature Conservancy in 1968. The preserve, a short and pleasant walk from town down the east side of Carvers Harbor and over a small bridge, has extensive views out to the south and the open bay, which on windy days can whip up a good pounding surf.

Overlooking the park is the high, plain white farmhouse that Timothy Lane built early in the 19th century (the house itself is not inside the preserve); Timothy Lane's monument, a stone obelisk now weather-smoothed and covered with orange lichen, rises above the small fenced family cemetery in the center of the preserve. Paths lead over the spruce-dotted hayfield and all around the shoreline. Wildflowers seem to take on deeper hues in the intense light reflected off the sea (in July I spotted beach peas, rosa rugosa, thistle and blue flag). Lane's Island is an ideal spot to commune—with nature, with the sea, with the birds, and with the mysterious essence of Vinalhaven, whose lobster boats work the waters in front of you and whose town rises up around its harbor behind.

On the way to Lane's Island you'll pass Armbrust Hill, the site of four major quarries as well as numerous smaller "motions" (pits), and now a town-owned wildlife reserve. Members of the Vinalhaven Garden Club and local schoolchildren cleared paths here and helped plant wildflowers and shrubs. From the top of the hill on a clear day you can see Matinicus, Wooden Ball and Seal Islands. The mountain ash comes alive with bright berries in the fall. The park abuts the island's Community Medical Center, and just back of the center there is a children's playground.

Geary's Beach, about four miles from town on the island's east shore, is a public sandy beach, considerably larger than the pocket beach on Lane's Island. Of course no one really *swims* in Maine's ocean (for swimming, try one of the abandoned quarries—see above), but Geary's Beach is pleasant for sunbathing, beachcombing or walking the trail through nearby Arey's Neck Woods. (For information and directions get hold of the brochure "Vinalhaven, Maine: Parks and Reservations and How to Get There," available on the island.)

Summer Folk and Island Folk

From most accounts, the old families of summer people and the old families of island people get along well here. They appreciate each other out of long acquaintance and for what they can give each other: The summer people bring in money (and taxes) and provide employment for caretakers; the island people provide services and, of course, lobsters. Both groups spend a good deal of time on the water. In the summer months, the fine old sloops and schooners of the summer people and the well-equipped, sturdily practical lobster boats of the island people cross each other's paths constantly in the coves and channels around the island. Most of the lobster boats go out from Carvers Harbor, Old Harbor and Sands Cove, all more or less on the island's south shore; the sailing yachts congregate on the north side in the Thorofare, in Winter Harbor and Seal Bay, though you can find them almost anywhere on a fair breezy summer afternoon, sailing across Penobscot Bay from neighboring islands and ports. In the summer months, Vinalhaven really belongs to the boaters, both commercial and pleasure varieties, and there is far more traffic on the water (and far more to see from the water) than on the island's bumpy roads.

One group of people who do *not* take regularly to the water are the small but growing band of artists who come here to work and play. In addition to Robert Indiana, who lives year-round right on Main Street, there is Carolyn Brady who spends summers here; and in recent summers the Vinalhaven Workshop and Press, established by native Vinalhavener Patricia Nick, has been attracting prominent master printers and artists to the island. The printers and artists collaborate in a large former schoolhouse overlooking Carvers Pond. But even with all the art being made here, Vinalhaven, unlike Monhegan, has no "art scene." The artists come here for the quiet; they're inconspicuous, they have no island galleries in which they display their work, and they seem to appreciate Vinalhaven for what it is. One thing it isn't is artsy.

While the summer folk yacht and the artists create and the tourists tour, the island people go on about their business. And their business is still predominantly the lobster business. Vinalhaven's commercial fleet of 200-odd boats is among Maine's largest, and island lobstermen send about $2 million worth of lobsters to market each year. A large percentage of the lobsters caught off the island's rocky shores are sold through the 100-member Vinalhaven Fishermen's Cooperative, established in 1974. Here's how it works: Cooperative members get their fuel and bait (usually herring) from the cooperative and at the end of the day they bring their catch to the station on Carvers Harbor. Here, after being weighed, the lobsters are stored in submerged 90-pound crates and then carried by Bunkers Trucking Service (a local concern) to East Coast markets, where they are sold wholesale. Prices at this writing (June 1989) are $2.50 a pound wholesale and anyone can also walk in and buy lobsters retail from the Cooperative for $3.50 a pound. The Cooperative holds onto the money from sales until the end of the year and then pays it out to members in the form of dividends. In addition to the Cooperative, there are four private lobster buying stations on the island.

Though the lobster season goes year-round on Vinalhaven, nearly all of the fishing is done between April and January. Cooperative manager Gerry Dowdy estimates that about 80% of the men on Vinalhaven support themselves through lobstering. Overfishing for lobsters is a problem here, as on other Maine islands: There's a vicious circle at work in which the men set more and more traps for fewer and fewer lobsters. "They're all concerned about overfishing," says Dowdy, "but nothing has been done about it. The men still get a living from lobstering, but they have to work harder."

Crab, shrimp and scallops (in winter) can also be found in the island waters, and fin fish caught here commercially include herring (caught at night in nets called seines), cod, hake, pollack, mackerel, yellowtail and haddock.

The fishing industry on Vinalhaven has been given a tremendous boost in recent years by the Penobscot Bay Fish and Cold Storage, a producers cooperative of 64 fishermen (nearly all of them islanders) that processes a wide range of fish and shellfish in its Vinalhaven plant. The company is the island's largest employer, with 75 Vinalhaveners working two shifts on shrimp and scallops from December to May (when there's very little other work on the island) and 30 people working the rest of the year.

Tourism and the summer resort trade are also doing their bit to boost the island's economy, though as they grow they threaten to undermine its "real working" character. Waterfront land prices have already risen beyond the means of most natives and Main Street seems to get more "gentrified" each year, with stores that cater to the day-trippers off the boats rather than to the people who live on the island. Tourism, like time, is relative and whether Vinalhaven's day-trippers strike one as descending hordes or merely eager mainland escapees depends very much on one's perspective. During the July weeks I was on the island, the local news weekly (really more like a family Christmas newsletter than a newspaper) wrote of the vacationers who "fill" Main

Street and "crowd" the shops—yet I found the town scene rather somnolent. And out of town, on the paved and dirt roads that wind around the island, one hardly meets a soul.

This is not to say that Vinalhaven is empty. At peak season, there may be two dozen people picnicking on Lane's Island; town streets will have their share of bikes, cars and mopeds; there will be a wait to check out your groceries at the stores and a much longer wait that may begin to seem like purgatory to get your car off the island. (The ferry is a real problem for resident and visitor alike and a subject of universal complaint: people must sometimes leave their cars on line for days, moving them up as ferries carry off the cars ahead.) In August, all the summer homes and cottages tucked away around the shore are filled, as are the island's motel, small inns and bed and breakfasts. But somehow, even in peak season the islanders continue to hold sway over their island. Part of it is simply the appearance of town and island. Vinalhaven, devoid of visible mansions, sloping lawns, manicured hedges, yacht or country clubs, *looks* like it belongs to working people. (There are, of course, mansions and estates, but they're discreetly tucked away along the Thorofare and seen if at all from the water.) Part of it is the size of the year-round community: Unlike Matinicus or Frenchboro, Vinalhaven has enough permanent residents to ensure the survival of the island as a place where people live and work. Twelve-hundred people by mainland standards make a village—but by Maine island standards they make a vital, ongoing community.

The Vinalhaven community has survived pretty much intact for all these years, but it rests today on some rather shaky supports: the grace of the surrounding bay in supplying lobsters and fish; the availability of affordable land in a real estate market more and more controlled by wealthy off-islanders; the continued health of the fish processing plant. What doesn't seem shaky in the least is the resourcefulness of islanders. Vinalhaven residents give the decided impression that they can manage to endure the vagaries of history and weather, as their families have managed for generations. On this jagged, rugged island of granite and spruce, the islanders seem here to stay.

MATINICUS

Area: 2 miles long; 1 mile wide at its widest; 720 acres.
Population: 30 to 40 year-round; about 250 in peak summer season.
Location: 20 miles off Rockland, Maine, at the entrance to Penobscot Bay.
Access: The *Mary and Donna* from Rockland (on regular schedule from June to September), foot passengers only; call 207-366-3700 days and 207-366-3926 nights. The *William S. Silsby* from Rockland, car ferry run once a month by the Maine State Ferry Service; call 207-594-5543.

Matinicus, the outermost of Maine's outer islands, is changing fast. Whether it's changing for the better or for the worse depends on how you look at it and whom you talk to. But there is no question that the pressures and pursuits of the present are blowing out to this small (720 acre), flat (a shade over 100 feet at its highest), beguiling island way out in Penobscot Bay. The once vital and tight-knit community of lobstermen and their families is dwindling and unraveling; people "from away" (as Mainers term non-natives) are buying up houses and land as they come on the market; tourism, albeit in a small and rather primitive way, has begun. Natives of the island, especially the older people, say sadly that the old spirit is gone.

What remains pretty much untouched is the beauty of the island itself: the amazingly varied rocky coast punctuated by two fine sand beaches and a number of coves; the idle farm fields growing up in tangles of wild roses, untended apple trees, raspberries and thick spruce forests—all alive with birds; the old farmhouses along

Looking south down Matinicus Island from the air. The island's harbor is at the middle left and Marky's Beach, one of two sand beaches, is two coves down at lower left. Most of the houses stand alongside the road that runs down the middle of the island. At lower right is the island airstrip. (Courtesy of Richard Moody.)

the island's unpaved central road; the marvelous blue vistas on clear days out to the bay, the islands near and far, the "mountains" of Camden, Mt. Desert and Isle au Haut, the distant mainland. But of course the physical aspect of the island is just as fragile as the human community—and intimately bound up with it. As the community shifts, the landscape, or at least our perception of the landscape, is bound to shift too. Matinicus won't "feel" the same.

The Matinicus I visited in the summers of 1987 and 1989 feels very different from what I had expected. Its reputation, though not exactly bad, lacks the allure of Maine's other outer islands—the haunting beauty and artistic heritage of Monhegan, the rugged splendors of the national park on Isle au Haut. What I had imagined, from books and travel pieces and stray secondhand impressions, was a remote, backward, craggy fishing village. I'd heard about the harbor with its 12-foot tides and rickety fish houses on stilts, and I'd heard about the island jalopies abandoned on the side of dirt roads. I knew that until 1986 the island had ferry service only one day a month, so I expected the islanders to be "queer" and creaky with their isolation. In short, I thought the place would be a downeast version of Tobacco Road. Instead, the Matinicus I found was welcoming, in the reserved Maine islands way; it was so prosperous that several islanders could afford their own private planes (there is a beautifully situated airstrip on the island's north shore). The boat trip out to the island was easy and even enjoyable; and islanders were quite enough plugged into the modern world to supply their visitors with T-shirts, hotdogs, and even snow peas at the farmer's market.

Despite being the outermost Maine island, Matinicus doesn't feel vastly remote; the islanders are not in the least bit odd (not to visitors anyway); the harbor is indeed rather sloppy with piles of lobster traps and lobster smell and a few jalopies do rust among the weeds, but the island houses are well cared for and some are even elegant in a stark, unadorned way. Matinicus is simple but it's not rude. It's old-fashioned but not impoverished. Though it has few amenities, it doesn't seem to need many. Without a town, a park or even a famous landmark, it still has plenty of character.

The changes on Matinicus have been brewing for a long time, but they've become really apparent only recently. As recently as 1982, Charles B. McLane wrote in his authoritative study, *Islands of the Mid-Maine Coast*: "The island has inevitably experienced an influx of summer vacationers...but their seasonal presence has not significantly altered the character of Matinicus, as has been the case on other islands. The rusticators [the Mainers' term for summer folk] are there on sufferance, as it were, for Matinicus remains above all a working island." Five years later, not one of the Matinicus islanders I talked to agreed with this portrait. It is estimated that more than two-thirds of the land on the island belongs to people "from away." As the old families have left, so has the old pride, the social life and the neighborliness that once were so much part of the island's character. With the lobster business in a slump that many fear is only going to get worse, the young men are fishing as hard and as fast as they can with no thought of the future—theirs or anyone else's. Nowadays, come winter, there are barely enough people to make a community. And in summer the island seems crowded with new faces, more each year.

Some islanders see Matinicus going the way of neighboring Criehaven, an island half its size that used to support a year-round community but now, without ferry service, is inhabited only in summers by a handful of lobstermen and rusticators. Others wonder whether their island is fated to become a second Monhegan, now a summer tourist haven that draws crowds of day-trippers to its galleries and hiking trails as well as overnight guests to its large inns. Neither alternative seems right for Matinicus. But elements of both seem to loom in the island's future.

The Island's Fledgling Tourist Industry

Tourism on Matinicus, which got underway about a year ago, can hardly be said to be booming yet. Subsisting with some bright prospects would be more ac-curate. The catalyst was the resumption of regular ferry ser-vice to the island after a nine-year hiatus. Richard Moody, who owns the island's only store and serves as postmaster, acquired the 40-foot *Mary and Donna* in 1986 and began taking a maximum load of 28 foot-passengers out to the island on a regular schedule from June to September. All at once Matinicus appeared on the tourist map. Although the island was accessible by airplane before this (on unfoggy days only, which

Fish houses, Matinicus Island. In recent years, a few of these pic-turesque old structures have been converted to summer homes, but island lobstermen still use most of them to store and repair their traps and floats. (Courtesy of Gladys Mitchell.)

appear randomly and sometimes rarely), island enthusiasts and purists (and some natives) wouldn't have dreamed of flying. "The boat ride is part of people's vacations," says Moody. "Flying out—they don't even think they're on an island." The *New York Times* did a story on Matinicus (July 20, 1986). A bed and breakfast opened and so did a restaurant. All available cottages were rented. All real estate on the market was sold. In the 1987 season taxi service started up. Now a small inn is slated to open and bikes will be available for rental. Matinicus is now "doable" in the same way that Vinalhaven or Swans Island are doable.

But tourists should still not expect too much. Though Matinicus is not the backward, barren outpost I imagined, it's still a far cry from Hilton Head. Accommodations range from the rustic to the spartan (some of the cottages have outdoor plumbing); the island store (dubbed the "inconvenience store" by one wry resident) stocks most basics but regularly runs out of some of them between ferry trips; the restaurant (which did not open during the summer of 1989) serves lobster and plain fish dishes (there's also a stand near the harbor serving hotdogs and pizza); in the summer there is a farmer's market of island-grown produce and baked goods. Matinicus, as one might expect, has no resort or recreational facilities: no yacht club, no pool, no golf or tennis. There is no museum or theater and the only sights to see are natural: the views, the paths, the beaches (Marky Beach at the north end and South Sandy at the south), the headlands, the cliffs at Southwest Point and gorgeous sunsets at West Point. One comes here not for entertainment but to walk on the roads and paths (all land is privately owned, but most of the island is open to the considerate public), to observe the stunning variety of birds, to gather berries, to look for some of the 700 varieties of wildflowers and ferns and 57 species of grasses and sedges, and simply to be on the outermost island.

Matinicus does offer one special activity that anyone interested in birds will want to take advantage of. On summer weekends, Richard Moody takes groups out on the *Mary and Donna* to see the nesting colonies of Atlantic puffins, razorbill auks, storm petrels and arctic terns on Matinicus Rock. (Trips to the Rock and other nearby islands can also be arranged informally with lobstermen.) The Rock, a forbidding-looking 32 acres of treeless granite five miles from Matinicus, is Maine's outermost lighthouse station and has had a light in operation since 1827. The twin, gray granite towers (erected in 1846), rising over the barren rock and the open sea, give the island a stark gothic aura. Today only one tower serves as a lighthouse (it's automated); the Coast Guard maintains an installation on the Rock and the Audubon Society sends people out to study the birds and keep intruders away.

The puffins are the main attraction here, for this is one of two nesting sites of the species on the Atlantic coast. (The other puffin colony is on Machias Seal Island near Canada and there is an experiment underway to introduce breeding pairs to Eastern Egg Rock in Muscongus Bay to the south.) The ungainly penguin-like birds with their outsized red and orange beaks and frantic way of flying are known as the clowns of the sea; the best time to catch their performances is from mid-June to mid-July. On the way out to the Rock there are ledges where seals frequently haul out; as the boat passes, they flop one after another back into the cold water.

Man's History on the Island

The landscape, resources and situation of Matinicus—its flat topography and the fine quality of its soil, its rocky shores and small coves rich in shell and fin fish, its relative proximity to the huge fishing opportunities of the Georges Bank—have in large part determined its human history. Before the white settlers came to stay in the mid-18th century, there were French and English and even Portuguese fishermen who used the island as a stopping off point on long fishing expeditions as far back as the 16th century (and perhaps earlier, with visits from the Vikings as well). And before the European fishermen, of course, there were native Americans, the Penobscot tribe of the Tarratine Indians, who came to Matinicus and its neighboring islands to hunt, fish and gather birds' eggs and grass. The name Matinicus is believed to be a corruption of the Indian word Manasquesicook, which some translate as "place of many turkeys" and others as "collection of grassy islands." The early European fishermen built huts on the island in which they stayed while they were drying fish, and by 1671 English traveler John Jesselyn noted in his journal that Matinicus was "well supplied with homes, cattle, arable land, and marshes." In the early years of the 18th century English fishermen had 20 boats based on the island, and in 1725 William Vaughan, a Harvard graduate from Damariscotta, Maine, tried to get a commercial fishing venture going on the island, but his scheme soon failed.

The history of Matinicus as an established, ongoing white settlement dates from 1751 when Ebenezer Hall came here from Portland, Maine, with his wife and children. Hall's own stay on the island was brief for he ran afoul of the Indians. As part of his farming practices, Hall burned over small, neighboring Green Island in order to improve the quality of the hay. The Indians objected because it destroyed the birds' eggs and grasses they gathered there and they sent a formal letter of protest to the governor. When the law failed to move against Hall, they took matters into their own hands, and in June 1757 they killed Hall and carried off his wife and young daughters. However, the two Hall sons escaped: one jumped through the window and the other, Ebenezer Jr., happened to be out fishing at the time of the massacre. (After several years and many adventures, Mrs. Hall Sr. was released by the Indians and she lived to be 81; according to some accounts, the young Hall girls lived happily ever after with the Indians.) In 1763, Ebenezer Jr. returned to Matinicus with his wife and soon her brother, Abraham Young, followed. And so the Halls and Youngs became established on the island and they remain to this day. Gladys Mitchell, who lives on Matinicus most of the year and rents her house out during the summer, is a direct descendant of Ebenezer Hall; she very kindly answered my questions about the island and allowed me to publish some of her old photographs.

The Hall massacre marks the highpoint of drama in the island's history. After this, the Indians left the white islanders alone and for about 100 years the whites increased in numbers and in prosperity. The 1790 census shows 10 families and a total of 59 people on Matinicus; in 1850, there were 220 people living on the island; and in 1870 the population peaked at around 275. During these growth years of the 19th century, farming was as important as fishing in the island's economy. The settlers cleared the original hardwood forests and planted apple orchards, kept oxen, cows and sheep and raised vegetables, particularly potatoes, cabbage and turnips. The soil was fertile, the land flat, the climate, at least by northern New England standards, temperate—and the farmers made out well.

The waters around the island were also fertile, and after the middle of the 19th century the men turned more and more to the sea to earn their livings. Herring and mackerel, once abundant in this region, brought the greatest profits in those years. By 1880, 40 Matinicus islanders worked the waters for these fish, and the island supported two operations, the Matinicus Fish Company and the W.B. Kittredge Company, which bought fresh fish from regional fishermen, cured it and sold it on the mainland. Gradually, the island farms declined, and after the Second World War farming pretty much ceased. Those who worked on Matinicus worked the sea.

Lobstering on Matinicus

Just as fishing supplanted farming on Matinicus, so lobstering supplanted mackerel and herring fishing, especially after the turn of the century. Lobstering remains the major—in fact, just about the only reliable—source of income on the island today

(tourism has not yet taken a firm enough hold to count). Herring and mackerel fishing continue in a small, occasional way: Though herring has again become scarce in these parts recently, at least one of the island men was netting mackerel during my visit. But lobstering is king on Matinicus. According to McLane, "more than a few Matinicus lobstermen today—excluding buyers—have incomes in the $30,000-$50,000 range, and several keep their own planes." Even though the last few years have been poor for lobstering, the men (and boys, for the islanders start lobstering as soon as they can use a boat) can still make out quite well if they work at it. Working at it today means having as many as 1,000 traps in the water, hauling several hundred traps a day starting at dawn nearly every day, all year round, in all sorts of weather.

Unlike the Vinalhaven fisherman, the Matinicus lobstermen have no island-based cooperative to market their catch. Instead,

Marky Young, a Matinicus islander, back in the days when lobsters could be plucked out of the rockweed at low tide. Marky's Beach, a fine sand beach at the island's north end, is named for this Matinicus luminary. (Courtesy of Gladys Mitchell.)

people from away own floats in the harbor where the lobstermen get fuel and bait (herring or red fish) and where they bring their haul at the end of the day. The float operators weight the catch and buy it (current rate is about $3 per pound) and periodically a lobster smack carries a load to the mainland. According to Emery Philbrook, a long-experienced lobsterman I talked to, one can expect to get 1/2 to 3/4 of a pound of lobster per trap. At $3 per pound, one would have to haul about 13,333 traps each year (assuming the higher yield of 3/4 lb. per trap) to earn $30,000. When you consider that getting outfitted with a boat and traps can cost more than $100,000 and that many lobstermen work in teams, it's not hard to understand why some of the younger men are driving themselves to work strings of 1,000 traps.

Of course in the long run everyone is going to lose if lobstering continues at this scale. The waters not only around Matinicus but also all up and down the coast of Maine are already dangerously overfished. Efforts to organize and impose trap limits, which one long-time lobsterman called "a damn good idea," have been tried here, but some of the men got greedy and broke the rules. Everyone agrees that the lobster business is going downhill, but no one seems to be doing much about it. As the wife of a middle-aged lobsterman told me, "The men keep doing it because it's the only thing they know. The young men have grown up with it. They get to be 40 or 50 and they can't retrain for another career so they stay with it."

What most people realize but few like to say is that as the lobstering declines, the islanders will have to look elsewhere for their livelihoods. Many have already sold out to summer people; for those who remain, the tourist trade seems to be an obvious, if not particularly welcome, potential source of income. But it won't be an easy fit. The men of Matinicus have been lobstering for generations. It's difficult to imagine these tough, independent people forsaking the sea to run bed and breakfasts, souvenir stands and craft galleries.

The Island Community

The community on Matinicus, like the lobster fishery that supports it, may be in decline, but it remains vital enough to support most of the crucial institutions of community life. The island's official status is "plantation," which in the hierarchy of Maine's local governments is one step up from unorganized territory and one step down from town. (Matinicus has had its own local government since 1840, the year it split off from Vinalhaven and became incorporated as a plantation.) Islanders elect three local officials, known as assessors, who administer the upkeep of the island's roads, the power company (which put in three new generators with automatic switching three years ago) and the school. The enrollment in the island's one-room schoolhouse is a good register of its decline. The island has had a school since the early 19th century and by 1869 there were 61 students. The schoolhouse was extensively modernized and remodeled in 1900, but by 1925, enrollment had dropped to 22; last winter only four students were in attendance. When these four reach the ninth grade, they will have to go off-island for their high school education (the plantation pays tuition).

There is a single church on the island, a sturdy, plain white structure that dates from 1906 and that provides sanctuary to a tiny Congregationalist congregation. Matinicus has no resident minister. During the two summer months, the Maine Sea Coast

Missionary Society sends a minister here to conduct services. The rest of the year, Matinicus, along with other offshore Maine islands, is served once a month by the *Sunbeam*, the Sea Coast Missionary Society's boat. In recent years, there have not been enough people for a service on the boat, so the minister visits islanders in their homes.

House and lobster traps on Matinicus.

Though none of the houses on Matinicus are particularly distinguished architecturally, there are several fine old farmhouses dating from the early to the mid-19th century that give the island's main road the settled, peaceful look of an old-time farming community. The best houses, to my mind, are mostly at the north end: the Young house, supposedly the oldest on the island (c. 1800), a simple white clapboard Cape-style dwelling with long extensions added on later; the Ames family home, a high, white rambling farmhouse with a big yard enclosed by a white picket fence; the gray-shingled Tolman farmhouse (c. 1850) that stands by itself on a gentle rise just beyond the other houses. Scattered around the island there are a few 20th-century bungalows. Some older homes have been renovated and one or two new homes are going up along the shore, but so far there has not been enough building anywhere on Matinicus to disturb its old-fashioned air.

Old-fashioned, to me, implies a deliberate adherence to the ways of the past—a matter of choice, not necessity—and that's the impression I gathered on Matinicus. Despite the decline of the island's working community, despite the discovery of the island by (gradually) increasing numbers of tourists and rusticators, Matinicus retains with a measure of pride the aspect and the habits of an earlier time. Laundry is washed in wringer-washers and hung on lines outdoors to dry; the islanders drive cars and pickup trucks that look (and sound) like they predate Henry Ford; the island fire department is a truck and a bell near the church. People greet each other on the roads and paths, keep track of each other's doings, help each other out in emergencies. Islanders share—their fish, their advice, their stories—not just with each other but with visitors and summer folk as well.

The island is scaled to distances one can cover on foot. A few days on Matinicus will put one in contact with a good part of the human population. An hour or two suffices for a stroll from the harbor to the north and south ends of the island and back. In the course of that stroll one passes the wharf, the store, the church, the school, the cemetery and the homes of most of the people who live here—all the essential places of a community. For the visitor, there is something immensely satisfying about being able to take in a community so quickly, to gain a feel for it, however inexact, to establish some sort of relation with it, however transitory. The Matinicus community lends itself ideally to this kind of rapid taking in because it is small, because it exists on an island and is thus sharply demarcated, because people walk—and of course because it is still, however precariously, a real community.

A real community, but a community sadly changed, in the eyes of island natives, from what it was. "I don't like to see Matinicus becoming like Criehaven," Gladys Mitchell said ruefully. "I'd like to see it as it used to be—a fishing village. I'd like to see it the way it was when just island people lived here." In those days, which Mrs. Mitchell said started to come to an end soon after World War II, there was pride in the island, pride in the community of the Halls and Youngs and Philbrooks and Ameses who had lived here for generations, pride in the independence that came with being way out and cut off from the mainland. Matinicus is just as far out in Penobscot Bay as it always was, but the mainland somehow seems closer today. Paradoxically, as the community grows smaller, it feels less isolated. The descendants of some of the old families remain, but more and more they're holdouts. The old-fashioned ways continue, but they're threatened. On Matinicus, everyone from the visitor of a week to the resident of a lifetime wonders: How much longer will even the forms and institutions of the old ways survive? No one, yet, has any clear answer.

MONHEGAN

Area: 1.5 miles long by .75 mile wide.
Population: 80 year-round; 600-700 in peak summer season.
Location: At the mouth of Muscongus Bay, 10 miles south of Port Clyde.
Access: By passenger ferry year-round from Port Clyde (207-372-8848) and in summer only from Boothbay Harbor (207-633-2284) and New Harbor.

Monhegan Island—tiny, lonely, mystically beautiful—has lured explorers and seafaring adventurers for centuries, perhaps millennia. According to legend, the Irish monk Saint Brendan spied its 160-foot cliffs rising up out of the ocean in 565 A.D. and sailed his open oxhide boat into the island's harbor. Vikings may have landed on Manana Island, the bleak, treeless speck of land that guards Monhegan's harbor, sometime around the year 1000; and European fishermen surely knew and used the island well before Columbus sailed to the New World. The island was the first American landfall on the routes of the great English explorers of the 17th century, and the last American landfall for Europe-bound sailing ships during the Colonial period. After the discovery by European mariners there was a rediscovery by American artists. As early as the 1870s, artists began making the 10-mile crossing to Monhegan, drawn hither by the cliffs, the meadows, the wild ocean views, the remoteness, the picturesque fishermen and fish houses and, soon, by the glowing words and pictures of other artists. The artists have kept coming ever since, but they haven't been able to keep Monhegan to themselves.

The island is now in the midst of another great age of discovery—by tourists and day-trippers, drawn hither by the same cliffs, meadows, ocean views, fishhouses and so on that the artists have painted so memorably, and drawn, of course, by the artists themselves. There is nothing like a group of artists to make a place fashionable, and nothing like fashion to drive up prices. Monhegan, like many other art colonies (the Hamptons, Cape Ann, Provincetown), has become too expensive for struggling artists—to say nothing of struggling fishermen—and too crowded (at least in summer) for seekers of solitude and escape. Monhegan may finally have been discovered too often and by too many.

It's easy to see why more than 300 artists, including Rockwell Kent, Robert Henri, Andrew Winters, Edward Hopper, Jay Connaway and Jamie Wyeth have fallen in love with the place. Even on a coast thickly gemmed with beautiful islands, Monhegan stands out. For the first generation of artists, Monhegan was a magnificent splinter of the American sublime—vast in power, if not in size; elemental, dramatic, new. Rockwell Kent, who first came here in 1905, was haunted by the looming masses of the steeply rising coast. ("It looks as large as the Rocky Mountains," wrote painter George Bellows, another Monhegan artist.) The dark, dangerous sea is at war with the blunt rectangles and triangles of fish houses in the works of Robert Henri, Kent's teacher. The island's fishermen, their nets and traps, were the subjects of the German-born artist Emil Holzhauer, who came to the island at intervals from 1914 to the 1950s. Andrew Winter, an artist who lived year round on the island from 1942 to 1958, memorably painted the cluster of steep-roofed wooden houses that front the island's harbor. Jamie Wyeth, the most famous artist now working on the island (he lives several months a year in the house Rockwell Kent built by the shore for his mother in 1908, one of three Kent houses on the island), frequently paints the people and animals that share the island. A hauntingly beautiful Wyeth painting called *Bronze Age* (1967) shows the bronze bell on Manana Island that keepers used to strike by hand as a warning to ships in foggy weather; today, the Coast Guard maintains a foghorn and radio beacon on Manana.

The fishermen, the cliffs, the rocks, the eerie hump of Manana Island, the crashing sea are all still here. The village and harbor today look much as they do in Winter's *Monhegan Village* of 1944 or Kent's *Monhegan, Maine*. The stark, geometric fish houses still take the curling salt spray along the shore, just as they do in Henri's *Storm Tide* of 1903. The shingled homes still cling to the open slope of the village hillside; above them rises the rambling Island Inn, and still farther inland at a height of land looms the island's granite-block lighthouse, whose keeper's quarters now houses a small museum open in summers with permanent exhibits on the human and natural history of the island and each year a different exhibit of the work of a local painter. Many visitors linger in the village area, where the few inns, restaurants and the Plantation Gallery are located. The flowers in houseyards, fields and meadows are exquisite: Wild iris and frost flowers bloom on the central meadow in spring; pink and white wild roses, the many blues of lupines, and purple vetches are the colors of early summer; violet-blue fringed gentians, rare elsewhere, bloom abundantly on Monhegan in the early autumn (picking the wildflowers is strictly forbidden on the island).

Away from the village, on the wild, uninhabited eastern backside, a magnificent spruce and balsam forest closes over the land. Although this is private land, mostly owned and preserved forever wild by the Monhegan Associates, which was founded in 1954 by Theodore Edison, the inventor's son, visitors may hike the needle-cushioned trails that lead through Cathedral Woods to the high cliffs at Black and White Head. These oft-painted cliffs are beautiful but deadly. The small library in Monhegan's village was built in memory of two victims of the cliffs, island children Jacqueline Stewart Barstow and Edward Winslow Vaughn, who were swept off the rocks to their deaths at ages 10 and 14 respectively, and there have been other tragic accidents here as well.

One will do a good deal of hiking if one stays on Monhegan for any length of time, for cars are not allowed here, and in fact only a handful of well-worn pickups belonging to islanders bump down the island's narrow, rutted dirt road. Seventeen miles of paths connect village with woods and shore. Until two years ago, a few private generators provided the only electricity on the island, and even now the central generator serves only about one-third of the island's homes; in some of the cottages people still light their way to bed by kerosene lamps. For the visitor, there is something unutterably quaint and charming about all this—to dwell far from civilization amid much-painted, much-loved scenery; to match the vistas one sees with the vistas one has admired in works of art; to live apart from cars and their noise; to walk with nature. Monhegan has everything people love about the Maine islands—*and* art. No wonder upwards of 300 day-trippers alight here whenever the fog lifts during July and August.

The Island Community

The 80 or so islanders who live here year-round know that nature can put on a sterner, grayer face than the one that smiles on summer crowds. The crowds thin out quickly in the autumn after the fall migration (of birds) ends and the last bird-watchers depart. The hotels close up by October. On November 1 the town water shuts off (the pipes are above ground and would freeze; winter residents must rely on their own wells or cisterns) and the mailboat service from Port Clyde drops down to three trips a week. Then the isolation really closes in. The primitive services and lack of cars that tourists delight in make the isolation that much deeper, but life goes on. Six island children attend the one-room schoolhouse (grades K-8; children must go off-island for high school), and there is a grocery store where islanders can buy their necessities. The islanders get to know each other very well during the long winter months, but somehow, as one islander commented wryly, they are all still friends come spring. It helps that most of them manage to get away for at least part of the winter, and the lobstermen travel frequently to the mainland in their boats.

Some 13 island men own lobster boats and support themselves from the sea, but lobstering off Monhegan does not commence until Trap Day—January 1 (or thereabout). The peculiar custom of lobstering only from Trap Day until sunset on June 25 became law in 1909, when the Maine state legislature closed the waters for two nautical miles out, making Monhegan the only island with a legally closed lobster season. (Swans Island has adopted a limit on the number of traps a lobsterman may set but not on the season; Monhegan also has an unofficial limit of 600 traps per boat, but enforcement is up to the individual fishermen.) By so limiting the lobster season to only six months a year, islanders have helped to conserve this precious resource, and they get the lobsters when they're plumpest and fetch the highest prices at market. But of course they have also consigned themselves to going out during the coldest, bleakest, dampest part of the year. The lobstermen used to sell their catch to a lobster smack that came out from the mainland about once every 10 days in the winter; but now, with larger and faster boats, they cross over to Boothbay Harbor themselves to market their catch.

When Trap Day dawns, just about the entire population—including any artists still in residence—troop down to the harbor to help move the stacks of lobster traps from the dock to the boats. Art and lobstering might appear to be strange bedfellows, but over the century during which artists have been coming here, the art community and the fishing community have mingled, and a number of the island's lobstermen are children of artists. Even in the early days of the art colony, notes Eunice Agar in an article about the island in *American Artist* magazine (May 1987), the island's artists "were an exuberant, hardy lot who actively pursued a vigorous life and believed in physical labor…No effete salon artists, they took an active part in the life and work of the island." Though most of these early artists painted in the summer, many of their paintings show Monhegan in its harsh wintery aspect: The human figure struggles against a nature immense and dark with ominous cliffs, a sea boiling with waves, and a sky intent on storm.

The island's present year-round community is composed of about half old island families and half families who have moved out here in the past 15 or 20 years. Some of the newcomers are summer people who chose to stay on, some are refugees from mainland pressures, some are fishermen who wanted to have a crack at Monhegan's lobsters. The newcomers and the old-timers form an integrated, cohesive community, said Willard J. Boyton, Monhegan's first assessor (an office equivalent to first selectman), just as the summer people and the year-round residents do. Perhaps because the original summer colonists were artists eager to participate in the life of the island rather than upper-crust vacationers determined to maintain their class distinction, no rigid divisions arose between island people and summer people.

Lobstering and art have both been vital to the island for a long time. And both now face a common threat: the rising cost of real estate, which has doubled the average price of a Monhegan home in the past 10 years or so. When a Monhegan home goes on the market these days, the buyer is likely to be a prosperous academic or writer who will come for a few weeks or a month or two in the summer, not a lobsterman who would live here all year or an artist who might stay for three or four months.

Monhegan does not seem to be in imminent danger of losing its year-round community, but islanders are aware of the possibility. "The fear is on everyone's mind," said Boynton. "The seeds have been planted."

History

Monhegan's mythical history begins, as mentioned above, with the voyages of Saint Brendan and the Vikings. Or perhaps not so mythical in the case of the Vikings—for the ledges of Manana bear strange runes that many believe were carved by the Vikings sometime around the year 1000. (Some claim the marks were left by Phoenicians; others, less romantically, insist they were scratched in by the sea.) In any case, the island's history is long, perhaps the longest of any North American island. Even if the Norse sailors did not come here, historians feel quite certain that Basque, Portuguese and Breton fishermen did. Monhegan was a landmark on their far-ranging western fishing expeditions, and the fishermen stopped off here for water and to dry their fish on the racks known as flakeyards. Some accounts claim that in 1497, shortly after Colombus discovered the islands of the Caribbean, John Cabot, a Venetian sailing under the English flag, made his first North American landfall on Monhegan. (However, in *The European Discovery of America: The Northern Voyages* Samuel Eliot Morrison, an authority on the subject of early exploration, says Cabot made landfall on Cape Degrat, Newfoundland, and never went anywhere near Monhegan.) Verrazano, sailing for the French in 1524, sighted the island and named it Anne (for one of the princesses of Navarre). The English sailor and adventurer David Ingram voyaged this way in 1569 and was the first to describe the island as "backed like a whale"—a comparison mariners still make when they see the high-humped island rise out of the sea (some claim it is visible from 60 miles away).

The first years of the 17th century brought a whole flock of explorers, including Bartholomew Gosnold, Champlain and Captain George Waymouth (sometimes spelled Weymouth). Waymouth anchored his boat, the *Archangel*, in the harbor in 1605, climbed ashore, named the island St. George, and planted a cross in the stony soil, the first Christian cross to stand in New England. According to A. Hyatt Verrill's *Romantic and Historic Maine*, he then proceeded to seize five Indians and pack them back to the English court. The most celebrated early Monhegan landing was that of Captain John Smith, who sailed north from the Virginia Colony in 1614 in search of gold, copper and whales (for more about Smith's travels, see Smith Island entry). What he found instead was abundant codfish and a field on top of the "rocky isle" on which to plant a garden for "sallets." While Smith continued his exploring, trading "trifles" with the Indians for beaver, marten and otter skins, a group of his men remained behind on Monhegan to fish.

Smith painted an enticing picture of Monhegan and other northeastern islands in *A Description of New England* (published in London in 1616). The book, as much promotional writing intended to rouse interest in future colonies as objective "description," did lure several hardy souls out to the island to fish in the summer, and there was a year-round English settlement as early as 1618. French and Indian raids during the 17th century—including a devastating attack of 1689 when the islanders' homes and fields were burned—forced the abandonment of the settlement, but fishermen and more settlers returned periodically.

It wasn't until after the American Revolution that three young men and their families, Henry Trefethren of Kittery, Maine, and his two brothers-in-law Francis Horn and Josiah Starling, planted an enduring settlement on Monhegan. Their descendants remained here to fish, but the community never grew very big. In 1820, there were 68 residents on the island—only 12 fewer than today. But of course nowadays, what Monhegan lacks in population it more than makes up for in popularity. For this, the island has its artists to thank.

Artist Colony

Aaron Draper Shattuck, who hailed from Connecticut and painted in the style of the Hudson River School, was the first artist known to visit and paint Monhegan. He came with another artist (possibly the Maine-born marine painter Harrison Bird Brown) in 1858 aboard the U.S. schooner *Vigilant*, which was making an inspection tour of the Maine lighthouses (Monhegan's light was built in 1824). Shattuck had enough time on the island to sketch the stormy sea beating against the cliffs, and later, back in his studio, he turned the sketches into paintings. In 1875, the artist Edward Norton spent some time on the island, and four or five years later the well-known marine illustrator Milton J. Burns made the voyage out and did some sketching; illustrations based on these sketches later accompanied an article in *Harper's New Monthly Magazine* called "Fish and Men in the Maine Islands" (September 1880). Other illustrators turned up and other articles appeared, and soon a steady trickle of artists and tourists were coming out to Monhegan.

The island's first boarding house opened for business in 1888, regular ferry service was inaugurated soon after, and by the 1890s, the art colony was established. According to Eunice Agar's article in *American Artist*, "Early in this century, just about every major American landscape painter visited Monhegan." One prominent exception was Winslow Homer, who, according to island lore, did make the crossing but became so violently seasick that he insisted on returning on the next boat back. Agar considers the period from about 1900 to 1914 Monhegan's "golden age," for it was in those years that Robert Henri and his many gifted students, including Rockwell Kent, George Bellows, Randall Davey, Edward Hopper, John McPherson, Sarah McPherson and Emil Holzhauer worked here.

Kent, perhaps the most famous and influential Monhegan artist, arrived in 1905 when he was 22 and lived much of the year on the island for five years, during which time he built three houses and a studio (all still standing), fished for lobsters, labored as a carpenter, well digger and gravedigger and completed some of his most impressive work. A fellow artist described his paintings of the island's cliffs, dark seas, and toiling fishermen as "splendid big thoughts…like prayers to God." In these canvases, Kent paints Monhegan as it must have looked to the first explorers—an island at the end of the world, a steep, luminous, primeval place that seems to rise newly created out of the sea. In addition to being a great painter, Kent was an outspoken socialist, and though his politics may not have sat too well with the islanders, they accepted him into the community and made good use of his skills as a carpenter. Kent was happy on Monhegan, but he snarled his life and his marriage by carrying on a romance with an island girl, and in 1917 he sold his Monhegan house. In 1947 he bought it back and began coming to the island again to paint. But the island, in Kent's view, had changed over the years to a "Down East Provincetown" and the islanders had changed as well. Now, in the age of McCarthyism, many of them no longer welcomed the socialist artist and he ceased coming to the island for good after 1953.

Over the years, a number of artists have lived year-round on Monhegan, including the English-born Samuel Peter Rolt Triscott and Eric Hudson, both of whom settled here early in the century; Jay Hall Connaway, who lived here from 1931 to 1947 and brought out many other artists to his art school; Andrew Winter, a summer visitor in

Storm Tide *was painted by Robert Henri in 1903, the year he first visited Monhegan. Although he didn't stay on the island very often himself, Henri ushered in Monhegan's "golden age" when he encouraged a number of his gifted students, including Rockwell Kent and Edward Hopper, to come to the island to paint. (Oil on canvas; 26 X 32 inches; collection of Whitney Museum of American Art.)*

the twenties and thirties and permanent resident after 1942; and James Fitzgerald, who moved here the following year and lived in one of the Kent houses from 1948 to 1971. Two long-time summer residents were the Russian-born artist Abraham J. Bogdanove and Leo Meissner, and later came Jamie Wyeth and Zero Mostel, who, though he made his name as an actor, received training as an artist and painted for many summers in his house on the shore. Charles E. Martin, best known for his drawings and covers for the *New Yorker* magazine, spends several months a year on Monhegan; his children's books set on the island, *Island Winter* and *Island Rescue* (both published by Greenwillow Books), vividly depict what life is like for island children once the summer crowds leave.

Today the artist colony has entered a period of transition. The generation of New York City artists who bought homes here after World War II is passing on, and their homes are coming into the hands of non-artists. There are now only three artists who live year-round (or most of the year) on the island: John Hultberg, who paints

Toilers of the Sea (1907) by Rockwell Kent. Kent painted this during his first, explosively creative period on Monhegan Island. In addition to painting, Kent worked on the island as a lobsterman, carpenter and gravedigger. Monhegan's 160-foot-high cliffs are a landmark for miles out to sea. (From the collection of the New Britain Museum of American Art, Charles F. Smith Fund; photo: E. Irving Blomstrann.)

large-scale abstract paintings; his artist wife Lynne Drexler, who records the island's changing landscape in colored pencil and oil; and Fred Wiley. Many more artists— perhaps 30 each year—still come to work in the summer, and about 15 to 20 of them set aside a day each week when visitors may come to their studios. But island life—and island land—are now more expensive than on the mainland, and artists with limited means can no longer afford to hole up here for long periods of work. They are now more likely to come for a few weeks, rent cottages or stay in one of the inns (where some of them also show their works in progress in their rooms). As Eunice Agar notes in her article "today, old-time residents say that another peak period has passed." These days, it is tourism, not art, that seems to be entering a golden age on Monhegan.

Monhegan may be the most heavily touristed of the unbridged Maine islands, but it is also one of the best protected. The artists and the well-off people who have followed them here over the years have seen to that. About two-thirds of the island is a nature preserve, and the settled part where people have their homes and summer homes is a kind of preserve as well: The old-fashioned, rugged character of the place is carefully kept intact. As George Dibner notes in *Seacoast Maine*, "Some of the buildings remain picturesque at considerable cost to their owners who love them." Inevitably, there has been some construction of less picturesque houses over the years, and a couple of the old homes have fallen into the hands of people whose appreciation runs more to the financial than the aesthetic. With so many visitors coming to the island, there is money to be made by converting single-family homes into bed-and-breakfast places and rental units. But there is a strict limit to how far such things can go here. Monhegan is small and held closely by those who care for it; village land seldom if ever becomes available anymore for new building, and land outside the village has been deeded forever wild. But there is less control over the number of tourists and day-trippers coming out to the island, and these numbers have been rising steadily in recent years. "Tourists have always been welcomed on Monhegan," said First Assessor Boynton, "but there is some concern about potentially unlimited numbers of tourists coming out."

For the most part, Monhegan has been lucky in the kinds of visitors it attracts. People come out not only for the art, but also for the nature—for the flowers that bloom so profusely in the warm months and for the amazing variety of birds that stop off here during the spring and fall migrations (usually mid-May for the former and the third week of September for the latter). Bird-watchers have identified some 200 to 250 different migrant bird species on Monhegan, which is situated right on the Atlantic flyway; hawks and peregrine falcons are particularly impressive here. As many at 700 different kinds of wildflowers bloom in the island's woods, along the rocky shore, in bogs and meadows. The trailing yew, a shrub in the white cedar family, is thought to be unique to the island. Frosts usually hold off until late in November, so there are flowers blooming here long after those on the mainland have turned brown.

The day-trippers come and go, but those who stay on Monhegan for any length of time almost always become passionate about the place. To its devotees, changing Monhegan would be a desecration. But preserving Monhegan is not as simple as creating nature sanctuaries and treating its old homes kindly. Monhegan is more than scenery, wildlife, flowers and architecture. Monhegan is also a community of 80 year-round residents—some from old island families, some from artist families, some relative newcomers—who stay on after the tourists and bird-watchers and summertime artists have left and greet them when they return. No one has yet figured out a way of preserving such communities from the threats they face, threats posed by rising real estate prices, the higher costs of services that have been expanded for large summer populations but must be paid for in part by tiny winter populations, the uncertainties of an economy based on fishing.

If history is any indication, Monhegan seems likelier than most Maine islands to survive. It has survived its artists, indeed, has been immeasurably enriched by them, and it seems to be surviving its day-trippers as well. Monhegan's haunting beauty attracts and holds people, it inspires strong emotion and great art. Perhaps its beauty—a beauty that lives in both the landscape and the people of the island—will prove to be the island's best protection.

CASCO BAY ISLANDS

PEAKS ISLAND
Area: 720 acres.
Population: 1,500 year-round; 3,000 in peak summer season.
Location: Maine's Casco Bay, 3 miles east of Portland.
Access: By car and passenger ferry from Portland (call 207-774-7871).

LONG ISLAND
Area: 988 acres.
Population: 200 year-round; 1,000 in peak summer season.
Location: Maine's Casco Bay, 4 miles east of Portland.
Access: By passenger ferry (and car ferry by arrangement) from Portland (call 207-774-7871).

GREAT CHEBEAGUE ISLAND
Area: 2,800 acres.
Population: 300 year-round; 2,000 in peak summer season.
Location: Maine's Casco Bay, 7 miles northeast of Portland.
Access: By passenger ferry (and car ferry by arrangement) from Portland (call 207-774-7871) and by passenger ferry from Cousins Island (call 207-846-3700).

Smelt fishermen and their nets on the shore of Great Chebeague Island. Lobster has long since replaced smelt, herring and cod as the major commercial fishery of the Maine islands. (Courtesy of the Chebeague Island Library.)

CLIFF ISLAND
Area: 125 acres.
Population: 80 year-round, 350 in peak summer season.
Location: Maine's Casco Bay, 8 miles east of Portland.
Access: By passenger ferry (and car ferry by arrangement) from Portland (call 207-774-7871).

GREAT DIAMOND ISLAND
Area: 349 acres.
Population: 5 families year-round; about 300 in peak summer season.

The Casco Bay Islands

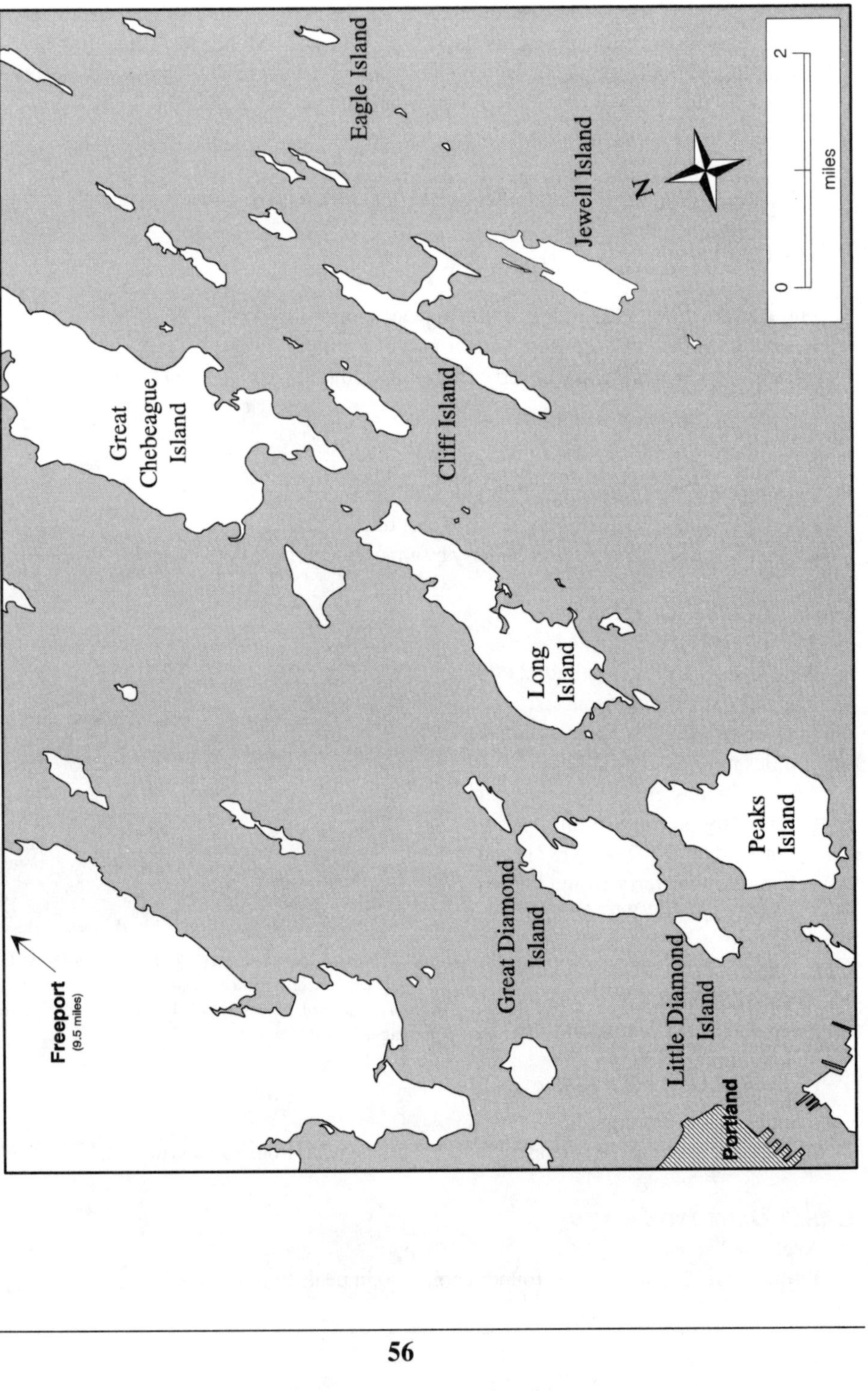

Freeport
(9.5 miles)

Great
Chebeague
Island

Eagle Island

Cliff Island

Jewell Island

Long
Island

Great Diamond
Island

Peaks
Island

Little Diamond
Island

Portland

N

0   miles   2

CASCO BAY ISLANDS

Location: Maine's Casco Bay, 2 miles east of Portland.
Access: By passenger ferry (and car ferry by arrangement) from Portland (call 207-774-7871).

LITTLE DIAMOND ISLAND
Area: 73 acres.
Population: No year-round residents; about 120 in peak summer season.
Location: Maine's Casco Bay, 1.5 miles east of Portland.
Access: By passenger ferry (and car ferry by arrangement) from Portland (call 207-774-7871).

EAGLE ISLAND
Area: 17 acres.
Population: 0.
Location: Maine's Casco Bay, 10.5 miles east of Portland.
Access: By passenger tour boat from Portland (call 207-774-6498).

Maine's Casco Bay has so many islands that they used to be known as the Calendar Islands on the belief that there was an island for every day in the year. In fact, the United States Coastal Pilot puts the number at 136, and other less official sources have counted 222 islands in the 200-square-mile bay that swings out 20 miles north and east from Cape Elizabeth near Portland to Cape Small at the mouth of the Kennebec River. However one adds them up, the Casco Bay islands are extremely numerous— more numerous than the islands of any other Maine bay—and, by Maine standards, quite easy to get to. The Casco Bay Lines offers frequent passage from Portland to four of the islands—Peaks, Long, Great Chebeague and Cliff—and frequent seasonal passage out to Little Diamond and Great Diamond; and in the summer months, there is a cruise boat out to Eagle Island. (See Maine Introduction for information on Bustins Island.) Five of the islands—Peaks, Great and Little Diamond, Long and Cliff—are part of Portland, Maine's largest city, and thus subject to city taxes and regulations. But, as one island resident put it, the islands have long been "unwanted step-children" of the city, and many islanders feel they get the worst of city life (crime, a polluted bay, complicated bureaucracy) without the benefit of city services. Occasionally, some of the islands threaten to secede from the city.

The accessibility of the islands and their nearness to Portland have brought the predictable changes to the Casco Bay group. Peaks Island, the closest to Portland harbor, has for decades now been primarily a suburban satellite of the city, to which workers commute by ferry; Great Diamond has recently seen a former fort converted into 134 condominium units; and development, tourism and rising real estate prices are putting pressure on the native communities on some of the outer islands. These changes and pressures are not unique to the Casco Bay islands: They are working their way north and east to nearly all of the accessible Maine islands. The Casco Bay islands have been hit first, and perhaps hardest, because they are the first in line, the closest not only to Portland, but also to the big East Coast population centers. The Casco Bay islands are the Maine islands' bellwether, leading the flock into a future that is likely to be much more crowded and expensive than the past.

THE ISLANDS OF MAINE

If you're traveling up to Maine from the south, the Isles of Shoals are the first Maine islands you'll come to (five of the nine Isles of Shoals belong to Maine, four to New Hampshire). But the Casco Bay islands, 50 miles northeast of the Shoals, are the first Maine islands that really look like Maine islands. With their jagged, rocky shores, precious strips of sand beach, thick stands of dark green spruce, cottages and lobster wharves, and blue vistas of water broken up by more and more islands, the Casco Bay islands have that unmistakable down east Maine feel. Suburbanization may be sprawling across the bay from Portland, but it hasn't hit too many of the islands yet. Chebeague Island remains rural and quiet, and on Cliff Island, lobstermen and their families still hold sway, at least during the winter months, as they have for generations.

Some of the Casco Bay islands are private estates owned by a family or an association of families, and some of the smaller ones have no residents, summer or winter, aside from gulls and the seals that haul out on the rocks. The early settlers, faced with such an abundance of islands, seem to have run out of traditional names, and they christened some of the smaller islands and ledges things like Irony, Pound of Tea, Junk of Pork, Pumpkin Knob, Scrag and Uncle Zeke. Forts have been built on several of the islands including Fort Gorges on Hog Island, Fort Levett on Cushing Island, Fort Scammel on House Island and Fort McKinley on Great Diamond.

When you're standing on one of them or sailing among them, the islands seem to be strewn this way and that without any pattern or plan; but in fact, if you look at a map, you can see that the islands and long trailing peninsulas of Casco Bay line up in parallel ranges running from southwest to northeast. The Maine writer Louise Dickinson Rich compares them to a "flotilla of ships all lying with their bows to the wind and tide." These parallel ranges of islands are, as Philip W. Conkling puts it in his book *Islands in Time*, "the weathered roots of resistant ridges." When the glaciers advanced they scraped out the valleys between these ridges, and when they melted, the rising seas filled the valleys and turned the ridges into islands and peninsulas. Christopher Levett, the first European to record his impressions of the Casco Bay islands, described them as "all broken islands," which is very much how they look from the sea.

History

Before Levett sailed this way in 1623, the Casco Bay islands were used by the Abnaki Indians as summertime fishing and berrying grounds. (Sources differ on the origin of the word Casco. According to some it is a corruption of an Abnaki Indian word meaning "muddy bay," others say the Abnaki word means "place of the herons," and still others claim that the 16th-century Spanish explorer Esteban Gomez named the bay Casco because it resembles a helmet.) The Casco Bay Indians later proved quite hostile to the white settlers in the region, but they welcomed the young Englishman Christopher Levett because he was careful to treat them with respect and to learn what he could of their customs and skills. After his return to England, Levett wrote a book about his travels titled *Voyage into New England* (published in London in 1628) in which he describes the Indians as "marvelous quick of apprehension and full of subtlety"; but he goes on to warn his readers that "they are very bloody-minded and treacherous among themselves…I would wish no man to trust them, whatever they say or do, but always to keep a strict hand over them, and yet to use them kindly and deal uprightly with them."

Levett, who had won favor at the court of James I, had been granted 6,000 acres in New England at a spot of his choosing, and he spent a good deal of 1623 sailing the Maine coast to determine where he would take possession of his grant. He found a good sheltered anchorage between four of the Casco Bay islands—Cushing, Peaks, Diamond and House—and landed with 10 men on one of the islands (historians dispute whether it was House, Cushing or York). Leaving his men in possession of the stone dwelling they had built on the island, Levett sailed back to England in 1624 with the intention of gathering new colonists. He failed in his mission and did not return to Casco Bay. The first Casco Bay island settlement died before it was really born.

Granite blocks being unloaded from The Lettie. (Courtesy of the Chebeague Island Library.)

But other settlements were not long in coming. Mackworth and Sebascodegan islands had English colonists during the 1630s, and Orrs, Bailey, Lower Goose and Moshier were settled during the succeeding decades. The early colonists preferred the islands to the mainland because it was easier to defend an island and easier to travel from island to island over the sea than to penetrate the vast unbroken forests of the New England mainland. However, the white settlers did not at first attempt to wrest the larger Casco Bay islands—Peaks, Long, Great Diamond, Chebeague—away from the Indians who used them each summer. One indication of the strength and hostility of the Indians of the region was the successful attack they made on the fledgling city of Portland in 1689, an attack launched from Peaks Island. It wasn't until the French and Indian Wars ended about 1760 that white settlers dared to claim the large bay islands as their own.

The Casco Bay islands, like the Penobscot Bay islands, supported farming and fishing communities during the 19th century. From the 1790s until after the Civil War, Chebeague Islanders built and operated a fleet of "stone sloops," powerful sailing ships used to transport granite quarried in Maine. When the craze for seaside bathing and vacationing took off after the Civil War, many of the Casco Bay islands became summer resorts, with grand hotels rising on Peaks, Long Island and Chebeague. During the Second World War, the U.S. government used a number of Casco Bay islands as a base for the North Atlantic fleet. Fort Scammel on House Island, Fort Levett on Cushing and Fort McKinley on Great Diamond were all garrisoned with Navy personnel; two coastal artillery batteries were set up on the back-shore of Peaks

Isles of Shoals

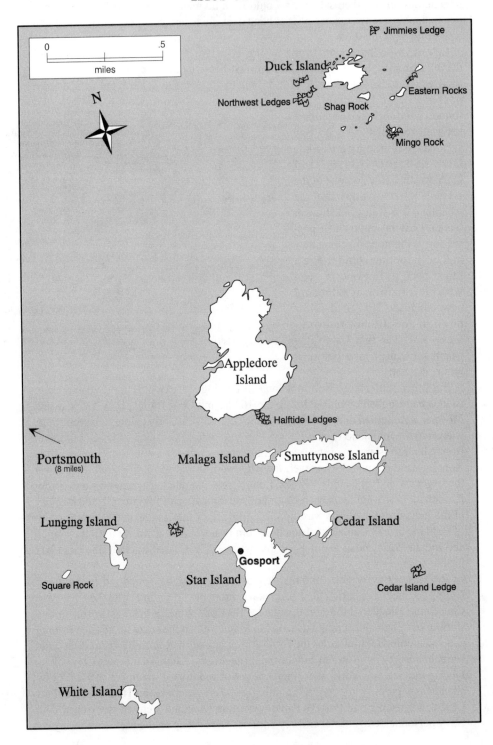

Island, and Long Island was used as a fueling station. After the war, all the island military installations were shut down and sold off.

Today, although most of the Victorian-era hotels are gone, summer people continue to flock to the islands. In the winter months, commuters to Portland far outnumber lobstermen on Peaks Island, the closest to the city. Long Island has a nice sandy beach, popular with summer day-trippers. Beautiful Great Chebeague has some fine old houses from the days of the stone sloops, and at low tide a sandbar connects Indian Point to Little Chebeague, an uninhabited 200-acre island owned by the state. Cliff Island, the most remote and rugged of the Casco Bay group, supports a small and independent-minded community of lobstermen, along with summer folk. Great and Little Diamond islands are for the most part summer resorts. And on Eagle Island the state maintains as a museum the house of Admiral Robert E. Peary, the American explorer who headed the first successful expedition to the North Pole.

THE ISLES OF SHOALS

Area: 206 acres on 9 islands.
Population: Only caretakers year-round.
Location: Atlantic Ocean, 9 miles from Portsmouth, New Hampshire.
Access: By passenger ferry from Portsmouth, New Hampshire (call 603-431-5500).

New Hampshire and Maine share the Isles of Shoals, a cluster of nine small islands that lie some nine miles out to sea from the mouth of the Piscataqua River that separates the two states. Maine has five of the islands (Appledore, Smuttynose, Cedar, Duck and Malaga) and New Hampshire has the other four (Star, Lunging, Seavey and White). Star and Appledore are used as conference centers during the summer months. Star hosts week-long religious and arts conferences sponsored by the Unitarian Universalists and the United Church of Christ; Appledore has scientific conferences for college students and adults at the Shoals Marine Laboratory. Visitors may also come to Star and Appledore for the day during the summer months, but there is a limit of 100 a day and the time is restricted to three hours between ferries.

Even with the restrictions, island-lovers will find the trip out to Star or Appledore well worth it, for the Isles of Shoals are lovely and fascinating islands, rich in history and literary associations. One of the first seaside summer resorts on the East Coast, the Isles of Shoals attracted some of the most famous writers of the 19th century, including Nathaniel Hawthorne, Charles Henry Dana, Harriet Beecher Stowe and James Russell Lowell. These and other literary lions came out to visit Celia Thaxter, a well-known and successful poet in her day, who grew up on the Isles of Shoals and celebrated them in her verse. Today the Star Island Corporation, which owns both Star and Appledore, is careful to preserve the beauty and serenity of the islands. A hushed and concentrated atmosphere prevails here, an atmosphere well-suited to spiritual contemplation and the pursuit of scientific knowledge for those who attend the conferences. For the day visitor, the islands offer a brief retreat from the din of modern life.

The landscape of the Isles of Shoals blends elements typical of the Maine islands and of the gentler islands off southern New England. Their coastlines, like those of nearly all the Maine islands, are rocky; but like Nantucket, parts of Martha's Vineyard, and Cuttyhunk on the Elizabeth Islands chain off Cape Cod, the Isles of Shoals are mostly open and moorlike, their vegetation low-growing tangles of shrubs, wild flowers and poison ivy. Above this shrubby, windswept landscape, the buildings on the islands—a rambling 19th-century hotel and stone church on Star Island, a scattering of cottages and labs on Appledore, a lighthouse on White Island—stand out sharply against the sky and the sea. Appledore, at 95 acres the largest of the nine islands, is also the highest, rising to 60 feet above sea level. The smallest island, Seavey, is a mere five acres.

History

The Isles of Shoals hold a place in history entirely out of proportion with their diminutive size. Prized for their location in the midst of rich fishing grounds (the "shoals" in their name refers to the schools of cod that once swam here in vast numbers), the islands were used by European fishermen as early as the late 16th century. Samuel de Champlain noted the islands in his voyage of 1605, and Captain John Smith fell in love with them when he journeyed up the coast of New England in 1614. "Of all four parts of the world that I have seene not inhabited," wrote Smith in his *Description of New England* (published in 1616), "could I have but the meanes to transport a Colonie, I would rather live here than any where." Smith dubbed the island group Smith's Isles, but fishermen had already named them the Isles of Shoals, and this name stuck.

The colony that Smith dreamed of became a reality quite soon. The British fishermen who used the islands as a base began to stay over for longer and longer periods during the early 17th century, and by the 1660s the Isles of Shoals supported a thriving, substantial colony of about 600 people. For a time, the Isles of Shoals were the wealthiest, most prominent settlement in New England, more important as a center of trade than Boston. The eponymous shoals of cod were the source of most of the islands' wealth during the Colonial period. Cod caught off the Shoals were prized for their size and for the special process that Shoalers used to cure them, and into the early 19th century Isles of Shoals cod fetched a higher price at market than Newfoundland dried cod.

Fishing made the Shoalers rich quickly, but they didn't stay rich for long. At the start of the 18th century the islands' glory days were already over, and the mainland settlements quickly outstripped the islands in the course of the 18th century. By 1767, the population had declined to 284, and during the Revolution, the islands were evacuated at the insistence of the Colonials, who suspected the political loyalty of the islanders. The evacuation marked the end of the Shoals as a vital community. Those who returned to the town of Gosport on Star Island were, for the most part, misfits who couldn't take to mainland ways, and in the course of the 19th century they grew increasingly poor, isolated and strange in their customs and even speech. The residents of Star Island were notorious for their drinking and their scorn for marriage.

The summer resort trade brought new life to the islands, though it didn't reverse the decline of the year-round communities. Thomas Laighton, a Portsmouth, New Hampshire, businessman who left the city to become keeper of the White Island light, pioneered the resort era on the Isles of Shoals. In 1839 he bought up a number of the islands, including Hog Island, which he rechristened with the more pleasingly romantic name Appledore when he opened up the Appledore House resort in 1848. The success of the hotel made the Isles of Shoals famous in the Northeast as a bracing seaside retreat.

Laighton brought his family with him out to White Island, and his young daughter Celia grew up on the Shoals. When she was 16, Celia married her father's partner Levi Lincoln Thaxter and the couple moved near Boston, spending their summers on Appledore. In the 1860s Celia began publishing her poetry, and as her reputation grew she made more and more friends in Boston's literary and artistic circles. These friends, who included John Greenleaf Whittier, Sarah Orne Jewett, Childe Hassam and Thomas Bailey Aldrich, began coming out to Appledore in the summer months as her guests, and Celia Thaxter's sunny parlor, filled with flowers from her fabled garden, became a kind of off-shore salon. In her verse and even more highly respected prose pieces, including *Among the Isles of Shoals*, published in 1873, Thaxter wrote of the history and legends of the islands and described the eerie, empty Shoals landscapes that haunted her all her life. In *Among the Isles of Shoals* she writes of the "strange beauty" and "the sadness of the place—the vast loneliness; for there are not even trees to whisper with familiar voices,—nothing but sky and sea and rocks." Thaxter is also the author of *An Island Garden*, a charming garden book with illustrations by Childe Hassam, published in 1894, the year of her death.

The summer resort trade spread from Appledore to Star Island in 1873 when Star Island's Oceanic Hotel opened for business. (The opening of the Oceanic on Star Island marked the end of Gosport as a year-round community, for most of the remaining islanders sold their land to the hotel developer, the wealthy John Poor.) The original Oceanic burned down three years later, but a new Oceanic Hotel was promptly built, and it still stands today. In 1914, the Appledore House, having fallen from fashion around the turn of the century, was also destroyed by fire, and the resort era on the Isles of Shoals ended.

The conference era got underway in the twilight years of the resort era. The founding father of the religious conferences on Star Island was Thomas Elliott, the president of a Unitarian Church conference group, who visited the island with his wife during the summer of 1896. The Elliotts liked what they found here, and the following summer the first conference of the Isles of Shoals Summer Meeting Association was held in the Oceanic Hotel on Star Island. Conferences continued and grew even more popular in succeeding summers. The Unitarians and Congregationalists organized the Star Island Corporation to buy the island in 1915, and the conferences have been held on the island ever since, except during the war years. In recent years, an arts conference for writers, musicians and visual artists has been added to the religious conferences held on Star Island each summer.

In the late 1960s, Dr. John Kingsbury of Cornell University received permission from the Star Island Corporation to offer conferences and courses on marine biology on Star Island. The Shoals Marine Laboratory began to restore some of the old cottages on Appledore and to put up new buildings in 1971, and the first summer session on Appledore was held in 1973. The Shoals Marine Laboratory, jointly sponsored by Cornell and the University of New Hampshire, offers classes on marine biology to students from colleges all over the country, and there are also shorter seminars open to the public. The Shoals Marine Laboratory is open from May to September.

For information about the summer conferences on Star Island, contact: The Star Island Corporation, 110 Arlington Street, Boston, Mass. 02116; 617-426-7988. For information about the Shoals Marine Laboratory, contact: Dr. John B. Heiser, Director, G-14 Stimson Hall, Cornell University, Ithaca, New York 14850.

Visiting the Islands

Members of the public who are not part of the conferences may visit Star Island and Appledore during the summer months as day-trippers. The ferry for day-trippers sails out of Portsmouth at 11 A.M., is open to 100 visitors (no reservations), docks at Star Island at noon and departs the island at 3 P.M. Those who wish to visit Appledore should arrange in advance to be picked up by the Shoals Marine Laboratory's launch (call 603-862-2994) for the half-mile crossing from Star Island.

Star Island's old Oceanic Hotel now serves as the conference center; day visitors are welcome on the main floor and basement. Visitors may also go into the island's very lovely stone meetinghouse, built in 1800 (Nathaniel Hawthorne noted his interest in the church, whose records date back to Colonial times). Each evening during the 11-week conference season, conferees hold a candlelight service in the chapel, preceded and followed by a silent candlelight procession. Not far from the Star Island meetinghouse, the Charles F. Vaughn Memorial Cottage has a room with exhibits of memorabilia of Celia Thaxter. Paths lead away from the little cluster of buildings to the coves along the island's rocky shore and to the cliffs. Near the island's western shore there is a monument to Captain John Smith's 1614 landing on the island. The Isles of Shoals, including both Star and Appledore, have the largest number of nesting gulls in the Gulf of Maine, and visitors who walk around the islands should avoid the nesting areas during the spring and early summer. Gulls and terns will dive at anyone who comes too close to their nests.

Devotees of Celia Thaxter will want to arrange to cross over to Appledore, for her wonderful island garden has been recreated here and nearby is the lonely, windswept Laighton family cemetery, where she is buried. Day visitors may, with permission, tour the classrooms and labs of the Shoals Marine Laboratory, and there are marked trails through the gull rookery. It is best to carry a stick to ward off dive attacks from the nesting gulls (there as many as 2,000 pairs on this island alone). In addition to the vast numbers of herring gulls and great black-backed gulls, snowy egrets, glossy ibis and blue and black-crowned night herons all have established successful nesting colonies on Appledore, which is at the northern limit of their range. More than 100 transient species have been identified on the island during the spring and fall migrations.

Although Star and Appledore are the only Isles of Shoals accessible by public ferry, a few of the other islands are open to visitors who have their own boats. Breakwaters connect Star Island to Cedar Island, Cedar to Smuttynose and Smuttynose to the tiny speck of Malaga. These three islands are private property, though visitors may row their own boats out to the Smuttynose pier and explore this island and Malaga. White Island, which has had a lighthouse since 1820 (replaced in 1859-60 and repaired in 1978), and Seavey Island are both government property. Celia Thaxter grew up in the shadow of the White Island light, which rises 82 feet above the ocean out of the bare gray rock. Privately owned Lunging Island, also known as Londoner's Island, is not open to visitors. Duck Island, which has a large colony of nesting cormorants at its south end as well as around 1,000 pairs of nesting gulls, is a wildlife sanctuary owned by the Star Island Corporation. The public is barred from this island as well.

The day visitor's three hours on Star or Appledore pass quickly. Just as one begins to get a feel for the strange, melancholy beauty that Celia Thaxter wrote of, the ferry summons one back to the mainland. One envies the conferees who can stay on to meditate or study while the sun slips down over the stretch of ocean to the west; and one thinks wistfully of the Victorian-era writers and artists who came for weeks or months to take the sea air, walk amid the birds and tangled shrubs, and converse in Celia Thaxter's parlor. Those who crave more than three hours on these exposed, treeless, poetic little islands may study their history in *The Isles of Shoals in Lore and Legend* by Lyman V. Rutledge or visit them imaginatively with Celia Thaxter in her vividly evocative books.

THE ISLANDS OF SOUTHERN NEW ENGLAND

INTRODUCTION

The southern New England states—Massachusetts, Rhode Island and Connecticut—may not rival Maine for sheer abundance of islands, but what their islands lack in numbers they more than make up in size, importance and variety. Massachusetts alone has the 30 islands of Boston Harbor, many of them easily accessible from the city for day-trips and camping; and south of Cape Cod sit the two largest unbridged islands on the East Coast: Nantucket to the east and Martha's Vineyard, which is nearly twice the size, to the west. Nantucket and Martha's Vineyard, along with Block Island to the west and New York's Long Island still farther west and south, are all part of the same terminal moraine, a vast deposit of ground-up rock and dirt that the last glacier left behind when it melted back from its southernmost advance. Though they are neighbors only 15 miles apart and kin geologically, the Vineyard and Nantucket feel like different worlds—the Vineyard world of woods, rolling hills, inland villages and old port towns, Great Ponds behind the south shore barrier beach and the spectacular Gay Head cliffs dropping down to the ocean at the western end; Nantucket, by contrast, "a mere hillock, an elbow of sand" in Herman Melville's famous formulation, a place of windswept moors and a gray-shingled town from which Quaker whaling men sailed around the world and to which they returned with fat profits. Having proudly gone their separate ways for centuries, Nantucket and Martha's Vineyard seem to be growing more alike these days, for both have been seized by tremendous development booms that are swelling their populations, taxing their resources, and filling up their countryside with expensive vacation homes.

Northwest of the Vineyard and forming a kind of land barrier between Buzzards Bay and Vineyard Sound are the Elizabeth Islands, a chain of 16 islands, of which only Cuttyhunk, the westernmost island in the group, is accessible by public ferry. Due to its small size and careful private ownership, Cuttyhunk has so far eluded the ravages of the late 20th century. Those who care to venture out from New Bedford will find a single small village built on a hill, a fine circular harbor, a rolling landscape of bayberry and beach rose, cliffs that drop down to desolate beaches, scores of deer and about a mile of paved road on which golf carts are more common than cars. Cuttyhunk has been identified by some scholars as the island setting for Shakespeare's *Tempest*, and it does in fact seem to be protected from time by some strong magic.

One particularly noteworthy bridged island in Massachusetts is Plum Island, north of Boston, site of the Parker River National Wildlife Refuge. One of the few true barrier islands north of New York, Plum Island has high dunes and sand beaches on the ocean side, an extensive salt marsh on its land side, mowed meadows and freshwater pools. Vast numbers of snow and Canada geese pass through during spring and fall migrations, and in the spring and early summer federally endangered piping plovers nest on the beach. Plum Island may be reached by bridge from the town of Newburyport. The wildlife refuge protects the southern two-thirds of Plum Island, and a beach cottage colony occupies the island's northern third. For more information, contact the refuge manager, Parker River National Wildlife Refuge, Northern Boulevard, Plum Island, Newburyport, Mass. 01950; 617-465-5753.

INTRODUCTION

Rhode Island, though not actually an island itself, has borrowed its name from an island—or rather from two islands. The explorer Giovanni da Verrazano sailed this way in 1524 and named the large island at the mouth of Narragansett Bay Rhode Island because it reminded him of the Greek island of Rhodes. Later on, the state took the name over for itself and the former Rhode Island became Aquidneck Island. Today Aquidneck, bridged at the north to Bristol and Tiverton and bridged at the west to Conanicut Island, is better known by the name of its most famous town—Newport, a summer resort of the super-rich since the late 19th century. Conanicut Island, similarly, is better known by the name of its primary town—Jamestown, which, compared to Newport, is a simple country village.

Newport today is a popular tourist destination for the so-called cottages (i.e., Gilded Age palaces) lining Bellevue Avenue, for its well-preserved 18th-century town center, for its yacht-filled harbor and for the spectacular sea views from Cliff Walk, Ocean Avenue and Brenton Point State Park in the island's southwest corner. Conanicut Island offers a quiet escape from the crowded magnificence of Newport. A particularly scenic spot on this island is the Beavertail State Park at its south end, with a lighthouse built in 1856 and the same magnificent ocean views as Newport's Ocean Avenue.

Aquidneck and Conanicut are the biggest islands of Narragansett Bay, which cuts 25 miles north into the state of Rhode Island, effectively dividing the state into two pieces. Together they guard the entrance to the bay and shelter a number of smaller unbridged islands, several of which have been incorporated into the Bay Islands State Park.

The Beavertail Lighthouse (1856) at the south end of Conanicut Island.

Of these islands, Prudence, accessible by public car ferry, makes a pleasant day-trip for its quiet country aura, its winery, its sleepy villages and its two large parks, one at each end. Neighboring Hog Island, a tiny bit of land that sits practically in the shadow of the Mount Hope Bridge, is also accessible by public ferry; but since the land is all privately owned and the island offers no facilities for visitors, I have not given it an entry of its own. About 75 to 80 families come here to vacation in the summer, but Hog Island has no year-round residents, no electricity or phones. Dutch and Patience Islands, both part of the Bay Islands Park, may be visited by those who have their own boats; Hope Island, though part of the park, is closed to the public from April to August to protect the nesting snowy egrets, night herons, terns and gulls.

Rhode Island's most popular and to many minds most picturesque unbridged island is not in Narragansett Bay at all but some 15 miles south of it, sitting all by itself in the Atlantic Ocean. This is Block Island, sculpted by the glaciers into the shape of a teardrop (some, less poetically, see a pork chop). Open, moorlike and nearly treeless like Nantucket, Block Island used to support a fishing and farming community until the hurricane of 1938 destroyed the fishing fleet and flattened the island's barns. The island's Old Harbor is dominated by huge Victorian inns that date from the resort boom of the 1870s and 1880s and that have found new life in the tourist boom of the 1970s and 1980s. Like Martha's Vineyard and Nantucket, Block Island has become increasingly popular and increasingly developed in the past 15 years. Islanders are now scrambling to save what they can of the open, rural character of this 6,460-acre island, and they have succeeded in setting aside some very lovely nature preserves.

Connecticut has a sprinkling of islands along its 250-mile coastline on Long Island Sound, but the only really substantial unbridged island off the Connecticut coast— Fishers Island— belongs to New York State, even though it is far closer to Connecticut and reached from the Connecticut town of New London.

Most of the other Connecticut islands are quite small and clustered in groups. The Thimble Islands off the little village of Stony Creek (a few miles east of New Haven) number over 300, though none is larger than 20 acres and most are much smaller. All the Thimble Islands are privately owned and off-limits to the public, but cruise ships out of Stony Creek sail by them in the summer months.

The Norwalk Islands, scattered off the shores of Westport, Norwalk and Darien, are a small archipelago of 16 islands, some privately owned, some protected as wildlife sanctuaries and some owned by the towns. From May to October, the Saugatuck Valley Audubon Society runs day-trips for groups out to a few of the islands, including Chimon, Sheffield and Shea. For more information call 203-227-7253.

Great and Little Captain Islands off Greenwich are served in the summer months by passenger ferries open to town residents; the locals, who call them the Beach Islands, use their sandy beaches for swimming and picnicking. Southern Calf Island, also off Greenwich, is open to those who have their own boats. This 28-acre island, owned by the Greenwich YMCA, is attached by sandbar to Northern Calf, which is private.

BOSTON HARBOR ISLANDS

GEORGE'S ISLAND
Area: 28 acres.
Population: Caretaker only.
Location: Boston Harbor, 7 miles east of Boston.
Access: By seasonal passenger ferry from Boston, Hingham, Nantasket and Lynn (call 617-723-7800, 617-749-4500, 617-227-4321 or 617-598-0260).

The Boston Harbor Islands

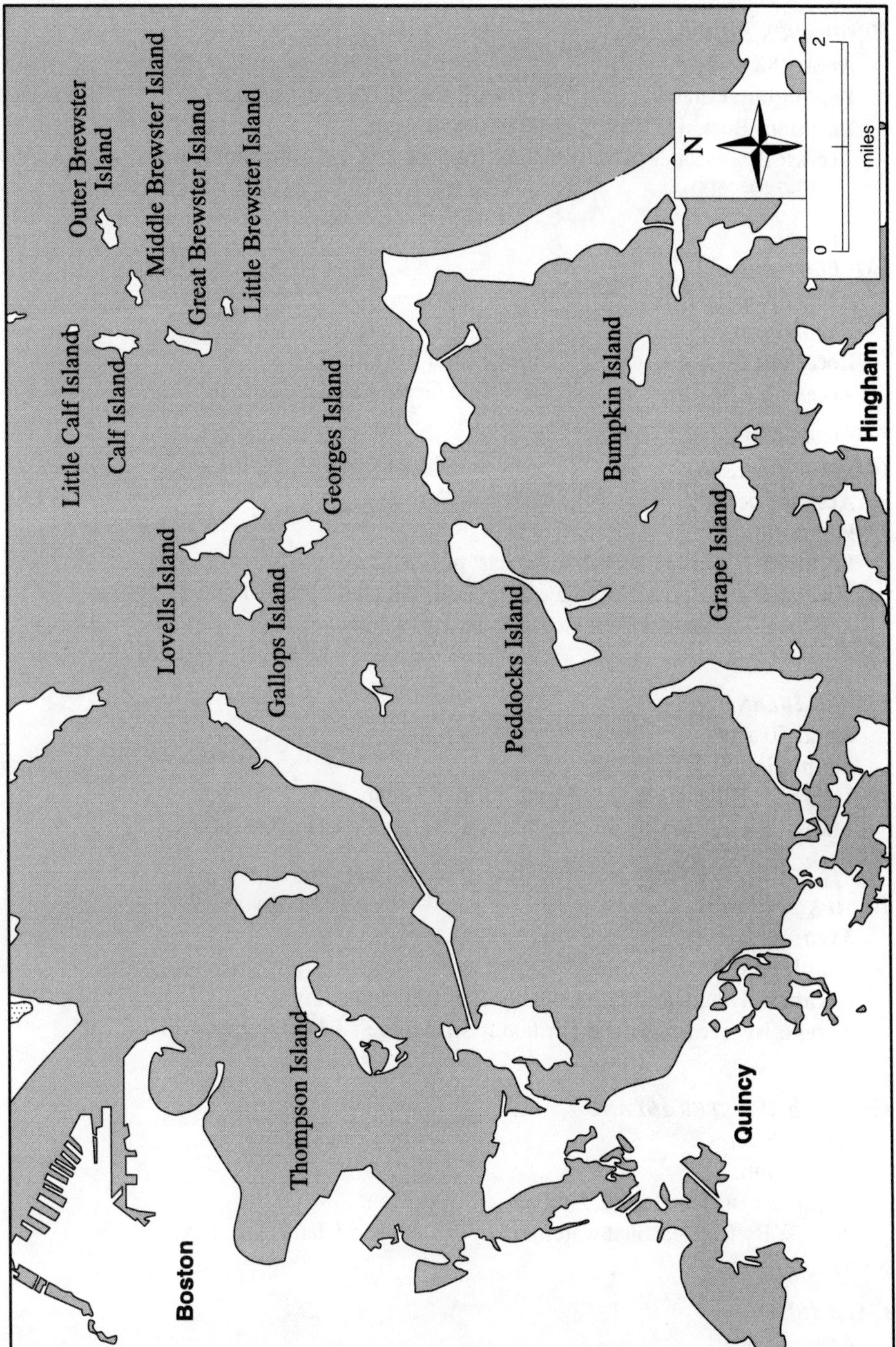

Outer Brewster Island
Middle Brewster Island
Great Brewster Island
Little Brewster Island

Little Calf Island
Calf Island

Georges Island

Lovells Island

Gallops Island

Bumpkin Island

Peddocks Island

Grape Island

Thompson Island

Boston

Quincy

Hingham

N

miles

PEDDOCK'S ISLAND
Area: 188 acres.
Population: Caretaker only year-round; about 100 in the summer.
Location: Boston Harbor, 5 miles east of Boston.
Access: By seasonal passenger ferry from Boston and Hingham (call 617-723-7800 or 617-749-4500).

LOVELL'S ISLAND
Area: 62 acres.
Population: 0
Location: Boston Harbor, 5.5 miles east of Boston.
Access: By free seasonal water taxi from George's Island (see above).

GALLOP'S ISLAND
Area: 16 acres.
Population: 0
Location: Boston Harbor, 5 miles east of Boston.
Access: By seasonal passenger ferry from Hingham (call 617-749-4500) and by free seasonal water taxi from George's Island (see above).

GRAPE ISLAND
Area: 50 acres.
Population: 0
Location: Hingham Bay, 0.5 mile north of Hingham.
Access: By free seasonal water taxi from George's Island (see above).

BUMPKIN ISLAND
Area: 35 acres.
Population: 0
Location: Hingham Bay, 1 mile north of Hingham.
Access: By free seasonal water taxi from George's Island (see above).

GREAT BREWSTER ISLAND
Area: 23 acres.
Population: 0
Location: Boston Harbor, 9 miles east of Boston.
Access: By free seasonal water taxi from George's Island (see above).

CALF ISLAND
Area: 17 acres.
Population: 0
Location: Boston Harbor, 9 miles east of Boston.
Access: By free seasonal water taxi from George's Island (see above).

BOSTON HARBOR ISLANDS

THOMPSON ISLAND

Area: 157 acres.
Population: 15 year-round; 30 in summer; with capacity for 200 students.
Location: Boston Harbor, 1 mile east of Boston.
Access: By special arrangement with the Thompson Island Outward Bound Education Center (call 617-328-3900).

Boston, unlike New York, is not an island city, but it does have 30 islands dotting its 50-square-mile harbor, and many of them are open to the visiting public. Over the years the city has found a number of different uses for its islands. Early settlers farmed the islands and gave them their names; John Winthrop, first governor of the Massachusetts Bay Colony, lived on Governor's Island for some years during his long term in office. The Boston Light, the first lighthouse built in North America—erected in 1716 and replaced after the British blew it up during the Revolution—stands on rocky Little Brewster Island in the outer harbor. George's Island is the site of Fort Warren, used as a prison for Confederate troops and political prisoners during the Civil War (Alexander Stephens, the vice president of the Confederacy, was an inmate for a time). During World War II, other Boston islands were fortified to protect the city and the Charlestown Navy Yard. For a time after the war, the islands fell into neglect, but in the early seventies they were incorporated into the Boston Islands State Park. Nine of the islands are accessible to the public in the summer by passenger ferries.

Although the Boston Harbor islands have nothing quite as grand as the Statue of Liberty or quite as historic as the Ellis Island immigration station, they do afford an easy escape from the crowded city into empty woods, undeveloped shores and interesting old ruins. Well within sight of Boston's skyscrapers and busy air and marine traffic, the islands are little oases of relative peace and calm, far more remote from the mainland in feeling than in fact. For those oppressed by the city, they offer the same pleasures as remote wilderness islands: clear vistas, open water, a chance to breathe, and on some of the islands a place to camp. Water pollution makes swimming a bit dicier, but several of the islands have smooth sandy beaches.

Two of the islands—George's and Peddock's—are serviced directly by ferries departing from the Boston waterfront, and ferries also run to George's from Hingham's Hewitt's Cove, Nantasket's Pemberton Pier and from the Lynn Marina. Six islands—Lovell's, Grape, Bumpkin, Gallops, Great Brewster and Calf—may be reached from George's by free water taxi service. Thompson, though privately owned by the Thompson Island Outward Bound Education Center, is part of the Boston Harbor Park and is open to groups by prior arrangement and to individuals in the summer on Thursday and Friday evenings. During the summer months all the islands have staffs in residence and there are self-guided trails and regular tours led by rangers. The islands are small—Peddock's, the largest unbridged island, is 188 acres—and in the course of a day a visitor can make a leisurely tour of two or three, taking the tours or just strolling around the old forts, the hiking trails and the beaches. Peddock's has a hill, forest, salt marsh and rocky and sandy coves. On Lovell's there is the remains of a fort, and supervised swimming at a beach. There are paths through the tangles of sumac, bayberry and blackberry bushes on Gallops, Bumpkin and Grape. Great

Nantucket Island

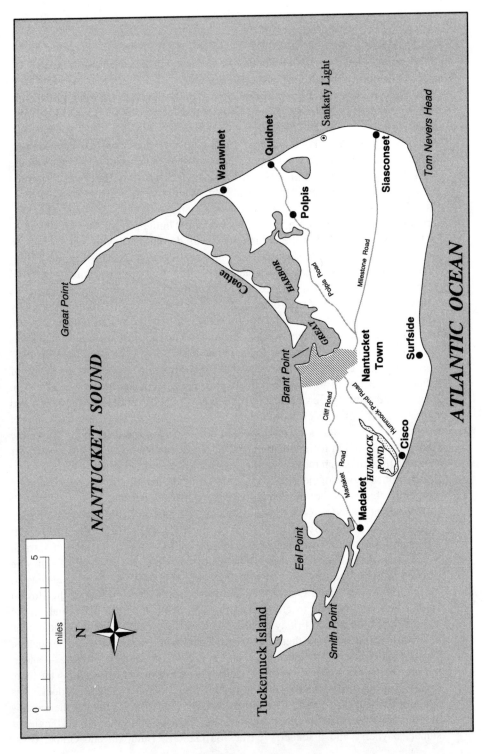

Brewster is an outer island, with a more rugged, windblown feel. Calf Island is a nesting site for snowy egrets and black-crowned night herons. George's Island is open to visitors from April through early November, and the other islands within the Boston Harbor Islands State Park are open during the summer months.

George's, Peddock's and Lovell's islands are administered by Boston's Metropolitan District Commission (for information call 617-727-5215); the other accessible harbor islands are administered by the Massachusetts Department of Environmental Management (for information call 617-740-1605). For information about visiting Thompson Island, call 617-328-3900.

Those interested in pursuing the histories and legends of the Boston Harbor islands should consult M.F. Sweetser's *King's Handbook of the Boston Harbor Islands*, first published in 1882; Edward Rowe Snow's lively book *The Islands of Boston Harbor*; and *All About the Boston Harbor Islands* by Emily and David Kales.

NANTUCKET

Area: 31,000 acres; 13 miles across and from 2.5 to 6 miles wide.

Population: 8,000 year-round; 40,000 in peak summer season.

Location: 30 miles south of Cape Cod and 15 miles east of Martha's Vineyard.

Access: From Woods Hole or Hyannis, Mass., by car or passenger ferry. Contact the Woods Hole, Martha's Vineyard and Nantucket Steamship Authority (car ferry): 617-548-5011; Hy-Line ferry company (passengers only): 617-778-2602.

An aerial view of the entrance to Nantucket's harbor. (Courtesy of the Nantucket Historical Association.)

Nantucket is a great island for history. Its rise and fall as the whaling capital of the world, the century-long sway of Quakerism on the island, the building of more and more elegant houses as wealth and worldliness increased, the laying waste of much of the town by fire, and the rebuilding on an even grander scale—all this is stirring stuff. Along the wharves and cobbled streets and narrow lanes of the finely preserved old town, the sense of the past remains alive and accessible to the imagination. The hum and buzz of the future is also in the air. Nantucket is preserved, but it's not embalmed. History continues to be made on the island, which seems to have arrived at a kind of crossroads of development. The historic events of today—the skyrocketing land prices, the $50 million sale of a large block of downtown and waterfront commercial real estate, the epidemic of shingled summer homes on the once empty moors and dunes, the fighting over how or whether to stem the rapid development— may lack the glory or the greatness of the island's past, but there is more continuity than one might think. One common thread is money: the pursuit, the acquisition and the disposal of considerable wealth. Commerce, it seems, has always been part of the soul of Nantucket.

This is not to say that there is anything cheap or grasping or vulgar about the island. Far from it. Part of the wonder of Nantucket is that the grubby business of whaling should have produced so magical, so enchantingly beautiful a town. The magic, though prettied away in places by gift shops and over-renovation, endures. But the balance on Nantucket is delicate. The commercial waterfront district that Green Stamp-heir Walter Beneicke Jr. bought up, restored and transformed in the 1960s has such a bogus "theme park" picturesqueness you almost expect to see a Disneyland parade of peg-legged Captain Ahabs and menacing white whales march down the wharves at the stroke of noon. Lower Main Street, with its worn-down cobbles, ancient elms and perfect proportions, looks right enough until you discover that almost every store contains pricy gifts, crafts, cards and sportswear. Federal-style mansions are now expensive inns; cottages that look like they've weathered for generations are actually newer than the foreign sports cars parked in front of them. But these aspects, while ominous, have not yet reached the status of blots on the landscape. And may never. Nantucket with its island-wide Historic District status (see below) may be able to protect itself from blots, but the danger is that while the landscape is preserved, the spirit will drain away.

For the moment, the spirit is there for the conjuring. You can still climb up the tower of the Congregational Church and look over the low roofs of a 19th-century town and out to sea. You can still walk among the shingled and clapboard houses on the hills and out to the graveyards on the edge of town and beyond to the moors and dream your dreams of mad sea captains, Quaker merchants and vats of whale blubber. You can still dream. There is still magic enough on this sandy, wind-bitten island 30 miles out to sea.

Of course, some of Nantucket's magical aura derives from its place in our literature. In *Moby Dick* Herman Melville launches the fated voyage of the *Pequod* from Nantucket, and though Melville never lived on the island and probably did not even visit it until a year after his masterpiece was published in 1851, it is his rhapsodic description of Nantucket that most excites our imaginations:

> Nantucket! Take out your map and look at it. See what a real corner of the world it occupies; how it stands there, away off shore, more lonely than the Eddystone lighthouse. Look at it—a mere hillock, and elbow of sand; all beach, without a background…they [the Nantucketers] are so shut up, belted about, every way inclosed, surrounded, and made an utter island of by the ocean, that to their very chairs and tables small clams will sometimes be found adhering, as to the backs of sea turtles.

Henry David Thoreau visited the island a few years later and records in his journal entry of December 27, 1854, that "There is not a tree to be seen, except such as are set out about houses…This island must look exactly like a prairie, except that the view in clear weather is bounded by the sea." Thoreau, unfortunately, enjoyed no such clear weather during his visit: His passage out to the island was rough and foggy, and a misty drizzle hung in for the duration of his stay.

NANTUCKET

It requires a powerful imagination to recognize Melville's wild and lonely "elbow of sand" in the Nantucket of today; but the island, though changed utterly by time, continues to enchant new arrivals. If you're coming by ferry from the Cape, Nantucket's magic starts working on you the moment you sight its low profile on the horizon. From afar the island seems to open its long, curved sandy arms: To the east, so distant it almost seems to rise from a separate island, is the blazing white cone of the Great Point Lighthouse (a replica of the 1818 lighthouse that a storm destroyed

The Great Point Lighthouse is the first landmark you see as you sail to Nantucket from Cape Cod. Built in 1818, the light was destroyed by a storm in 1984 and a replica now stands in its place. (Courtesy of the Nantucket Historical Association; photo: John McCalley, c. 1965.)

in 1984); due south is the grayish landmass on which the town sits, its gentle rise crowned by a gold-topped steeple (the Unitarian Church), a pure white spire (the Congregational Church) and a black standpipe (the town's water supply) to the west. Linking Great Point and town is the sweeping sandbar called Coatue (pronounced "ko-too' "), a natural area partly under the management of the Nantucket Conservation Foundation (see below). Approaching still nearer, you make out imposing summer "cottages" behind Jetties Beach and atop Cliff Road; and then, as the boat enters the long jetties at the entrance to Nantucket Harbor, the much photographed, diminutive Brant Point Lighthouse (built in 1746, the nation's second oldest) comes into view.

Minutes later the car ferry has docked at Steamboat Wharf and the town is spread out before you. But for the cars, Nantucket on first view seems untouched by modern life. You won't find a skyscraper, a McDonald's, a highway, a neon "strip," a traffic light or any of the other standard features of late-20th-century towns. The first impression is of narrow streets, one or two-story houses, and gray shingles—everywhere on every conceivable structure in a muted spectrum ranging from the tan of freshly split white cedar to pale gray, silver, steel and the black-streaked, somber gray of the oldest and most weathered shingles.

Nantucket is the kind of town that invites walking—and in fact, a car is a positive hindrance in high season because of the traffic and limited parking. Walking is the best way to get the lay of the land and to put yourself in tune with Nantucket's moods. One discovery that you make almost instantly is that Nantucket is a real town—not an overgrown village, not a country market crossroads that grew into a settlement, not a hodgepodge of houses with a shopping street down the middle. Nantucket is a classic port town, oriented to its harbor, shaped by the oddity of its island location, settled and built up as a place of commerce and industry, enhanced by its prosperity, and preserved by that prosperity's collapse. It is, in the words of historian Samuel Eliot Morison, "the one unspoiled seaport town of New England, a town in which every house built before 1840—and few were not—was sired out of the sea."

The harbor and the sea determined the shape and style of the town of Nantucket, but today it is the land that sustains it. Though the contemporary Nantucketer may fish or yacht, depending on his background, he no longer "resides and riots on the sea." Commerce on the sea has taken a backseat to Nantucket's new boom business: real estate and construction, which have edged out even tourism as the island's number one source of income. Today's Nantucketer is firmly tied to his ever more valuable land. The *Wall Street Journal* estimates that two-thirds of the islanders make a living off real estate (the island is home to 340 licensed real estate brokers) and reports that the price of an average home on the island has nearly quadrupled in the past 10 years from $75,600 to $300,000, with 300 new ones going up each year. There are now 7,000 houses on the island, one for nearly every year-round Nantucketer (though of course most of them are occupied by part-time Nantucketers); and, if the current rate of construction continues, there will be 7,000 more houses built in the next 20-odd years.

The island's seaward orientation is now more important for its scenic value than its commercial opportunities (in fact, the island isolation is a positive nuisance when it comes to transporting building supplies and construction crews, some of whom must be ferried in daily from the mainland because housing is so expensive on the island). Outside the whaling museum on Broad Street, the souvenir shops and the names of hotels and restaurants, you'd be hard-pressed to find any tokens of the island's whaling heritage. Nantucket natives, seasonal residents and vacationers alike have their eyes fixed on the land. "Nothing stirs emotions the way land does," the *Wall Street Journal* stated flatly in a front-page news story (May 6, 1987) about a bitterly contested sale of 66 acres by the Wannacomet Water Company.

When, if ever, will the bottom fall out of the giddy real estate market? How many more houses can be built on the moors before the island's essential character is irreversibly altered? How can native islanders survive in a closed community in which it's impossible to find a house for less than $200,000, a community in which gift shops and designer clothing stores have forced "normal" stores like the Five and Ten to close, a community in which, as one resident put it, "there's no place to buy curtains, sheets, ladies' underwear, or an egg slicer"? Will Nantucket become a kind of gilded ghetto of wealthy natives and even wealthier summer people?

These are the burning issues on Nantucket today. To understand how it got this way, it's instructive to look at the island's history.

History: Early Settlement

Nantucket, like all the Eastern islands, was inhabited by Indians before the coming of the white settlers; and it is believed that four separate Indian civilizations dwelled here, the earliest dating back some 9,000 years. When the English arrived on the island in the 17th century, there were around 700 Narragansett Indians (part of the Algonquian family) living in six villages, most of them on the island's east shore. There is not a single descendant of these Indians on the island today. All that survives of their culture are names and legends. Nantucket itself is derived from an Algonquian word that most historians translate as "far away island" but Eugene Green and William Sachse in their book *Names of the Land* render it as "at the point of land on a tidal river." According to one of these Indian legends, a giant named Maushop created

Nantucket and Martha's Vineyard when he kicked his moccasins out to sea while trying to rid his feet of Cape Cod sand; in another legend, the island consists of the ashes that Maushop knocked from his pipe. (For the geologists' version of how Nantucket was formed, see below.) In *Moby-Dick* Melville recounts an Indian legend that explains the island's settlement: An eagle carried off an Indian babe in his talons and flew off over the "wide waters." The babe's parents followed the eagle's flight in their canoe and "after a perilous passage they discovered the island, and there they found an empty ivory casket—the poor little Indian's skeleton."

The English explorer Bartholomew Gosnold is credited with the first sighting of the island in 1602, and three years later Captain George Weymouth fixed its nautical position and described the cliffs off Sankaty Head. In 1641 one Thomas Mayhew of Watertown, Massachusetts, purchased Nantucket along with Martha's Vineyard and the Elizabeth Islands (see Cuttyhunk) with the intention of converting the Indians to Christianity and setting up a manorial estate after the English style. Mayhew, who settled at Edgartown on Martha's Vineyard, never got very far with his plans for Nantucket, and in 1659, when a planter named Tristram Coffin from Salisbury, Massachusetts, surveyed the island and offered to buy it, Mayhew agreed. The price he set was 30 pounds "in good Marchantable Pay" and "two Beaver Hatts one for myself and one for my wife."

Nantucket's original white settlers were, in a sense, refugees from refugees. Coffin went in on the deal with eight partners from Salisbury, all men eager to escape the repressive Puritan theocracy of the Bay Colony. Of the nine original buyers, Thomas Macy was most eager to take up residence on Nantucket and he made the journey from the mainland with his wife, five children, his friend Edward Starbuck and the boys James Coffin (age 18) and Isaac Coleman (age 12) in an open boat in the fall of 1659. Other partners followed the next year and the settlers laid out the first homes not at the great harbor around which the town was later built but at the smaller Cappamet Harbor farther west (sands later closed up the mouth of the harbor, creating the present-day Capaum Pond) and on the west side of Hummock Pond. The settlement, originally part of the New York Province, received the name Sherburne in 1673 from New York's Royal Governor Francis Lovelace. In 1692 Massachusetts took over jurisdiction of Sherburne, and in 1795, long after the present town had been established, town and island were named Nantucket. (As local boosters are quick to point out, Nantucket is the only locale in the country in which a town, a county and an island all bear the same name.)

The Rise of Nantucket: Whaling and Quakerism

The Sherburne settlement prospered in a modest way. The soil was too poor for much farming, so the settlers raised sheep, pasturing them on the open moors. The Indians had known for centuries that the true wealth of the island lay offshore, and the English settlers learned from the Indians how to harvest the sea. In the Edenic first years of the white settlement, whales were so plentiful that they could be spotted from shore and pursued in small boats. Shore whaling became a growing source of revenue in the last decades of the 17th century. Then, as the local whale populations became depleted in the early years of the 18th century, Nantucketers began to pursue these giant marine mammals in boats fitted out for deep-sea hunting. One turning point in Nantucket whaling came in 1712 when Nantucketer Christopher Hussey, blown off course, spotted a school of sperm whales not far from the island and succeeded in killing one. Previously, right whales had been the preferred species, but Hussey's sperm whale changed all that. Soon after Hussey's encounter with the sperm whale, islanders acquired a 30-ton vessel for deep-sea sperm whale hunting, and five other sloops were added to the Nantucket commercial fleet by 1715. By the 1720s there were 25 vessels in the islands's whaling fleet. Thus began the long and profitable association of Nantucketers and the sperm whale.

At the same time that sperm whaling was becoming the chief economic enterprise on the island, the Quaker sect was becoming its dominant religion. Quakerism took the island pretty much by storm. For 50 years after its initial settlement, Nantucket had no established church. Quakers, whose sect was outlawed in Massachusetts, visited the island in its early days, and in 1708 they brought into their fold the influential Mary Coffin Starbuck, the wife of Nathaniel Starbuck. She began holding Quaker meetings in her house near Hummock Pond (the house was later moved in part into town) and the religion took. Whaling and Quakerism were to hold sway on Nantucket for the next century and a quarter, and most historians attribute the island's prosperity to the two forces working together. The shared religion bound the islanders into a

The Quaker Meeting House on Fair Street, built as a school in 1838, is the only house of worship still used by Quakers on Nantucket. The sect, which dominated the island during its whaling days, died out in the late 19th century. Today services are held in this Meeting House only during the summer months.

tight-knit, frugal and efficient community, and the stable island community supported the increasingly arduous and complex business of whaling with a network of related industries.

Quakerism (called the Society of Friends by its adherents) as it was practiced in the 18th century was a religion of radical simplicity: Its followers, who held to no creed or dogma, valued plain and peaceful living and an honest dedication to work. They shunned all worldly display, including bright color, music, art, flowers, and ornamental beauty in their homes, their persons, their habits and their places of worship. At their meetings, Quakers sat in silence until moved to speak; they marked their graves with no monuments or headstones. (The few headstones huddled together in a corner of Nantucket's Friends Burial Ground on Quaker Road are from the most recent past when splinter sects departed from this custom; the older sections of the burying ground remain an open field.) Nantucket's first Quaker meeting house was put up in the old Sherburne settlement in 1711 and 21 years later the sect, now well-established on Nantucket, erected a much larger meeting house at the end of Main Street in the new town. Quakerism, writes Nantucket historian Edouard A. Stackpole (*Nantucket in Color*), soon controlled the religious, social and economic life of the island: "No other place in America was so controlled and in no other community in the new world was such a large proportion of the inhabitants members of this faith."

And so by the third decade of the 18th century, Nantucket—a Quaker community supported by whaling and growing rapidly around its great harbor—was set on the course of its history. Its rise as the world's whaling capital was swift; its prosperity, though goodly, was brief and erratic.

As the town prospered and grew, more and more houses went up. Here, too, the Quaker influence is apparent in the simple, clean lines of the "typical Nantucket" house: A two-and-a-half story rectangle fronting the street, with four-bayed facade (two windows on one side, door and narrower window on the other), a central chimney and often a "walk" on the roof. (The term "widow's walk" is a popular misnomer; walks were used as much for putting out chimney fires as spying ships on the horizon and, as one historian points out, a widow would not be up on her roof looking out for returning ships anyway.) The Nantucket house of this period was an advance over the more primitive Puritan lean-to dwelling (the New England "saltbox") with its two-story front and roof sloping down to a low wall in the back.

According to Clay Lancaster's *The Architecture of Historic Nantucket*, of the 800 pre-Civil War houses still standing in the town of Nantucket, about 175 are in this "typical Nantucket" style. These are the houses that give the town of Nantucket its characteristic "feel"—serious, spare, consistent, unadorned, in harmony with its setting and open to the commerce and communion of town life. A good example is the Hezekiah Swain House at 1 Vestal Street, the birthplace of Nantucket's distinguished 19th-century astronomer Maria Mitchell. The Nantucket-style house has none of the elegance (or pretensions) of the later Federal and Greek Revival-style houses that stand on Upper Main Street. Like the religion that helped determine its form, its grace derives from its plainness, its good sense and its elegant suitability to the demands of everyday life.

The American Revolution brought an abrupt halt to everything on Nantucket: whaling, building, trade, prosperity, growth. The war that set the American Colonies free was a disaster for Nantucket. Compelled by the pacifist principles of their religion and by their economic dependence on the two warring parties, Nantucketers tried to remain neutral and succeeded in becoming the target of both sides. Rebels and Tories alike raided the island and the fishing fleet, and the British navy utterly crushed Nantucket's whaling industry. During the course of the war, the British took 134 Nantucket ships and captured or killed over 1,200 Nantucketers. The island lost more than a third of its population, and among the survivors there were over 200 widows and 342 orphans.

The Golden Age

Nantucketers were back on the sea even before the Treaty of Paris was ratified: It was a Nantucket ship, the *Bedford*, under the command of Nantucket Captain Mooers, that first showed the Stars and Stripes in British waters in February of 1783. But recovery was slow and the island suffered another serious setback during the War of 1812 when Nantucketers again were caught in the middle of a conflict they wanted no part of. At the war's end, only 23 ships of the 116-ship fleet remained and the island was sunk in a depression. The War of 1812 marked a nadir from which Nantucket would rise very quickly to its zenith, for the decades following—particularly the 1820s and '30s—were the golden age of whaling. Not long after the Revolution, a Nantucket ship rounded Cape Horn for the first time and entered the Pacific hunting grounds. After the War of 1812, Nantucketers discovered the tremendous sperm whaling opportunities of the Japanese fishing grounds. The so-called Southern Whale Fishery industry boomed, and Nantucket was its capital. By 1820, the island's population had topped 7,000 and a fleet of over 60 whaling ships and some 75 trading vessels sailed from the great harbor.

Nantucket's wealth during her golden age was considerable, with the largest share going to the merchants who owned the ships. Many tourists make the mistake, when strolling along Upper Main Street, of identifying the fine Federal and Greek Revival mansions as ship captains' homes. In fact, these homes were built and lived in by merchants; whaling captains were likely to live on the more modest Orange Street, home to 126 whaling captains over the course of 100 years. The homes of the wealthy whaling merchants swell in opulence and style in their ascent up Main Street. The most famous houses in town are the so-called "Three Bricks," matching brick Georgian houses built for three Starbuck brothers at 93, 95 and 97 Main Street and the so-called "Two Greeks," two splendid, soaring, white clapboard Greek Revival mansions (one with Corinthian columns, the other with Ionic columns) that William Hadwen built for himself and his adopted niece at 94 and 96 Main Street. These five houses date from the palmy days of whaling wealth, the Bricks built between 1836 and 1838 and the Greeks in the mid-1840s.

Other fine expressions of Nantucket's mercantile wealth are the Henry and Charles B. Coffin houses (1831-33), built across from each other at 75 and 78 Main Street in a transitional Federal-Greek Revival style; the three-story brick Greek Revival Jared Coffin house (1845), now an inn at 29 Broad Street; Moor's End, a lovely, rambling Federal-style house (1829-34) that Jared Coffin built at 19 Pleasant Street; and the Pacific National Bank (1818), a fine example of the early Federal style that sits at the top of Lower Main Street. The bank's name testifies to the importance of the Pacific Ocean in Nantucket's whaling economy.

These expensive, substantial dwellings and public buildings with their Greek columns or pilasters, porticoes, decorated cornices and roof parapets represent a sharp break with the earlier, Quaker style of building. Where the typical Nantucket-style house was plain and functional, the 19th-century mansion is showy and sophisticated. These are houses built not merely for survival, but also for the enjoyment of comfort, culture, luxury—all the ease and refinement that money could buy. Not surprisingly, as Nantucket's wealth increased, the influence of the Quakers waned. The religion was not well-suited to a town whose leaders were vying with each other in architectural ostentation, and internal dissension hastened the sect's decline. The last Nantucket-born Quaker died in 1900. Today the few Quakers who make their home on Nantucket use the Friends Meeting House at 7 Fair Street for their services during the summer.

All of this wealth and the refinement it purchased flowed from an industry notorious for its danger, its grubbiness, the extreme hardship of its working conditions. The quest of the *Pequod* that Melville describes in *Moby-Dick* is perhaps more frenzied and apocalyptic than the typical whaling voyage, but it does give a good sense of the rough living conditions aboard ship, the peril of setting out in a fragile whaleboat after an animal that could be 100 feet long, of hooking oneself to this beast with a harpoon and being towed by it on a so-called "Nantucket sleigh ride" as it dove and writhed in the open sea.

The very length of the fishing voyages played a part in the decline of Nantucket's whaling economy. As the voyages grew longer, the ships had to become bigger and carry more supplies. There came a point when the ships drew so much water that they could no longer get over the sand bars that kept forming at the mouth of Nantucket's harbor, and the lucrative business of fitting out the ships moved to Edgartown on Martha's Vineyard and New Bedford on the mainland, which in time displaced Nantucket as the world capital of whaling.

Even more disastrous was the great fire of July 13, 1846, the worst in the island's history, which destroyed one-seventh of the town's total area, including nearly the entire commercial district. Nantucket rose from its ashes grander and finer than ever. Main Street was widened by 23 feet and the burned-out wooden shops replaced with brick buildings. The Pacific Bank at the head of Lower Main Street is the only building that remains from before the fire and it marks the westward extent of the blaze. Merchants commissioned some of the town's most resplendent dwellings; warehouses and candle factories were replaced. But though the town rose again, Nantucket had already passed its high-water mark. Three years after the fire came the California Gold Rush and 400 Nantucketers abandoned the hardships of whaling to seek their fortunes out West, creating a serious shortage of experienced crew for the whaling ships. The deathblow of whaling came in the 1850s when petroleum oil was first produced commercially (in 1854) and then discovered in large quantities in Pennsylvania (in 1859). All at once, America and the world had kerosene, a new and better source of illumination, and the bottom fell out of the whale oil market. The Civil War pretty much finished off what was left of Nantucket's whaling fleet. The last Nantucket whaling ship sailed in 1869, and then the island's whaling industry rolled over and died.

With its economy gone, Nantucket collapsed. By 1870 only 2,120 people remained of the 9,700 who had lived here at the peak of prosperity. Grass grew up between the cobbles of town streets. Many once prosperous islanders left their houses derelict and others had their houses lifted from their foundations and floated to the mainland. Nantucket was a ghost town. While the Industrial Revolution raged on the mainland, pumping up the economies of Eastern towns and cities even as it ravaged their architecture, Nantucket languished. Of course the island's loss during these years is our gain today: Because the town lay dormant, it was spared not only industrial development but also the excesses of Victorian architecture. Nantucket's depression preserved its lovely, simple 18th- and early-19th-century architecture nearly intact.

Nantucket lay dormant, but its slumber was not totally undisturbed. Stirrings of a new economy began in the 1860s and '70s when the first ads for Nantucket summer rentals appeared and the first cottages went up along Cliff Road and Brant Point. The summer trade came gradually and gently to Nantucket. Hotels and summer homes were built in town and in 'Sconset (see below), but for the most part they were discreet compared with the enormous Gilded Age "cottages" of Newport and Bar Harbor or Block Island's rambling resort hotels. Nantucket, though it had lost its indigenous industry, retained its character—at least its visual character. And this character is precisely what has been drawing visitors to Nantucket for over 100 years now. From the 1870s until today, the history of Nantucket has pretty much been the history of the tourist and resort trade, the history of an island and town opening its doors to paying guests. Some of the islanders have earned, and still earn, their living from commercial fishing (particularly from scallops); but tourism has been the mainstay of the island's economy for most of the 20th century.

Has been…because things are changing on Nantucket again. Now that construction has edged out tourism as the number one source of revenue, Nantucket has entered a new phase of development, development at a pace unknown on the island for 140 years. What impact the current building boom will have on the tourist industry and on the overall look and feel of the place remains to be seen. For now it's enough to say that this island is, after all these years, still making history.

Exploring the Island: Town and Country

It you're coming to Nantucket by boat, you will first make contact with the wharves along the waterfront, a good place to begin an informal tour. The town's five wharves, built in the 18th and 19th centuries, bristled with commercial activity in the days when Nantucket was an active, working port. Today the primary trade along the wharves is in human bodies—the bodies of visitors coming and going from Steamboat Wharf (where the Steamship Authority car ferry docks) and Straight Wharf (the terminal for the Hy-Line foot passenger ferry from Hyannis). Straight Wharf, which lines up straight with Main Street, is and has been the town's most important. Built by Richard Macy in 1723, this wharf carried the greatest volume of commercial traffic in the whaling days and today it is the centerpiece of the extensive waterfront renovation that Walter Beinecke Jr. carried out in the 1960s. Straight Wharf, together with Old South and Commercial (or Swain's) Wharves, forms a kind of waterfront shopping mall. There are craft and gift shops, snack bars and restaurants, a supermarket and big parking lot (partially hidden by trees), all done up in gray shingles, cobblestone squares, gaslights and other authentic-seeming details. The total effect is tastefully ersatz. One building worth examining on Straight Wharf is the Thomas Macy Warehouse, built in 1846 for the purpose of outfitting whaling ships for long voyages. The building, now maintained by the Nantucket Historical Association, houses the Artist's Association of Nantucket with a gallery open to the public. If Straight Wharf is Nantucket's most important, Old North Wharf, built in 1750, is probably the most photographed. With its row of old shacks built out over the harbor and its genial, carefully unkempt air, Old North Wharf is decidedly picturesque.

A few steps up from Straight Wharf take one right onto the cobbles of Main Street's Market Square, the wide open stretch of Lower Main Street that has been the hub of the town from the start. Despite the distinctively American style of the brick buildings (all erected after the great fire of 1846), Market Square has something of a European aura about it. Perhaps this derives from the comforting human proportions—the buildings are low but not squat, the street broad but not vast—or perhaps from the long-accustomed activities that go on here outdoors: the selling of produce and flowers from curbside farm trucks, the gathering of pedestrians to stroll, windowshop, or simply take the air beneath the famous elms (planted in 1851 by Henry and Charles Coffin, the brothers whose impressive Federal-Greek Revival houses face each other across Main Street a few blocks up).

Unlike commercial Lower Main Street, Upper Main is entirely residential. Within a few blocks it offers a survey of almost every major architectural style used in the town. The house at number 139, built for Richard Gardner sometime before 1688 and thus one of the oldest on the island, is in a style similar to English cottages of the period. The lean-to at the back was added later, in the early 18th century, when lean-to-style dwellings dominated the island. A lean-to house (also called a "saltbox") typically rises to two stories in the front (which on Nantucket often faces south) and then the roof slides sharply down to a low wall in back. The house at number 153 is a two-and-a-half-story, shingle lean-to house built in 1723, with later additions. The Christopher

One of the "Two Greeks" constructed for William Hadwen on Upper Main Street in the mid-1840s. These imposing Greek Revival mansions were built when Nantucket was at its peak of whaling prosperity. They represent an extreme departure from the plain, unadorned, shingled houses favored by earlier generations of Nantucket Quakers. (Courtesy of Nantucket Historical Association; photo: H. Marshall Gardiner, c. 1920.)

Starbuck house at number 105 (the older part built about 1690, the newer part in the mid-18th century) is a good example of the joining together of the lean-to style and the slightly later, typical Nantucket style. This style, widely employed on the island from the 1760s to the 1830s, reflects the Quaker influence as well as the growing prosperity of Nantucket and its transformation from settlement to town.

The typical Nantucket house has neither symmetry, grandeur nor eye-catching ornamentation, but it does have undeniable charm. It is above all the *look* of Nantucket.

Examples of the type can be found on Main Street at numbers 81, 87, 91 (with doorway treatment added later), 109, 120.

Main Street may have the densest concentration of architectural landmarks, but almost any street in town rewards the stroller with something worth looking at. In the midst of old ship captains' homes on Orange Street rises the Unitarian Church (known as the South Tower) built in 1809. In the tower's gold-capped belfry hangs Nantucket's most famous bell, cast in Lisbon in 1812 and first rung in 1815. No one is quite sure why, but for decades the South Tower bell has been struck 52 times at seven in the morning, at noon and at nine at night.

Center Street, off Main Street, will take you past two other important town churches: the Methodist Church (at number 2 Center Street), built in 1822-23 and adorned with a massive Greek Revival portico in 1840 (thought to be the work of Frederick Coleman); and at number 62 the First Congregational Church, known as the North Church, built in 1834 in a style Lancaster describes as transitional Rococo Gothic and Gothic Revival.

These are a few of the "must-see" buildings in town; but if you really want to get a feel for the place, you might want to wander down Pleasant Street, Gardner Street, Beach Street, Lily Street or Fair Street, all of which contain excellent examples of Nantucket architecture at its best. Or lose yourself (which isn't hard since few of the streets have identifying signs) along the back streets of Academy Hill or among the little lanes such as Ray's Court or Darling Street that run into Fair and Pine Streets. If you haven't the time or inclination to get lost, you should take the excellent leisurely walking tour of Nantucket off-the-beaten-track offered by Roger Young, an island native who is as charming as he is knowledgeable. (Contact him through the Historical Association.) Mr. Young will show you the houses where he grew up, take you down back alleys you might never have noticed, point out obscure but fascinating architectural features, entertain you with local gossip and anecdotes, and generally evoke a feeling for the town as a real, living community that no guide book could ever manage.

Before leaving the subject of "must-see" attractions, I should mention the excellent museums, houses and exhibits maintained by the Nantucket Historical Association. In all, there are 13 historic buildings scattered around town that are open to the public. The most important is the Whaling Museum on Broad Street (at the head of Steamboat Wharf). The museum building was originally a factory for the refinement of spermaceti built in 1846; today it contains a variety of maps, objects, replicas, dioramas and paintings related to the great whaling days. Two of the museum's prizes are the only spermaceti press still in existence and the complete skeleton of a 43-foot finback whale. For historic displays on all aspects of Nantucket not related to whaling, take a look at the collections of the Peter Foulger Museum, next door to the Whaling Museum. Here are exhibits of artifacts and paintings relating to Nantucket's Indians, its farming period, the Quakers, the China trade, the island's railroad, and the village at 'Sconset. Scholars, students and genealogists are welcome to use the collection of documents, books, manuscripts, ships' logs and photographs housed at the Foulger Museum's Research Center.

Outside of the town of Nantucket, the island's east shore is probably the area of greatest interest to the visitor. Here are the little villages built originally as escapes from the hubbub of town: 'Sconset, Quidnet and Wauwinet. 'Sconset (the official name, Siasconset, which means something like "at the little muddy place," is never used except on maps) is the oddest and most famous of the three. As far back as the late 17th century, island fishermen began coming here to fish for cod and blue during fishing season and they put up little one-room shacks to sleep in when they weren't fishing. In time their wives followed them here and began to insist on additions to the shacks: "Warts" built on one side of the shacks served as bedrooms, and porches on the other became enclosed kitchens. Houses grew in a patchwork fashion and so did the village perched on a bluff over the open sea. Between 'Sconset and the ocean is an open, dunesy area known as Codfish Park where the fisher folk dumped fish heads and entrails and where squatters took up residence. 'Sconset, with its superb location, extensive beach, and comic little shacks, became too charming to be left to the fishermen: Nantucket town-dwellers and town-weary whaling men fastened on the place as the perfect summertime retreat, and the "Patchwork Village" became a kind of resort (once called "the Newport of the Nantucketoise") well before the island's tourist era commenced.

If native Nantucketers were charmed by 'Sconset, the off-islanders who began coming in the 1870s were intoxicated by it. New York theater people went mad for 'Sconset's quaintness, and the village took on a new identity as an actors' colony. So many of the shacks became summer homes of actors, producers and directors, that 'Sconset's main street—the lane most thickly planted with shacks that leads to its famous pump—became known as Broadway. As demand for the shacks grew, an enterprising soul named Edward Underhill in 1881 undertook to boost the supply by putting up replicas of the original fishing huts, so that today it's not always easy to tell the genuine article and the fakes apart. One genuine article we can be sure of is Auld Lang Syne (see photo on page 87), the oldest shack in 'Sconset and perhaps on Nantucket as well.

On the island's east shore just south of Wauwinet is Quidnet, once a fishing village, now a small summer colony with a scattering of homes on the oceanfront and on Sesachacha Pond. South of Quidnet is the Sankaty Head Golf Club (private) and beyond it the Sankaty Lighthouse, built in 1849. Another jump down the east shore takes you to 'Sconset.

Nantucket's long, gently curving south shore has perhaps its greatest allure for those who love the beach. Fifty-five miles of fine sand beaches fringe the island, and on the south shore the beaches are wide and the waves often roll in with the long, slow-breaking crests that surfers like. You can get down to the south shore beaches at Surfside, Cisco and Madaket. Cisco is the preferred spot for surfing, and from the bluffs above the beach you can really feel the force of the waves pounding at the shore. In fact, the pounding waves are gradually swallowing up the shore. The spring I was on the island, the remains of a large beach house hung over the bluff at Cisco, and the sea was visibly eating away at the structure's last hold on earth. The sea has already removed a mile and a half from Nantucket's south shore since the glaciers (see below) deposited it, and the sea's advance continues at an average rate of eight feet a year (and sometimes much more). The road to Cisco runs alongside Hummock Pond, a glacially formed freshwater pond that is a lovely spot for bird-watching. A small road off Hummock Pond Road takes you to Bartlett's Farm, an island institution for decades. This 200-acre farm, one of three on the island, has been in the Bartlett family for seven generations and grows an assortment of vegetables and flowers. The Bartlett Farm truck is a familiar curbside sight in Main Street's Market Square during the summer and well into the fall. Because of the moderating influence of the surrounding ocean, Nantucket's growing season extends well beyond that on the mainland, and as late as the first week of December the Bartletts continue bringing squash, potatoes, broccoli and cauliflower to town.

On its east side, Nantucket ends abruptly at the bluffs that stretch from Sankaty head to 'Sconset. But the island's west side at Madaket peters out gradually in long reaches of sandy islands and shoals. The status of these westernmost reaches of Nantucket keeps changing. Tuckernuck Island to the far west used to be connected to the rest of Nantucket (depending on the tides), and Smith's Point, which became Esther Island when Hurricane Esther broke through the narrow sandbar in 1961, has (for the moment anyway) been joined up again by shifting sands. Madaket with its crescent-shaped harbor sweeping north from Hither Creek to Eel Point is an area of contrast. The Nantucket Conservation Foundation (see below) has extensive holdings around the harbor at Little Neck and Eel Point, and in these protected wetlands gray and harbor seals, oldsquaw ducks, sandpipers, oystercatchers and

The Nantucket Life Saving Museum on Polpis Road is a replica of the island's first life saving station, which was erected on the shore at Surfside in 1874.

many other shore birds abound. But there is also considerable development going on all around Madaket. This former fishing village, now a burgeoning second-home community, has earned a certain notoriety for containing Tristram's Landing, Nantucket's first condominium development, which, despite its historic Nantucket name, is pretty much indistinguishable from beach condos anywhere.

In good weather when the wind is not blowing too hard, a bicycle is the ideal way to explore Nantucket's outlying areas. There is a bike path leading from town to 'Sconset along Milestone Road and another leading to Surfside. The Polpis Road, Madaket Road and Hummock Pond Road also make pleasant biking routes.

Even though it is by any mainland standard small, the island feels vast when you're on foot or biking in the empty parts. One is lulled by the sameness of the land, the open expanse of the moors and then beyond them the endless expanse of the sea. Nantucket's land, a moored chunk of glacial spill, puts one in mind of the forces that formed it, the ice and sea that heaved it far from the continent. It's closer to the elements and thus, though confining, seems to comprehend a sense of infinity. As it turns out, the land's sameness is itself an illusion, for the island is stocked with life forms both terrestrial and avian in seeming infinite variety.

Preserving Nantucket

The species increasing most rapidly on Nantucket's moors is not a variety of bird or plant, but our own humankind. Our increase, as mentioned above, has been especially marked of late. *The New York Times* estimates that the 7,000 houses already standing on the island will be joined over the next two decades by 7,000 more houses, many of them rising on once open moors. No one can say with any exactness what impact this will have on the island's ecology or its delicate water supply, but there is no doubt the impact will be tremendous. There are, however, a number of organizations working to blunt that impact and protect natural Nantucket. The most important is the Nantucket Conservation Foundation, founded in 1963 by Roy Larsen, a vice president with Time Inc., Walter Beinecke Jr., heir to the Green Stamp fortune, and other

"Auld Lang Syne" in 'Sconset, considered by many to be the oldest house on Nantucket. It is typical of the shingled shacks that island fishermen built here in the 18th and early 19th centuries. When New York theater people started buying up and restoring the shacks in the 1870s, 'Sconset's main street was renamed Broadway. (Courtesy of the Nantucket Historical Association; photo: H. Marshall Gardiner.)

wealthy Nantucket summer people who owned large tracts of land. The purpose of the NCF is to preserve and protect the open spaces on the island, and through donations of land and money over the years the organization has managed to acquire about one-quarter of the island's total acreage. Among its holdings are the cranberry bogs on 'Sconset Road and the Windswept Bogs at the junction of Wauwinet and Polpis Roads. The NCF leases the bogs out to an operator called the Nantucket Cranberry Associates, which harvests the cranberries and markets them through the Ocean Spray cooperative. Other choice NCF parcels include Sanford Farm (halfway between town and Madaket), Eel Point north of Madaket Harbor, Madequecham Valley east of Nantucket airport, and various holdings on Coatue. Except for the bogs, NCF lands are open to the public for passive recreation, such as fishing, hunting (deer, pheasant, rabbit, ducks and geese), walking and bird-watching.

In 1983 the town of Nantucket also moved to save the island's open land: Starting that year a "land bank" was formed, funded by a 2% tax levied on every real estate transaction. The receipts, which last year came to about $5.1 million, are used to buy up and preserve land for public enjoyment. (In 1987, the tax was raised to 2.5%, with the added 0.5% designated to buy land on which lower-priced housing would be built, thus preserving some of the island's human features as well as its natural ones.) So far about 650 acres have been purchased through the land bank, much of it remote moorland. The guiding principle is that if outer lands are protected, new development will be confined to areas around town, thus keeping intact the island's traditional character of thickly settled town surrounded by open moor. Those who cherish this traditional character say that at least half the island's land must be kept open if the character is to survive. To date, about one-third of Nantucket's acreage is protected by either private or public preservation organizations. But as land prices soar, NCF and "land bank" dollars buy less and less. The future of natural Nantucket, particularly the 87-mile shore line, of which only a mile and a half is publicly owned, remains uncertain.

Though little is being done to control the *volume* of development on Nantucket, the nature and style of development is stringently regulated by the Historic District Commission, whose five locally elected officials review plans for every new structure or renovation project on Nantucket to make sure it conforms with certain stylistic guidelines. The result is a striking architectural uniformity, in which cedar shingles, like some rampant lichen, cover houses old and new, large and small, suitable and unsuitable.

Nantucket Today: Working, Playing, Prospering

Island natives are notoriously proud of being island born and island raised, but on Nantucket this pride sometimes rises to the level of fanaticism. Nantucketers have been known to refer to the mainland as "America," with the clear implication that their island must not be lumped together with the rest. And the story goes that if you're born off-island (even by accident), no matter how many generations of your family have been Nantucket natives, you're considered an off-islander. When I asked Gayl Michael, assistant curator of research materials with the Nantucket Historical Association, about this attitude, she told me about the hierarchy of status on Nantucket:

NANTUCKET

1) Day-trippers: those who come as foot passengers on the Hy-Line, buy a few plastic whale souvenirs and return to America.

2) Tourists: those who come to stay for a weekend, a week, a month (day-trippers and tourists numbered 450,000 last summer).

3) Summer people: second-home owners, usually with school-age children, who descend in June and vanish after Labor Day. They're the ones largely responsible for the island's building boom.

4) Year-round residents: anyone who lives here but was not born here.

5) Semi-natives: anyone born off-island whose parents were born on Nantucket.

6) Natives: true-blue Nantucketers born on the island to parents born on the island.

Although one might assume that for many, this ranking system is a bit of joke, the fact that it exists at all is some reflection of the Nantucket social climate. On this island, the more insular the better.

Whatever one's place in the hierarchy, if one comes to Nantucket for any length of time, and most especially if one wants to live or own a home here, one had better be well-to-do. The average house on the island now sells for $300,000, and no house, even one that is uninhabitable, goes for less than $200,000. Nantucket's real estate boom reflects conditions that apply up and down the entire East Coast, but a number of factors have made prices especially steep here. Walter Beinecke Jr., the man who has had the most influence in determining the aspect and atmosphere of contemporary Nantucket, had a hand in raising the price of just about everything on the island. Beinecke, who in the late '50s and '60s amassed a small empire of 160 commercial and waterfront properties in town, including stores, hotels and the vital Straight Wharf area, made a deliberate decision to go for "class" not "mass" on the island. His stated policy was to "have fewer bodies spending more time" and of course more money on Nantucket. Perhaps his most notorious move was to prevent a commercial ferry from docking at his wharf unless it cut the number of people coming across on each boat from 2,000 to 500.

Anyway, Beinecke spruced up the town, transforming the ramshackle into the picturesque, and he did what he could to ensure that only a better class of tourist could come to enjoy it. Downtown real estate prices rose, then real estate all over the island, then rents on town shops and naturally prices of things sold in them. Prices have risen so high that "normal" stores such as the Five and Ten and normal people can no longer afford to be on Nantucket. Now it's easier to buy designer sportswear than an ironing board on which to press them. At the end of 1986, Beinecke sold his Sherburne Associates—the company through which he controlled his two major hotels, 36 buildings, 40 cottages and the boat basin—to First Winthrop, a Boston-based real estate concern. The price was $56 million. "Whether by the grace of God or inflation," Beinecke told the *New York Times*, "we managed to make a profit in the end." No one yet has any clear idea what impact this sale will have on the island. Meanwhile, business, particularly the real estate and construction business, continues to boom.

Of course Beinecke alone did not turn the island into an enclave for the rich. The rich have been around for some time. The Nantucket rich are not for the most part the flashy celebrities who summer on Martha's Vineyard or the high-rolling artists and authors who retreat to Long Island's East End. They're the quiet, unobtrusive, staunchly rich, like IBM chairman John Akers and Senator John Heinz. Rock stars, hotshot writers and film people do come to Nantucket (there's TV's Mr. Rogers, Peter Benchley, David Halberstam, frequent appearances by Billy Joel and Christie Brinkley), but they don't dominate the scene. The scene, like the shingles and clapboards and moors, is subdued. There is little in the way of glitz, chic or ticky-tack. This is not to say that at peak summer season the town is quiet: When the waves of day-trippers join those in the higher status categories, Nantucket is swamped. But these invasions are like the extreme tides at the full or new moon, known as spring tides: They're a temporary occurrence and when the high water recedes, the old outlines of the island reemerge.

Nantucket is prospering. No matter where you go on the island, everything looks neat and fine and well cared for. There are no old cars rusting in abandoned fields, no junkyards, no rickety wharves rotting into the sea. There are no glaring eyesores, unless you consider new development on once empty moors an eyesore in itself. Some feel that the island has become *too* neat, that prosperity has brought preciousness, that restoration, no matter how carefully authentic, has straightened the queer, old, sea-bitten soul out of the place. And many worry that the island is going to sink under its very success, that it is becoming too popular, too populated, too built up, too expensive, too much cherished by too many devotees. Nantucket is clearly entering another peak period. But it is a peak that many regard with bitter regret. "You should have seen it ten—even five years ago" is a refrain one hears frequently from those who were here then. In a way I do wish I could have seen it then—but even more I wish I could have seen it 150 or even 250 years ago, when Nantucketers were building their town around the great harbor and discovering the wealth of the surrounding area.

History has left her mark on this island for a long time, long at least by American standards. What was great in Nantucket is gone. But one suspects that somehow what is beautiful will survive.

MARTHA'S VINEYARD

Area: 19.25 miles long by 9.37 miles wide at its widest; 96 square miles; 64,000 acres.

Population: 12,690 year-round; 94,708 in peak summer season.

Location: 5 miles south of Cape Cod between Vineyard and Nantucket Sounds and the Atlantic Ocean.

Access: By car and passenger ferry from Woods Hole, Massachusetts (call 508-540-2022); by passenger ferry from Falmouth, Massachusetts (call 508-548-4800); by passenger ferry from Hyannis (call 508-775-7185); by passenger ferry from New Bedford, Massachusetts (summer only, call 508-997-1688).

The cliffs at Gay Head.

Martha's Vineyard

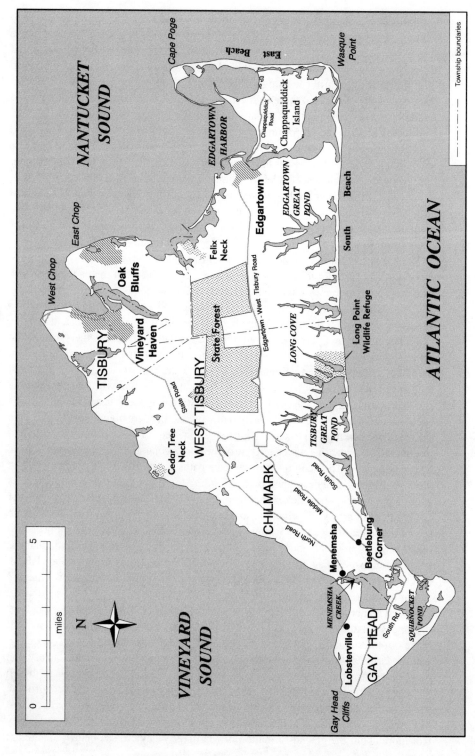

VINEYARD SOUND

NANTUCKET SOUND

ATLANTIC OCEAN

Cape Poge

East Beach

Wasque Point

West Chop

East Chop

EDGARTOWN HARBOR

Chappaquiddick Road

Chappaquiddick Island

Oak Bluffs

Vineyard Haven

Felix Neck

Edgartown

EDGARTOWN GREAT POND

South Beach

TISBURY

State Forest

Edgartown - West Tisbury Road

WEST TISBURY

LONG COVE

Long Point Wildlife Refuge

Cedar Tree Neck

State Road

TISBURY GREAT POND

CHILMARK

South Road

Middle Road

North Road

Menemsha

Beetlebung Corner

MENEMSHA CREEK

South Rd.

SQUIBNOCKET POND

Lobsterville

GAY HEAD

Gay Head Cliffs

N

0   miles   5

Township boundaries

91

Martha's Vineyard is pioneering the way for Eastern islands into the late 20th century. The largest unbridged East Coast island is also the most advanced in the trends, issues and new developments that are creeping—or in some cases rushing—out to sea from Maine to Florida. If Martha's Vineyard leads in tourism, it also leads in land preservation; cluster housing projects cropped up on former farmland here as long ago as the 1960s, but there also came swift public awareness of the dangers of uncontrolled development. There are more real estate developers trying to take Martha's Vineyard and more conservation organizations trying to save it. The island also leads the Eastern islands in fame and fortune. Although it is difficult to measure such things precisely, it is probably safe to say that the Vineyard has a higher concentration of high-power celebrities than any other unbridged island; and that of all islands, with the possible exception of neighboring Nantucket, it is the most expensive to live on and to visit. These are boom times on the Vineyard, and if you want to share in the fun, even for a few days, you'd better bring a lot of money along. If you want to *own* a piece of the fun, you'll need a fortune.

The boom has roused a reaction, sometimes a bitter one, among those who love Martha's Vineyard. Rape is a brutal word for a brutal act—but this is the word you hear most often in connection with this island. "Poor Martha, I can't believe they raped the whole thing" reads a bumper sticker popular with grieving devotees. *Martha's Vineyard, An Elegy* is the title of a fine book of reminiscences of the past and laments about the present by Everett Allen, a journalist who grew up here. Others have taken a more personal and practical approach to protect themselves and their property from the rising tide of popularity. Edgartown, the Vineyard's most elegant settlement and thus a prime target for day-trippers and tour buses, fairly bristles with "no trespassing" and "keep out" signs. Much of the magnificent stretch of ocean beach on the island's south shore is similarly branded, and in many places there are high fences to reinforce the message. Parking—in towns, near beaches, in scenic areas—can be difficult; and in summer, visitors bring with them one of the horrors of mainland life, the traffic jam. Even biking can be difficult on crowded bike paths and narrow roads; and mopeds, in the eyes of many islanders, are a plague rivaling the Black Death. ("Ban mopeds" is another popular bumper sticker and the rallying cry of a growing island movement.)

"We used to crave fall when the tourists left," said one Vineyarder. "Now at the height of the season we want *winter* when things are really quiet." The pioneer East Coast island is an island under siege—or perhaps, more accurately, an island that has surrendered to its besiegers. On Swan's Island, Maine, on Block Island, Rhode Island, on Ocracoke in the Outer Banks they worry about the future; on Martha's Vineyard the future is here. Islanders and visitors are living, and dealing, with the consequences.

At first glance, the future doesn't look so bad. If you've never seen the island before, the rape is not that obvious. The beauty has been marred but not effaced. You can still make out the stunning, glacially sculpted landscape that has lured and fascinated so many. Martha's Vineyard is not only the largest unbridged Eastern island, but also the most diverse in topography and in its settlements. Unlike Nantucket—"all beach without a background" as Melville called it—the Vineyard has beach *and* background, or rather many backgrounds. The landscape varies from the green, rolling, morainal hills of Chilmark to the vast, flat outwash plain south of Edgartown and West Tisbury (for more about the glacial formation of Martha's Vineyard, see below). There are farms and forests, moors and ponds, the famous cliffs of Gay Head at the west end and the long white sand beaches of Katama and Chappaquiddick at the east.

Politically, the Vineyard is divided into six townships, each distinct in character. The three major population centers at the east end of the island are built around three fine harbors: At the northern apex of the island's triangle sits Vineyard Haven, a working port and commercial center, the least given over to tourism; Oak Bluffs just a few miles down the triangle's east side is an historic tourist town, a layered confection of Victorian gingerbread and modern honky-tonk; and farther still down the east side lies Edgartown, a fine and refined New England port town built with whaling money back in the late 18th and early 19th centuries and beautifully maintained with money of one sort or another ever since.

A 19th-century photo of Edgartown's Old Whaling Church, built with money made in the whaling trade from 1842 to 1849. The 92-foot-high tower is a landmark by sea. Edgartown's Main Street is now paved and, for lack of congregation, the former Methodist church has become a performing arts center. (Courtesy of the Dukes County Historical Society.)

Together, Vineyard Haven, Oak Bluffs and Edgartown are referred to as "down-island" and the more rural portions of the island to the west are called "up-island." (The terms are nautical in origin and refer to degrees of longitude as measured from England's Greenwich at zero: A ship sailing east is running *down* its longitude, a westbound ship running *up*.) There are three up-island townships to balance the three down-island townships: West Tisbury occupies the center of the island, which might almost pass for southern Vermont with its agricultural cast and large stands of forest; farther west is Chilmark, where stone walls follow the rolling hills right off to the ocean; and all the way to the west is Gay Head, one of two Indian townships in

Massachusetts, a countryside of moors, scrub woods and ancient cranberry bogs where the island terminates abruptly at the famous multi-colored cliffs.

Up-island is country, at least compared with down-island, and Chilmark and Gay Head have the kind of beauty that can take your breath away. But country on Martha's Vineyard does not mean the same thing as country in Wyoming or even upstate New York. Little networks of dirt roads fan out from the two-lane highways, and fanning off the dirt roads there are driveways leading to homes and second homes, working farms and gentlemen's farms, private estates, cottages and condos. Many of the homes are new, and more and more of them belong to the privileged and monied people who come to Martha's Vineyard to vacation, to retire, and in some cases simply to live. Homes are just about everywhere on the island: It's difficult to find a vista that does not take in a group of them. This is what the development of the past 20 years has brought. The development is too tasteful and opulent to be called blight; but it has spread too far and too wide. Martha's Vineyard has become a resort island, a rich, strange hybrid landscape that has lost the sense of emptiness and endless open space we associate with the American countryside. The island is filling in and closing up. With a few notable exceptions, the island's greatest remaining beauty is private and off-limits.

Fortunately, the exceptions include some of the most spectacular pieces of Martha's Vineyard. The movement to preserve open land and wild spaces on the Vineyard began more than 30 years ago, pioneered in part by celebrated *Vineyard Gazette* editor, outspoken author and conservationist Henry Beetle Hough. It was the work of Hough and the Sheriff's Meadow Foundation he set up in the late 1950s that helped preserve the Cedar Tree Neck Sanctuary on the northwest shore, perhaps the finest natural area on the island. The Long Point Refuge which encompasses one-half mile of South Beach as well as considerable frontage on Tisbury Great Pond is another superbly beautiful area. On Chappaquiddick Island the Cape Poge Wildlife Refuge and Wasque Point protect long stretches of the island's east coast. These and other sanctuaries, small as they are, are prizes. Along their beaches, salt marsh, dunes and woods we are all privileged to see Martha's Vineyard in its pristine state. These areas are sanctuaries not only for wildlife, but for people. Since Hough began his work back in the fifties, a number of other conservation organizations have grown up on Martha's Vineyard, and today they are working together to save what land can still be saved. (For more about the natural areas on the island and the conservation groups, see below.)

Early History: Indians and Settlers

Though they have diverged considerably over the years, Martha's Vineyard and Nantucket were linked in their early history (that is, their white history). Both islands were discovered by Captain Bartholomew Gosnold in his voyage from England on the *Concord* in 1602, the voyage during which he planted a short-lived colony on Cuttyhunk. We believe from accounts left by John Brereton and Gabriel Archer, members of Gosnold's expedition, that the Englishmen went ashore on the Vineyard, probably at Cape Poge. Brereton later wrote of the "incredible store of vines, as well in the woodie part of the Island where they run upon every tree, as on the outward parts." It was these vines that led Gosnold to name the island a Vineyard, but the identity of Martha remains in dispute. The contestants range from Gosnold's infant daughter, to his mother-in-law, his wife and his mother. Charles Banks, the preeminent Martha's Vineyard historian, has muddied the waters even more: He claims that Gosnold used the name Martha's Vineyard for the small satellite island to the southwest now known as Noman's Land (currently used as a bombing practice site by the U.S. Navy) and that he called the large island *Martin's* Vineyard, for Captain John Martin. In any case, whoever Martha was or whether Martha was really Martin, her name eventually became associated with the 96-square-mile "vineyard" in the New World.

Four decades after discovery, in 1642, Thomas Mayhew Jr. landed on the island with a small group of white colonists and founded the settlement that later became Edgartown. Mayhew's father had the previous year purchased Martha's Vineyard, Nantucket and the Elizabeth Islands for £40. His intention was not only to colonize the islands but also to convert the Indians to Christianity, and his son embarked on this project forthwith. Mayhew Senior soon joined his son at Edgartown (named in honor of the Duke of York's three-year-old son, the heir to the British throne, who, unknown to the Mayhews, had already died when they selected his name). A few years later Mayhew sold Nantucket and devoted himself exclusively to Martha's Vineyard, and four generations of Mayhews after him carried on his work of Christianizing the Indians.

When the Mayhews and their band of white settlers arrived on the island, there were perhaps as many as 3,000 Indians living on it. They were members of the Wampanoag Indian Federation, part of the Algonquin family that dominated the eastern region of North America. The Vineyard Wampanoags were divided into four tribes: the Takemmies who dwelled at Tisbury; the Nunapugs at Edgartown; the Aquinnahs at Gay Head; and the Chappaquiddicks at the separate island that bears their name. Native Americans had been on the Vineyard for a long time when the whites arrived. Archaeologists have found evidence of Indian culture on the island going back to 2270 B.C., and they believe that the island people were originally hunters of deer and did not begin to fish or farm until after 1000 A.D. The land was sacred to the Indians and they held it in common. The concept of buying and selling land was alien to their culture, though the Wampanoags soon learned all about it from the whites.

The history of the Martha's Vineyard Indians is sad, but not as sad as most North American Indian histories, for at least some Indians remain on the island. In the first years after the coming of the whites, Wampanoags died in great numbers from the diseases transmitted by the new settlers. Most of those who survived converted to Christianity, believing that the religion offered some magic protection to its adherents. By 1674, the island's Indian population had fallen by half; in 1720, their numbers were reduced to 800 and in 1764 to 313. The Indians who remained continued to live by fishing and farming, and they shared the secrets of the land and the sea with the whites, particularly the secrets of whaling, which in time proved most profitable to the white settlers.

The Indians did not fare quite so well on land. As the whites bought up the fertile lands at the center of the Vineyard, the Indians moved to the fringes, to Chappaquiddick at the east and Gay Head at the west end. During the 19th century, Gay Head became an Indian reservation, in which the members of the Wampanoag Tribe held the land in common. In 1870 Gay Head was incorporated as a town, and the land was divided among individual owners, though some common land remained. In the histories written by whites, the establishment of the township is portrayed as a benefit to the Indians; but some of the Wampanoags say it was done against their wishes so that whites could buy and sell the land. This, in fact, has happened, and white landowners now outnumber Indian owners in the town of Gay Head.

The Age of Prosperity

The first white settlers had been farmers in England, and farmers they remained when they established themselves on Martha's Vineyard. To their credit they did pay the Indians for the land they wanted, and they soon had thriving farms all over the island. Much of the original forest was cleared off for sheep grazing, and the islanders grew corn and potatoes, kept pigs and cattle, and erected mills along the streams that run down into Vineyard Sound in the northwest section of the island. The settlers' greatest wealth, however, came from the sea, and especially from whaling, which became a major industry on Martha's Vineyard in the early 19th century. Edgartown was the principal whaling port, and though it never rivaled Nantucket or New Bedford, it made out quite well in the hugely profitable, hugely dangerous and fairly short-lived venture of worldwide whaling. (For more about the great age of whaling, see the Nantucket entry.) Edgartown's golden age lasted from about 1830 to 1845, and it was in this period that many of the town's stately white homes were built on Water Street, Main Street, South Summer Street and School Street.

Meanwhile, Vineyard Haven—originally called Holmes Hole and also known as the town of Tisbury—was also prospering as a commercial port. The town's harbor became a major stopping-off place in Colonial times when there was a good deal of maritime traffic from the West Indies up the East Coast and into New England. Vineyard Haven's waterfront, like Edgartown's, was crowded with businesses that built and serviced ships, though Vineyard Haven depended less on whaling than on trade. Vineyard Haven was also the port of entry for hostile British forces during the Revolutionary War. In 1778, a fleet of 83 British ships under the command of Major General Gray entered the harbor in order to requisition supplies. From their head-

quarters at Vineyard Haven, the British ransacked the island, carrying off most of its sheep and cattle and stripping the local militia of their arms. The town recovered from the ravages of the war, but later it suffered even more from the ravages of a fire that destroyed the center of town and most of the houses along Main Street in 1883. Edgartown has preserved much of its early-19th-century character, but because of the fire, Vineyard Haven is a much newer and visually less interesting town.

The Dr. Daniel Fisher House at 99 Main Street was built in 1840 by one of Edgartown's most prosperous citizens.

For both towns, the mid-19th century was the era of greatest prosperity, and for both decline came fairly rapidly. Edgartown, like Nantucket, went into a slump when the widespread use of petroleum put an end to the whaling industry after the Civil War. Vineyard Haven lost a good deal of its business when trains began to replace ships as freight-carriers and when the opening up of the Cape Cod Canal in 1914 permitted Boston-bound ships to bypass the island. The island's

The pavilion at Ocean Park where summertime concerts have been given for over a hundred years.

glory days were over before the 20th century began, but with the new century, a new kind of glory descended on Martha's Vineyard—the fashionable glory of a summer resort.

The Resort Era: From Camp Meetings to Condos

Actually, the summer resort business got started on the Vineyard well before the 20th century. Originally it was religion, not relaxation, that brought visitors here. Religious revivals started on the island back in 1835, when a zealous Edgartown Methodist named Jeremiah Pease gathered his coreligionists at a camp meeting in an oak grove in the bucolic area that was to become Oak Bluffs. The idea caught fire, and the next year and in successive Augusts, the Methodists were back, flocking here in ever greater numbers from the island, the mainland and eventually all over the country. In the course of the 19th century, the spirit of summer holiday supplanted the spirit of religion, and Cottage City (the Victorian name for Oak Bluffs) became a pleasure-seeker's summer resort, complete with carousel, boardwalk, roller-skating rink, large hotels, dance halls and more and more ornate gingerbread cottages.

The revival meetings at Oak Bluffs opened the way for island-wide tourism. West Chop, one of the two headlands that protect the Vineyard Haven harbor, attracted well-off Bostonians in the late 1880s; East Chop, the other headland, was a camp meeting ground for Baptists. And at the turn of the century, wealthy New Yorkers began buying up the elegant Edgartown whaling captains' homes as summer places. Emily Post bought a house out on Fuller Street and helped to establish Edgartown as a very proper, very exclusive, and very conservative retreat.

Although the resort trade was in full swing by the first decade of the 20th century, it was for the most part limited to the summer colonies in and around the down-island towns. The "developments" of those days were huge shingle-style cottages built along the shore at West Chop and on Tower Hill just south of Edgartown's harbor and Starbuck Neck just north of it. It was not until after World War II that significant numbers of summer people began to infiltrate the more rural up-island areas, and not until the late sixties and seventies that the character of the island began to change beyond recognition. Within the memories of older Vineyarders, nearly everyone who lived outside of the towns had a few farm animals; Gay Head had no summer homes and even Chilmark very few; the majority of the islanders worked in agriculture, fishing or forestry.

Today there are a handful of farms left, a small commercial fishing industry based mostly in the lovely little village of Menemsha, some shellfishing, particularly for scallops—but tourism and building account for more than 95% of the island's economy. Development is island-wide, and the Vineyard has become not just a summer resort, but more and more a year-round resort, with crowds of visitors hanging on well into the fall and returning in the spring. The souvenir T-shirt and ice cream culture has invaded even staid Edgartown, and Oak Bluffs is more than ever a colorful commercial carnival. The history of Martha's Vineyard in the 1970s and eighties is largely the history of real estate. On the island where fortunes were made by sending ships around the world in pursuit of sperm whales, now there are fortunes being made by exchanging plots of land. Prosperity has returned with a vengeance.

The Island Before History: Geology and Natural Features

Despite the development that is spreading over the face of the island, Martha's Vineyard's distinct and varied landforms are still striking even to the casual visitor who traverses the island quickly by car. Like Nantucket, Block Island and Long Island, the Vineyard is a terminal moraine, formed when the Wisconsin glacier melted and dumped its load of ground-up stones and gravel. Barbara Blau Chamberlain in *These Fragile Outposts*, her very interesting book about the geology of the Vineyard, Nantucket and Cape Cod, gives a vivid description of the glacier's role in forming the Vineyard:

> Martha's Vineyard is almost entirely an ice-molded island. Its rolling hills and valleys, its great plain, its stone walls, blue coves and refreshing scenery—even its shape—it owes to the glaciers. The only changes here since the days when ice first exposed the Vineyard to the air have been wrought about its shores where the sea has played, taking land from here and tacking it on there—and across its surface, onto which winds and rainwaters, vegetation and people have brushed the colors and shadings of a landscape.

What makes the glacial formation of the Vineyard particularly fascinating is that one can still see quite plainly how separate lobes of ice descended on and retreated from the island. Glaciers advance not in a solid wall of ice but by radiating ice out in scallop-edged lobes. The Vineyard's up-island was covered by the Buzzards Bay Lobe, which left behind, in Chamberlain's words, "a rough, bouldery highland some three miles wide, parallel to the shore [with] long wrinkles, pronounced dips in the topography...Here are [the island's] highest hills, its only streams, and nearly all its small ponds." The down-island moraine, left behind by the earlier Cape Cod Lobe, is a markedly different landform, much flatter and gentler, with low hills that rise gradually, not abruptly like the roller-coaster terrain of Chilmark. The highest down-island point is 120 feet, in Oak Bluffs, compared with Chilmark's 308-foot Prospect Hill, the highest point on the island. In addition, there were far fewer boulders carried by the Cape Cod Lobe. The lacy stone walls, which Vineyard farmers deliberately built loosely so the wind would pass through and not knock them over, are a characteristic feature of the up-island landscape; down-island, stones were too scarce to build many walls. (On Nantucket, which was also covered by the Cape Cod Lobe, stones of any size are nearly impossible to find.)

The Buzzards Bay Lobe and the Cape Cod Lobe met at Lake Tashmoo, and it was the meeting of these two rounded tongues of ice that gave the Vineyard its triangular shape with the head of Lake Tashmoo at the apex. South of the morainal hills lies the vast flat outwash plain, formed by the lighter sands and gravels that washed down from the ridges of the moraine. In the center of the outwash plain is the 4,500-acre Martha's Vineyard State Forest, and in the center of the forest is the island's airport.

A party of 19th-century picnickers at Gay Head. (Courtesy of the Dukes County Historical Society.)

The Vineyard's south shore Great Ponds are also of glacial origin. With the melting of the ice, streams gouged out the soft outwash sediments, and as sea levels rose, these stream beds filled with ocean water. In succeeding millennia, sand thrown up from the ocean blocked off the mouths of these inlets, the salt water drained out and the inlets became the freshwater Great Ponds—Chilmark Pond, Tisbury Great Pond, Edgartown Great Pond are the largest—that now lie behind the expanse of South Beach. The South Beach itself along with Cape Poge on Chappaquiddick and Lobsterville Beach to the east of Gay Head all postdate the glacial retreat.

Gay Head, the 150-foot cliffs at the Vineyard's west end—named by British sailors in the 17th century for its bright gay colors—is a formation far more ancient than the glacial moraine and outwash that covers the rest of the island. In Gay Head's streaks of luminous white, gray, pink, tan, red, yellow and black one can read, in Chamberlain's words, "New England's most complete record of its past hundred million years." The cliffs are a complex, composite formation, laid down initially in horizontal layers but thrust upward, folded and jumbled by the glaciers. There are sand, gravel and clay layers, layers rich in fossils, and others composed of decayed primeval forests. By "reading" the cliffs, scientists have learned that the land has fallen and risen several times: Forest floor became sea floor where clay

Gay Head Lighthouse *(1935) by Adolf Dehn.* (Lithograph, 12.5 X 18.875 inches; collection of the Whitney Museum of American Art.)

accumulated, and then ocean levels dropped and Gay Head again became dry land, only to sink again beneath the sea. When the Wisconsin glacier descended on the area, it pushed the Gay Head cliffs up until they towered above the ice like an island in a frozen sea.

Gay Head has been steadily eroding for thousands of years, and man hastened the erosion in the late 19th century by scooping out white Cretaceous clays for use as pottery and cannon molds. Erosion continues to sculpt the cliffs, which look rather like a small multi-colored mountain range whose flanks have been deeply eaten away. Already erosion has claimed much of the red clay that was once so vivid, but as pieces of Gay Head slide down into the sea, new sections emerge. Contrary to appearances, it is not the ocean that is the primary agent of erosion, but seepage from groundwater behind the cliffs. Because of erosion, the public is now prohibited from walking on the Gay Head cliffs, but one can still take in their startling beauty from an observation platform above. The U.S. Department of the Interior registered the cliffs as a Natural Landmark in 1966.

Seeing the Sights: Down-Island

Probably the worst way to see the sights of Martha's Vineyard is to board one of the tour buses that collect tourists at the ferry docks and circle the island in a brisk two-and-a-half hours of narration and pitstops. Yes, you'll get to see where Jacqueline Onassis's

The Gay Head Lighthouse today.

driveway is and the picturesque little cemetery outside of Chilmark Center where Lillian Hellman and John Belushi are buried. But, as one island resident put it, the buses are not permitted to "disgorge their contents" except at a few designated spots up-island, so you will see much of the Vineyard as a green, rolling blur. You are far better off conducting your own tour by car or bicycle.

Vineyard Haven

If you come to the island by ferry, you're likely to disembark at Vineyard Haven (ferries also run to Oak Bluffs), so I'll start there and cover the down-island towns before moving on to the up-island countryside. Because so much of the central part of town was destroyed in the 1883 fire, Vineyard Haven has far fewer beautiful old homes than Edgartown. Its Main Street could be that of any New England coastal town, and its waterfront has more of the gritty, disheveled atmosphere of a real working port than the gussied-up, gentrified Edgartown harbor, where tourism has blotted out all vestiges of the old whaling days. The two "chops," east and west, give Vineyard Haven a superb, V-shaped natural harbor. (The derivation of "chop" in this sense is obscure; some say it once referred to the side of a vise, others claim it means entrance to a harbor.) Fine as the Vineyard Haven harbor is, it offered no protection from a vicious northeaster that blew in in 1898 and destroyed 50 boats at anchor here.

Right at the Vineyard Haven ferry dock is the Seaman's Bethel, a building that was once the local branch of the Boston Seamen's Friends Society, and is currently open as a museum. Though it's a rather drab, squat-looking building, it is one of the few structures on the waterfront that dates from the old days of the port's commercial peak.

As you walk or drive up from Vineyard Haven's harbor, you will ascend a hill that puts you in the center of town and also on the broad back of the terminal moraine that runs southwest to Gay Head and southeast to Edgartown. William Street is perhaps Vineyard Haven's finest town street for strolling, for the fire did not reach it and many of the old captains' houses still stand. At the corner of Church and William streets rises the square fieldstone tower of the town's Methodist Church, built in 1922.

The Tisbury Museum is on Beach Road, just off Main Street, in a Federal house dating from 1795. The small museum has exhibits relating to the history of the town.

Beach Road is the eastern way out of town and on to East Chop and then to Oak Bluffs. It follows the harbor contours past a big shipyard and crosses the narrow spit of land that separates the main part of the harbor from the more sheltered Lagoon Pond, where local fishermen harvest scallops and where cautious seamen move their boats when a big northeast blow is forecast. Beach Road will take you to Highland Drive, which ascends a bluff on whose high point the East Chop lighthouse (1877) sits. There are fine views north to Cape Cod from here. The views are equally good on West Chop, which you can reach by following Main Street out of town until it becomes West Chop Avenue. West Chop also has a lighthouse and some large, enviably situated summer homes, many in the picturesque shingle style that seems so redolent of long, slow, turn-of-the-century holidays.

Edgartown

Elegant Edgartown is a very different affair from Vineyard Haven. It is a white town of gleaming white houses, white picket fences, white steeples—all perfectly painted and kept up in flawless repair. For an old port town, Edgartown is remarkably *un*-weatherbeaten. It has an aura of wealth and good taste—if less wealth, then better taste than the town of Nantucket, where the early houses were severe and radically plain in the Quaker period and then grew grand and showy at the height of the whaling days. Edgartown's height was never so high as Nantucket's, the town was never so big, and the social scene was dominated by ship's captains, not the ambitious merchants who imported oriental luxuries into Nantucket. Also, Edgartown's Congregationalist origins put it more in the New England mainstream than Nantucket. If one relieves Edgartown of the summer homes that went up on its outskirts at the turn of the century and the crass commercial element that has been plastered on its center in the past 10 years, one can see that it was once a rather compact town and a very fine one, with a remarkable number of lovely Colonial, Federal and Greek Revival homes.

One of the best things about Edgartown today is that, aside from its waterfront, it still looks much as it did in the whaling era. Even with the intrusions of resort elements and tourist trade, Edgartown is wonderfully well-preserved. The waterfront, sadly, is a bit of a blight; the introduction of a municipal waste treatment plant a few years back allowed sizable restaurants catering to tourists to grow up along the harbor, replacing the collection of charming old shanties and hole-in-the-wall eateries. The waterfront is also the headquarters of the yacht club, a notoriously snobbish institution that for many years has stopped the social clock of Edgartown at conservative, Republican and old rich.

The Dukes County Historical Society at School and Cooke streets is worth a visit for its small display of whaling memorabilia, including scrimshaw, old maps and miniature portraits of 110 whaling captains and for the Thomas Cooke House built in 1765 and now a house museum. On the lawn outside the museum stands the 1854 Fresnel lens that once refracted the beacon in the Gay Head lighthouse. The streets around the Historical Society—School, Cooke, Davis Lane and South Summer—all contain beautiful old homes, old trees and the real feel of old Edgartown. If you follow Cooke Street all the way to the water you'll be on the site where Thomas Mayhew, the founder of Edgartown, had his homestead. The Mayhew house, built about 1670, after the original house burned, stood here until it was torn down in 1910. The small beach, called Collins Beach, is open to the public and affords good views of the harbor to the left and Tower Hill out to the right, where the town's first cemetery was laid. The early generations of the Mayhew family are buried on the left side of South Water Street as you head away from town.

Oak Bluffs

Oak Bluffs is at the opposite end of the Martha's Vineyard-style spectrum from Edgartown. Where Edgartown is reserved and elegant, Oak Bluffs is jovial and a bit tacky; where the characteristic Edgartown homes have the simple, clean lines and white color of the Federal and Greek Revival styles, Oak Bluff houses and cottages riot with the elaborately fanciful curls and scrolls and cut-outs of Victorian architecture and the varied palette of an Easter parade. Oak Bluffs takes the gingerbread style of decoration to the limit, the style seeming all the more playfully exaggerated because the houses for the most part are so tiny. Oak Bluffs is a gingerbread fantasia with its "wooden tents" ringing the grand wrought-iron Tabernacle of Trinity Park and lining up cheek by jowl on the side streets that radiate out from the inner circle. Though religion gave Oak Bluffs its start, the spirit of fun soon wafted it high in the air like an iridescent soap bubble. While the faithful preached and prayed in their campground behind a seven-foot wall (later removed), holiday-makers promenaded up and down the commercial boulevard of Circuit Avenue and listened to bands play from the gazebo in the vast semicircle of Ocean Park, which sprouted slightly more opulent cottages than the wooden tents of Trinity Park.

The mingling of the spirit of worldliness and religion gave the town a very odd atmosphere. Cornell's president Andrew D. White mentions in his autobiography seeing rollerskaters going round and round the floor of the town's mammoth old skating rink to the accompaniment of "Nearer my God to Thee." At Oak Bluffs piety and levity embraced in the golden air of Victorian summers. It was wonderful while it lasted, but it didn't last long: The town was overbuilt by get-rich-quick operators on a shaky financial foundation and the panic of 1873 dealt it a serious blow. During the 1890s many of the big hotels—the town had 20 in its heyday—burnt down, and by the First World War the big crowds had ceased to come. But many of the Methodists remained loyal even after the town's decline, and later in the 20th century, Oak Bluffs became one of the first seaside resorts to attract large numbers of black Americans.

Ocean Park at Oak Bluffs at the height of the Victorian resort boom. (Courtesy of the Dukes County Historical Society.)

When tourists rediscovered the Vineyard in the 1960s, Oak Bluffs rode a new crest of popularity, and it continues to be a favorite with day-trippers, overnight visitors and the thousands who own and rent the vast number of cottages in the former Cottage City. The highpoint of the Oak Bluffs summer season is Illumination Night, a tradition dating back to 1869 when revivalists first marked the end of the camp meeting by lighting lanterns. Today, on the designated night in August, cottagers all over the town still deck their houses, porches, picket fences and trees with ornamental lanterns, and the old meeting grounds shimmer like a celestial city.

Seeing the Sights: Up-Island

Up-island, away from the congested, closely-built towns of Vineyard Haven, Edgartown and Oak Bluffs, Martha's Vineyard becomes an island of farms and villages, stone walls and oak forests, ponds, moors, rolling hills and shoreline cliffs. Of course, there are vacation homes and new subdivisions along the quiet dirt roads, and in summertime lots of tourists biking and driving all over the place—but tourism and development do not dominate the up-island landscape as they do down-island. With few hotels, inns or restaurants, up-island retains the vestiges of the Vineyard's rural past.

West Tisbury, the largest up-island township, includes a good-sized chunk of the 4,000-acre State Forest, Tisbury Great Pond on its south coast and a lovely stretch of Vineyard Sound shoreline on its north coast. The West Tisbury Center has all the elements of a farming village: a mill pond (the 18th-century mill now houses the Martha's Vineyard Garden Club), a general store, a fine white Congregational church, a town hall and an agricultural hall with big grounds for the annual country fair in August. Never mind that Jacqueline Onassis turns up now and then in Alley's General Store ("dealers in almost everything"), that art galleries have cropped up in the village and that the few remaining farmers are sitting on top of a fortune in real estate. West Tisbury still *looks* rural if you don't look too closely. West Tisbury occupies 25.46 square miles and has a year-round population of 1,400.

Chilmark, the next township west, at 20.58 square miles is not much smaller in area than West Tisbury, but it has only 520 year-round residents. Development has been slower to arrive here because the steep hills and glacially-transported boulders make construction more costly and deep pre-glacial clay deposits make it difficult to locate water and drain off sewage reliably. To many minds, Chilmark's landscape is the most beautiful on the island. Its South Road offers the exquisite sight of sheep graz-

Menemsha from across Menemsha Creek. Though tourism is encroaching, Menemsha remains essentially a fishing village. The Coast Guard station here was towed over from Cuttyhunk some years back.

ing on old, rough hillside pastures that seem to fall off the end of the world into the dark blue ocean. Everywhere one looks there are stones piled into loosely built walls, walls that never fall down and never need repairs.

Chilmark has two small villages, Chilmark Center inland and Menemsha on the water. Chilmark Center is at the intersection known as Beetlebung Corner for the small grove of beetlebung trees growing here. (Elsewhere known as tupelo, this species of hardwood was used to make mallets—once called beetles—and bungs, plugs for bungholes in wooden casks.) There is a community center not far from the intersection, a town hall, a two-room schoolhouse, a Methodist church and a cluster of houses. Menemsha is Chilmark's fishing village on Vineyard Sound. It is a wonderfully picturesque place of old shacks and fishhouses, a long hill rising up from the water's edge, a white Coast Guard Station, rickety little docks, coils of rope, stacks of fishing gear and a harbor jammed with boats—both pleasure craft and the real-McCoy fishing boats that go out from Dutcher's Dock.

If you continue on the South Road west past Chilmark, you eventually end up at the Gay Head cliffs. On the way you pass through the small Gay Head village and wide expanses of high moors and oak and pitch pine woods.

Island Beaches and Nature Sanctuaries

You'd think that going to the beach on an island with 124.6 miles of shoreline on the Atlantic Ocean and the Vineyard and Nantucket Sounds would be as simple as rolling out of bed and jumping in your car. It's not. As more and more tourists descended on Martha's Vineyard in the sixties, seventies and eighties, island residents and summer people became more and more possessive of their beautiful, tawny sand beaches. Now a good deal of 16-mile-long South Beach on the Atlantic is off-limits except to town residents and property owners. Chilmark has its Lucy Vincent Beach and Squibnocket Beach for Chilmark folks only; Gay Head has its residents-only town beach on the ocean and restricted Lobsterville Beach on the Sound; West Tisbury has its residents-only piece of sound and ocean shoreline; and so on. For the non-resident, the choices are a bit more limited. The only south shore ocean beach that is open to all and easy to get to on main roads is the Katama Beach, three miles out of Edgartown. Not surprisingly, it is quite packed on hot summer weekends. There is also an easily accessible public beach that runs along two miles of Nantucket Sound shoreline between Oak Bluffs and Edgartown. This is the popular Joseph A. Sylvia State Beach on Beach Road.

Enterprising visitors can enjoy far-less-crowded beaches, on both the ocean and the sound side, if they are wiling to take the time and effort to get to them. These are beaches that lie within island nature preserves, including the 200-acre Wasque Point Reservation and 490-acre Cape Poge Wildlife Refuge on Chappaquiddick Island; the 580-acre Long Point Wildlife Refuge along the south shore, a prime gathering spot for waterfowl; and the 300-acre Cedar Tree Neck Sanctuary, which preserves a splendid chunk of the up-island moraine. For more information about visiting these and other nature preserves, see Ann Hale's *Moraine to Marsh: A Field Guide to Martha's Vineyard*. Preserved through the hard work of a variety of island conservation groups and the generosity of island residents, these areas are worth visiting not only for their beaches, but also for their wildlife, their forests and wetlands, their hiking trails and for the opportunity of experiencing the island's landscape in its pristine state.

Five Vineyard conservation groups have recently set up a shared headquarters at the Mary Wakeman Conservation Center in Tisbury. Together they buy and manage scores of parcels, large and small, scattered around the island.

Island Trends

Though these conservation groups have managed to preserve some choice sections of the island, they have not succeeded in preserving the Vineyard from many of the side-effects of increasing population and popularity. The county of Dukes County, which encompasses the Vineyard and the Elizabeth Islands, is, according to the National Association of Counties, the fastest growing county in the five New England states (all the growth is on the Vineyard, for the population of the Elizabeth Islands is declining). Statistics compiled by the Martha's Vineyard Commission show that from 1980 to 1986 the Vineyard's year-round population jumped 38.1% from 9,190 to 12,690, and the seasonal population soared 71.2% in that period, from 55,313 to 94,708. The MVC also reports that the number of building permits issued in Edgartown rose by 290% from 1977 to 1987, 500% in Gay Head, 137% in Oak Bluffs and 157% in West Tisbury. These figures look all the more ominous when you consider that in 1930 there were only 4,953 year-round residents on the island, and that even back in the good old days of 1970, the average summertime population was only 40,000. The MVC projects that by the year 2000, there will be 17,600 year-round residents on the island and 130,450 in the summer.

In a democracy with a free market economy, there is no equitable way of keeping people off the island or preventing them from buying and building homes if they have the means. In *Martha's Vineyard, An Elegy*, a very moving personal view of the changes on the island over the past 50 years, Everett S. Allen quotes an editorial that appeared in the *Gazette* back in 1970: "We have room for only so many. Who is to be welcomed and who is to be excluded? Some said in 1964—that was not the first year of consideration of the island's growth, but it was a year of omens—that the island should be for the right people. Who the right people are is difficult to define." It is indeed. Are the right people the celebrities and writers, including Jacqueline Onassis, William Styron, Beverly Sills, Carly Simon, Patricia Neal and Mike Wallace, who have made the island chic and glamorous? Are the right people the Wampanoag Indians who are attempting to hold on to the land that had been the home of their ancestors not for centuries but for millennia? Are the right people the descendants of the early white settlers—the people who carry on the family names of Mayhew, Norton, Vincent, Pease, Allen, Arey, Ripley, Athearn, Merry, Tilton, Skiff? Or are they the people with the new names and new money earned in big cities, the people who can afford to buy land and build houses here today?

No one really has the right or the power to answer these questions. And even if someone did, it is unlikely that the answer would be just. Through land preservation, zoning and planning, Vineyarders are doing what they can to retain the island's character—if not its spiritual character then at lest its visual character. Critics argue that these tools are not doing enough; but, though one may sympathize with them, it's hard to see what else can be done. Islanders and island lovers can't stop others from loving the island too. Martha is acquiring too many lovers for her own good.

CUTTYHUNK

Area: 2.5 miles long; .75 mile wide.
Population: 20-40 year-round; about 400 in summer season.
Location: 14 miles off New Bedford, Massachusetts, in Buzzards Bay.
Access: The *Alert II* (foot passengers only) from New Bedford (call Cuttyhunk Boat Lines, 617-992-1432).

Family of geese on Cuttyhunk Harbor.

Cuttyhunk is a holdout. A small, hilly outpost 14 miles from New Bedford at the western reaches of Buzzards Bay and Vineyard Sound, Cuttyhunk clings to its oddness, its remoteness from mainland ways, its peculiar charm and extraordinary, unspoiled beauty. Cuttyhunk has history—mostly a history of events that did not quite manage to transpire here. It has amenities—power (from four generators), phones (seven altogether), an inn with a restaurant, a bakery—but not so many that you take them for granted. It has its institutions—a church, a school (two students currently attend), a town government (Town of Gosnold, governed by three selectmen), a five-person police force—but in miniature. It has its tiny year-round population (as few as 20 people after Christmas), its summer colony of "nice" families who love the island and have been summering here for years, and the fishermen who come for the bass and blues. But mostly it has its character: its scattering of unpretentious shingled and clapboard houses perched high above the harbor, its miles of grassy paths through thickets of bayberry, *rosa rugosa* and wild cherry, its bluffs dropping precipitously down to rocky shore, its magnificent vistas out to Gay Head on the Vineyard, out to Buzzards Bay and beyond to the open Atlantic.

Cuttyhunk harks back to another era, a slower, quieter time before highways, motels and ticky-tack gobbled up the seashore. (There are cars on the island, but not many, and the islanders prefer to get around in golfcarts—used exclusively for transport, since there is no golf course.) It is the kind of place where even in high season dogs snooze undisturbed in the middle of Main Street, where deer come into town at dawn to nibble people's fruit trees, where young children can be turned loose to explore. It has that real island feel—unpolluted, largely undeveloped, distant enough from the mainland to seem a place apart—and that is just the way most Cuttyhunkers like it.

Cuttyhunk's diminutive size accounts for many of its charming peculiarities. Two-and-a-half miles long and three-quarters of a mile wide, Cuttyhunk has roughly the shape of a "mermaid's purse" (those strange black pouches, the casing of the skate's eggs, that you often see washed up on Atlantic beaches): a plump, boxy middle

Narragansett Bay and the Elizabeth Islands

NARRAGANSETT BAY

RHODE ISLAND SOUND

BUZZARDS BAY

VINEYARD SOUND

Bristol

Prudence
Island

Conanicut
Island

Newport

New Bedford

Woods Hole

Nonamesset
Island

Martha's
Vineyard

Naushon Island

The Elizabeth Islands

Pasque Island

Nashawena Island

Cuttyhunk Island

N

miles

0

5

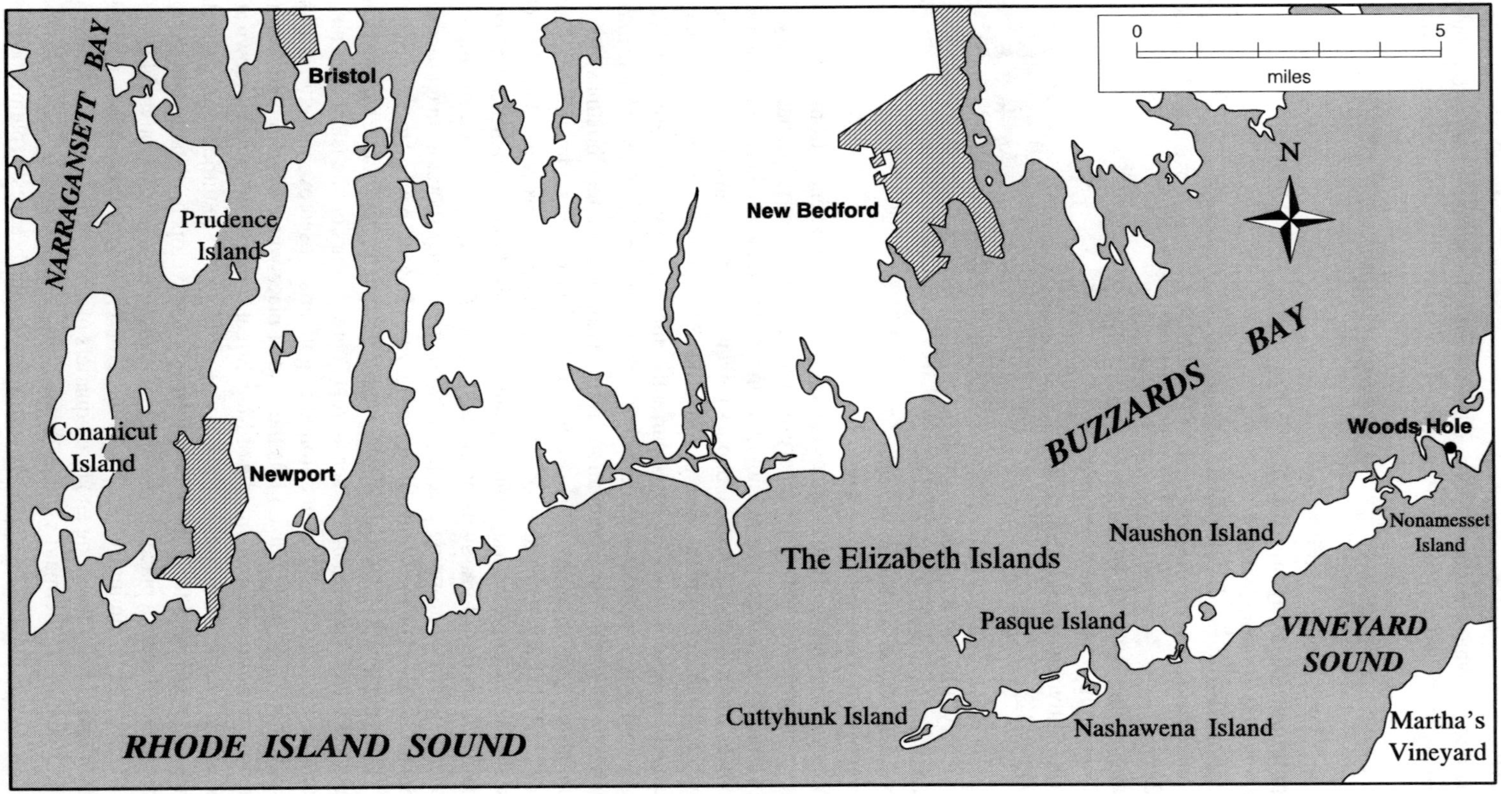

with four tendrils curling from the ends. Its highest point, the Lookout above the town, is 154 feet above sea level. You can walk all over the island in a few hours, and walking is very definitely the way to explore. Cuttyhunk's ferry, the *Alert II*, does not take cars and since the island has only about a mile of paved road, there is little point in bringing a bike. Luckily, Cuttyhunk is blissful to walk: Though the island is almost entirely held in private hands, most of its paths are open to the public. Well-worn tracks will take you out to the lighthouse and Gosnold monument (see below) at the western end of the island, to the sandy reach of Barges Beach (the southeast tendril) and most of the way around Cuttyhunk Pond, the island's working and playing harbor. Small as it is, however, Cuttyhunk is still large enough to get lost on. There are few signs or landmarks away from town, and a half mile of bayberry tangle can seem like a vast wilderness if you don't know where you're going and have a ferry to catch.

Cuttyhunk is isolated, but it's not alone. It is one of the 16 Elizabeth Islands, a glacially formed archipelago that trails off southwest of Woods Hole roughly parallel to the northwest side of Martha's Vineyard. The chain, with a total of 8,268 acres, separates Buzzards Bay to the north from Vineyard Sound to the south. Cuttyhunk, the westernmost Elizabeth Island and thus the last link in the chain, is the only one with a town and year-round community.

Bartholomew Gosnold and the English Discovery of Cuttyhunk

Though all of the individual islands have "uncouth Indian names," the chain itself bears a name of a distinctly English cast. The bestower of this name was Captain Bartholomew Gosnold, the Elizabethan explorer who discovered Cuttyhunk as well as Cape Cod, Martha's Vineyard and Nantucket. Gosnold set out from Falmouth, England, in March of 1602 with a company of 32 men aboard the bark *Concord*. Their intention was to land at Virginia and establish a colony there (in fact, four years later Gosnold assisted with the colony at Jamestown), but winds took them farther up the East Coast. Gosnold, who hailed from an established Suffolk gentry family, had the support of the Earl of Southampton, Shakespeare's patron, and it's possible that Gosnold and Shakespeare were acquainted. There is a tradition that Cuttyhunk was actually the island the Bard had in mind as the scene of *The Tempest*. Edward Everett Hale, 19th-century American clergyman and scholar, first made the case for this view in his essay "Prospero's Island ": He draws convincing parallels between the Cuttyhunk depicted in the narratives of Gosnold's voyages (see below) and the island Shakespeare conjures up in his play, and concludes that "there is no doubt that the local coloring of *The Tempest* is in part derived from the narrative of Gosnold's adventures." In any case, Cuttyhunk seems at least as likely a setting for the play as Bermuda, the island frequently cited by modern scholars.

The *Concord*'s mariners first sighted the New World near Kennebunkport, Maine; they made land at Cape Cod, which Gosnold so named, and then sailed around the Cape and south of Martha's Vineyard (which Gosnold named, possibly for his daughter), passing close to the cliffs at Gay Head (Gosnold called them Dover Cliff). Toward the end of May 1602, Gosnold and his company landed at Cuttyhunk, and chose this as the place they would settle. Gosnold named the place Elizabeth's Isle, possibly for his queen but probably for his sister. We have detailed accounts of Gosnold's voyage and brief stay on Cuttyhunk in the reports written by John Brereton

Gosnold at Cuttyhunk *(1858)*, an oil painting by Albert Bierstadt. Bierstadt is faithful both to history and the actual landscape, for Bartholomew Gosnold did indeed plant his settlement, the first on the New England coast, on the island at the center of the pond—an island within an island—and his depiction of the Cuttyhunk terrain is quite accurate. Bierstadt, who grew up in New Bedford, could easily have made the trip across Buzzards Bay to Cuttyhunk. (Courtesy of the Whaling Museum, New Bedford, Massachusetts)

and Gabriel Archer, both among the *Concord*'s company. Brereton describes the island as a kind of maritime Eden "in comparison whereof the most fertile part of all England is but barren...Coming ashore, we stood a while like men ravished at the beauty and delicacy of this sweet soil...This island is full of high timbered oaks, their leaves thrice so broad as ours; cedars straight and tall, beech, elm, holly, walnut trees in abundance, hazel-nut trees, cherry trees, sassafras trees..." The plentiful water fowl are "much bigger than ours in England," the nuts "as big as hen's eggs...[and] as good as potatoes."

On the first of June, Gosnold directed his men to erect a fort at the island's west end; the site was the tiny island that sits in the middle of the body of water known today as Gosnold's Pond.

The end of his colonizing venture came swiftly. The men lost heart when Gosnold left to explore nearby islands, and they insisted on sailing back to England when he returned. Though the colony failed, Gosnold returned with a good load of Cuttyhunk sassafras, much prized then as a cure for syphilis.

Cuttyhunk changed hands several times in the mid-17th century, but it did not harbor a permanent English settlement until 1688. Even the Indians, as far as can be determined from existing records, did not live on Cuttyhunk but rather used it as a summer hunting and fishing ground. The early English settlers were more interested in the island's timber, and they soon stripped it of the hardwood forests that Gosnold's men describe. Those familiar with the island in the latter half of the 19th century report that it was a treeless place, its open hilly fields grazed and trampled by flocks of sheep.

Now that the sheep have been gone for several generations, trees grow again on Cuttyhunk, but the groves of wild cherry, pitch pine, scrub oak, sassafras and bayberry thickets have more the look of overgrown moors than forests. If we could visit the Forbes preserve on Naushon, we could see what Cuttyhunk looked like to Gosnold and his men, for this Elizabeth Island, the last remaining climax oak-beech forest in New England, still has virgin stands of oak, maple, birch, hickory, beech, cedar and pitch and white pines. But Naushon, like all the Elizabeth Islands aside from Cuttyhunk, is off-limits to the general public.

The Sporting Era: The Cuttyhunk Fishing Club

Not a great deal of historical note took place on Cuttyhunk during the 18th century and most of the 19th. In 1693, Peleg Slocum acquired Cuttyhunk as well as Penikese and Nashawena, and in 1858 his descendant Otis Slocum sold the island to three whaling men from New Bedford for $50. In 1864 the Town of Gosnold was incorporated, largely through the influence of John M. Forbes, known as "Master of Naushon." At the early town meetings, held on Naushon, it was decided to raise money for a school, which was duly built on Cuttyhunk in 1874. Population showed no very startling growth (and never has): It is estimated that around 90 people lived on all of the Elizabeth Islands in 1761. The census of 1790 records 103 Elizabeth Islanders (13 on Cuttyhunk) and today Cuttyhunk claims about 40 year-round souls. ("But don't you believe it," one old lady on the island told me. "Most of the younger folk go off-island from Christmas until April.") If Gosnold and his crew of 32 had remained on the island, Cuttyhunk would have started off with nearly as many people as it has today. The Town of Gosnold now numbers 100 voters.

The dedication of the Gosnold monument on September 1, 1903. The monument was begun the previous year to celebrate the tercentenary of Gosnold's landing and brief settlement on the spot. Compare the landscape in this photograph to the oil painting by Albert Bierstadt on p. 110. (Courtesy of the Whaling Museum, New Bedford, Massachusetts)

The year 1864 marks not only Cuttyhunk's incorporation as a town but also the start of the island's sporting era. In this year Cuttyhunk caught the attention of a group of 50 wealthy New York businessmen looking for a new retreat for their fishing vacations. They quickly bought up the better part of the island and established the Cuttyhunk Fishing Club. These men, mostly prominent and well-connected bankers and industrialists, were in pursuit of striped bass, and Cuttyhunk was their idea of paradise because they could catch quantities of magnificent stripers right off the island's rocky shores. The mode of fishing these affluent anglers employed may sound odd, but it seemed to work, at least while the supplies of bass held. They fished from "stands"—a couple of wooden planks supported on iron rods on which the sportsmen could walk out to fish beyond the boulders of the shore. Attending the New York fishermen were Cuttyhunk boys known as chummers (or chums) whose job it was to attract the bass, which they did by tossing bits of lobster tail off a "chum-spoon" so as to "chum up the fish." The bass would swim in toward the stand, the fisherman, perched at the stand's precarious end, would catch the fish, and the chummer would receive a dollar for each bass snagged (more for bigger fish). At its peak, the Cuttyhunk Club commanded 26 stands around the island and numbered 75 members, all of whom were millionaires "at least once or twice over" according to the booklet entitled *Cuttyhunk: Bartholomew Gosnold's Contribution to Our Country and the Plymouth Colony* by Asa Cobb Paine Lombard Jr. The record bass weighed in at 73 pounds.

Cuttyhunk Under William Wood

The glory days of the Cuttyhunk Club, though brief, were exceedingly glorious. According to Asa Lombard's booklet, "It was not unusual to see five or six of New York's and Newport's largest yachts—Morgan's, Rockefeller's, Mellon's, Carnegie's and others—anchored in Cuttyhunk Harbor at a single time." But by the early years of the 20th century, the bass around Cuttyhunk were much diminished and the millionaires were losing interest. In 1921 the Cuttyhunk Club members sold out to William W. Wood, president of the American Woolen Company.

Wood's purchase of the Cuttyhunk Club was actually a stage in his personal quest for total control over Cuttyhunk. Earlier in the century, the Cuttyhunk Club had blackballed Wood: Though he was a millionaire, the wool magnate was evidently not the right kind of millionaire, and the club members wanted no part of him. Wood, a tenacious and acquisitive man, had retaliated by building his own Avalon Club, a rambling shingled affair, a stone's throw from the Cuttyhunk Club house. Later he also had a large stone summer house built for himself at the top of the hill in town. Wood lived by a kind of latter-day Gilded Age ethos of buying up everything the heart desired with cold cash, be it galleries of Old Master paintings or sections of Gothic churches. Wood didn't want art or architecture, but he did want Cuttyhunk; and when the Cuttyhunk Club members, tired of the island, the fishing and Wood's pressure on them, signed over their holdings, he got most of it. He had to be satisfied with most but not all. The few fishermen and pilots (a number of Cuttyhunk salts had been piloting boats into New Bedford harbor for money as far back as the whaling days) on the island wanted to retain their land, and they did. But for all intents and purposes, Cuttyhunk was Wood's island, and even today most of it remains in the hands of his heirs and connections.

William Wood loved Cuttyhunk and he did what he could to preserve its beauty while improving its amenities. It is to Wood that Cuttyhunk owes its telephones, sewage system, town water, the stone walls that run down the hill through town, its power supply, paths and roads, harbor improvements and its regular ferry service. The *Alert*, the picturesque if rather unlikely looking oaken-hulled craft that served as Cuttyhunk's ferry from New Bedford for generations, was actually built in 1916 to bring supplies over for Wood and his various houses. The *Alert* served Cuttyhunk long and well and, except for a hiatus during World War II, during which Cuttyhunkers had to rely on two smaller boats they dubbed the *Less Alert* and *Least Alert*, it remained in service until 1987. In that year the *Alert II*, a nine-year-old oil rig personnel boat that seats 36 passengers, took over. Cuttyhunkers and long-time summer visitors mourn the changeover, insisting that the new boat lacks the character of the grizzled old *Alert*, which remains moored at Pier 3 in New Bedford.

The Island Today

The changes on Cuttyhunk from William Wood's day to our own are noticeable, but not startling. There are more houses, but not that many more. In the summer the harbor fills up with boats, most of them piloted not by the staffs of tycoons but by middle-class people out for a good time. Fishing remains a source of income for islanders and a popular sport for visitors. Cuttyhunkers go out for bass and lobster and four or five islanders dig clams commercially. (The island's clams are much prized because they are miles from any source of pollution, and are quite pure.) Half a dozen island men use their boats for charter fishing expeditions; charters, usually booked well in advance, can be arranged through the Allen House.

Cuttyhunk has what might be called a protected island economy. According to Ginger Cooper, a young Cuttyhunker who owns the island's general store and is one of the island's five constables and three selectman, the workforce consists of six or seven "able bodies" who do everything from carpentry and plumbing to maintenance and machine repair. "There are a lot of wealthy people here," says Cooper, "who don't do anything but watch their stocks." Land rarely goes out of the hands of the families who bought it from Wood and his heirs and who have been coming here for years. There is no such thing as real estate listings on Cuttyhunk, and even summer rentals are scarce and usually accounted for a year ahead of time. There is a small circle of Cuttyhunk families—a few year-round residents, a few more most-of-the-year residents and many more who come for the summer—who own the island and want to keep it just the way it is. They don't want development; they don't want commercialization; they don't want to lift the current prohibition of the sale of alcohol. They want Cuttyhunk to remain a holdout.

The church in the little village of Cuttyhunk.

Visiting Cuttyhunk

Cuttyhunk welcomes the visitor of a day, a week or a summer to join in its pleasing slumber. As long as one does not expect too much in the way of activity, one will not come away disappointed. Though there is no country club, no nightlife, no movie theater, no art gallery or shopping mall, Cuttyhunk has one of just about everything a tourist absolutely needs. The Allen House offers plain, informal accommodations in rooms and cottages and fine

The Alert II, *Cuttyhunk's lifeline to the mainland.*

meals in a very nice dining room. There is Ginger Cooper's general store for picnic supplies (remember, Cuttyhunk is a dry island so one must bring one's own liquor, beer and wine). The Vineyard View Bakery, a short stroll west, serves light meals indoors or at outside picnic tables. One can pick up souvenir T-shirts, crafts or antiques at the two tiny island shops, Dot's Gifts or Cuttyhunk Crafts. Fishing charters are available at the fish dock near the Gosnold marina or can be arranged through the Allen House. The season for all these facilities is May to October: Outside of that you're on your own. Cuttyhunk also has a church, technically Methodist but all denominations hold their services here in the summer; a small library; and the island's historical society mounts occasional exhibitions at the schoolhouse.

The real draw of Cuttyhunk is island life and island nature. On Cuttyhunk, a few minutes' stroll from the ferry landing or from town will take one out into the island's beaches, fields and low woodlands. Cuttyhunk does not have a wilderness, but it does have plenty of wildlife and wild spaces. Deer abound on the island. If you wake up early enough, you can spot them browsing in the village. But if you're quiet and you walk long enough, you'll see them almost anytime. I glimpsed a few on the northeast lump of the island that maps identify as Copicut Neck but that Cuttyhunkers call simply the Neck, a rugged bluff with a few modern houses tucked away off dirt roads.

A house in Cuttyhunk's village. The village is so quiet that deer frequently come to feed on the lawns and trees. The island's population falls as low as 20 in the winter.

Cuttyhunk is notorious for wrecking ships, particularly on the treacherous Sow and Pigs Reef off the island's western tip.

CUTTYHUNK

Cuttyhunkers have done, and continue to do, their part in rescuing mariners in distress. For many years starting in 1889 the U.S. government ran a lifesaving station at the island's southeast peninsula, and later the Coast Guard established a station here. (The Coast Guard Station was towed to Menemsha on Martha's Vineyard some years ago, and today the house and boathouse are used primarily for R&R by Coast Guard officers.) Whenever a ship is in trouble off the island's waters, Cuttyhunkers turn out to a man to offer whatever help they can. But the islanders are not above appropriating any useful items that wash up on their shores after shipwrecks, and it is perhaps this habit that gave rise to the old legend that Cuttyhunkers are pirates.

During its May through October tourist season, Cuttyhunk offers an idyllic retreat for the visitor. But one wonders here, as on all remote offshore islands, what life is like for those who remain when the tourists leave. From Columbus Day to Memorial Day, the ferry comes only twice a week, which means only two mail deliveries per week and two opportunities to come or go. The handful of families who make their homes here are intimately ac-quainted and have been for generations. "You sneeze twice and everyone on the island figures you have a cold," one resi-dent said only partly in jest. The two children, ages nine and 13, who are now taught in the Cut-tyhunk one-room schoolhouse, will attend high school on the mainland after they complete the eighth grade. They will board with New Bedford families (the Town of Gosnold will pay their room and board) and return to their island for vacations.

The Coast Guard boathouse on Cuttyhunk. Part of the Cuttyhunk Coast Guard station was towed to Menemsha on Martha's Vineyard some years ago.

Those who make Cuttyhunk their home are a proud and independent lot, proud of their little island and fierce in their loyalty to each other in times of need—proudest and fiercest of all about the individual spirit that gets each of them through the long winters. "You have to know yourself and like yourself to live here year-round," one year-rounder told me. Lots of people who have fallen in love with Cuttyhunk in the summer decide they want to stay on through the winter. The Cuttyhunkers take bets on how long they'll remain. Few make it past Thanksgiving.

The Cuttyhunkers themselves, one feels, remain here not so much out of necessity but of love. Certainly, there's more opportunity of every sort on the mainland. But Cuttyhunk seems a world and a century away from that life, and those who know and love the island want to keep it that way. And perhaps they'll succeed. Its size is definitely an advantage in keeping the island undeveloped. Cuttyhunk is too small to harbor the kind of building and tourist frenzy that is descending on Martha's Vineyard and Nantucket. (Though if development does come, it could gobble up the island overnight.)

Cuttyhunk has been known to us ever since Bartholomew Gosnold landed here in 1602; yet in the intervening centuries, few have come and fewer still have stayed. Small, rugged, lonely, old-fashioned, the island has always been isolated. Aside from its brief moment in the sun during the sporting era, Cuttyhunk never really caught on. And this seems to suit Cuttyhunk—its year-round residents and summer people, its deer and rabbits, its gulls, ducks, plovers and eiders, its quiet paths, oceanside bluffs and rocky shores—just fine.

PRUDENCE

Area: 3,627 acres; 7 miles long and about 1 mile wide.

Population: 80 year-round; over 2,000 in summer season.

Location: 4 miles off Bristol, Rhode Island in Narragansett Bay.

Access: From Bristol, Rhode Island, on the *Prudence Ferry* (10 cars, 149 passengers); trip lasts 20 minutes. Phone 401-253-9808.

The Garland mansion on Potter Cove. Its owner, James Garland, died before the 36-room house was completed early in the century.

Prudence is a bay island, Narragansett Bay to be precise, and it has the quiet, sheltered atmosphere peculiar to bay places. The larger bridged islands of Conanicut and Aquidneck (better known by the names of their major towns, Jamestown and Newport, respectively) guard the mouth of the bay and protect Prudence from the open waters of Rhode Island Sound. The island is neither remote nor rugged. Its hills, for the most part, are gentle; the channels of water that set it off are limited in extent. From its east shore, the bustling town of Portsmouth (the northern half of Aquidneck) seems only a stone's throw away; from Providence Point at the north end of Prudence, one can see the office towers of Providence rise up at the head of the bay. The high arches of two bay bridges—Mount Hope, the link between Portsmouth and Bristol, and the Newport Bridge, the link between Jamestown and Newport—are clearly visible from many points along the eastern and southern shores.

All of these vistas to the mainland, to the larger bridged islands and to the bridges themselves give Prudence the sense of affording a quiet vantage point on a familiar world. The very nearness of Prudence to that surrounding world of traffic and tall buildings enforces the sensation of being sheltered. That world is close enough to see and sometimes hear—but as long as Narragansett Bay intervenes, it won't touch Prudence too much. Prudence is just separate, just protected enough.

Narragansett Bay, which cuts 25 miles up into Rhode Island, protects Prudence, and Prudence has also acted to protect itself. Over one-third of the island's acreage at the north and south ends has been set aside as public parkland. The island's Heritage Foundation is a private group that owns and protects another 500 acres in the center of Prudence (walkers are welcome on their trails); and another 400-acre parcel is in the hands of a single family that intends to keep it together. (Prudence Island Vineyards grows grapes on part of this land—see below.) Though there is talk of development on Prudence, as on so many of the Eastern islands, development seems unlikely to go too far. Prudence really is well protected.

Prudence has a nickname—the Whale in the Bay—and it is perfectly apt, for the island really does have the shape of an immense cetacean swimming nearly due south for Rhode Island Sound. The whale's head is the South Prudence State Park, part of the 23,000-acre Bay Islands Park system that includes parts (or all) of nearly every island in Narragansett Bay. Its tail, which flips to the north, is the island's other public park, the Narragansett Bay National Estuarine Sanctuary, 2,500 acres of federally protected land that also encompasses the smaller Hope and Patience Islands and the surrounding waters to a depth of 18 feet. The whale even has flippers: one, a jut on the island's east shore on which rests the compact Sandy Point Lighthouse, built on Goat Island in Newport Harbor and towed here in 1852; and the other, a jut on the west shore at the termination of Broadway, the incongruously named paved road that traverses the breadth of Prudence, all one mile of it. The island's resemblance to a whale is apparent only on a map or from the air: Viewed from the water or across the bay from the mainland, the Whale in the Bay has a low, green, lightly wooded aspect. Unlike some of the bare, rocky Maine islands that really do look like whales skimming along the ocean surface, Prudence is unmistakably a wedge of land, a gentle wooded crest rising gradually, undramatically out of the bay.

The Settlements: East and West

Prudence seems even less whale-like once one has landed on the island and begun to explore. To get the lay of the land it's best to forget about the whale analogy and apply instead the distinction that New Yorkers make so adamantly on their own Manhattan Island: There's an east side and a west side, and the differences between them are more marked than the distances. If you come from Bristol by ferry, you'll be deposited on the island's east side at the little settlement called Homestead. (At the moment this is your only option aside from private boat; over the years various ferries from Portsmouth, Melville and Bristol, Rhode Island, have landed at North Prudence, Homestead, Sandy Point and South Prudence, but only the Bristol-Homestead link is currently in operation.) The crossing from Bristol is four miles and it's over in less than half an hour.

The first thing one notices about Homestead are houses—lots and lots of tidy little beach cottages with names like Dunworkin', Snug Harbor and La Gioconda, stretching north and south in an unbroken row along the shore. Prudence has some 375 houses, most built in the past 50 years and most of them lining the island's east shore from Northeast Point near Nag Pond to Broadway and the edge of South Prudence Park. The Homestead shoreline is summer vacationland and for the most part indistinguishable from colonies of beach cottages anywhere on the East Coast.

To get to the island's west side, you go south on Narragansett Avenue (for a small island with so few streets, Prudence does a remarkable job of identifying them with rather imposing names) past Sandy Point Lighthouse and the now defunct inn (see below), turn right on Broadway and proceed across the island to the water. Here is the settlement known as Prudence Park: Its houses are fewer, older, larger and endowed with more character than those on the east side; some of the larger and older ones were boarding houses during Prudence's brief resort period in the late 19th century. There are porches and lawns and turrets and views. A couple of streets thread among the houses and a gravel road leads north along the shore past a few more houses. To cross from the east to the west side of Prudence is to jump from mid-20th-century beach sprawl to late-Victorian bayside retreat.

The island's east shore and the area around Prudence Park on the west shore feel rather built up, but development is only skin-deep on Prudence Island. Aside from the cottages, the former rooming houses and the scattering of year-round residences, there isn't much. Once you add in the winery, the two food stores in Homestead, the church (built in 1926), the library and the gift shop, you pretty much have the sum total of civilization on the island. On Broadway is the Prudence Park School, a charming little schoolhouse complete with bell tower, that dates from 1896 and once claimed to be America's smallest school; but it closed a few years back and the island's two remaining students are now being privately tutored. There used to be an inn, but it too closed a while ago, and with it closed the island's only restaurant. Perhaps it should be said that one does not come to Prudence for its civilization but for its nature, and this it has in plentiful supply in its two very special parks.

The Island Parks: South and North

Prudence Island's north and south ends have been parks only since 1980, and they still bear traces of their previous uses. If you have only a day on Prudence it makes sense to visit the south park first, for it's closer to the ferry landing and it has more facilities for the visitor, including an information booth staffed by naturalists who will answer your questions and provide you with maps and self-guided trail booklets for both parks.

The south park, officially called the Bay Islands Park at South Prudence, was part of the network of U.S. Navy installations on Narragansett Bay. During World War II the Navy stored ammunition here in bunkers built into the hills and covered with grass. You can still see a number of them from the nature trail: Now empty, they look like giant concrete walk-in closets. The large T-wharf at South Point, where the park's headquarters and information center stand, was put in by the Navy and used as a depot, and the paved roads and quonset huts around the park are all of Navy vintage. South Prudence, though heavily fortified, got off easy compared to tiny Gould Island directly to the south: During the War the Navy used this bit of land to test torpedoes.

The Navy presence at South Prudence can be distracting or fascinating, depending on your interests. If you want to ignore it, you can wander along the shore and admire the views out to Hope Island (a state-owned bird rookery and important nesting site for snowy egrets, night herons and various sorts of terns and gulls—closed to the public from April to August), the north end of Conanicut Island, and Coddington Point at the northwest of Newport.

The park supports a wide variety of plant life, and the best way to get acquainted with it is to take the park's well-marked self-guiding nature loop. Prudence, like Cuttyhunk Island, had fine, dense forests before the white settlers came and cut them down. On Prudence early settlers cleared the land so that they could graze sheep on the island; and what the settlers didn't cut, the British burned during the Revolutionary War. Grandparents of contemporary Prudence Islanders can remember when Prudence was still largely a place of open fields and low brush. But today, as one can see on the South Prudence nature loop, the forests are coming back with black oak, pitch pine, tupelo, black cherry, tamarack, red cedar, along with bushes and vines, including bittersweet, wild grape, high-bush blueberry, sweet pepper, greenbriar, bayberry and wild flowers such as Queen Anne's lace, milkweed, rabbit-foot clover, St. Johnswort.

As for fauna, the most plentiful and visible wildlife on Prudence Island are deer. Prudence supposedly has more deer per square mile than any

A quiet corner of South Prudence Park.

other place in New England. The current count is 300 at fawning time in the spring. There are so many deer on the island that it's difficult to be on Prudence for any length of time *without* running into several (I saw six during a single afternoon). Graceful and fleet-footed as they are, deer do bring problems with them. They eat the gardens of islanders, even hopping over fairly high fences, and the tick species *Ixodes dammini*, also quite abundant on Prudence, can spread the very serious Lyme disease from deer to humans. (Ticks carry the deadly Rocky Mountain Spotted Fever as well.) If you're on Prudence during warm weather, check yourself carefully for ticks at the end of the day and try to stay out of the tall grasses where ticks live. In addition to deer and ticks, Prudence also supports healthy populations of pheasant, rabbits, red foxes, raccoons, mink, voles and shrews.

The park at South Prudence can accommodate overnight visitors at 15 individual camp sites (maximum of six people) and one group camping area (with room for 50). There are also seven very nice picnic spots along the shore, and drinking water is available. Dutch Island, a smaller island in the Bay Islands Park system off the west shore of Conanicut and accessible only by private boat, has 12 individual camp sites. For camping information and reservations, call Colt State Park in Bristol (401-253-7482).

The hand of man rests even more lightly on the park at Prudence's north end. Officially called Narragansett Bay National Estuarine Sanctuary, this park takes up the whole of the whale's tail and a bit of its narrow dorsal section. It was established in 1980 in cooperation with the National Oceanic and Atmospheric Administration as part of the National Estuarine Sanctuary Program. (Other East Coast sanctuaries that are part of the same program include Sapelo Island, Georgia, *q.v.*, four sites in coastal North Carolina and two in Chesapeake Bay.) The North Prudence park is a bit farther from the ferry landing at Homestead than South Prudence. To get there follow the road up either the east or the west side of the island; the two roads join right before the whale's body narrows down to its tail, and a single road takes you up past scenic Potter Cover (a good place to dig quahogs) and into the sanctuary. The road is barred at the entrance to the sanctuary so no cars can get in (one wouldn't want to drive along the grass and sand track anyway), but it is possible to ease a bicycle under the bar and ride it all the way to Providence Point at the northern tip. In fact, biking is an ideal way to get around the island in clement weather. The summer ferry schedule gives you all day on the island, and you can bicycle around its entire circumference on paved and gravel roads without much exertion. (Bikes are also a good deal cheaper to bring across on the boat than cars.) The distance from Potter Cove to Providence Point can be covered in about two and a half hours on foot, or about 45 minutes on a bike.

If you are planning to visit the north park, try to get a copy of the "Hikers Guide to the North End of Prudence Island," available at the information building on the T-wharf at the south end. This little booklet is the key to the self-guiding trail that wanders through the north park's light woods, grassy field and marshes.

Near the entrance to the park on a rise facing Potter Cove stands an imposing and rather forbidding stone mansion. This was the summer home built in the first decade of this century by millionaire James Garland. The land and house have an interesting history. In the mid-17th century Richard Parker gave the 600 acres of land around Potter Cove as a gift to his daughter Sarah when she married John Paine. The British burned the original Paine farmhouse during the Revolutionary War, but another farmhouse was built and generations of farmers at Cove Farm, as it was called, raised corn, rye, oats, barley and hay as well as cows, sheep, pigs and horses. Garland, a visitor to Prudence, fell in love with the farm and the views it commanded of Potter Cove, and in 1904 he bought the place. But Garland wanted a mansion, not a farmhouse, to summer in, and he brought over a team of workmen to build his 36-room home, housing them in the old farmhouse during construction. Garland never got to live in his summer retreat: he died before the place was completed.

The Narragansett Bay National Estuarine Sanctuary is a silent enclave on a quiet island. On the bright June afternoon I biked along its paths I had the park to myself: I didn't come across another person. I heard only the trill of redwing blackbirds and the slipping of tall grass through my bicycle spokes. With its overgrown fields and old stone walls, the sanctuary has the hushed, haunted aura of abandoned places. The tenant farmers—and the Narragansett Indians who used the land before them—have long departed, but their presences seem to linger along the fringes of their fast-disappearing clearings. It's strange to think that in the old days, centuries before beach condos and weekend speed boats, north Prudence was an active, human community, where families lived and worked the land and children walked down the roads to school. Today, in the crowded late 20th century, when so many of the natural places on the East Coast are being turned into real estate, north Prudence is quietly returning to nature.

Prudence Through the Centuries

The history of Prudence is, like the landscape of the island, for the most part gentle and undramatic. With the exception of a brief episode of violence at the founding of the Republic, it is an even-keeled history of land settled and farmed, of families coming and staying for generations, of relative isolation and gradual change arriving a few steps behind the changing times. The place to go to get the history of Prudence firsthand is the winery, Prudence Island Vineyards, located in the center of the island up the hill a bit from the last houses of Homestead. This is for Prudence an historic place and its owners, William and Natalie Bacon, are themselves part of the history of the island. The family of Mrs. Bacon, nee Chase, has been on this island for seven generations and her people have been farming this land since the rambling old farmhouse (impressively situated and picturesque, but in need of repair) was built in 1783.

Before the coming of the white settlers, Prudence, as mentioned above, was part of the territory of the Narragansett Indians. The Indians did not live year-round on the island, but used it through the warm weather months for hunting, fishing, digging quahogs and perhaps farming. They called the island Chibachuwese, meaning something like "separation of the passage." These were a friendly, trusting people, and they did not long survive their brush with the representatives of European civilization.

Actually, their initial contact with the Europeans was deceptively positive, for it was the tolerant and enlightened Roger Williams, the Father of Rhode Island, who was the first white to come to the island. Williams had been banished some years earlier from the Massachusetts Bay Colony for his criticism of its theocracy and for his advocacy of the Indians' rights to their land. He settled at Providence and it was from there in 1636 that he paddled a canoe down to Chibachuwese and, with Governor John Winthrop of the Bay Colony as his equal partner, bought the island from the Indians for 20 fathoms of wampum and two coats. As the Indians understood the transaction, they were selling not the land itself, but the rights to share in its natural resources. Williams acknowledged and respected the Indians' right to continue using the land; in fact, Williams, more than any other Colonial leader, attempted to take the Indians on their own terms and treat them fairly. He learned their language and customs and, though he tried to convert them to Christianity, his intent was not, as one historian puts it, "to make over the Indians into a poor type of English." Williams preached to the Indians of Prudence (the name he chose for the island) in the open air at Pulpit Rock, which happens to stand on the land of William and Natalie Bacon. He made many converts and lived at peace with the Narragansett people. Unfortunately, most of the English settlers who came after him did not follow his example. They soon had stripped Prudence of its trees, planted crops, and brought in livestock that spoiled the quahog beds. The Indians were denied the resources they had enjoyed and preserved for generations, and Prudence became the exclusive domain of the whites.

The white farmers prospered, though few grew rich. Prudence was never to have a booming economy or large population. Great events seem to have given the island a fairly wide berth. In the 1650s the Duke of York authorized a scheme to turn the island into a feudal estate called Topley or Sophy Manor, but the plan was not long-lived. Despite its shape and nickname, the island never supported a whaling industry, leaving that pursuit to the communities on the ocean islands of Nantucket and Martha's Vineyard, to Sag Harbor on Long Island and New Bedford on the Massachusetts mainland. Prudence did see action in 1776 during the American Revolution when the British troops stationed down the bay at Newport came here to requisition hay; island farmers refused and the redcoats put their farms to the torch. Farms were established again after the war; it was common then on Prudence for landowners from the mainland to build the farmhouses and then lease them and the land to tenant farmers on the island.

In the late 19th century America's middle and upper classes discovered the pleasures of seaside vacations on the Eastern islands and coastal towns, and the resort boom hit Prudence, but only in a very modest way. The handful of Victorian homes at Prudence Park are relics from this era. Summer home construction continued at a trickle until after World War II, when the trickle widened into a brook as the cottages on the east shore went up. Today, some Prudence Islanders worry that the brook may turn into a stream as new houses are going up at a significantly faster rate than they did a decade ago. There is even talk of condos on the site of the closed-up Prudence Inn. But, as the anti-development faction point out, development can only go so far on Prudence since a good part of the island is locked up in public parks and in large private parcels held by families who do not intend to sell (at least not now).

Though its farming days are pretty much over (and not too likely to return), Prudence retains the friendly, neighborly spirit one associates with farming communities. Island isolation has made the islanders here, as elsewhere, a self-reliant lot. Since they can't count on mainland services, they learn to do things for themselves, be it fixing the plumbing or finding entertainment on long winter evenings; but when neighbors need each other, islanders pitch in without hesitation. The visitor benefits from this community spirit right along with the resident. Though there is no longer an inn or restaurant on Prudence and little else that caters to tourists, the islanders provide welcome enough. They'll set you on your way if you get lost, chat about their island if you show the interest, recount its history and point out its sights. As lovely as it would be to spend a summer here dreaming beside the bay, it's also lovely to come to Prudence for the day, or, if you're prepared, to camp at South Prudence for a longer stretch. A day is sufficient to bike the length and breadth of the island, picnic in its parks, tour its winery and grow very fond of the place.

On Prudence one won't find the elemental energy and intensity of outer islands; There are no crashing waves or limitless vistas out to sea, no granite cliffs gnawed by the surf or barrier beaches continually refashioned by wind and tide. Instead there is the serene pleasure of sharing abandoned farm fields with herds of deer, of gazing at herons feeding in the salt marsh, of contemplating the boats on Narragansett Bay. Because history has handled Prudence so gently, the deep past, the time before Roger Williams when the island was a seasonal hunting and fishing ground of the Narragansett Indians, remains alive to the imagination. The traces of the whites' occupation—the deforestation, the farms, the military installations—are growing fainter with time. And though the tokens of the most recent invasion—the summer homes along the shore—seem destined to endure and increase, they haven't really marred the essential character of Prudence and probably won't. Prudence, by virtue of its location, its parks and its careful, large landowners, seems likely to remain protected.

BLOCK ISLAND

Area: 6,460 acres; 11 square miles; 6 miles long by 3.5 miles wide.

Population: 700 year-round; about 15,000 in peak summer season (about 20,000, including day-trippers).

Location: Block Island Sound, 8 miles south of the Rhode Island mainland and 13 miles east of Long Island's Montauk Point.

Access: Year-round car and passenger ferry from Point Judith (call 401-789-3502); seasonal passenger ferries from Newport (call 203-442-7891) and Montauk, N.Y. (call 516-668-2214 or 516-668-5709).

The Northeast Light, built of granite in 1867. The Sandy Point area around the lighthouse is an important nesting site for many species of birds. (Courtesy of the Rhode Island Department of Economic Development.)

For those with a taste for moralizing, Block Island's recent history is a tale of the fickleness of man's desires and nature's favors. Forty years ago this island of moorlike open landscape, fragrant fields set off by low stone walls, small ponds, long beaches and dramatic cliffs was a forgotten place. It had no real economy to speak of and barely enough people to make up a respectable village. Its fishing fleet had been smashed by the disastrous hurricane of 1938 and most of its farms had closed up. Its hotel and rooming houses—huge Victorian wooden piles that went up after the Civil War when the first wave of summer resort mania broke over the Eastern islands—stood empty and undefended against vandals and the elements. Block Island, cut adrift from her past, seemed to have no future.

But Block Island rose again. Like many other Eastern islands, Block Island was rediscovered in the prosperous decades after World War II by a new generation of vacationers. Visitors and yachtsmen began coming again to admire the beauty of the land and sea, the serenity of an island gliding into oblivion, the curious spectacle of a big, serviceable but largely empty harbor gaping at a collection of sleeping wooden giants—the Victorian white elephants. Some of these newcomers fell in love with the place and bought old farmhouses for a song. More and more visitors learned the secret. In the wake of new summer people came tourists and in the wake of tourists came day-trippers. One by one, the sleeping giants awoke under new management, fresh paint, modern plumbing, expensive renovation. Restaurants opened. New vacation homes appeared on the hillsides and moors and along the shore. Block Island began to boom.

Today, rediscovery is still going strong. The pace of building continues to accelerate, with as many as 40 new houses built each year. Real estate prices nearly quadrupled from 1978 to 1988. The sweet-smelling moorlike landscape has begun to close up. In the tourist season, the narrow country lanes are busy with cars, bikes and mopeds, and the Old Harbor commercial area where the big hotels and restaurants are clustered can feel (and smell) like Coney Island. The year-round population is rising but the summertime population is exploding. Water, sewage and garbage disposal have become serious problems during the summer months when upwards of 15,000 people are flushing, washing, laundering, and dumping into facilities built to serve 500. In short, discovery and development are now threatening to obliterate Block Island—at least what is most precious and special about the place—just as they are threatening so many other Eastern islands. It's the old story: too many people, not enough land, and a race between developers and conservationists to win control over what is left.

First Impressions: Getting the Lay of the Land

Block Island has been called a poor man's Nantucket, and there is something to this (although poverty, one must remember, is a relative condition). Like Nantucket, Block Island is well out to sea, off by itself and far from the mainland or any other island. Both islands have large harbors that afford safe anchorage (see below for the construction of Block Island's two harbors) but the surrounding waters of both are notoriously

Block Island landscape. The island's rolling moors are a terminal moraine, formed by the retreat of the last glacier some 10,000 years ago. Various conservation groups are trying to preserve the open character of Block Island's countryside. (Felice Nudelman)

Block Island

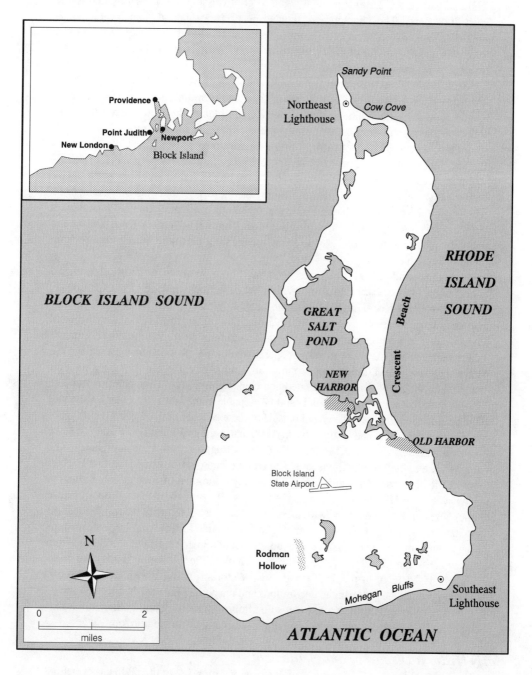

treacherous to navigate on account of their shoals and tricky tides. (In one year, 240 boats stranded on Block Island; and by one reckoning, Block Island's waters have claimed half of the 2,000 ships that came to grief off southern New England in the past 200 years). The characteristic landscape of Block Island, like Nantucket, is moorlike (though not technically moors), with low scrub and tangles of honeysuckle, bayberry and blackberry covering the hillsides and hardly a tree to be seen aside from ornamentals planted around houses.

Geologically, Block Island and Nantucket, along with Martha's Vineyard and Long Island, are close relatives: All are part of the same terminal moraine, vast heaps of gravel, boulders and sediment that the Wisconsin glacier dumped when it began to retreat from its southernmost terminus some 10,000 years ago (for more about glacial moraines, see the Nantucket entry). The glacier also created Block Island's numerous ponds: Technically, these are kettle-holes formed by large blocks of ice that broke off from the receding glacier; as they melted, the ice blocks left depressions in the sandy ground that subsequently filled with water. Local lore says there are 365 such ponds on the island—one for each day in the year. Over the millennia, many of the island's kettle ponds filled in and became peat bogs; peat, known as "tug" on the island for the way the islanders got it up, was an important heating fuel here before coal became readily available.

Although winds of 91 miles per hour have been recorded on Block Island and windbreaks are necessary to protect orchards, the island looks and feels less exposed than Nantucket. Block Island has a softness that harsh, windbitten Nantucket lacks. It also has better soil, good enough to support extensive farming in the 19th century whereas Nantucket's stark commons were used for little aside from sheep grazing. When Nantucketers were circling the globe in hunt of sperm whales, Block Islanders were staying put on or near the island, farming the rolling hills and fishing the surrounding waters for swordfish (the island's most celebrated and challenging catch), tuna, bluefish and cod. Until summer visitors made Block Island fashionable in the late 19th century, there was little economic activity on the island outside of these two pursuits.

Perhaps because it had no industry to rival whaling, Block Island developed no town to rival Nantucket town or Martha's Vineyard's Edgartown or Vineyard Haven. The farms were scattered over the island. The commercial district around the Old Harbor, where the big ferries dock today, grew up largely during the first resort boom after the Civil War. Old Harbor is not a natural harbor (oddly enough, the island doesn't have one) but is protected with an artificial breakwater constructed with federal funds from 1870 to 1878. It was the completion of a harbor capable of receiving large steamships that ushered in the resort era. The huge hotels that dominate the island's "skyline" from the water—the Hotel Manisses, the Surf Hotel, the National Hotel, the New Shoreham—date from the 1870s and '80s. Victorian in style, with mansard roofs, spacious verandas, gingerbread decorations and the occasional cupola, they conjure up an image of long dresses, white linen suits, floppy straw hats, and golden afternoons spent rocking on the porch and gazing at the steamers off on the horizon.

Early History: Discovery and Settlement

To get a feel for Block Island's early history, one must leave the Old Harbor behind and travel to the island's north end where the Settler's Rock memorial stands near the shore of Cow Cove. Settler's Rock is a large fieldstone that marks the spot where the first white settlers landed on Block Island in 1661. In 1911, the descendants of these 16 men and their families commemorated the 250th anniversary of the island's settlement with a bronze tablet set into the rock and engraved with the names of their ancestors. The island's original settlers were from the Boston area and they were for the most part people of means—farmers, merchants, a physician, surveyors. They came

"Smilin' Through," one of the oldest houses on Block Island, is named for the popular song composed here by Arthur Penn in the 1920s. (Felice Nudelman)

not out of economic need but in search of religious and intellectual freedom from the oppressive theocracy of the Massachusetts Bay Colony. Roger Williams had founded the Block Island colony nearly 30 years earlier after he was banished from Massachusetts for the same cause, and the first Block Islanders followed where Williams led. The island was to be their refuge, a safe haven remote from the influence and political control of the Puritan church. They paid the considerable sum of 400 pounds for the security of owning the 11-square-mile island eight miles offshore. To them, the island's distance from the mainland and from any other island was part of its value.

Block Island's first settlers were of English stock, but it is named for a Dutchman, Adriaen Block, a navigator and fur trader who in 1614 sailed around it, charted it and named it "Adriaen's Eylant," a name that time transformed to Block Island. Block had been hired by the merchants of New Amsterdam (later New York) to explore the coast of New England and assess its commercial possibilities. His ship, the *Onrust* ("restless"), was the first vessel built on Manhattan Island. Block was not the first European to sight and name the island. The Italian explorer Giovanni da Verrazano sailed this way in 1524 under the service of the French and described the island as a hilly, densely forested and populated island (the trees were later cut down by the settlers and have never returned). Verrazano named the island Luisa, for the mother of Francis I, the French king, and the French renamed it Claudia, for the queen.

Before it had been Block or Claudia or Luisa, the island was known as Manisses, meaning Island of the Little God, the name given it by the tribe of Narragansett Indians who lived here. Manisses was a prize much fought over by the Indians of southern New England and Long Island, for its soil was fertile, its shores rich in clams and its surrounding waters teeming with fish. In 1590 the Manisses Indians repulsed a raiding party of 40 Mohegans from Long Island by forcing them over the edge of the 200-foot cliffs, since known as Mohegan Bluff, at the island's south end. The Manisses soon after ran afoul of the Massachusetts Bay Colony when they murdered a Boston trader named John Oldham who had anchored here in 1636. In revenge, the colony sent over a raiding party of 100 men who killed what Indians they could find and burned their wigwams and corn fields. The raid took the starch out of the Indians, and when the first settlers came here 25 years later, the Manisses no longer had the strength to cast them back to the sea. The whites and Indians lived in peace, but the Indian population fell off steadily over the years. The last Manisses Indian, Isaac Church, died in the late 19th century.

Fishing boats tied up in the Old Harbor. Block Island has no natural harbor, and before the breakwater (in the background) was constructed with federal funds from 1870 to 1878, island fishermen tied their boats up offshore to long poles driven into the ocean floor. Despite the breakwater, the hurricane of 1938 destroyed the Block Island commercial fishing fleet, and today only a handful of islanders support themselves by fishing. (Felice Nudelman)

The 16 white settlers divided the island among themselves and set to work clearing and farming the land. In 1672 the settlement was formally incorporated as the Town of New Shoreham, which remains Block Island's official name. The first Block Islanders came here to find peace and freedom from intolerance, but the very remoteness that attracted them to the island proved to be a lure for privateers, outcasts and army deserters as well. From the end of the 17th century until after the American Revolution, the island was plagued by marauders and criminals of various stripes and nationalities. Supposedly Captain Kidd buried treasure on Block Island, but other pirates were more prone to seize what little treasure the inhabitants had. The Revolution was a particularly severe period for the islanders, who suffered at the hands of both the British and the Colonials. During the War of 1812, however, the situation was reversed. Block Island had a kind of neutral status and the islanders, exempt from American military service and taxes, made out quite well by selling their produce for inflated prices to the English men-of-war.

The Resort Era: From Popularity to Oblivion and Back Again

The next invasion to interrupt the peaceful farming and fishing of the islanders was launched not by hostile armies but by enthusiastic vacationers. The island's popularity as a resort, as mentioned above, took off with the construction of the Old Harbor in 1870, peaked in the 1890s, and declined precipitately after World War I. Most of the grand old hotels are still standing today, but the grandest and most fashionable of all, the sumptuous Ocean View, burned to the ground in 1966. Ulysses S. Grant came here as a guest while he was in office, as did members of the Supreme Court and many, many wealthy society people. Block Island, though it never attained the wealth, exclusiveness and social cachet of nearby Newport, was a recognized and approved port-of-call on the Eastern seaboard social circuit.

When the winds of fashion shifted and the visitors stopped coming to the grand hotels, the islanders were left to fall back on their old means of support—farming and fishing. But even these were to fail them. The cost of exporting produce to the mainland made farming increasingly unprofitable, so the islanders began to rely more heavily on fishing. The harbors that were opened in the late 19th century were as much of a boon to fishermen as to tourists. For centuries the island fishermen, lacking a good natural harbor, had to steer their boats in to shore on the crests of waves or tie them up to long poles driven into the ocean floor. The man-made harbors allowed them to fish from larger boats and increase their haul.

According to the WPA guide to Rhode Island published in 1937, island fishermen were at that period shipping 30,000 barrels of fish to markets on the mainland each year. But the disastrous hurricane of September 21, 1938, one of the worst natural catastrophes in America's history, dealt a death blow to fishing on the island and wiped out what was left of farming as well. The hurricane coming in the wake of the Great Depression pretty much finished off the economy that had sustained Block Islanders since 1661.

Ferry packed with tourists arriving at Block Island's Old Harbor. (Courtesy of the Rhode Island Department of Economic Development.)

It wasn't until tourists began coming back in the 1960s that a measure of prosperity returned to Block Island. Today, tourism and construction are the major sources of income on the island. Block Island is even more popular and, in its way, fashionable now than it was in the 1890s. The island has some 30 hotels and guest houses and 20 restaurants to receive and feed its visitors, whose numbers can swell to nearly 25,000 on a peak summer weekend.

Up and Down the Island: Seeing the Sights

Old Harbor, the island's commercial hub, is where most visitors to Block Island disembark and many are content to spend their time and money on its hotels, shops, restaurants and tourist "scene." But for those who have come to the island to get a break from shops and scenes, the Old Harbor is easily and quickly escaped by following almost any road out of town. A mile to the West on Ocean Avenue is the island's New Harbor on Great Salt Pond, a 1,400-acre body of salt water that very nearly cuts this pear-shaped island in two, leaving a small tapering stem end to the north and the broad base to the south. Great Salt Pond originally offered no access to the ocean and early attempts to cut a passageway failed. Although settlers first petitioned for help in creating a harbor here in 1694, it wasn't until 1895 that crews began the work of digging out the present 24-foot-deep, 300-foot-wide channel to the west. Great Salt Pond now serves as a vast marina for pleasure craft, which unfortunately have polluted its waters and spoiled its quahog beds. It was along the shores of this protected body of water that the Manisses Indians lived, and archaeologists have unearthed many important artifacts here. A Coast Guard Station stands at the entrance channel to Great Salt Pond, and there is a little beach beyond the station that is a nice place for picnics, fishing and boat-watching. For land-based visitors, the New Harbor offers a couple of restaurants and a few shops.

Corn Neck Road, which you can pick up off Ocean Avenue just outside of the Old Harbor area, is the way to the island's north end. Just outside of town you'll come to

Fountain Square and the statue of Rebecca at the center of Block Island's Old Harbor. The old drugstore with its mansard roof, verandas and fancy woodwork is typical of the island's Victorian architecture. (Felice Nudelman)

the long, smooth, sandy Crescent Beach, which, like all of Block Island's 25 miles of beach, is open to the public. The strip of beach known as State Beach, which lies nearest the Old Harbor, has a bathing pavilion and a lifeguard is on duty during the summer months.

A few miles north of Crescent Beach, Corn Neck Road takes you to the Clay Head Nature Trail, known locally as the Maze, a network of 11 miles of mowed grass trails traversing a beautiful 192-acre nature preserve (privately owned but open to the public). You can follow the trails to the cliffs that front the sea at the northeast end of the island, where Settler's Rock (see above) is located.

Sandy Point, Block Island's northern tip, is one of the most beautiful sections of the island, a place of rippling dunes, long sweeping shorelines and wide water views. Corn Neck Road comes to its northern terminus at Settler's Rock, and from there paths lead to the Sandy Point area through tawny beach grass and tangles of beach roses, beach plums, beach peas, goldenrod and pearly everlasting. A path skirts Sachem Pond (which became salt water after the hurricane of 1938 breached the narrow bar that separates it from the sea) and climbs the dunes to the North Light. This serene, nobly proportioned granite building was erected in 1867 and abandoned by the Coast Guard in 1972. Now owned by the Town of New Shoreham, the building is undergoing extensive renovation with the aim of opening it to the public as an interpretive center. Three other lighthouses have stood on this site: The first two were washed off the dunes and the third destroyed by fire.

To the north, Block Island peters out: The land narrows to the aptly named Sandy Point, gradually merges with the sea and then runs under it for some distance in a reach of treacherous shoal and sandbar. At the south end, where the island is widest, the land comes to an abrupt halt: High cliffs drop down to the Atlantic and take the full force of its surf, which grinds away as much as three feet of land each year. Spring Street is the road that leads from the Old Harbor, past the Spring House Hotel (the oldest and largest on Block Island; one wing dates from 1852), to the island's dramatic south shore. The most impressive man-made monument here is the Southeast Light, a Gothic revival building with sharp-peaked gables built of brick on a granite foundation. Erected in 1873 and first illuminated in 1875, the light is the highest in New England, its lantern rising 52 feet above the ground and 204 feet above sea level. The beam refracted by the light's Fresnel lens travels 35 miles out to sea and is supposed to be the strongest on the Atlantic coast. But the light, which before automation required eight keepers to tend it, is in danger of imminent destruction as the sea tears down the bluff on which it stands. The Southeast Lighthouse Foundation, which recently leased the lighthouse from the Coast Guard, is trying to raise $2.5 million to move the lighthouse 60 feet back from the eroding cliff.

Just west of the lighthouse on the south coast rise the Mohegan Bluffs, the island's highest bluffs and surely its most impressive natural feature. The Bluffs, whose private owners recently sold them at a reduced price for use as a nature preserve, stand about 200 feet above the ocean. The views are magnificent: south out to the limitless sea; west down to the island's craggy southern coast, terrain that brings to mind the rugged, romantic Scottish Highlands; and still farther west, on a clear day, straight across the ocean to Montauk Point. A long flight of wooden steps descends to a sand beach at the base of the bluffs.

On the west side of the island's broad south base are two substantial nature preserves ideal for walking, bird-watching and contemplating the image the island presented to early settlers and farmers. Rodman's Hollow is a ravine that the glacier scooped out so deeply that it is actually below sea level. The hollow did not become a pond because its sandy soil is too porous to hold rainwater, and it never became a farm because the soil is too poor to support much grazing grass. It did, however, very nearly become building sites until its 169 acres were saved from development

The Mohegan Bluffs on the south coast of Block Island. These bluffs, like parts of Martha's Vineyard's Gay Head, are composed of blue Gardiners clay, deposited during an intermission between glaciers. The area is now protected as a nature reserve. (Felice Nudelman)

through the efforts of Captain John Robinson Lewis and the Block Island Conservancy he helped to found in 1971. Rodman's Hollow, now open to the public, offers an

important habitat to the Block Island meadow vole, a species unique to Block Island. To reach Rodman's Hollow, follow the Mohegan Trail past Mohegan Bluffs, go right on Lakeside Drive and left on Cooneymus Road. Black Rock Road, which leads left off Cooneymus, will take you there.

Adjoining Rodman's Hollow is a superb 218-acre tract of former farm land known as the Lewis-Dickens Farm. Previously owned by Bill Lewis and Keith Lewis (now president of the Block Island Conservancy), this rolling coastal grassland was preserved as a nature sanctuary through the combined work of the Nature Conservancy, the Town of New Shoreham, the efforts of Rhode Island Senator John Chafee and the generosity and

Block Island's Southeast Light, erected in 1873, is in imminent danger of toppling over the eroding cliffs. However, islanders are trying to save the light, and if sufficient funds can be raised, the lighthouse building will be moved 60 feet back from the ocean. (Felice Nudelman)

vision of its owners. The Rhode Island Department of Environmental Management offers guided walks through parts of the farmland in the summer months.

BLOCK ISLAND

Perhaps it's overly dramatic to speak of "saving" Block Island. Much of what is most beautiful—Sandy Point, Mohegan Bluffs, Crescent Beach—is safe already. Much of the land that remains up for grabs is protected, at least to some degree, by zoning. The island, though increasingly popular, is in no danger of going the way of the barrier islands of the New Jersey Shore, where unbroken ranks of beach cottages squat depressingly beside the polluted ocean beaches. Block Island will not be entirely spoiled nor will it be entirely preserved from the consequences of its own popularity. The Block Island of the future will no doubt fall somewhere in the middle—with regulated development, a patchwork of open space and filled space, bigger crowds but better facilities to accommodate them, tighter controls on sewage, pollution and water use, a bike path to relieve congestion of the roads. The complexities of the future make the past look sweet and innocent, but as many islanders remember, the old days were not all that golden. If the past was quiet, it was also poor; when the island slept, it slept in neglect and abandonment, not peaceful fulfillment. Out of wisdom and perhaps even more out of necessity, Block Islanders have put the past behind and turned their anxious, wistful faces to the future that is bearing down on them.

THE ISLANDS OF NEW YORK

INTRODUCTION

New York, like Venice, is a city built on islands, but one would hardly call it an island city. The 65 bridges, four automobile tunnels and 13 train and subway tunnels that link up these New York islands with each other and with the mainland have reduced the city's island status from an essential quality of life to an inconvenience of transportation. Not only do New Yorkers forget that they are islanders, they positively repudiate it. To New Yorkers, "the Island" (that is, Long Island) begins only where "the City" leaves off. Never mind that on a map Brooklyn and Queens make up the head of the whopping fish that Long Island so uncannily resembles: To New Yorkers the City is an entity that takes precedence over mere geography. Long thin Manhattan at its epicenter, squat, lush Staten Island off to the vague southwest, the west end of Long Island, the scattering of river and sound islands including Wards, Rikers, Randalls, Roosevelt, City Island: The City has assumed its islands into its own vast being. It has swallowed them up and obliterated their individuality, their "island-ness." The City's numerous bridges and tunnels, infuriatingly inadequate as they are to handle the City's ever-mounting traffic, have made the City's islands irrelevant as islands.

Of course, it wasn't always this way. Back before Manhattan's first link to Long Island, the Brooklyn Bridge, was opened in 1883, New York still felt like an island city. Or, rather, two cities, one great city in Manhattan, one rather small one in Brooklyn— with Staten Island an outlying country district and the Bronx the sole mainland outpost. (The High Bridge over the Harlem River, which linked Manhattan and the Bronx in 1848, was technically the first New York bridge; but the Brooklyn Bridge is so much bigger and more beautiful and so much greater a feat of engineering that people tend to forget about its predecessor.) Walt Whitman's "Crossing Brooklyn Ferry," probably the greatest piece of verse ever inspired by an island ferry ride, gives ample evidence of just how separate these New York "islands large and small" were before the bridges and tunnels hooked them up. The shape and isolation of the New York islands played a major role in the architecture and layout of the city. The skyscraper, arguably, evolved to its gigantic proportions on Manhattan Island precisely because it is an island (and a rather small island at that, of only 22 square miles) that could expand only by ascending.

The neglected High Bridge and the celebrated Brooklyn Bridge have been followed by a complex network of additional bridges, tunnels, footbridges, even an aerial tramway connecting Roosevelt Island to Manhattan. Nevertheless, a number of New York islands, significant in history if not in size, have escaped the arteries of steel and concrete. The islands of New York harbor—Liberty, Ellis[*] and Governors—remain true islands, attainable only by confronting the flood tide "face to face," as Whitman did when he crossed to Brooklyn with "countless crowds of passengers." The Statue

---

[*] A temporary bridge was opened up between Ellis Island and Jersey City, New Jersey, in 1988 to facilitate the restoration project. It will be taken down when the work is completed in 1992, and Ellis Island will become a true island once more.

of Liberty and the Ellis Island Immigration Museum are monuments whose significance is immeasurably enhanced by their island settings. Governors Island, the site of Fort Jay, built in 1797, is currently a Coast Guard facility and home to about 5,000 people; twice a year, in the spring and fall, the ferry from Manhattan's Battery is open to members of the visiting public (for information, call 212-668-7366). In a strange twist of history, ferry travel to Manhattan is coming back into vogue as bridges and tunnels grow ever more congested and decrepit. There is now ferry service to New York from a number of New Jersey locations, including Weehawken, Fort Lee and Elizabeth, from Brooklyn's Rockaway and Fulton Street, and additional ferry links may open up soon.

Long Island, extending 188 miles from east to west and covering 1,723 square miles, is not only the largest by far of the New York islands, it is also the largest island on the East Coast (and the fourth largest island in the United States, after Hawaii Island, Kodiak Island in the Gulf of Alaska and Puerto Rico). With nearly seven million residents it is also the most populous of the East Coast islands. (Manhattan, however, with 64,922 people per square mile, is the most densely populated). Though firmly knit to the mainland, via bridges and tunnels to Manhattan and Staten Island, Long Island does carry a number of unconnected satellite islands in its orbit. Shelter Island, snagged between the North and South Forks of Long Island's East End, is a quiet island of green fields, woods and protected coves that has a small year-round community and a growing number of summer homes. It also holds the record for the shortest ferry ride to any Eastern island—just three minutes for the half-mile South Ferry crossing. Plum Island, less than two miles off Orient Point, is the site of the U.S. Department of Agriculture Plum Island Animal Disease Center; the boat out to Plum is accessible by government permission only. East of Shelter Island and south of Plum lies Gardiners Island, the private domain of the Gardiner family for 10 generations, dating back to 1639.

Long Island's South Shore is protected by a series of barrier islands and beaches, including Long Beach, Jones Beach and Westhampton Beach, that have been bridged to the main island and turned into public parks or private beach communities. The longest and most interesting of the Long Island barrier islands is Fire Island, a kind of hybrid island—bridged at its two ends, but accessible only by passenger ferry in between. Fire Island has a reputation as a hedonistic beach resort for homosexuals and swinging singles; but actually it is better preserved from development than most East Coast barrier islands. Large public beaches occupy the two bridged ends; and the unbridged middle was declared a National Seashore in 1964. The beach communities (many of them nice wholesome family places) were allowed to remain and grow within set boundaries, but the rest of Fire Island is safe from development. An eight-mile stretch near the island's east end is New York State's only official wilderness area.

Fishers Island can hardly be considered a satellite of Long Island since it is so much closer to Connecticut; but politically, this extremely exclusive retreat of the Eastern elite is part of the Long Island town of Southold and thus it belongs with the New York islands. Fishers takes the prize for the most closely guarded of all the accessible Eastern island resorts (runners-up are Islesboro and North Haven in Maine): though anyone can take the ferry over from New London (for information, call 516-788-7463 or 203-443-6851), two-thirds of the island is sealed off to all but property owners and country club members. Fishers is suffering from the embarrassment of its quite literal riches: the 5,000 or so uppercrust seasonal residents have driven property values up so high that the island's small year-round community (about 250 people) can no longer afford to live here. No islanders in the winter means no "help" in the summer. Such are the perils of island life in the late 20th century.

SHELTER ISLAND

Area: 7,800 acres; 4 miles wide by 7 miles long.
Population: 2,277 year-round; around 10,000 in peak summer season.
Location: Between the North and South Forks of Long Island's East End, between Gardiners Bay and Peconic Bay; 0.9 miles south of Greenport and 0.5 mile north of North Haven.
Access: By car ferry from Greenport (call: 516-749-0139) and from North Haven (call: 516-749-0007).

Shelter Island, as its name suggests, is a protected place. Lodged safely between Long Island's North and South Forks, the island enjoys the relatively calm waters of Gardiners Bay to the east and Peconic Bay to the west—waters made even quieter by the island's numerous natural harbors, coves and creeks. The landscape is also peaceful, gently rolling in places and broad and flat in others, lightly wooded or cleared off in open fields, smooth and green and settled, with bands of sand and clumps of golden beach grass softening its deeply indented shores. No cliffs or rocky promontories break the surface of the land; only at Shelter Island Heights in the island's northwest corner does a high bluff rise 110 feet above the water. This is idyllic country, well-suited to the summer homes, marinas, yacht and country clubs that have gradually but relentlessly covered the island and turned it into a summer resort. With farming and fishing pretty much pur-

The Union Chapel, or Chapel in the Grove, built in 1875-76 on Shelter Island Heights.

Shelter Island

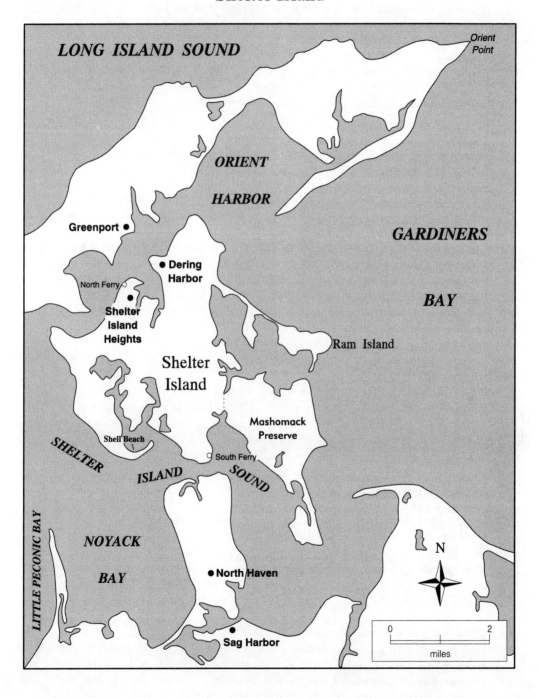

suits of the past, Shelter Island has settled down to the business of entertaining its summer folk, caring for their homes and boats, running the restaurants and the few inns that cater to tourists, a small but growing presence on the island. For those who come here, Shelter Island is sheltered indeed—sheltered from both the pressures of city life and from the fashionable frenzy that has seized the Hamptons on the South Fork.

There are two ferries that serve Shelter Island: the North Ferry that sails from Greenport and the South Ferry from North Haven. Together these ferries hold the distinction of making the shortest trips of any Eastern island ferry—seven minutes for the 0.9-mile North Ferry crossing and three minutes for the half-mile South Ferry crossing. At various times in the past there has been talk of building a bridge to Shelter Island. Such an undertaking would require no great feat of engineering and the gain to islanders in time and money saved would be considerable. But the idea proved unpopular and has been shelved, probably forever. Yes, a bridge would eliminate the ferry lines, which at the North Ferry particularly can grow maddeningly long on summer weekends. But a bridge would also eliminate what is left of the island's old-fashioned charm. Though it is only a jump away from the "mainland" of bridged Long Island, Shelter Island still feels different. It's quieter, slower, just a touch removed from the highway and subdivision culture that dominates Long Island. From the shore or from the water, Shelter Island and the surrounding landmasses of Long Island are nearly indistinguishable, except to those who really know. The arms of low-lying land seem to blend together. But they don't. Less than a mile of quiet unspanned bay water sets Shelter Island apart. It's a tiny distance, but it still makes a difference.

Getting Oriented

Shelter Island is not all that big, just seven miles long and four miles wide at its widest, but it is so irregular in shape that getting a feel for the place can take some time. Route 114 cuts more or less straight across the island, connecting the North and South Ferries and passing through the main business district at the island's center, but if you stick to 114 you'll miss all the juts and jags of land that make Shelter Island so special. On the east side there are two long appendages to the main body of the island, the Ram Islands, Little and Big, which are connected by a sandy causeway; and to the south, hooked on like a claw, is the 2,039-acre Mashomack Preserve, a peninsula of varied terrain entirely protected in its wild state by the Nature Conservancy. Mashomack and the Ram Islands enclose Coecles Harbor, which has a marina and a town dock at the head of Congdons Creek.

Across Shelter Island's narrow northern neck from the Ram Islands lies the Village of Dering Harbor, an exclusive 200-acre enclave set apart within the Town of Shelter Island. Dering Harbor is the name of both a village and a small and pretty harbor scooped out of the island's northwest corner. Facing west across the harbor to the yacht club, Shelter Island's grandest mansions stand shoulder to shoulder like country cousins of the gargantuan Gilded Age "cottages" of Newport. Shelter Island Heights, rising to the south and west of Dering Harbor, presents a very different aspect indeed. On this steep hill a maze of roads was laid out and a little colony of Victorian gingerbread cottages (real cottages, not mansions) was planted a little more than 100 years ago. Wooded, secluded and pleasantly sedate, Shelter Island Heights retains the aura of earnest religious spirit on which it was built (see below).

South of Shelter Island Heights the island's west wide is defined by an elbow of land known as West Neck and a long peninsula that curls to its southern terminus at Shell Beach (one of four public beaches), a very pretty sandbar bordered by West Neck Harbor to its north and Shelter Island Sound to its south. By water, Shell Beach is less than half-a-mile from Wades Beach (another town beach), which is right in the middle of the island's south shore; but in order to get from one to the other by car, you have to drive over five miles. Driving miles around coves, creeks and harbors

An old photograph of Shelter Island's West Neck. (Courtesy of the Shelter Island Historical Society.)

to reach a destination that is only yards away as the crow flies can be a nuisance if you're in a hurry; but there is not usually much to hurry for on Shelter Island. And in any case, most of the summer folk prefer to travel by water whenever they can. The coves, creeks and harbors that impede land travel make Shelter Island ideal for boating, and pleasure craft abound on the sheltered waters.

History

For so quiet a place, Shelter Island has a surprisingly long and impressive history. The Manhanset Indian tribe, who lived here before the coming of white settlers, called the island Manhansack-aha-quash-awamock, which means "an island sheltered by islands"—whence its English name. Pogatticut (also known as Yoco), a grand sachem whose power may have extended to nearly all of Long Island, was the leader of the Manhansets when the English first appeared in the area. Pogatticut's people welcomed the first English settlers in 1652, and most of the Indians soon left the island for other parts of Long Island.

Even before they settled here, the English were busy transferring title to Shelter Island and changing its name. Originally part of the Plymouth Colony grant that King James I made in 1620, the island passed into the hands of William Alexander, Earl of Stirling, in 1637 and then into the possession of his American agent, James Farrett, who promptly named it for himself. Farrett sold it to one Stephen Goodyear in 1641, and 10 years later Goodyear sold it to four merchants who had interests in the Barbados sugar trade. The price was 1,600 pounds of Muscavado sugar. Of these four buyers, Nathaniel Sylvester alone came to settle here in 1652, bringing his gently-born 16-year-old English bride Grissel with him. Sylvester ruled Shelter Island benevolently, as a sort of feudal domain. He had a manor house built and his slaves cleared fields and farmed them. A man of unusual open-mindedness and toleration, Sylvester made

Shelter Island a haven for Quakers, who were being persecuted, tortured and killed in 17th-century New England. Sylvester twice received and entertained George Fox, the founder of the Society of Friends, and Fox preached on the island. A small Quaker cemetery and monument stand on the grounds of Sylvester Manor in memory of the last four Quakers put to death on Boston Common.

Although the Sylvester heirs sold off sections of the island, Sylvester Manor, which was rebuilt in 1773, still stands on the largest private estate on the island, and, astonishingly, it is occupied today, as it always has been, by a descendant of Nathaniel Sylvester.

Shelter Island suffered greatly during the American Revolution and many of the 170 or so residents were forced to flee to Connecticut while the English plundered their lands and cut most of the island's valuable timber. After the war, the refugees returned and Shelter Island settled back into the quiet rhythms of a farming community. The island had 200 residents in 1790 and by 1845 the population had risen to 446. In addition to farming, the islanders fished commercially and after 1853 the menhaden fishery became important on the island; menhaden were valued not as food but as a source of oil and fertilizer. Unfortunately, the business of boiling down the fish,

The Manhanset Chapel was built in 1890 to satisfy the religious yearnings of Manhanset House guests. The building now serves as the museum of the island's historical society. (Courtesy of the Shelter Island Historical Society.)

pressing out their oil and drying the scraps for fertilizer was extremely malodorous and this brought the menhaden fishery into direct conflict with Shelter Island's other emerging industry—summer tourism. Eventually tourism won out and the "pot works"—so-called because of the large pots used to boil down the fish—were banished forever from Shelter Island.

The Resort Era: Past and Present

Shelter Island rose as a summer resort on the same wave of enthusiasm that swept up Block Island, Newport, Mount Desert and many other fashionable Eastern islands and coastal communities. All at once, after the Civil War, America's leisure class went mad for seaside bathing, and huge hotels and elaborate, rustic "cottages" sprung up where once only fishing shanties and farm fields had stood. The pioneer summer folk on Shelter Island were Brooklyn Methodists in search of an inspiring natural setting for their camp meetings. They found it in 1871 amid the peaceful woods of the high bluff then known as the Prospect and now known as Shelter Island Heights. In a twinkling, the Shelter Island Grove and Camp Meeting Association of the Methodist

Episcopal Church was formed and by the summer of 1872, the Association had laid out a camp meeting ground and opened up the Prospect Hotel complete with community dining hall and groups of cottages quite similar to those at Martha's Vineyard's Oak Bluffs (then known as Cottage City), another Methodist summer retreat of the period attended by some of the same faithful.

The Manhanset house destroyed by fire in 1896. A similar fate befell grand wooden hotels on Martha's Vineyard, Block Island, Islesboro and other Eastern resort islands of the Victorian era. (Courtesy of the Shelter Island Historical Society.)

Though the religious zeal faded in time, the zeal for the beauties of Shelter Island only grew more fervent. The next year another, even larger and more luxurious hotel rose across Dering Harbor from the Prospect Hotel; this was the Manhanset House, which stood in what is now the posh Village of Dering Harbor (see above). The Manhanset House was a very swanky place indeed, catering not to religious enthusiasts but to a worldly crowd of rich East Coast yachtsmen and their families. In the summer months, expensive pleasure craft crowded into Dering Harbor and the New York Yacht Club made a yearly cruise to the Manhanset House, where it had a station for its members.

Tennis on the lawn of the Manhanset House, an even grander and more fashionable 1870s resort than the Prospect House, which preceded it by a year. (Courtesy of the Shelter Island Historical Society.)

Shelter Island's resort boom peaked in the 1890s and declined fairly rapidly after that. Fire claimed Manhanset House in 1896; the hotel was rebuilt but never attained its original chic. It burned again in 1910. The Prospect Hotel, which had changed its name to the New Prospect House, burned to the ground in 1942, but Shelter Island's era of elegance had long since come to a close.

Shelter Island may have fallen out of fashion in the early 20th century, but, unlike Block Island, it did not close up altogether as a summer resort. After the big hotels burnt down, smaller inns and hotels continued to cater to visitors, and during the thirties and forties and then increasingly after World War II summer people bought up land and put up vacation homes. Once the preserve of a very few aristocratic families, Shelter Island and its large estates were carved up into summer colonies with comfortable cottages occupying small plots along the shore. West Neck, Montclair at the south end, Westmoreland Farm, Silver Beach, South Ferry Hills, Ram Island, Hay Beach—these were among the first areas to sprout summer homes. Today, development has spread pretty much all over the island, and each year about forty new houses go up. Farming, like commercial fishing, is pretty much a thing of the past, and the islanders depend on the summer folk and retirees for their livelihood.

The Mashomack Preserve

One area on the island where new houses are not going up and never will is the Mashomack Preserve, which at 2,039 acres makes up nearly one-third of Shelter Island's total area. The existence on Shelter Island of so extensive a tract of undeveloped and undivided land is due to a happy coincidence of history, luck and struggle. Mashomack, formerly known as Sachem's Neck, passed from Giles Sylvester to William Nicoll in 1695. The peninsula remained in the hands of the Nicoll family for 230 years, and then in the 1920s the New York financier Otto Kahn bought it and later sold it to the Gerard Brothers, who owned a number of other pieces of real estate and buildings. As the real estate market on Shelter Island took off, developers began to formulate great plans for Mashomack. With 10 miles of pristine shoreline, sandy beaches and prime frontage on Coecles Harbor, the land was a developer's dream, ideally suited to condos, marinas—the whole works. But late in the 1970s, the Gerards approached the Nature Conservancy about buying the land as a preserve, and the Conservancy launched a major fund-raising drive. With a good deal of help from the Shelter Islanders, the Conservancy raised the $5.6 million needed to acquire the property, and closed on it in January of 1980.

Aside from a few structures, including an 1820s-era gatehouse that now serves as a visitor's center and trail house, the 1891 Nicholl manor that stands near the center of the property, a keeper's cottage and barn, Mashomack is wild and open land. An oak/hickory hardwood forest, a forest-type characteristic of this area, covers about 1,300 of its acres. Dogwood, red maple, sassafras, gray birch and American beech are also common tree species in the forest. There are 500 acres of freshwater and tidal wetlands, including salt marsh, and a number of kettle-hole ponds, rounded depressions formed by large, slowly melting ice blocks left behind by the retreating glacier.

Of the many species of birds that nest on the preserve, the most highly prized are the osprey, which have made a small comeback in recent years. In 1988, there were 16 osprey nests on Mashomack.

Mashomack is a wild and beautiful place, a place set apart from the rest of Shelter Island, which man has been taming and smoothing and subdividing for more than 300 years now. Among the many pleasures it offers, perhaps the most exhilarating is the pleasure of wandering freely amid miles of open space on a small and increasingly congested island.

Seeing the Sights

Despite the increasing number of bed and breakfast places and small inns and restaurants, Shelter Island attracts relatively few tourists, especially compared with islands like Nantucket, Block Island or even Smith and Tangier in Chesapeake Bay. Summer people, not day-trippers, hold sway here, and the island has the feel of a relaxed but private summer resort. Still, unlike such forbiddingly exclusive islands as Fisher's Island in Long Island Sound or Maine's North Haven, Shelter Island welcomes those tourists who do come and gives them nearly the whole island to explore. Visitors can keep themselves busy biking the pleasant island roads, walking the beaches, wandering in Mashomack and seeing what sights there are to see.

The island has no grand monuments or fabulous summer palaces, but there is some nice Victorian-era architecture, particularly in Shelter Island Heights, where the Methodists ushered in the island's resort era back in the 1870s (see above). The Chequit Inn, just up the hill from the North Ferry, preserves part of the old Prospect House's dining hall. Higher up on the Heights on Wesley Street is the very lovely Chapel in the Grove—or Union Chapel—built in 1875-76 in a gentle, restrained neo-gothic style and surrounded by gingerbread-bedecked cottages. The chapel's windows are marine mosaics that local artist Walter Cole Brigham fashioned of shells, wave-worn stones and beach glass. Perhaps the most fantastic efflorescence of high Victorian architecture on the island is the Gingerbread House at 37 Grand in the Heights. Built by Squire Frederick Chase in 1875, the house has a gabled tower and pointed gothic windows, and its balcony and veranda are iced with so much fancy woodwork it makes your teeth ache. The Greek Revival Crook-Hassel House (1849) at Route 114 and Winthrop Road, with its cool white portico and fluted pillars, is a relief from Victorian excess.

The Shelter Island Historical Society maintains two noteworthy buildings on the island. The Manhanset Chapel, built in 1890 as the chapel to the Manhanset House Hotel, now serves as the Historical Society's museum, with displays on the history and industries of the island. The chapel, which originally stood in the Village of Dering Harbor, was moved to its present location at Route 114 and Thomas Avenue in 1924. The Havens House on Route 114 just south of Smith Street was completed in 1743 and served as the Havens family homestead for 170 years. The Historical Society acquired it in 1968. The simple but graceful white house, with a veranda on two sides supported by square pillars, is open to the public as a house museum; its interior is furnished with pieces dating to the mid-19th century.

The Village of Dering Harbor, as mentioned above, has a cluster of grand summer mansions along the shore on Shore Road; although the homes are all privately owned, visitors are free to walk down the road and admire the houses on one side and the water views over the harbor on the other. Little and Big Ram Island also merit a visit

Fire Island

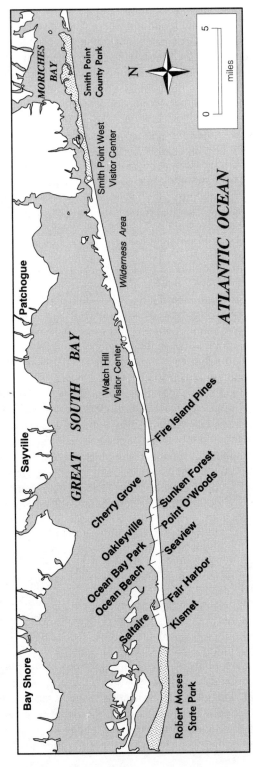

for the ospreys that nest on the causeway that connects them, for the superb views north into Gardiners Bay and for glimpses of fine homes tucked away in the woods.

Shelter Island's beaches lack the drama of crashing surf and endless ocean vistas, but they are clean, uncrowded and free. You can walk for a long way down the sandy beach on the north side of Little Ram. Crescent Beach, a jump southwest of the Heights, is a long, thin strip of sand backed by two rambling hotels. Shell Beach and Wades Beach face each other across shallow West Neck Harbor, and when the tide is low you can wade from one to the other with just a brief swim across a channel deepened for the boat traffic. Both are open to the public, but cars must have a town sticker in order to park.

Many once peaceful Eastern islands are now the scenes of pitched battles between real estate developers and conservationists, with island natives often caught in the middle. On many Maine islands, including Swans, Islesboro and the Casco Bay islands, rich summer people are forcing the price of land and homes out of the reach of island people; natives whose families have farmed and fished for generations are selling out—because they have to, because the prices are too tempting not to, because they know there is no future on the island for their children. On Block Island, Nantucket and Martha's Vineyard there is a scramble to save and preserve what open land remains undeveloped. On Shelter Island, however, the battle is pretty much over, the crisis has passed. Development has won out. As Mike Laspia, preserve director for the Nature Conservancy at Mashomack and a Shelter Island native, puts it, "It's reached the point where the island is gone other than Mashomack. There just aren't any big parcels of undeveloped land left."

Much remains, however, for the visitors, summer people and vacationers who come here. Island-wide development has changed the face of Shelter Island but it has not spoiled its charm. Though much of the shoreline is dotted with houses, it is still a beautiful, gentle shoreline; though most of the estates and farms have been sold off and divided up, the land still looks rich and green and promising. This is fertile land and the long centuries of settlement have been kind to it. If the islanders and summer people of the present have squeezed the land just a little too hard, at least they have also had the foresight to set aside the Mashomack Preserve. Mashomack offers everyone a resort of a very different kind from the rest of this expensive, sheltered island.

FIRE ISLAND

Area: 6,700 acres; 32 miles long and 0.5 mile wide at its widest.
Population: 200 families year-round; about 15,000 people in peak summer season (with 25,000-30,000 day-trippers).
Location: Between Great South Bay to the north and the Atlantic Ocean to the south; 5 miles (at the maximum) south of the shore of Long Island; east of Jones Beach Island and west of Westhampton Beach.
Access: By bridge from Long Island to Robert Moses State Park at the west end and to Smith Point County Park at the east end. By passenger ferries from May to November from Bay Shore (516-665-5045, 516-665-3600, 516-665-2115) for Kismet, Saltaire, Fair Harbor, Dunewood, Ocean Beach, Seaview and Point O'Woods; from Sayville

(516-589-8980, 516-589-0810) for Cherry Grove, Fire Island Pines, Barrett Beach and Sailors Haven; from Patchogue (516-475-1665) for Davis Park-Ocean Ridge and Watch Hill.

Fire Island is a classic barrier island, a long, narrow, ever-shifting strip of sand that runs for 32 miles parallel to the South Shore of Long Island. On its "front" side, Fire Island's wide white beaches take the force of 8,000 Atlantic Ocean breakers each day; behind the island and sheltered by it lie the wide shallow waters of Great South Bay. If this fragile ribbon of sand, less than 200 yards across at its narrowest, were suddenly to disappear, enough ocean water would come rushing across the bay to swallow up 1,500 feet of the South Shore. The barrier island thus protects thousands of people and millions of dollars of property—but of course its own people and property are that much more vulnerable to the force of the ocean.

The swale between the primary and secondary dunes on Fire Island. The Sunken Forest grows behind the secondary dune. Boardwalks protect the vegetation from hikers and protect hikers from poison ivy.

Geologically, Fire Island is a pure barrier island; but from the point of view of the traveler, it is a hybrid, part bridged and part accessible only by boat. HIghways carry cars over bridges to its two ends, where there are large public beaches—Robert Moses State Park to the west and Smith Point County Park to the east. But in between lie 20 miles of island on which there are no bridges, no paved roads and no cars aside from a limited number of four-wheel-drive vehicles used by the few year-round residents during the winter. But of course, no cars and no roads doesn't mean that Fire Island has no people. Just 45 miles from New York City, Fire Island has served as a summer resort for over 100 years, and in that time some 17 very different summer resort communities have grown up on the island. Best known, perhaps, is the gay community of Cherry Grove and the various swinging singles communities where "groupers" team up to rent beach cottages on a rotating schedule. But there is also the stodgily respectable Point O'Woods, which has erected an eight-foot-high chain and barbed wire fence to keep the riffraff out, and such wholesome family communities as Saltaire and Seaview. In fact, there is a Fire Island community to suit just about every (prosperous) lifestyle, and those who can't afford to buy or rent a place can come for the day. With an estimated 15,000 people living in the island's 1,500 private homes and as many as 30,000 day-trippers joining them on peak summer weekends, Fire Island can be a very crowded place.

Fire Island might have succumbed to its own popularity and become lined with beach cottages from one end to the other had it not been declared a National Seashore in 1964. (Another big threat to the island came from New York State Parks Commissioner Robert Moses, who in 1962 nearly pushed through his dream of constructing a four-lane highway running the length of the island, supposedly as an anchor to the shifting sands. Islanders rushed to the defense of their unpaved paradise and saw that the idea was scrapped.) The National Seashore, administered by the National Park Service, comprises all of the island between the two parks at its east and west ends; the resort communities, technically inside the National Seashore, retain control over most of their own affairs and have been allowed to continue to grow and develop, so long as new houses are single-family dwellings and built within the boundaries set in 1964. (The same situation obtains at the Cape Hatteras National Seashore in the Outer Banks of North Carolina; see the Ocracoke entry.) But outside the communities, particularly east of Point O'Woods, there remain long stretches of open land preserved in its wild state. The eight miles from Smith Point West to Watch Hill at the island's east end was designated a wilderness area by Congress in 1980, the only such area in New York state. Another precious feature of the National Seashore is the Sunken Forest (described below) at Sailors Haven.

Although the National Seashore was created with the aim of "conserving and preserving…certain relatively unspoiled and undeveloped beaches, dunes, and other natural features," there have been complaints that it is not doing enough to protect the island's character from residential development; whatever the validity of these complaints, the National Seashore has at least done *something* to protect and preserve Fire Island. Thanks to the National Seashore, we can turn our backs on the frantic sun- and body-worshipping "scene" for which Fire Island has become famous and wander freely amid the flickering shade of the Sunken Forest or hike down the miles of untouched wilderness beach. It is strange and wonderful that pristine wilderness and densely packed resort villages share the same narrow strip of sand.

Barrier Island Formation

From the air, from the water, and most particularly when you are on one of them, barrier islands are unmistakable. Their narrowness, their long straight lines, their sand, and the way they parallel the mainland coast set them apart from other islands. They really do look like chalk lines drawn just off shore down the length of the continent from New Jersey to North Carolina. Fire Island has the distinction of running east-west instead of north-south like most East Coast barrier islands, and of paralleling an island instead of the mainland. But otherwise, it is a perfect representative of its island type. It offers the special exhilaration of having ocean and bay at its front and back doors, so close you feel you can also straddle the island and stand with a foot in each.

For islands so common and so easily identified, barrier islands remain something of a mystery to science. We still don't really know how they got there. The theory that has gained most credence recently is that the islands were formed some 4,000 to 6,000 years ago, or about 6,000 years after the recession of the last glacier. As water levels rose, the ocean pushed up sand and sediment to form the barrier beaches of the East Coast and then broke through these sandy deposits to create the sounds and lagoons that make them islands. The action of waves, storms and the continuing rise in ocean levels together are pushing the barrier islands closer to the mainland. According to some scientists, Fire Island will eventually merge with the South Shore of Long Island. (Others say that the same forces that are pushing Fire Island northward are pushing Long Island as well.)

The Sunken Forest

Barrier islands do not usually contain forests, but Fire Island has two natural conditions that have permitted a maritime forest to grow: shelter from the salt spray and sufficient fresh water to support tree growth. Rain is the sole source of this freshwater supply; over the centuries it has collected in a natural well—or lens—as deep as 130 feet, which floats on top of the denser, surrounding sea water and keeps it from intruding. On few other barrier islands has such a large supply of fresh water collected, which is why the Sunken Forest is so rare a feature. Some visitors have supposed from the name that the Sunken Forest is below sea level, a notion that seems to be supported by the presence of bogs and pools of water scattered on the forest floor. These are actually the top of the freshwater lens that reaches ground level in very low-lying areas.

Inside the Sunken Forest on Fire Island.

Although the forest floor is a few feet above sea level, the forest canopy is below dune level and thus hidden from the shore. The extraordinary feature of the canopy is its uniformity of height. There are a number of different varieties of trees in the forest, among them the evergreen American holly, the dominant tree, sassafras, tupelo, red oak, red maple and shadblow. But strangely, nearly all the trees rise to the same height, about 38 feet. Any growth that reaches higher than this loses the protection of the dune and will be swiftly shorn away by the salt winds (the one exception is the salt-tolerant red cedar, which protrudes above the canopy in places). You can actually stand on top of the secondary dune and look down at the green carpet of forest treetops that rolls out at your feet. The Sunken Forest, though a mere 300 years old, is a climax forest, which means that it will not be succeeded by another forest type. The oldest holly tree in the forest has been dated back to 1804, the oldest sassafras specimen to 1880.

Descending from the dune into the forest is like passing through the portal to a twilight fairly land. The forest trees are delicate and lacy, their shorn-off tops extend laterally like leafy umbrellas, and flecks of light fall on the undergrowth of catbrier, ferns, poison ivy, sarsaparilla and moss. Characteristic birds of the forest include catbird, yellow-bellied sapsucker, black-capped chickadee, yellowthroat, eastern wood pee-wee and brown thrasher. Among the prominent mammals are Virginia white-tailed deer (the Fire Island herd is estimated at 500), red fox, cottontail rabbit, long-tailed weasel and mice—and there are also hognose snakes, black racers and Fowlers toads slithering or hopping on the forest floor.

Precious and magical as it is, the Sunken Forest very nearly fell to developers' bulldozers in the late 1950s. A group of private individuals from the Point O'Woods community down the beach intervened just in time, buying up the land and holding it as a wildlife preserve. When Fire Island became a federally protected National Seashore, the National Park Service took over management of the Sunken Forest. The Park Service put up a mile-and-a-half-long boardwalk trail through the forest, which protects the fragile forest plants and thin layer of topsoil from being trampled and protects walkers from poison ivy, as common in the forest as it is everywhere on Fire Island. The easiest access to the Sunken Forest is from Sailor's Haven, where the Park Service maintains a marina and visitor's center.

History

Before the age of vacationing dawned after the Civil War, America's white settlers had little use for barrier islands, and Fire Island was no exception. The English colonists who came down from Massachusetts and Connecticut to settle eastern Long Island in the 17th century (the western end of the island was in the hands of the Dutch, who had made New Amsterdam their stronghold on Manhattan Island) regarded Fire Island as a wasteland, fit for grazing cattle, harvesting salt hay and not much else. As late as 1850 the island was virtually unpopulated. Fearful legends had attached themselves to Fire Island over the centuries. The island was supposed to be haunted by ghosts. Pirates used the barrier beach as a hiding place for treasure in the late 17th and 18th centuries; and treasure-hunters have actually dug up pots of gold in the vicinity, some of it supposedly the loot of Captain Kidd. "Wreckers" were believed to have lured ships into breaking up on the island by setting beacon fires on the beach. (Some claim this is the origin of the island's name; others say that "fire"is a corruption of the Dutch word "vier" meaning four, the number of inlet islands drawn on certain 18th-century charts; still others insist it was a misprint for "five," the number of islands that dotted Great South Bay in the late 17th century.) Originally, the island seems to have been valued chiefly by shore whalers, who set up winter whale watching stations on the coast from the mid-17th to the mid-18th centuries. (The fires that these whalers kept going for days as they boiled down the blubber in try pots is another possible source of the island's name.) By 1750, the local waters had been fished out and shore-whaling ceased (for more about whaling, see the Nantucket entry).

For a tract of land so little valued, Fire Island has a remarkably complex history of ownership. The first owner of note was William Tangier Smith, a page at the court of King Charles II and for a time lieutenant governor of Tangier, who arrived in the New World in 1686 and acquired the island from the Indians in 1693. Fire Island was divided between Smith's oldest son (who got the western end) and his younger sons (who got the eastern), and in 1789 a descendant of the oldest son sold off his portion to "twenty yeoman of Brookhaven" who held the land in common. Starting in 1845,

David S.S. Sammis, Fire Island's first resort developer, began buying up shares from the Brookhaven families, and by 1855 he felt he owned sufficient interest in the commonly held land to take 120 acres and erect a hotel on it. This was the rambling Surf Hotel, which stood on the site of the present-day community of Kismet, east of the lighthouse. After years of fighting among the shareowners, who wanted to continue to pasture their cattle on the dunes, and Sammis, who wanted the beasts kept away from his guests, one of the shareowners challenged Sammis's title to the land and took him to court. The case dragged on for seven years, until in 1878 all of Fire Island from the lighthouse to Long Cove was divided up into 78 parcels. Wrangling continued into the 1920s, but the Great Partition held.

It was this partition that opened the way to the development of the summer home communities. The first was Point O'Woods, which began in 1894 as a summer

A boardwalk through the salt marsh on the bay side of Fire Island near Sailor's Haven.

gathering place for the Chautauqua Assembly, a group promoting cultural and educational summer activities that grew out of the religious revival movement of the Methodist Episcopal Church. When the Assembly fell into debt, two summer people formed the Point O'Woods Association, which assumed ownership of the property. Point O'Woods is still owned by the Association: Members, who must have children in order to join and are rigorously screened before getting approval, lease their homesites from the association (though they own their homes). The communities of Oakleyville, Lonelyville and Ocean Beach soon followed, and by the 1920s, most of today's 17 communities were in place, the majority of them rising on the western section of the island. Homosexuals arrived on Fire Island in the 1920s and '30s, and in time came to dominate the communities of Cherry Grove and Fire Island Pines. During the 1960s and '70s, the Fire Island gay rituals became notorious: the beach cruising, the tea dances and drag shows. It was quite a scene, and it gave the whole island its risqué reputation. Celebrities who have visited Cherry Grove include W.H. Auden, Christopher Isherwood and Greta Garbo.

Architecturally, Fire Island is a grab bag: The homes in Point O'Woods are genteel, sober and either old or old-fashioned looking; Dunewood, at the opposite end of the design spectrum, has been dubbed "Levittown-by-the-Sea;" in Fire Island Pines, Seaview and Saltaire the little old beach bungalows have been greatly overshadowed by elaborate modern and post-modern confections of glass and wood, beach mansions that cost a mint and look it. Different as they are in style and lifestyle, all of the communities share a kind of never-never land aura due to the absence of cars and roads. Grown-ups become children again as they transport luggage in little wagons and pad down boardwalks and sandy paths to do their errands or go to the beach, tennis courts, boat slips or parties. The ubiquitous sand, the ocean and bay waters less than half a mile apart, the impermanence of the sandy land that is always blowing and washing away—all of these contribute to the feeling that Fire Island is not part of the "real world," is not even really terra firma. On this island, without much human history or industry, one is free to pursue one's pleasures.

There is, however, one major threat to the pursuit of pleasure on Fire Island, the threat posed by the weather. Barrier islands are the land areas most vulnerable to storms and hurricanes, and Fire Island suffers major storm damage on the average of once every seven years. Most memorably awful have been three hurricanes: that of September 23, 1938, which carried off 265 Fire Island houses, nearly flattening Saltaire and Cherry Grove and eroding vast areas of beach; the Ash Wednesday storm of March 7, 1962, a severe northeaster that tore down over 100 Fire Island houses and damaged 130 others; and hurricane Gloria of 1985, which ripped porches and roofs off many island homes, including that of fashion designer Calvin Klein.

The very narrowness, sandiness and impermanence that make Fire Island such a delightful playground for people also make it the fragile plaything of nature. Our 17th- and 18th-century ancestors knew better than to build their homes on exposed barrier islands like Fire Island and left the land open for cattle and salt hay; with every big storm, nature reminds us of the wisdom we have forgotten.

LIBERTY ISLAND

Area: 12 acres.
Population: 5 year-round (National Park Service personnel).
Location: New York Harbor, 1.5 miles from Manhattan's Battery Park.
Access: By passenger ferry from Battery Park in Manhattan (call 212-269-5755) and Liberty State Park in Jersey City, New Jersey (from April to November only; call 201-435-9499).

It is a monument to rival the seven wonders of the ancient world. It is a symbol of one of the sacred truths on which our nation is founded. It is an image that retains its pure, ennobling splendor despite a century of commercial reproduction. The Statue of Liberty—or Liberty Enlightening the World, to use her formal name—is without question the grandest, most famous work of man to grace any Eastern island. That the statue rises, indeed towers, from a tiny island in New York Harbor magnifies her grandeur and exalts the power of her symbolism. The island location makes the statue inviolable, as liberty itself is supposed to be. The island makes the visit to Liberty like a pilgrimage to a shrine. The crossing of the water, to the poetic-minded, is a symbolic voyage, a passage from the ordinary world to the realm of the spirit, a reenactment of the crossings of immigrant ancestors whose first vision of the New World was the New Colossus, as the poet Emma Lazarus called her. On a more practical level, the island location ensures that the sight-lines to Liberty will always be open from all points in the harbor. When the statue was set on her pedestal in 1886, her torch, rising to 305 feet above sea level, was the highest point on the New York skyline. But in the succeeding century, the skyscrapers of lower Manhattan have grown up like a gigantic, fantastically mutated forest. Liberty would have been lost had she been planted among them. Her island home keeps Liberty free.

Size is essential to the impression the Statue of Liberty makes, and to appreciate that impression, it is worthwhile knowing some of the statue's vital statistics. Liberty is a stern, forward-gazing woman who stands 151 feet and one inch high from heel to torch. Garbed in flowing Roman robes, she holds her 42-foot-long right arm aloft and in her right hand grasps a 21-foot-high torch. (When the statue was restored between 1984 and 1986, a new "flame" of solid copper gilded with gold plate was set in place on the torch.) Her left hand holds a tablet on which is written July 4, 1776 (the numbers in Roman numerals). Liberty is newly liberated, for she is shown stepping free of broken shackles, and she is Liberty universal and triumphant, for she wears a diadem with seven rays, repre-

The Statue of Liberty, rising from the star-shaped ramparts of Fort Wood on Liberty Island. (Courtesy of the New York Convention and Visitors Bureau.)

senting the seven continents and seven seas. Her head measures 17 feet and three inches from chin to top and 10 feet across, each eye is 2.5 feet wide, her mouth is three feet wide and her nose is 4.5 feet long. The immense statue is hollow, its outside skin made of more than 350 sheets of copper hammered by hand to .09370 of an inch thick (about the width of a silver dollar); the total weight of the copper skin and the inside iron skeleton and support framework is 225 tons. Liberty stands on an 89-foot-tall pedestal made of granite sheathing an inner core of concrete. The statue's pedestal in turn rests on a 53-foot-tall foundation, and the foundation is set atop the walls of Fort Wood, which predates the statue. In order to ascend from ground level to the crown of the statue, one must climb 354 steps, with 154 steps rising through the statue itself. (Much to the regret of adventurous children, the climb up the raised right arm to the little platform at the base of the torch has been closed since 1916; structurally, the right arm has always been the weakest part of the statue.)

Liberty was beautiful when she was born, and time has been kind to her. Over the years, her reddish-brown copper skin has acquired a patina of softest, palest green, and in the recent restoration the black blotches were removed from Liberty's face. Today, we are privileged to behold Liberty as fair and as sound as she was when she

Liberty's head measures 17 feet and 3 inches from chin to top and 10 feet across; each eye is 2.5 feet wide; her mouth is 3 feet wide and her nose is 4.5 feet long. (Courtesy of the New York Convention and Visitors Bureau.)

was set in place in 1886. An instant success with the American public, Liberty has soared ever higher in popularity since her grand centennial celebration and reopening on July 4, 1986. In the year following that much-publicized event, 3.3 million visitors ferried out to Liberty Island (the high water mark before that was 1.8 million visitors in 1981). The enthusiasm for Liberty is still going strong. On a summer Saturday or Sunday as many as 20,000 people visit the statue; and even in the depths of November, the wait to climb up to the crown can be three hours long. Overwhelming numbers figure in every aspect of this monument. Waiting in the company of so many others in the shadow of so immense a work, shuffling slowly, person by person, closer and closer to the portal at the pedestal's base, one cannot but be awed and humbled by the experience of Liberty.

History

Before the statue shared its name and its glory with the island on which it stands, the 12-acre speck of land in New York Harbor's Upper Bay was called Bedloe's Island. It was a rather obscure little outpost with a checkered and not terribly noteworthy past. The Indian name for the island was Minissais (lesser island), the colonists dubbed it Great Oyster Island, and then it acquired the name Bedloe's from its first white owner, Isaac Bedloe, a farmer of Dutch origin who bought it in 1667. At various times in the 219 years between Bedloe's and Liberty's occupation, the island was home to a farm, a pesthouse, a gallows, a quarantine station and a dump. The state of New York took over title in 1796 in order to use the island as a fort, and Fort Wood, whose star-shaped ramparts now serve so admirably as the platform for Liberty's pedestal, was constructed between 1808 and 1812.

The history of the statue begins quite separately from the history of the island. The idea for a statue of liberty originated with Edouard René Lefebvre de Laboulaye, a French professor of law and the author of a massive history of the United States, a nation he fervently admired. The monument was to commemorate the centennial of the French-American alliance during the American Revolution. Supposedly Laboulaye brought up the idea in 1865 at a dinner part at his country house—at which the sculptor Frederic-Auguste Bartholdi was a guest. For Bartholdi it became an *idée fixe* from then on. Bartholdi visited the United States in 1871 and scouted out the site for the statue that he had already sketched and made models of. From then on, it was Bartholdi's vision and determination, indeed obsession, that saw the project through to its completion. To raise money for the work, Laboulaye set up the Franco-American Union in 1874 and he formally proposed the idea to the United States. Bartholdi finished a four-foot model of the statue in 1875, the Franco-American Union gave its immediate approval, and money began pouring in, at least in France. Bartholdi set to work at once on the task of translating the four-foot model to the 151-foot-high copper statue. The statue's massive right hand holding the torch of liberty was shipped to Philadelphia for America's Centennial Exhibition, and this got the American fund-raising campaign underway.

The fund-raising proceeded more rapidly in France than in America. There, the $400,000 (approximately two million francs) needed for the building of the statue had been gathered by 1880. But the United States, which was responsible for the design and financing of the pedestal, was unable to come up with the necessary $300,000 until 1885, and only then because Joseph Pulitzer used his newspaper, the *New York World*, to launch a final, frantic fund-raising drive. Richard M. Hunt, the architect appointed to design the pedestal, altered his design to make it smaller and cheaper, and the work on the pedestal was finally finished in April 1886. The statue itself was already at hand—it had been shipped to New York the previous May in 214 crates stowed aboard the French ship *Isere*. The work of riveting the molded copper sheets of the statue onto the ingenious wrought iron skeleton designed by Gustave Eiffel (designer of the Eiffel Tower) commenced in July 1886, and finally, on October 28, 1886, a day of fog and drizzle, President Grover Cleveland dedicated the statue before a crowd of one million.

The American people immediately took Liberty to their hearts, and among her most fervent devotees were the immigrants, the millions of new Americans who sailed by the "Mother of Exiles" on their way to the immigration station on neighboring Ellis Island. In the year the statue was dedicated, 334,203 immigrants entered this country, and between 1892 and 1954, some 12 million immigrants were processed on Ellis Island on their way to new homes in the United States. The Statue of Liberty and Ellis Island have become linked symbols of the freedoms of the New World—the statue representing the spiritual aspect of these freedoms and Ellis Island their more practical and, for some, bitterly disillusioning side. Since 1984, the immigration station at Ellis Island has been undergoing total renovation, and it is scheduled to reopen as a museum in 1989.

Although she was cherished by the American people, Liberty was rather neglected by the American government. There was no official machinery for caring for such a monument, and the statue was passed from one federal agency to the next—from the Lighthouse Board to the War Department in 1901, and then to the National Park Service in 1933. The statue was declared a national monument in 1924. Despite their enthusiasm, the visiting public did not treat the monument kindly: They defaced the inside of the statue with graffiti and littered the island with peanut shells. In 1916, a new torch designed by Gutzon Borglum (who went on to design the monument to the presidents at Mount Rushmore) replaced the original Bartholdi light, which shone but feebly; Borglum's torch, made of amber-tinted glass and illuminated by 15 500-candlepower, gas-filled lamps, did indeed shed a more powerful light, but it was badly flawed in

Liberty, with the skyscrapers of lower Manhattan rising across the harbor. (Courtesy of the New York Convention and Visitors Bureau.)

its design. The joints between glass and copper leaked, and in time the torch was corroded beyond repair. During the 1984-86 restoration, the Borglum torch was taken down and replaced by a completely new torch with a solid copper flame gilded with layers of gold leaf. The Borglum torch is now on display in the statue's ground-level lobby.

The torch was not the statue's only structural flaw. Inside, the iron skeleton was steadily rusting away, in part because the statue was unheated and thus always damp. A major overhaul undertaken in 1938 cleaned the inside of the statue, attended to the weakening of platforms and stairs, repaired some of the spikes in her crown, but left the iron supports alone. The job of replacing the iron ribs and flat bars with supports of stainless steel was done during the 1984-86 renovation. At this time, the support to the statue's right arm was also strengthened.

The island on which Liberty stands has also had a few alterations over the years. The Army, which had maintained some of the facilities of Fort Wood after the statue went up over the fort's ramparts, finally pulled out of Bedloe's Island in 1937, and the National Park Service then took over the jurisdiction for the entire island (the Park Service had administered the two acres occupied by the statue since 1933). The last of the Fort Wood buildings were not cleared away until after World War II, when Congress set aside $110,000 to spruce up the island, re-landscape and build a new seawall and new pier. In 1956, Bedloe's Island was officially named Liberty Island after its most famous resident. The statue is not, however, the island's only resident. Today, there are five National Park Service workers and their families living in a cluster of buildings at the west end of Liberty Island. When the final ferry of the day carries off the last of the visitors, these five residents have the island and its statue to themselves.

Visiting the Monument

Most of the two to three million visitors a year who ferry out to Liberty Island come with the intention of ascending as high as they can inside the statue. As visitors approach the base of the monument they are divided into two lines—one for the 354 steps that lead up to the statue's crown and one for the elevator that rises 10 stories to the top of the pedestal. The waits on either line can be daunting: When I visited the statue on a recent sunny November Saturday, the wait to climb the steps was nearly three hours, and the wait for the elevator over an hour and a half. For some, the thrill of gazing down on New York Harbor from the little windows set into the statue's crown or from the balcony at the top of the pedestal is well worth the hours of standing and shuffling closer. (The thrill is not without risk, for in the summer months, five people a day on average faint

The celebration of the Statue of Liberty's centennial and the reopening of the restored statue on July 4, 1986. (Courtesy of the New York Convention and Visitors Bureau.)

from waiting in the sun and climbing the stairs.) Those who have less patience, time or strength may prefer to limit their visit to the monument's museum exhibits and the promenade on top of the old Fort Wood ramparts. (You still must wait on one of the two lines to get inside the statue's lobby, but once you've entered, you can explore the museums without any further delay.)

The Statue of Liberty exhibit at the second level of the base was installed during the 1984-86 restoration; it has exhibits on the history of the statue, its fabrication and restoration, as well as hundreds of replicas and models. As of this writing, the

American Museum of Immigration, which used to occupy the next level up, is being dismantled and many of its exhibits are being transferred to the Ellis Island Immigration Museum in the main building at Ellis Island, which is slated to open in the fall of 1989. Exhibits include maps, photos, filmstrips, tape-recorded interviews, dioramas and a variety of artifacts that together tell the great story of the peopling of the United States by immigrants from all over the world. At the base of Liberty's pedestal there is a promenade with excellent views out to the harbor, and, if you crane your head back, you see the statue shooting right into the sky.

Liberty is thrilling even for those who never set foot on her island. To glimpse her from the sky out the window of an airplane or, better yet, to stand on the deck of a homebound ship and see her "ris[ing] out of the ocean on a pedestal of petrified waves," as the exiled Russian write Maxim Gorki put it, is enough to set one shivering with patriotic awe. The Statue of Liberty symbolizes what is finest about America, and whatever one thinks about what we have done with our liberty, one finds oneself responding to the statue with the wide-eyed zeal of childhood. The Statue of Liberty, a monument that all can love and that offends no one, has transformed the former Bedloe's Island from fortress to a secular shrine. No Eastern island claimed by man has been put to better use.

ELLIS ISLAND

Area: 27.5 acres.
Population: 0.
Location: New York Harbor, 1 mile from Manhattan's Battery Park.
Access: By passenger ferry from Battery Park in Manhattan (call 212-269-5755) and Liberty State Park in Jersey City, New Jersey (from April to November only; call 201-435-9499); and by shuttle ferry from Liberty Island.

If Liberty Island with its colossal statue stirs the heart to celebrate all that is grand and noble in our democracy, Ellis Island, Liberty's sister island just half-a-mile away in New York Harbor, arouses more complicated emotions and a more troubling chain of associations. For 62 years, from 1892 to 1954, Ellis Island served as the processing

Immigrants traveling in steerage arrived by the millions in New York City in the first decades of the 20th century. The Ellis Island Immigration Station, the nation's busiest, processed approximately 12 million immigrants between 1892 and 1954. (Library of Congress)

center for approximately 12 million immigrants to the United States. On this 27.5-acre island, boatloads of refugees from all over the world were unloaded and the newcomers inspected and documented, tested and in some cases renamed and, if they failed the inspection, detained, observed and retested before being permitted to pass on to the New World. Ellis Island served as the "golden door" that Emma Lazarus writes of in "The New Colossus," her poem for the Statue of Liberty.

For most, the golden door swung open after several hours of processing. But for about 20%, the door remained shut for days or weeks while the bureaucracy of immigration ground its rusty gears. About 2% of the immigrants never entered the door, but were sent back to the countries they were hoping to escape. For all the immigrants who landed here, Ellis Island was a kind of purgatory, a place of slow, shuffling lines, endless confusion and rumor, a constant din of strange languages, overcrowded and often squalid conditions, sometimes rough or even brutal treatment by guards, and the terror that they would be deported. Though paradise, at least as so many imagined it, lay just across the water, the dim uncertainty of purgatory had to be endured before the boat would take them there. It was an experience that would live in the memories of immigrants with the sharp clarity of trauma.

The peak years for the immigration station at Ellis Island were 1900 to 1915, with 1907 the high-water mark, when nearly 1.3 million immigrants entered the country via this island. (There were a total of 70 stations open to process immigrants at this time, but 90% of them passed through the Ellis Island station.) During the 1920s, quotas were set to limit the number of immigrants from each country, and the crowds on Ellis Island grew sparser and sparser. The Great Hall of the Registry in Ellis Island's main building began to seem like a vast, empty cavern; eventually this and other facilities built to process and detain immigrants were put to other uses, including a hospital, a Coast Guard station and a detention center for the soon-to-be-deported. In 1954, the immigration station was closed, the island abandoned by the federal government. For nearly three decades the buildings decayed and the island drifted into ruin. The rehabilitation of Ellis Island began in 1982 when the federal government formed the Statue of Liberty/Ellis Island Centennial Commission to raise money to restore the statue and the historic buildings on Ellis Island. The restored statue was reopened on July 4, 1986, and the Ellis Island Immigration Museum in the main building is slated to open during the autumn of 1989. The other, smaller buildings on the island will be used as a conference center.

History

When the Dutch controlled New Amsterdam in the 17th century, Ellis Island was known as Oyster Island and Liberty Island as Great Oyster Island. Oyster Island was a mere three acres in size—the additional 24.5 acres that make up today's Ellis Island are landfill dumped there from 1898 to 1905. The island acquired its name from one Samuel Ellis, a Manhattan tradesman who bought it late in the 18th century. New York state bought the island in 1808, and sold it off at once to the federal government for $10,000. During the early 19th century, the government erected Fort Gibson on the island and later used it as a storage place for ammunition and gunpowder.

In 1890, the government realized that Castle Garden (the former Castle Clinton) in Battery Park, which had been in use as an immigration station since 1855, was too small to handle the increasing number of newcomers, and Ellis Island was designated as the replacement. The new station opened in 1892, but a fire destroyed the rambling wooden building in 1897; by a stroke of pure luck, no lives were lost. Three years later Ellis Island's new fireproof main building with its four domed spires was ready to receive immigrants. On December 3, 1990, the *New York Times* described the Ellis Island facilities as "a pleasing addition to the picturesque waterfront metropolis...The main building, situated in the center of the island, is 385 feet in length and 165 feet in width...the four towers at each corner are 100 feet from the ground to the top of the domes. The style is a conglomeration of several styles of architecture, the predominating style being that of the French Renaissance...The spires of the towers are copper-covered, and in the top of each is an observatory from which a splendid view of the harbor and city may be had."

The main building was impressively outfitted with amenities, including roof gardens, a restaurant, laundry, beds for 600 and showers for 200 (these facilities were expanded several times). The great hall of the registry was on the second floor of the main building, and there was an observation gallery from which visitors could look down on the immense line of immigrants that was present during the station's peak years. Later, two hospitals were built on the newly created sections of the island. (The landfill sections, originally separate islands known as islands #2 and #3, were subsequently joined together by causeways.)

The new facility at Ellis Island, built at a total cost of $1.2 million, was without question an improvement over the old, but the corruption that had plagued the station's administration from the start was not suppressed, and overcrowding became a more and more serious problem as the tide of immigrants swelled in the first years of the new century. Those who landed on Ellis Island from 1900 to 1902 were routinely cheated by moneychangers, forced to bribe inspectors to clear their passage, and fed under appallingly unsanitary conditions. But in 1902, President Theodore Roosevelt appointed William Williams the new commissioner of immigration for New York, and Williams moved quickly to clean up the administration of Ellis Island. Williams also insisted that both government workers and the staff of the various concessions on the island treat the immigrants with kindness and consideration. He replaced the concessionaires in charge of food, moneychanging and baggage handling with less corrupt outfits, and cleaned up and relandscaped the island. Williams served as commissioner from 1902 to 1905 and again from 1909 to 1913.

Processing the Arrivals

The new Ellis Island station was built to receive as many as 5,000 immigrants a day, but in the peak year of 1907, when 1,150,000 immigrants passed through Ellis Island, there could be twice that number. Some immigrants during this period had to wait up to four days on their anchored ships before being ferried to Ellis Island to join the long line leading up to the canopied entrance to the main building's baggage room. The immigrants were directed to deposit their possessions in the baggage room, and then the processing began. As they moved up the staircase leading to the registry room on the second floor, doctors (unbeknownst to the immigrants) were watching from above to see if they were strong enough to ascend without difficulty. At the top of the stairs, they were divided into lines and subjected to a more thorough medical examination. According to an immigration regulation passed in 1891, "all idiots, insane persons, paupers or persons likely to become a public charge, persons suffering from a loathsome or dangerous contagious disease" as well as convicted felons, polygamists, and persons unable to pay for their passage were to be barred entrance to the country. The Ellis Island doctors would scrutinize all immigrants for signs of the medical conditions, and if they found one, the doctors would initial the immigrant's shoulder in chalk—B for back, H for heart, X for mental retardation—and send the person off for further inspection. Those who failed the medical were sent to the hospital for treatment, and if they recovered they were permitted to complete their processing and enter the country. In 1909, of the 1,506 babies treated for infectious disease at the Ellis Island hospital, 205 died.

The processing of immigrants on Ellis Island included a medical inspection, a test for mental fitness, and questions regarding their finances and employment prospects. About 2% of the immigrants failed and were sent back to their country of origin. (National Archives)

Those who passed the medical exam were sent on to the main area of the registry room where they waited in another line for the legal aspect of their processing. Once they reached an inspector, the immigrants would be asked a series of questions concerning their prospects for employment in this country, their ability to pay for the trip to their final destination, their ability to read and write. The questioning period usually lasted no more than three minutes, and about 80% of the newcomers got through. This concluded the official part of the processing. From the registry, the approved immigrants went back downstairs and made arrangements for the final leg of the journey to their new homes in America. Many contacted relatives, by postcard or telegram, and all exchanged their foreign currency for American money (often getting cheated in the process). Various social service agencies were stationed in this area to help immigrants with the details of travel arrangements and contacting relatives. Immigrants who planned to go West bought train tickets at the Ellis Island ticket office; those planning to settle in New York City took a government ferry over to Manhattan. They were now free to begin their new lives in the United States.

In most cases, immigrants passed through Ellis Island in a matter of hours. Those who failed the medical or legal exam, however, were detained on the island until their problems could be resolved. Most detained immigrants were waiting for money or for relatives to contact them, and seldom did they wait longer than two weeks. During the period of detention, the immigrants received free housing, food and medical care, although in the peak years the dormitories and hospitals were terribly overcrowded. The worst of the concessionaires served the immigrants nothing more than prunes and bread, but when a more humane caterer held the food contract, the detained immigrants ate rather well. While they waited on Ellis Island, the immigrants could exercise on the roof gardens and let their children play in the playground. There was little else to do to pass the time.

Even those who passed through Ellis Island without a hitch were often traumatized by the experience. In the first-hand accounts and reminiscences that have come down to us, immigrants speak of abusive guards, filthy conditions, the fear and confusion that they experienced as they waited on endless-seeming lines. Some say they were herded like cattle, others compare the experience to the Day of Judgment. In the early years of the 20th century, a number of writers published exposés of the conditions that arriving immigrants encountered on Ellis Island and in their first years in this county; these accounts include Broughton Brandenburg's *Imported Americans* and Edward Steiner's *On the Trail of the Immigrant.*

The flood of immigrants slackened considerably during World War I, and once America entered the war, Ellis Island was taken over by the military as a hospital for wounded soldiers. After the war, the Immigration Service resumed its work on the island, but in 1921, the government pushed through the first immigration quotas and the number of arrivals on Ellis Island dropped from 560,971 in 1921 to 209,778 in 1922. During the '30s, the immigration station stood largely empty, its buildings used primarily to detain rejected immigrants before deportation. The once jam-packed registry was converted into a recreation hall in the late 1940s, and in November of 1954, when the last detainee was sent back to his country, the immigration station was officially closed.

The Ellis Island Immigration Museum

Interest in restoring the immigration station on Ellis Island and opening it to the public as a museum dates back to 1963, when the National Park Service first proposed that the island be incorporated into a historic and recreational area that would also include the Statue of Liberty and Liberty State Park in New Jersey. Two years later, when Ellis Island was made part of the Statue of Liberty National Monument, the Park Service took over official jurisdiction of the island. But the Park Service lacked the funds to undertake any restoration work beyond stabilizing the already seriously decayed buildings, and there was no consensus on what other sort of work might be done. In 1976, the Park Service was granted sufficient money to clean up the island and open it to visitors; the buildings, although not restored, were refitted with utilities, relieved of most of the debris that had accumulated since 1954 and staffed with guards.

The restoration project that is nearing completion now got underway in 1982, when the Statue of Liberty-Ellis Island Centennial Commission was formed and Chrysler chief executive officer Lee Iacocca was named as its chairman. The commission was given the task of raising money from private sources to finance the joint restoration projects, and it succeeded in raising more than $230 million, despite the much-publicized dispute between Iacocca and Secretary of the Interior Donald P. Hodel, a dispute that led to Iacocca's being fired as chairman of the federal advisory commission on the Statue of Liberty and Ellis Island (though not from the private fund-raising commission). Iacocca and the Park Service (which is part of the Department of the Interior) agreed that the Ellis Island main building should be restored and converted into a museum of immigration; the dispute focused on what to do with the former

Admitted immigrants look across the water from the Ellis Island dock to Manhattan Island, the golden land of opportunity that has just been opened to them. (Library of Congress)

hospital and recreation buildings scattered around the south end of the island. Iacocca wanted to turn this section into what he called an "ethnic Williamsburg," but the Park Service has rejected this idea and instead is going ahead with its plan to convert the area into a conference center to be run by a private concessionaire. An earlier plan that incorporated a hotel and marina into the conference center was shelved; although there will be overnight accommodations on the island, they will be limited to participants in conferences. Completion of this facility is slated for 1992, Ellis Island's centennial as an immigration station.

The museum in the main building, however, is to open in the autumn of 1989. It will incorporate some of the exhibits formerly housed at the American Museum of Immigration at the Statue of Liberty's base, and many new features will be added. There will be an oral history room, a library, displays of photographs and objects, maps, exhibits devoted to how the immigrants were processed on the island, and a theater. One eagerly awaited feature of the museum is a computerized genealogical center where individuals can retrieve information about their immigrant ancestors' first journey to America, including the ship their ancestor sailed on, the date of their arrival, their port of origin, and the amount of money they had with them when they arrived at Ellis Island. (As of this writing, more money must still be raised to complete this project.) It is estimated that 100 million Americans, or about 40% of our current population, are descended from immigrants who passed through Ellis Island during its 62 years as an immigration station.

ELLIS ISLAND

The immigration station's vast central registry room, which is 180 feet long with a 58-foot, barrel-vaulted ceiling, is being restored to the way it looked from 1918 to 1924. The registry will have no exhibits but be left empty as a place of contemplation. The baggage room, the dormitory rooms, and the railroad ticket office may also be restored and incorporated into the museum. When the museum is open, visitors will probably be able to retrace the steps that immigrants took as they were processed on Ellis Island. With a total of 100,000 square feet of exhibition space, the museum will be the largest of its kind in America. Very likely the museum in its first decade will receive more visitors than the island received immigrants in its 62 years as an immigration station.

For most of us, the name Ellis Island conjures up an image of the "huddled masses" Emma Lazarus wrote about: long lines of Eastern European peasants and Jews, their faces tense, bewildered with apprehension and hope, their bodies burdened with huge bundles of possessions and overdressed children hanging on their arms. Ellis Island, during its years as an immigration station, was the site of 12 million private trials held on a vast, numbing public stage that Kafka might have designed. That history of Ellis Island is really the history of these trials, a history of personal yearnings, individual emotions, events that made a difference only to ordinary people and their families. The Ellis Island Immigration Museum with its oral history room and its genealogical computer will preserve whatever can be preserved of this most ephemeral type of history. For the rest, the restored buildings, the views across the harbor to the Statue of Liberty and the New York skyline, the ferry ride, and even the long lines that are sure to form at dockside, museum entrance and refreshment stands, will help us imagine the immigrant experience of Ellis Island. Ellis Island's history may not be a history that America is proud of, but it is nonetheless a history worth saving. For the approximately 12 million immigrants who landed here and their 100 million descendants, the experience of Ellis Island touches deeply and intimately on the American history of their family.

THE ISLANDS OF THE MID-ATLANTIC AND CHESAPEAKE BAY

INTRODUCTION

The story of the mid-Atlantic islands is the story of barrier islands. Barrier islands do crop up occasionally on the glaciated coast north of New York—Plum Island north of Boston is a barrier island and so is Drake's Island in southern Maine—but, starting with the south shore of Long Island, barrier islands really take over. Except for gaps at Delaware Bay and Chesapeake Bay, barrier islands run in an almost unbroken chain from New York City down to Miami, Florida.

Though scientists still don't know exactly how barrier islands came into being, any visiting layman can identify a barrier island at a glance. Long, narrow, straight and sandy, barrier islands unspool like tawny threads just off the continent's edge. On their ocean side, their wide, flat sand beaches take the force of the Atlantic breakers; behind the islands are quiet, shallow bays or lagoons, with the tall grasses of a salt marsh frequently growing up at the edges of the land. Seldom wider than a mile and often far narrower, barrier islands support maritime forests only when their dunes are high enough to shelter the trees and their soil is deep enough to trap sufficient fresh water. As the tidal range gets smaller, the islands tend to narrow, as on the Outer Banks of North Carolina. The broader tidal ranges (six to 13 feet) of South Carolina and Georgia, for example, create wider islands, characteristically in the shape of drumsticks. On the barrier islands of the north, the dunes along the ocean beaches are anchored primarily by American beach grass, and behind the dunes grow thickets of bearberry, beach heather, bayberry and beach plum; in the south, the primary dune vegetation changes over to sea oats, and common plants behind the dunes include sand myrtle, silverling and yaupon holly. The dwarf bear oak on northern barrier islands is replaced by live oak on the southern islands. As one moves from north to south, the pines tend to get taller, more spindly of trunk and longer of needle.

Barrier islands are the islands of choice for millions of vacationers because the waters of ocean or bay are never far, the wide sand beaches are great for swimming and sunbathing, and the open, exposed landscape catches every ocean breeze. Not surprisingly, development is swallowing up the Atlantic barrier islands at a clip. According to *Landprints* by Walter Sullivan, the total area of developed land on the barrier islands increased from 90,000 acres in 1950 to 280,000 acres in 1980.

Development has hit the 10 New Jersey barrier islands particularly hard because they are close to major cities and because most of them have been linked to the mainland by bridges or causeways. Island Beach State Park and the Brigantine National Wildlife Refuge protect stretches of the New Jersey barrier islands; but outside of the public lands, beach cottage communities or major resorts have overspread Long Beach Island, Brigantine, Absecon Island (site of Atlantic City), Ludlum Beach, Seven Mile Beach and Wildwood. The barrier islands and beaches of the Jersey shore have made the news in recent summers for the pollution, hospital waste and dead dolphins that have washed up on their shores—depressing evidence of the perils of fouling the ocean alongside an overdeveloped coast.

INTRODUCTION

Development threatens not only the ecology of these barrier islands but also their very existence. Barrier islands are fragile, dynamic landforms, their sands constantly shifting, their shape and even location changing as wind and tide play over them. As we have learned at enormous cost, building houses on the barrier island dunes is a sure way of hastening erosion. In recent years, scientists have discovered that even such protective measures as snow fencing, sea walls, groins and jetties, far from preserving the barrier islands, may actually be contributing to their demise. The prevailing wisdom now is to let the islands alone, to limit development on the beaches, to let natural beach grass anchor the dunes, to allow the sands to migrate as they have migrated for thousands of years.

Of course such wisdom is not always easy to follow. Every major storm that comes roaring out of the Atlantic gobbles up vast amounts of barrier beach and brings the ocean that much closer to the doorsteps of beach homes, many of which have been destroyed already. It is estimated that the mid-Atlantic barrier beaches are eroding at a rate of between 1.5 and 4.5 feet per year. Hurricanes and northeasters, such as the devastating Ash Wednesday storm of March 7, 1962, have flattened beach communities and claimed lives all along the Atlantic coast in the past and can be expected to do so in the future. Our ancestors knew better than to build their homes on these perilously shifting sands: They used the barrier islands for grazing livestock and set their farmhouses well back from the ocean. Today we are learning the hard way just how foolish our craze for waterfront property can be.

The mid-Atlantic barrier island picture is by no means entirely bleak. The government and private conservation organizations have acted together to save many barrier islands from development and open them as parks. At present, of the 295 barrier islands along America's Atlantic and Gulf coasts, the government has preserved 80 islands, including 15 of the largest islands, as natural areas or national seashores; and 120 islands remain undeveloped by their private owners.

The premier barrier island preserve on the mid-Atlantic coast is Assateague, a 37-mile-long island shared by Maryland and Virginia. Maryland protects its stretch of the island with the Assateague State Park, and the federal government protects the Virginia end with the Chincoteague National Wildlife Refuge. Both ends of the island are bridged to the mainland. Assateague Island is famous for its wild ponies, which travel in two large herds, one at each end. Ponies have been running free on Assateague since Colonial times (some believe that the original ponies swam to the island from shipwrecked Spanish galleons). The roundup and penning of the Virginia herd in July is a colorful event attended by thousands of tourists. Assateague also has a herd of diminutive Sika deer (technically Oriental elk), which were introduced to the island in the 1920s. The island is an important habitat to the endangered piping plover and a major wintering ground for vast flocks of waterfowl, including brant, tundra swan, snow geese, gadwell, American widgeon, oldsquaw, black scoter and bufflehead ducks. Some 307 bird species have been spotted on Assateague Island. Each year, some 1.5 million people visit the Virginia end of the island and 800,000 visit the Maryland end.

The good news for Atlantic barrier islands continues south of Assateague Island down the Eastern Shore of Virginia. Of the 18 major barrier islands situated here, 13 islands are part of the Virginia Coast Reserve, owned by the Nature Conservancy, a private organization dedicated to preserving land for threatened plant and animal species. (The Nature Conservancy has holdings on many other Eastern islands, including Vinalhaven in Maine, Shelter Island in New York, several of the South Carolina Sea Islands, and the Florida Keys.) The total protected area on the Virginia barrier islands comes to about 35,000 acres. None of the islands within the reserve, which encompasses all or parts of Metomkin, Cedar, Parramore, Revel's, Sandy, Hog, Rogue, Cobb, Ship Shoal, Myrtle, Smith, Mink and Godwin, is bridged to the mainland and none is accessible by public ferry; but private boat owners are welcome to sail out to most of them for day use and the Nature Conservancy runs occasional field trips and birding trips out to the islands. Scientists conduct a number of ecological studies on these islands, which have been altered less by man than any group of barrier islands on the Atlantic coast. For more information about visiting the islands or joining a field trip, contact the Nature Conservancy, Virginia Coast Reserve, Brownsville, Nassawadox, Virginia 23413, or call 804-442-3049.

Chesapeake Bay, which cuts up into the East Coast for 200 miles from Virginia's Cape Charles north almost to the Maryland/Pennsylvania border, is the largest estuary on the North American continent. Scores of islands rise out of the vast, shallow bay waters, though *rise* conveys a false impression, for these bay islands sit low to the water, and many are hardly more than marshland. On just about every Chesapeake island that is high enough to keep your feet dry, there is a community of watermen—the people who harvest the Chesapeake's edible marine life. These days, the watermen support themselves mostly from the bay's crabs, for the oysters that they used to dredge up in the winter months have largely succumbed to a mysterious disease known as MSX.

Wild ponies and cattle egret on Assateague Island. (Felice Nudelman)

Most of the Chesapeake islands lie fairly close to the mainland and have been linked to it by bridges. But the bridges have not really altered the character of the watermen communities on Hooper Island, Tilghman Island or Deal Island all that much. Kent Island, in the middle of the bay, is the stepping-stone for the bridges that connect Maryland's eastern and western shores; and the inevitable motels and condos have grown up around the highway that cuts across it.

There are two Chesapeake islands that will never be bridged because they are too far out in the bay. These are Smith and Tangier, both of which are accessible by public passenger ferry. Though they are in different states—Smith in Maryland, Tangier in Virginia—these are sister islands, dominated alike by their Methodist churches and by the waters of the bay. In recent years, both Smith and Tangier have become popular with tourists, who sail out for the day to eat huge seafood lunches, gaze at the bay waters and salt marsh, and eavesdrop on the islanders, whose accents have been traced to the West Country of Elizabethan England. The watermen communities on both islands seem little affected by the influx of tourists, though their numbers have been dwindling steadily since World War II. On Smith Island, the larger and prettier of the two, there is a plan afoot for waterfront condos and a marina, an ominous sign indeed for islands that until quite recently had been practically unknown to the outside world.

SMITH ISLAND

Area: 9 miles long by 4 miles wide.
Population: 550.
Location: Chesapeake Bay, 12 miles from Crisfield, Maryland.
Access: From Crisfield, Maryland, by passenger ferry; trip lasts 40 minutes; phone 301-425-4271 for the *Island Belle II*; 301-425-5931 for the *Captain Jason*.

Smith Island landscape: pier, bank float and salt marsh.

Smith Island, set off from Crisfield, Maryland, by 12 miles of Chesapeake Bay, is unquestionably an island, but just barely land. With an average elevation of two feet and a maximum of five, Smith Island (or islands, for the name covers a small, marshy archipelago) does not so much rise out of the bay as merge with it. Though on a map the islands measure nine miles by four miles, "fast land" (as the islanders call terra firma) is rather scarce here. Long stretches of salt marsh and winding channels of water separate Smith's three communities: Ewell (the unofficial capital and the largest), Rhodes Point (about a mile away down the island's sole connecting road) and Tylerton (accessible from the other two only by boat). Surrounded by water, often submerged in water and penetrated by water in countless creeks, guts, thoroughfares, swashes, drains, Smith also lives on the water. This is Chesapeake waterman country, where nearly every able-bodied man goes out on the bay and takes from it an astonishing number of crabs (and, with the passing years, a more and more disappoint-

Chesapeake Bay

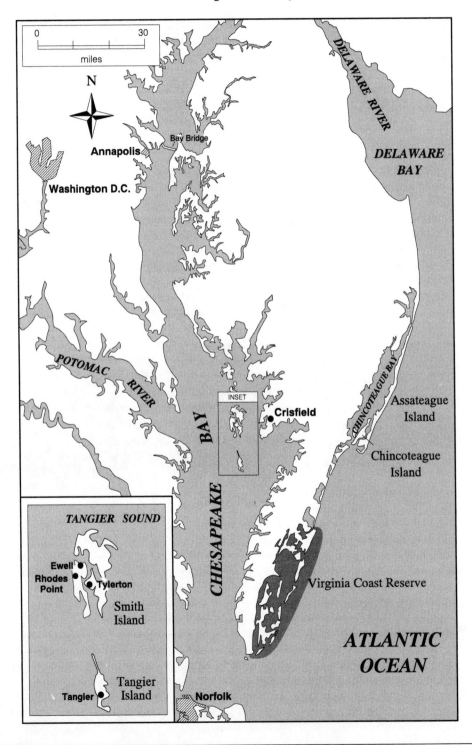

ing number of oysters). The salt waters of the Chesapeake are as necessary to Smith Island as they are inescapable. Smith is an island that harks back to the deepest roots of that word in the Old High German, *auwaland*, meaning something like "watery land."

Perhaps it's this watery quality—and the waterman culture that has grown up from it—that makes Smith Island seem so different, so cut off from the rest of the world. In fact, Smith Island is neither remote, inaccessible or undiscovered. Right on the axis of a semicircle of major East Coast population centers, the island is quite easy to get to on a number of seaworthy (or, rather, bayworthy) passenger ferries, and it is becoming more and more popular with that host of fast-moving tourists known as day-trippers. These days, come 1:15 on a summer afternoon, a good number of them will jump off the ferries in Ewell and commence wandering its narrow, blessedly shaded streets and crowding into the growing number of island restaurants that specialize in, what else?, soft-shell crabs, crab cakes, crab soup and such distinctive Smith Island trimmings as corn pudding and baked tomatoes. And yet despite the tourists, the restaurants, the small fleet of ferries and "cruise boats" that keep visitors circulating, Smith remains very much a place apart: It looks different from the mainland, it feels different, its people act and speak differently, it forces certain differences on its visitors. Smith holds onto its spirit: It is still an isolated island, more so than islands farther out to sea, less populated, less touristed.

Of course there are threats to Smith's spirit, the most serious being the recently stalled proposal to put up 100 condominiums along with 80 pleasure boat slips over at Pitchcroft, a dreamy, reedy jut of land on the outskirts of Ewell. Since Smith has no government, islanders discovered that they were ill-equipped to deal with this threat—but they fought it nonetheless. And, at least for the moment, they have won.

What may yet happen on Smith Island has already happened elsewhere around the Chesapeake, with alarming results. Chesapeake Bay, the largest estuary on the North American continent (its total shoreline measures some 4,000 miles), has already lost a part of its superfecund marine life to pollution. The Chesapeake, as we are learning a bit too late, is not only our largest estuary, but one of the most fragile. The human ecology of bay islands like Smith is just as fragile, and the impact that 100 condos might have on the character of a close-knit human community of 550 is incalculable. Strangely but typically of island politics, the fight against the condos was led by off-islanders and the decision to halt them was made on the mainland. On Smith Island itself, the condo question, though hotly debated, never came to a vote.

For the moment, however brief and however threatened, Smith Island holds onto its traditional character, its culture, and its exceptional beauty. This beauty—in essence a fine accord among landscape, waterscape and village—came as something of a shock to me. I suppose I was expecting the Chesapeake equivalent of Appalachia. What I found instead, on two absolutely stunning October days, was a place of glowing cord grass marshes and silvery views out to the bay; an active waterfront where herons perched on crab shanties and mallards made ripples in the reflections of tilting piers; a village at Ewell of tall, white, neatly kept, peak-roofed frame houses presided over by a stately Methodist church. Make no mistake: This is no Nantucket. Smith Island has not been gentrified. This is a working island, and its beauty is the beauty of the watermen's work—rough, spare, lonely, scaled to the bay and the weather that blows off it. Though houses are trim, harbor scenes picturesque and village roads quaintly narrow and winding, nothing has been prettied up.

The living community here has its own odd ways, some of them a bit unsettling to the day-tripper in search of serene escape from mainland civilization. Each evening what appears to be the entire population of Ewell and Rhodes Point takes to the island road in cars, pickup trucks, motorcycles, mopeds and, if age or engine trouble necessitates, bicycles to cruise around in a prolonged roaring Chesapeake island *passeggiatta*. They all go ricocheting from town to town across the darkening salt marsh, back and forth, back and forth on the single mile of open road. Islanders greet each other, and visitors too, with a wave, a horn toot, a shout, and island kids zipping by may heckle the tourists in a good-humored sort of way. Night descends, the roaring subsides and silence returns to the island—at least until 3 or 4 A.M. when the watermen get up and out on the water in their boats.

In the evening hours, once the *passeggiatta* is winding down, groups gather in Lee Roy Evans and Son General Convenience Store or Ruke's store/restaurant to talk—what else?—crabbing. Eavesdropping visitors, however, may not be able to make out much of the conversations. Smith Islanders, like their neighbors on Tangier and like the "hoigh-toiders" farther down the coast on North Carolina's Ocracoke Island, have their own very distinctive accent, an accent so strong it almost rates as a dialect. On Smith Island oysters are arsters, dredge is drudge, wire is ware, peel is pail, men address each other as "honey" when they want to add emphasis and heap their sentences with double and triple negatives. Islanders tend to soften their speech when they're talking with outsiders ("forcigncrs"), but when they're talking together the accent and idiom grow thick and their words seem to be formed somewhere deep in their throats. If you're eavesdropping and you lose the thread (which is easy to do, since the crabbing business has its own jargon, in which Jimmies are male crabs, sooks breeding females, rank crabs are ready to shed their shells and become softs etc.), you may not be able to pick it up again easily. It's rather like watching an unfamiliar Shakespeare play when the actors start tossing out the puns and verbal flourishes too quickly—a particularly apt comparison, since some linguists believe that the accents of Smith and Tangier islanders are living fossils of the English spoken in England's West Country in the 17th century, with New World waterman jargon thrown in. The theory is that island isolation arrested the speech of the first settlers and preserved it from the changes mainland American English underwent as waves of immigrants washed up on our shores.

Along with its speech, Smith has kept its bloodlines fairly pure: There are only a handful of surnames in the island cemeteries—Evans, Tyler, Bradshaw, Whitelock, Smith, Marshall—and these are the same names islanders bear today. But Smith Islanders worry because there are fewer and fewer members of these old families to carry on the tradition. Not only is the population of the island in decline (from 650 to about 550 in the past 12 years), but the community is getting older and older. The young people go to high school on the mainland, and after school many of them choose to stay on and work in jobs that demand less and reward more than following the water. When the old folks die, more and more of their children are putting the family homes on the market, and more often than not the buyers these days are non-islanders and non-residents. Ewell has many attractive homes dating from the late 19th and early

20th centuries, so there's plenty of raw material to work with. There isn't exactly a Smith Island real estate boom—yet—but house prices are going up and more and more summer people are establishing themselves on the island. Outsiders now outnumber insiders as homeowners at Rhodes Point, and the trend is the same at the two other Smith Island communities.

On other low-lying Chesapeake islands such as Holland and Sharps the communities were forced to leave as fast land drifted away to the rising waters of the bay; on Smith it seems the community itself is drifting away. In another generation, some predict, the island will be without a permanent population.

Tourists on the Island

Smith Island, as Frances Kitching, cookbook author and proprietress of the island's sole (and rather rudimentary) motel, informed me right off the bat, does not have much in the way of tourist attractions. Still, people come in droves to visit, but once they've been here, they tend not to come again. For all its haunting beauty, Smith Island offers very little for its visitors to *do*. There's no good beach for swimming, and even if there were the bay's summer jellyfish population makes swimming a somewhat risky affair. Nor is there a usable park. There is a huge wildlife refuge—the 4,423-acre Glen L. Martin National Wildlife Refuge, established in 1954—that takes up the island's northern half, a crescent of preserved salt marsh that wraps around Ewell, but its surrounding waters are accessible only by private boat and its land is not open to visitors anyway.

Aside from the close-set houses and narrow streets of Ewell, the somewhat shabbier Rhodes Point, the remote and smaller Tylerton (a mere 35 acres of terra firma), the expanse of salt marsh that separates them, their churches, cemeteries, trees and flowers—there are no sights to see. So you eat delicious crab in the island restaurants, stroll or bike from Ewell to Rhodes Point and back, chat with the islanders and eavesdrop on their famous accents. Smith Island has plenty of atmosphere to soak up and it's fascinating in its very strangeness, but this is not a place you'd come to for a week's "getaway" vacation and certainly not for a honeymoon or romantic island idyll. Though Smith Islanders welcome their tourists (and their summer people, particularly those who go to church), they haven't changed a whit for them and neither, in fundamental ways, has their island. As the ferry departs Ewell and pulls into the Big Thorofare leading into the bay, one leaves the islanders to their harvests of crabs and oysters, to their cars and motorcycles, their school, general stores and post offices (one for each community), and to their fierce loyalty to each other, their

The Methodist church and graveyard at Ewell. The Methodist Church has been the dominant institution on Smith Island since the Reverend Joshua Thomas, the "parson of the islands," converted the islanders in the early 19th century.

religion and their island. That is life on Smith Island. As a visitor, one has seen it but one really hasn't touched it.

The Island Past and Present

Smith Island is named for Captain John Smith, famous for leading the first Virginia colonies and for being saved by Pocahontas, and it is with him that the island's recorded history begins. In 1608 Smith set out from the colony at Jamestown (the first English settlement in North America to endure) in search of salt and harborage. He sailed up from the mouth of Chesapeake Bay, "a faire Bay" he called it, "compassed but for the mouth with fruitful and delightsome land." Smith's expedition took him past the island that would later be named for him and he remarked in his ship's log that the surrounding waters were thick with fish. Smith dipped up a skilletful of bay water to examine the marine life more closely and received a stingray sting for his pains. Nonetheless he concluded of the Chesapeake's lowlying islands and shorelines that "Heaven and earth never agreed better to frame a place for man's habitation."

Man's habitation arrived later and in numbers far fewer than Smith's encomium would suggest the island deserved. The early Smith Islanders, who came here in the mid-17th century as religious dissenters from St. Clements Island, are notorious for nothing so much as their lawlessness. They eked out a living from their shallow soil and from the bay (catching mostly fish, since oysters and crabs did not become prized delicacies until later); they drank and hunted and, by all accounts, raised a lot of hell. During the Revolution, the Chesapeake's Eastern Shore was infested with "picaroons," privateers loyal to the crown who raided patriots' tidewater plantations and shipping. Picaroons hid out between raids in the empty marshes fringing the islands and were extraordinarily successful in evading capture. The Smith Island community of Rhodes Point used to be known as Rogues Point for the pirates who lived there.

Remote from the centers of civilization in the days of sailing ships and controlled by men who considered themselves outside the law, Smith Island seemed ungovernable. Religion changed all that. In the early years of the 19th century, Methodism literally took Smith Island (along with the other bay islands and the rest of the Eastern Shore) by storm. There were mass conversions, and the newly awakened religious zeal sometimes bordered on public hysteria. Contemporary accounts speak of a "sudden and spontaneous outburst that...rolled out over the waters," of hordes of repentant sinners falling prostrate "as by an earthquake shock," of shouting and rejoicing and adulation. The lawless reprobates of Smith Island had found the way and they haven't lost it since.

The man who brought the Word to the Chesapeake islands was the Reverend Joshua Thomas, known as "the Parson of the Islands." Thomas, who grew up in poverty on nearby Tangier Island and was converted to Methodism during a Tangier camp meeting, devoted his life to spreading his religion to all the bay islands—Watts, Holland, Spring, Tangier and Smith—that Episcopal ministers and other Methodists had neglected because of the inconvenience of getting there. He sailed his log canoe *The Methodist* all over the bay and left scores of converts in his wake. Methodism settled the islanders down to sober, hardworking, steady lives. The era of the rogue is long gone on Smith and the island watermen are now renowned not for their hell-raising but for their clean living.

Religion continues to be a powerful cohesive force on Smith Island. "The island churches are alive and full of God's love," a sign in front of the Rhodes Points United Methodist Church proclaimed when I visited the island. The islanders I talked to confirmed that this was true. The island's three churches (all Methodist) dominate their communities physically, spiritually, socially and politically. The *New York Times* reports that "Smith Island is about as close to a theocracy as any place in the United States." Smith Islanders sell no alcohol on their island and, though they may raise their voices in argument, they seldom swear. "Lordy" is about as strong as their language gets.

Aside from the Methodist churches, Smith Island has little in the way of public institutions. I asked an islander whether there was a local government and his response was, "What do you mean?" Perhaps my question sounded odd because Smith, which has never become incorporated into Somerset County, has never had a mayor, a board of selectmen, a jail or even local taxes—and most islanders agree that they have no need of such things. "We don't have that much trouble," is how one retired waterman put it. For what trouble they do have, they rely on the church. Islanders do send a representative to the county sewage commission—that's about as far as civic organization goes here. Other communal needs they handle on a voluntary, ad hoc basis.

Smith Island may strike visitors as a backward, clannish, old-fashioned sort of place, but in fact the island is a veritable hotbed of modern technology compared to what it was 40 years ago. Smith had no telephone hookup to the mainland until 1941 (though residents of the three island communities could communicate with each other via a few old-style crank phones as early as 1904); electricity did not arrive until 1949; and before 1940, when the Army Corps of engineers dug deep-water channels leading into the harbors, boats of any size would have to anchor offshore and discharge passengers and cargo into rowboats.

Harvesting the Bay: Oysters and Crabs

Ferry, phones, electricity and, of course, television and tourists have hooked up Smith Island with the mainland and with the late 20th century; pollution, development, competition, chemical fertilizer, disease and population growth have brought the late 20th century to the Chesapeake Bay waters as well. Disease has particularly ravaged the bay's oysters, which used to be the major breadwinning fishery on Smith Island and the bay in general. The oyster killer is a mysterious disease called MSX (for Multinucleate Sphere Unknown) that began spreading up

A bank float at Ewell where hard-shell crabs become the delicacy known as soft-shell crabs. Watermen place the "peelers" (crabs about to shed their shells) in shallow trays, pump water over them, and keep a close eye on them. As soon as the crabs molt, they are snatched out and packed off to market. The Methodist church is in the background.

the bay in 1959. Since then just about the only thing scientists have been able to learn about the disease is that it destroys oyster tissue and that it thrives in waters with higher salinity. A string of drought years in the 1980s has created ideal conditions for MSX by raising salinity levels farther and farther up the bay, and the oystering has fallen off drastically of late. The National Fisheries Institute estimates that in 1956 the Chesapeake supplied half of all oysters harvested in the United States; now that figure is down to one-quarter.

Luckily, MSX has not affected the Atlantic blue crab, which seems to be as abundant as ever in the Chesapeake. According to William W. Warner's superb *Beautiful Swimmers: Watermen, Crabs and the Chesapeake Bay* (a must for anyone interested in any one of these topics and also full of interesting information on both Smith and Tangier Islands), "the Chesapeake has provided more crabs for human consumption than any body of water in the world, great oceans included." And according to Smith Island watermen, the bay between their island and Tangier has the most productive soft crab bottoms in the world. Of course productive waters don't give up their crabs for the asking: You have to know how to catch them, and Smith Islanders are most surely expert at that. Theirs is an expertise born of patience, hard work, long hours, ingenuity (particularly in the design and variety of the boats they use), lore passed down from father to son and a surprising openness to new ideas.

Forty odd years ago, much of the island's crabbing fleet traveled the bay under sail. Crab pots, wire-mesh cages with the look of contraptions that have been around since Adam, really came into widespread use only after World War II. Now most of the islanders are potters, but a few still use trotlines, a primitive but effective technique in which you tie chunks of bait (preferably salted eel) at short spaces along a line, throw the line over the side of your boat, and then after a decent interval, haul the line in over a roller while you use a wire net to dip up the crabs dangling from the bait. Perhaps the *concept* of trotlining is primitive, but the proper execution is anything but. Potters usually work the bay from about 3 A.M. to 6 P.M., and trotliners may go out even earlier. In the high summer months Smith Island watermen catch softs and peelers by scraping. They take their boats into the marshy shallows where eelgrass grows and use scrapes—contraptions made of steel rods and heavy netting—to scoop up masses of eelgrass in which peelers and soft crabs love to hide. The eelgrass clump is deposited on the deck of the waterman's boat, and he picks through it to find the crabs he wants and often creatures he doesn't want as well. It's a bit like a hunt for a buried treasure, and treasure is exactly what soft crabs are to the watermen.

Just as demanding as the catching of the crabs is the handling of the peelers—green and rank crabs (in Eastern Shore idiom) that are ready to shed their shells and become the delicacy we call soft-shelled crabs and waterman call simply softs. Unless they're removed from the water, soft crabs stay soft for only a few hours. In 12 hours they'll have "paper shells," in 24 hours the paper has hardened to a brittle texture known as "buckram" and two days later they're hard again. And while they're without shells they're vulnerable to attack from other crabs, so the peelers and softs need constant monitoring if they're going to make it to market. That's what the raised trays set out on rickety piers with strings of lightbulbs overhead are for—constant monitoring by the watermen and their families. Crabs about to shed (watermen can "read" their condition at a glance and they have names for every stage of the molting process) are set in the tanks (called bank floats or shore floats, even though they aren't really floats, as the old-style shedding pounds were) and water is pumped over them. As soon as the crabs have shed their shells, the watermen (or their wives or children) fish them out in nets and pack them carefully in eelgrass to be shipped off to hungry seafood lovers all over the country. The process is exhausting and laborious, and even with the vigilant monitoring many softs die, but of course those that make it fetch more at market than hard crabs. As Warner points out in *Beautiful Swimmers*, nursing along peelers is a specialty of the watermen of the Chesapeake islands and small Eastern Shore towns. No one else has the patience, the expertise or the abundance of peelers to work with.

The Smith Island family is big, but not as big as it used to be. There are signs that the family is breaking up. The young are moving away from home, the old unable to keep them or lure them back. School enrollment is down. Young couples are having fewer children and having them later in life than their parents did. And, of course, if the Pitchcroft condos ever do go through, it would mean the introduction of 200 or more newcomers into a community of 550. In the face of these threats, the native population that remains on Smith Island holds tightly to its identity, its character, its waterman culture and economy. "We feel we're altogether different from the mainland," one islander said with utter conviction. "Our talking is different, our jokes are different. We depend on the water for everything. If it's not out there you just have to tighten your belt." So far, though the oysters are failing, plenty of crabs are still out there. Belts haven't been tightened too much of late. The watermen can still get by with it. But one wonders. Even if the water continues to provide as it always has, for how many more generations will the waterman hold on to Smith Island?

TANGIER ISLAND

Area: 3.5 miles long by 1.5 miles wide.
Population: 700.
Location: Chesapeake Bay, 14 miles from Crisfield, Maryland.
Access: Year-round passenger ferry service by mailboat from Crisfield, Maryland. Seasonal passenger ferries from Crisfield, Maryland (call 301-968-2338); from Onancock, Virginia (call 804-787-8220); and from Reedville, Virginia (call 804-333-4656).

Rough weather on the Chesapeake off Tangier Island. (Felice Nudelman)

Although Smith and Tangier are separated by a state line, the former falling on the Maryland side and the latter on the Virginia side, the two Chesapeake Bay islands are sisters and the family resemblance is very clear. Both islands lie low to the water and are belted by salt marsh; the people on both islands depend on the bay for their livelihoods, especially the crabs it yields in unfailing abundance. Both islands support long-established, tight-knit communities, communities that have retained the accents and some of the diction of their Elizabethan English forebears. On both islands Methodism took firm root in the 19th century and continues to hold the islanders fast (in addition to the Methodist Church, Tangier also has a New Testament Church). And both islands have entered the modern world rather abruptly as increasing numbers of tourists discover the charms of taking the ferry out for the day, feasting on shellfish and strolling amid quaint old-fashioned homes and picturesque crab shanties.

Tangier is, if anything, the more heavily touristed of the two, perhaps because of its very exotic name, the invention, it is said, of Captain John Smith, who imagined he saw resemblance between the island and the coast of North Africa when he sailed through the Chesapeake in 1608. (Smith Island, which inspired no such flight of fancy, has had to make do with the prosaic name of its discoverer.) Tangier is both smaller and more populous than Smith, and in the summer months, when tourist party boats are coming at the island from three different locations on the mainland, the island can be very crowded indeed. Unlike Smith Island which has three distinct communities separated by expanses of salt marsh, Tangier has a single settlement. To many minds, the little village fails to live up to the island's exotic name. The white clapboard houses are packed in tight together and press close to the road behind an unbroken line of chain link fences (the more picturesque white picket fences were taken down when the road was widened some years back).

Tangier lacks the grace of stately, shaded Ewell on Smith Island; some say it lacks grace altogether. But the tourists don't seem to mind. Some 300-400,000 of them come each year from April to November for the food, for the ferry ride and for the experience of being on a remote island with an odd name and an odd way of life.

Despite the tourists, the oddness persists on Tangier Island. The watermen, here as on Smith Island, go about their business as they have for generations; the

Tangier's Methodist church, the major island institution since the Reverend Joshua Thomas converted his fellow islanders in the early 19th century. (Felice Nudelman)

landbound islanders pick up some extra money from the visitors but otherwise seem untouched by their island's newfound popularity. Tourists have invaded but they haven't conquered Tangier. Though the land is shallow here, roots run very deep.

History

Over the centuries since John Smith first spotted the islands in 1608, Smith and Tangier have developed along very similar lines. White settlers came to both late in the 17th century. On Tangier, the founding father was one John Crockett, who bought a section of the island in 1686 and moved out with other fisherfolk who hailed originally from England's West Country. Today, if you shout the name Crockett on the Tangier waterfront, nearly half the men will probably look up. The early Tangier settlers were, in all probability, watermen, just as the islanders are today; but they were also, it seems, a rough living, lawless, godless lot, who readily turned to piracy as "picaroons" during the American Revolution (see Smith Island entry).

Both Smith and Tangier were considered ungovernable islands of the damned until the early 19th century when the great wave of the Methodist Revival broke over the region. The Reverend Joshua Thomas, "the Parson of the Islands," hailed from Tangier and was converted to Methodism as a young man during one of the early Tangier camp meetings. Thomas devoted the rest of his life to spreading the Word to all the bay islands, traveling from island to island on his sailing canoe *The Methodist*, and he had extraordinary and enduring success. Once they heard the Reverend Thomas preach, the people on Tangier, as on Smith, cast off their lawless ways and settled down to

Abandoned house and family cemetery on Tangier Island. The island's population has declined in recent years, despite its growing popularity with day-trippers. (Felice Nudelman)

live strict, steady lives. The water and the Methodist Church became their guides and have remained so ever since. As one islander put it, "We trust in the Lord for our livings and to keep us safe from storms." Tangier, like Smith, still abides by the old ways of old-time religion: no work on Sunday, no liquor, no swearing, and, between the Methodist Church and the more recently established New Testament Church, just about universal church attendance.

For an island so distant, so small and so different in outlook from the mainland, Tangier has a surprising number of modern conveniences and civic institutions. Tangier, unlike Smith, has a local government with an elected mayor and six-member council and a deputy sheriff appointed by the county. The island school runs from kindergarten through 12th grade, has about 150 total enrollment and graduates about 10 seniors a year. Telephone service is supplied by microwave and there is even cable television on the island. Between harvesting the bay waters and satisfying the hungry tourists, there is plenty of work for islanders to do. But even so, the young are moving off Tangier, just as they are moving off Smith. It's becoming more and more common for the islands' high school graduates to go to college, and once they get a taste of the mainland, they lose their appetites for the old island ways. Tangier's population has dropped steadily in the past 50 years, from about 1,300 people in the early forties, to 900 in the late seventies, to around 700 today. At least there is some consolation on Tangier that most of the young married couples are staying put and having children. On Smith, where the young couples are either selling their homes and moving away or postponing having kids, the situation seems more dire.

Visiting Tangier

The standard visit to Tangier goes something like this: You board a ferry or cruise boat in Crisfield, Maryland, or in Reedville or Onancock, Virginia, and you sit out on the deck with your fellow day-trippers to soak in the sunshine and the salt breeze blowing off the bay. Soon the flat featureless mainland shoreline disappears behind you and you're well out on the silvery bay waters. Before long, Tangier appears as a smudge on the horizon. It too looks flat and nearly featureless from the water. As you approach,

Two young Tangier Islanders on one of the six wooden bridges that cross the Gut. (Felice Nudelman)

you can see that stretches of marsh link together the patches of higher (but never high) solid land. The Tangier skyline consists of a huddle of houses, the steeple of the Methodist church and a radar dish resting on a steel tower. The island sits by itself in the bay. Its closest neighbor is Watts Island, which lost its community as the solid land drifted away.

As you enter the channel leading to Tangier's harbor, you get a good waterside view of the paraphernalia of the crabbing fishery—the pots and tackle, the shanties and shedding floats, the beat-up little wharves and the shallow draft boats. The entrance to the harbor is perhaps the most picturesque sight you will encounter on your island excursion. Once you disembark from the ferry, you have little choice but to follow the crowd up King Street, the main street of Tangier's village, past the Swain Memorial Methodist Church, the post office and the inevitable gift shops selling nautical souvenirs and T-shirts. The destination of most day-trippers and all overnight guests to the island is Hilda Crockett's Chesapeake House, where you can dine sumptuously (if simply) with about 160 fellow tourists on island specialties (crab cakes, corn pudding, pickled beets and clam fritters are standouts). After lunch, you can visit the Tangier Nautical Museum, which has displays on the major island fisheries.

After you've exhausted the possibilities of the village area, you can choose one of six wooden bridges to cross a marshy creek called the Gut. The land rises high enough here to have earned the name of West Ridge (the ridge crests at about five feet above sea level) and there are a few houses planted on the high ground, bigger, grander and more spread out than the houses lining King Street. Beyond them lies the western reach of the bay.

By mid-afternoon, the ferries are waiting to take you back to the mainland. If you choose to stay on (few do), you can linger by the harbor to watch the watermen returning in the late afternoon, hang around while the islanders gather to play dominos and talk crabbing, or tackle another substantial seafood meal. Like it or not, you will be part of the evening parade of beeping scooters and flashing bikes that takes over the island road until sunset. Once it's dark everything quiets down fast. In a few hours, the men will be up again and back on the water. And then, round about lunchtime, fresh boatloads of tourists will be delivered.

The Tangier Islanders have gotten used to their tourists, indeed they have come to rely on them. Like the tides, the tourists ebb and flow quite regularly and predictably, flooding the island in the summer and receding altogether come Halloween. One good thing about the Tangier tourists is that all they usually want of the island is a single day. Tangier is not the kind of place that inspires dreams of returning for retirement or for a protracted summer vacation or a bucolic escape from the "real world." The old homes don't have much potential as summer cottages, and no one has proposed to put up condos here, as they have on Smith. Aside from crabbing and looking after summertime tourists, there isn't much to do on Tangier. Though lots of people come to see the island, no one aside from the watermen really wants to live here. In that regard the Tangier Islanders are lucky. It's reassuring to think that Tangier, no matter how many tourists come out, will always be a waterman's island. No one else really belongs here.

The Outer Banks of North Carolina

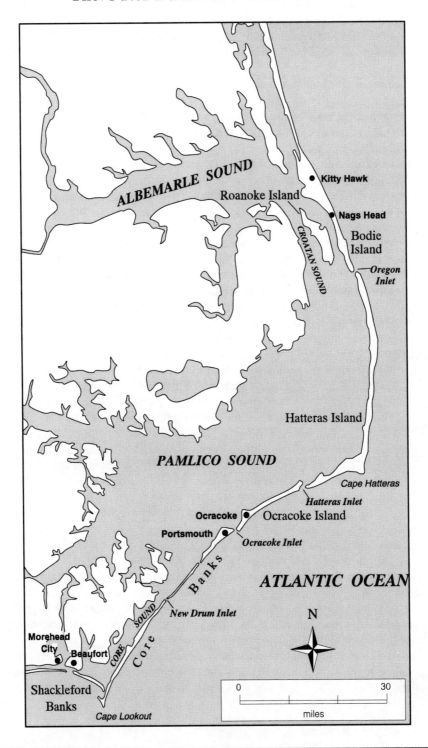

ALBEMARLE SOUND

Roanoke Island

Kitty Hawk

Nags Head

Bodie Island

CROATAN SOUND

Oregon Inlet

Hatteras Island

PAMLICO SOUND

Cape Hatteras

Hatteras Inlet

Ocracoke   Ocracoke Island

Portsmouth

Ocracoke Inlet

ATLANTIC OCEAN

B a n k s

New Drum Inlet

N

CORE SOUND

Core Sound

Morehead City

Beaufort

Shackleford Banks

Cape Lookout

0   30
miles

THE OUTER BANKS OF NORTH CAROLINA

INTRODUCTION

Hanging off the middle of the East Coast like a slender bent arm, the Outer Banks of North Carolina are an exception to the barrier island rule. Instead of running alongside the mainland and staying close to shore, the Outer Banks plunge out into the Atlantic, extending as far as 30 miles from land. As a result, the Banks are even more fluid and shifting than most barrier islands, more vulnerable to hurricanes and storms, more frequently washed over by the ocean and the sound, more drastically and rapidly altered as wind and sea ceaselessly rework the sand. The inlets between the sounds and the ocean divide the 180-mile-long arc of the Banks into a number of separate islands whose measurements and even existence have changed frequently over the relatively short span of America's recorded history. At present, the section of the Banks from the Virginia-North Carolina border down to the Oregon Inlet is connected to the mainland, although part of it is still known as Bodie Island. South of Oregon Inlet, there is the first true island on the Banks, Hatteras Island, which has been bridged to Bodie Island since the late 1960s. The next link in the chain is Ocracoke Island, and southwest of this unbridged island come Core Banks and Shackleford Banks, also unbridged. Core Banks is actually two islands, divided halfway down by New Drum Inlet. Shackleford Banks, proposed as a wilderness area, has no regular ferry service at present.

Although development has gobbled up the upper sections of the Banks, all the land from just south of Nags Head down to Shackleford Banks is protected as National

Fishermen cleaning nets on Roanoke Island. Commercial fishing is second to tourism as the major source of income on the Outer Banks. (Courtesy of the Dare County Tourist Bureau; photo: Drew C. Wilson.)

Seashore. The Cape Hatteras National Seashore protects about 70 miles of shoreline, including all of Hatteras and Ocracoke Islands; inside the Cape Hatteras National Seashore there are eight villages that have been allowed to grow within designated boundaries. The Cape Lookout National Seashore, which encompasses all of the Core and Shackleford Banks, is entirely undeveloped, its sole village, Portsmouth at the north end of the Core Banks, a ghost town abandoned by its last two residents in 1971. Altogether,

The Atlantic Ocean pounding the fishing pier at Rodanthe, Hatteras Island.

there are 120 miles of protected shore on the Outer Banks, the longest stretch in the nation. The Outer Banks are unique on the East Coast, and it is truly a marvel that so much of their land has been set aside for all of us to enjoy.

OCRACOKE ISLAND

Area: 16 miles long, 5 to 2 miles wide.

Population: 660 year-round; about 2,000 in the summer.

Location: North Carolina's Outer Banks, southwest of Hatteras Island and northeast of Portsmouth Island, between the Atlantic Ocean and Pamlico Sound.

Access: Free car and passenger ferry from Hatteras (40 minutes; no reservations necessary); pay car and passenger ferry from Swan Quarter, N.C. (2.5 hours) and Cedar Island, N.C. (2.25 hours)—reservations needed for

Silver Lake, the harbor of Ocracoke Village. Although tourism is growing in the village, the harbor remains an important center of commercial fishing. The Ocracoke Lighthouse is in the background and beyond it is the ocean. (Courtesy of the National Park Service, Cape Hatteras National Seashore.)

both in season (phone: 919-926-1111) for departures from Swan Quarter; phone 919-225-3551 for departures from Cedar Island).

The village of Ocracoke clings to Ocracoke Island like a green oasis in a desert of buff. If you have driven down here from the north, you will have had time to get accustomed to the almost featureless, nearly monochrome, eerily two-dimensional aspect of the chain of barrier islands and beaches known as the Outer Banks. From Bodie Island a single road, Highway 12, takes you south through long stretches of

Sea oats, sand and beach cottages: the landscape at Nags Head on the Outer Banks. (Courtesy of the Dare County Tourist Bureau.)

sand dune and salt marsh, an empty, treeless terrain of sea oats, cord grass and American beach grass punctuated at intervals by half a dozen villages with their clusters of wooden houses on stilts. At the end of Bodie Island, Highway 12 rises to cross Oregon Inlet over the high-arching Herbert C. Bonner Bridge and then it continues flat, straight and south down Hatteras Island. At Cape Hatteras, the crooked elbow of the Banks, Hatteras Island widens and makes an abrupt turn back to the mainland and Highway 12 swings west to follow the lay of the island. The highway pauses at the village of Hatteras, where a free ferry picks up cars for the 40-minute ride across Hatteras Inlet; and then on the Ocracoke side the road resumes, making its final 15-mile sprint down the island to Ocracoke Village. The drive down the length of the Cape Hatteras National Seashore from Bodie Island to Ocracoke Village is 70 miles, and if you do it all in one rush you may feel you've entered some endlessly repeating lunar loop, not so much real solid land as a vast ribbonlike sand bridge thrown from the mainland 30 miles out into the Atlantic Ocean.

At the end of the road, at the finish line, is Ocracoke Village. It announces itself, like the other Outer Banks villages, with billboards advertising motels and gift shops—but it begins, not with the now familiar beach cottages on stilts, but with trees. Red cedars, yaupon hollies, live oaks, loblolly pine, groundsel trees. Low, wind-pruned, gnarled, bending, some very old and many clearly struggling to hang on, these trees are the distinctive token and pride of Ocracoke. They shade and soften it. They given it color and character and set it apart from the wild remainder of the island. And these days, they hide some (but not all) of the new features that are rapidly transforming this once remote fishing village into a full-fledged tourist town.

Old Ocracoke, the village that predates the tourist boom, fits snugly under the trees. It is a village of low wooden houses with porches and hipped roofs built around a large, circular and extremely picturesque harbor called Silver Lake (it would indeed be a lake but for a narrow passage known as "the ditch" leading out to Pamlico Sound). Old Ocracoke has something of the charm of old Nantucket, a smaller, slower, humbler, southern Nantucket that never grew rich. Like Nantucket, Ocracoke invites

The Chicamacomico Life Saving Station at Rodanthe on Hatteras Island. Built by the Life Saving Service in 1874 and abandoned by the Coast Guard in 1954, the station is now being restored as a museum. (Courtesy of the Dare County Tourist Bureau.)

ambling down backstreets of close-set houses. Like Nantucket, the village of Ocracoke commands fine views over sheltered salt water and the air of the village is quickened by the sense of the open ocean rolling only a few miles away. Both Ocracoke and Nantucket are (or were) towns doubly surrounded by wastes—the waste of the water and the waste of the open, barren-seeming island land—and thus both have the feel of being refuges from the elements. But on Ocracoke, by virtue of the Cape Hatteras National Seashore that owns the entire island outside the town, the land will remain empty, a blessing that private ownership has failed to bestow on Nantucket. No matter what happens to Ocracoke Village, Ocracoke Island will go on being a wild, stark, rather desolate place, a truly Outer Bank inhabited only by flocks of gulls and the migrant Canada geese. Ocracoke Village has been built as a protected human enclave, and Ocracoke Island has been maintained as a protected natural sanctuary. The contrast and the balance are part of Ocracoke's appeal.

Old Ocracoke has the charm of the out-of-the-way and the time-worn and Ocracoke Island has the intensity of the pure and the elemental. New Ocracoke is something else again. New Ocracoke is like a coating of a thick, glary varnish over the village on Silver Lake. New Ocracoke is gift shops and restaurants, traffic that clogs up the narrow streets, a harbor loud with pleasure craft and charter boats; it is new motels and summer homes that spoil the old proportions by rising too high and spreading too wide and it is flocks of tourists who come to occupy all the spaces cleared for them. In new Ocracoke, the feeling of island remoteness in time and space has gone; new Ocracoke doesn't feel that different from any of the other small, almost painfully quaint East Coast harbors and fishing villages that have been made over into middle-class tourist towns. The gift shops adhere to the same vaguely nautical themes; the restaurants feature fancy seafood (not all of it caught locally); the motels boast of water views and charge more for it. Were it not for the water and the ferry ride, one might forget that new Ocracoke is an island at all.

To conjure up the sense of island isolation and separateness, the sense of what Ocracoke must have been like only 30 years ago before the highway and the regular ferry service linked it up to the other Outer Banks and to the world, to remove oneself at least mentally from Ocracoke's present and savor its past takes some wandering and some imagining. It's an exercise, but not an impossible exercise, for the past has not altogether vanished from the village. The varnish of the new covers much of the old, but it has not obliterated it.

Old Ocracoke still lurks under the tangled live oaks and yaupon hollies that conceal the old houses of Howard Street, a sand track that connects the harbor with the school road. It haunts the private graveyards of the village, some 84 of them, that poke up in odd corners of people's yards. Ocracoke's small, plain white lighthouse (built in 1823 and thus the oldest light on North Carolina's coast) is a relic of the old; and so are the fishing boats that go out from Silver Lake for flounder, gray and spotted trout, mullets, croakers, channel bass and blue crabs.

And of course there is history, somehow always more tangible, more palpably part of everyday life in the South than in the North.

The Ocracoke Lighthouse built in 1823 is the oldest on the coast of North Carolina. (Courtesy of the Dare County Tourist Bureau.)

Ocracoke's own history, though by no means illustrious, has its odd quirks and winding ways. It is for the most part a history determined by geography, the island's remoteness from the land and its strategic position on the coast, by the ocean and the sound and the men who knew and worked them.

Island History: Colonists, Pirates and Pilots

Geography put Ocracoke in the path of the first English colonizing expeditions to North America, those fabled and doomed missions sponsored by Queen Elizabeth's sometime favorite, Sir Walter Raleigh. Under Raleigh's direction, Sir Richard Grenville set out for the New World with 600 colonists and soldiers in April of 1585; Grenville's ship the *Tiger* ran aground on Ocracoke Island, and the expedition paused here for repairs before moving north to the more sheltered Roanoke Island. Sir Walter

Raleigh sponsored another attempt to colonize Roanoke Island two years later: This ill-fated venture, whose total disappearance remains a mystery to this day, became known as the Lost Colony. Today visitors to the Fort Raleigh National Historic Site on Roanoke Island can walk through the woods to a reconstruction of the fort that was to have protected the "Cittie of Ralegh." And those with a taste for seeing history brought to life can watch the play *The Lost Colony,* a dramatization of the fate of the settlement. *The Lost Colony,* performed at the Historic Site's Waterside Theater on the shore of Roanoke Sound, has been running each summer since 1937, with a hiatus during World War II.

Having failed in their attempt to colonize Roanoke Island, the English moved on with greater success to Jamestown Island in Chesapeake Bay. Ocracoke, passed over in the 16th century, remained unsettled for another century and a half. The English explorers named it and mapped it, but otherwise pretty much left it alone. (The island appears as Wococon, probably after the Woccon Indian tribe, on the 1587

Sir Walter Raleigh (1552?–1618) sponsored the first English settlements in North America, including the Lost Colony on Roanoke Island. (Courtesy of the National Park Service, Cape Hatteras National Seashore.)

map of the Outer Banks drawn by John White, a skilled artist and one of the leaders of the Lost Colony who survived because he had returned to England for supplies; in the course of time the island's name had some two dozen variant forms, including Wococock, Occacock, and Okercock before finally settling down to Ocracoke.)

Though official England planted no colonies and built no forts on the island during most of the Colonial period, unofficial England in the person of pirates flocked to Ocracoke. The secluded island made an ideal hideout for outlaws and here for R&R came such notorious brigands as Christopher Moody, Robert Deal, Charles Vane, "Calico Jack" Rackham, Anne Bonney and Mary Read. By far the most famous figure in the "Golden Age of Piracy" (1713-1718) was Edward Teach, more familiarly known by his nom de guerre, Blackbeard. Blackbeard's celebrity derives from both his success—by early 1718 he commanded four boats, 400 men, and had chalked up twenty-five ships captured—and his flamboyant personal style. The pirate, with a gift for the violently theatrical, would enter the fray looking like a demon of destruction: He decked his person with pistols and knives, he brandished an enormous cutlass, and to cap off the hellish impression, he tied burning ribbons and cannon fuses to his beard and tucked them under his hat so that he literally smoked as he fought. Blackbeard in full battle array must have cut a very terrifying figure, but in the end, smoking ribbons and all, he was not equal to the Royal Navy. Lieutenant Robert Maynard, summoned to Ocracoke by the governor of Virginia, gave chase to Blackbeard's *Adventure* in his ship the *Ranger*, and on November 22, 1718, after a terrific battle, Maynard's men succeeded in killing the pirate near Ocracoke Inlet. Supposedly 25 sword and pistol wounds were needed to cut him down, and a legend has grown up that after Maynard decapitated Blackbeard and tossed the body overboard, the headless brigand swam seven times around the ship before settling to the bottom of the channel in Pamlico Sound known today as "Teach's Hole." Whatever the truth of the pirate's demise, Blackbeard was dead and with him died large-scale piracy on the Outer Banks.

At about the same time that pirates were launching raids from Ocracoke, the island's first permanent white settlers were establishing themselves around Cockle Creek (later to be dredged and renamed Silver Lake). These first Ocracokers were pilots, stationed here by an act of the North Carolina Assembly to guide ships through Ocracoke Inlet, which in the first decades of the 18th century became North Carolina's major passage for ocean-going vessels.

In 1760 the North Carolina government made provision for the pilots by putting aside 50 acres of land around Cockle Creek for them, and in 1766 the government purchased 20 acres and leased them to pilots. Today's village of Ocracoke was then known as Pilot Town and by the 1770s Pilot Town and the town of Portsmouth (brought into existence by the state assembly in 1755 for its strategic position and also as a home base for pilots; see Core Banks entry) across Ocracoke Inlet on Portsmouth Island were the largest settlements on the Outer Banks. It was not unusual in the 18th and early 19th centuries for as many as 40 ships to wait inside Ocracoke Inlet for one of the Ocracoke pilots to guide them out to the ocean.

With the pirates gone, Ocracoke Village settled into a quiet prosperity based on piloting, livestock raising and, later, commercial fishing. A traveler recorded his impressions of the Ocracokers in 1783: "All the people…seemed very robust and fat to me…The people of that country attribute their fleshiness to their food which consists entirely of fish, oysters, and some few vegetables which they grow in the small gardens they cultivate not far from their houses." A description of the village written by Jonathan Price in the 1790s remains remarkably apt today: "Its length is three miles, and its breadth two and one half. Small live oak and cedar grow abundantly over it, and it contains several swamps and rich marshes, which might be cultivated to great advantage." Apparently, the advantage of cultivation was never much realized, for the Ocracokers had the even greater advantage of the sea right at their doorsteps.

In 1798 a lighthouse went up on Shell Castle Island inside the entrance to Ocracoke Inlet, but as the channel shifted it soon proved worthless. Later Shell Castle Island served as an important trading depot and a number of warehouses, grist mills and stores were built on it. Ocracoke's present lighthouse, the oldest on the coast of North

Carolina and the second oldest in use in the United States, was built by Noah Porter of Massachusetts in 1823. The cost was $11,359.95 for the 65-foot-high lighthouse made of brick covered with white-painted mortar and the adjoining three-bedroom keeper's house (since enlarged and today in private hands). The lighthouse tower has a beauty of its own, a severe and innocent beauty it shares with American primitive art. The Ocracoke Lighthouse not only protects oceangoing ships but also has served as a refuge for village residents when bad hurricanes submerged the island. Behind the light, hidden in a tangle of shrubs and trees, is a private cemetery of the Gaskill and O'Neal families.

Ocracoke Inlet, important commercially during the 18th and early 19th centuries in times of peace, was crucial strategically in times of war. During the American Revolution, the British succeeded in blockading Charleston to the south and the Chesapeake Bay ports to the north, but the pilots of Ocracoke together with a militia company kept supplies for the patriots moving through the inlet and preyed on British shipping. Through Ocracoke Inlet slipped some of the much-needed supplies that kept Washington's army alive during its terrible winter at Valley Forge. During the Civil War, both Ocracoke Inlet and Hatteras Inlet, which by then had supplanted Ocracoke Inlet as the major Outer Banks access route for oceangoing ships, fell quickly to Union forces. The success of General Benjamin F. Butler and General Ambrose Burnside in taking and keeping the Outer Banks in 1861 and 1862 marked some of the first Union victories of the war. Control of the Banks inlets gave the North a significant maritime advantage throughout the war.

The Outer Banks again saw maritime action during the two World Wars of our century. The Germans mined the waters off the Banks during the First World War and on one occasion lifesavers from the Chicamacomico Lifesaving Station rescued most of the crew of an exploded British gasoline tanker. During World War II, in the early

An early photograph of the keeper's quarters at the Ocracoke Lighthouse. The quarters have been enlarged and altered since this photo was taken, and the building is now privately owned. (Courtesy of the National Park Service, Cape Hatteras National Seashore.)

months of 1941, German U-boats inflicted heavy damage on Allied shipping off the Outer Banks. In that year, the bodies of four British seamen, crew members of the HMS *Bedfordshire*, which went down somewhere between Norfolk and Morehead City, washed ashore on Ocracoke. The sailors were buried in a small private cemetery near the edge of town (follow the road that leaves Silver Lake Harbor behind the Anchorage Inn; the British Cemetery is a few blocks up on the right). Later in the war, Silver Lake Harbor, which had been dredged in 1931 and made suitable for large boats, served as a U.S. Navy base for antisubmarine patrols.

The Life of the Village

The wars and the brief reign of pirates were the high-water mark of action in Ocracoke's history. Its civil history has unfolded quietly and rather uneventfully. Until very recent times, the sea has been the basis of the island's economy; the first Ocracokers worked as pilots, later generations manned the island's two life-saving stations and gradually, during the 19th century, fishing became the major source of revenue for the islanders. But commercial fishing, though still important on the Outer Banks, is no longer the keystone of the island's economy: These days tourism creates more jobs and brings in more money than any other pursuit.

Tourism came more slowly to Ocracoke than to the Banks islands to the north for the simple reason that Ocracoke, being unbridged, was harder to get to. Before 1950, there was really no reliable way to make the crossing to Ocracoke unless you had your own boat. In that year an islander named Frazier Peele started up a primitive four-car ferry across Hatteras Inlet. Peele's ferry consisted of two boats lashed together and ran only at low tide; since there was no road running the length of the island, disembarking cars had to drive to the village along the beach. In 1957 the state of North Carolina took over the ferry service and offered free passage. Work on the paved road from Hatteras Inlet to the village began the following year. Regular ferry service and a road made the trip down to Ocracoke possible for casual visitors, and once the visitors began to arrive, motels and restaurants opened up to serve them. Tourism and tourist facilities have increased steadily during the 1970s and '80s, and today Ocracoke Village offers 17 hotels, motels and guest homes, two commercial campgrounds as well as 130 oceanfront camp sites near the village in the National Seashore, numerous cottages for rent, about a dozen gift shops and a handful of restaurants and fast-food stands. Tourists are very much a fixture of life in the village. As one local put it, "We can't resent the tourists because starting at around age fourteen, virtually everyone here depends on them for their livings."

Beyond the tourist accommodations, Ocracoke Village has all the usual institutions and services necessary to sustain a year-round community of about 660 people. The first island school opened in 1808, a new school took its place in 1917, and the current school, North Carolina's smallest with around 100 students in grades K through 12, opened in 1971. The island gained a post office in 1840. Electricity came in 1937-38, though island electrical service remains precarious: The power seems to fail routinely whenever the wind blows. Telephone service arrived in 1956. Ocracoke's Methodist church was built in 1943, but Methodism had been the island's major sect well before this and remains so today. There is also an Assembly of God chapel out past the lighthouse. Ocracoke has no local government to speak of, and the islanders traditionally have resisted this form of meddling. Ocracoke citizens elect one county commissioner to sit on the Hyde county council at Swan Quarter and the county sends sheriff's deputies to keep the peace. The village has a fire hall and next door there is a public library. There is a local water association to regulate the flow of the desalinated water from the village's 600-foot-deep well: The slightly salty tasting water is sometimes in short supply at peak summer season when the village's population more than triples. Ocracoke's year-round and summer populations are both rising; the new year-round residents are likely to be retirees, summer people who have decided to stay on, artists, craftspeople and small business owners.

Ocracoke's recent changes cannot all be blamed on the crowds of newcomers. The 20th century has come to the old Pilot Town, and Pilot Town has gone off to meet the 20th century. "Even if the tourists never came, the mere fact that we can get off the island makes a difference," said Philip Howard, a seventh generation Ocracoker. "Back in 1974, it was unusual for an Ocracoke kid to have been in a cafeteria, to have ridden on an escalator. Now they frequently go on trips, they get off-island. We can get to malls. We're more exposed to the mainland, and of course television has an effect." Gradually, the village of Ocracoke and the people who reside here are becoming more like villages and people everywhere. The remote, charming, unspoiled fishing village of yesteryear has become an accessible, convenient, popular tourist haven—tamely quaint and easily "doable."

But, while the village succumbs to (and embraces) the pressures of the 20th century, the island, thanks to its protected status as National Seashore, remains free from all pressures save those brought to bear by the elements.

The Life of the Island: Formation and Features

Geologically, Ocracoke Island and the entire 175-mile stretch of barrier islands and beaches that make up the Outer Banks is a fascinating region, unique in its formation and ever-changing in its interaction with ocean and wind. Like all barrier islands, the Banks are essentially a narrow chain of sandbars running roughly parallel to the mainland's shore. What is distinctive about the Outer Banks is the "outerness": Unlike the other East Coast barrier islands—or those anywhere in the world—that hug the continent's shoreline, the Outer Banks loop far out to sea, as far as 30 miles out from the mainland at their easternmost reach. From the air on an airplane flying south from New York, it looks as if a ditch had been dug just inland along the East Coast from New Jersey south to Virginia (with a gap at Chesapeake Bay) and then suddenly, at North Carolina, the ditch widens into a lake as the ribbon of land along the continent's edge bellies out into the Atlantic.

We are not quite sure why or how this happened, but one current theory suggests that the Outer Banks were composed of soft sediments carried from the mainland to the ocean by slow-moving rivers and that they once hugged the shore like other barrier islands. Then, after the worldwide rise in sea level that followed the melting of the glaciers, the vast coastal plain to their west flooded to become Pamlico and Albemarle Sounds, leaving the Banks adrift. The Banks, along with all barrier islands, are adrift in another sense as well: Like boats come loose from their moorings, these anchorless land forms go where the wind, the tide and the coastal currents take them. As anyone who has been on the Banks in a high gale can attest, the islands are not a stable landmass but a constantly shifting, fluid aggregate of beach, sand dunes and marsh.

The Outer Banks, protruding into the Atlantic 150 miles beyond the major East Coast axis, are particularly vulnerable to storms; and storms together with the steady rise in sea level are moving the Banks westward at the rate of one foot per century. In a continuous dynamic process, the islands literally roll over on themselves as sand from the exposed ocean side retreats west to the sound side. The storms and currents that batter the island chain also rearrange the gaps between the islands, called inlets, that connect Pamlico and Albemarle Sounds to the ocean (actually "outlets" would be a more appropriate term because the greater flow of water is *out* from sound to ocean). Old

The Ocracoke Island Coast Guard Station, near Hatteras Inlet, before and after the devastating storm of 1955. Hurricanes and powerful storms sweep regularly over the Outer Banks, opening new inlets, changing the shape of the islands, and carrying off the structures built by man. (Courtesy of the National Park Service, Cape Hatteras National Seashore.)

inlets shoal up and close and new ones open, separating, rejoining and reshaping the islands. Over the centuries of recorded history there have been as many as 11 inlets and as few as three punctuating the barrier chain. According to David Stick's history, *The Outer Banks of North Carolina*, "The changes and movements have occurred so frequently...that there is hardly a section of the entire Banks which has not, at one time or another, been cut through by an inlet."

Beach erosion has been aggravated on many of the barrier islands by overgrazing and lumbering in the 19th century and, more recently, by oceanfront development. From Southern Shores south to Nags Head there is an almost unbroken line of beach cottages.

Luckily, Ocracoke Island is protected from shorefront development and the destruction it brings in its wake, for all the island outside the confines of the village on Silver Lake Harbor is part of the Cape Hatteras National Seashore, owned and managed by the National Park Service. Established by an act of Congress in 1937 and finally realized in 1953, the Cape Hatteras National Seashore is the nation's first protected shoreline and together with the Cape Lookout National Seashore to the south it comprises about 120 miles of natural ocean beach, the longest stretch in the country. From north to south the Cape Hatteras National Seashore encompasses Bodie Island (no longer really an island but an extension of the Kitty Hawk-Nags Head barrier beach), Hatteras Island (whose north end, designated the Pea Island National Wildlife Refuge, is maintained by the U.S. Fish and Wildlife Service; Pea Island, like Bodie, is no longer a separate island) and Ocracoke Island. Within the national seashore there are eight villages—Rodanthe, Waves, Salvo, Avon, Buxton, Frisco, Hatteras and Ocracoke—that the park planners intentionally left in private hands as places for residents to continue living and for park visitors to stay. Boundaries around the villages were generous to permit them to expand to accommodate more people, and expand they have, particularly in the past few years. These days the Cape Hatteras National Seashore draws well over a million visitors a year.

The Life of the Island: Plants and Animals

A good many of the visitors to Ocracoke congregate in the village; the island outside the village tends to swallow up those who wander over it. The ocean beaches, with their unbroken expanses of smooth light-tan sand and long-rolling waves, attract surfers, surf-casters, bathers and sunbathers. The waters off the Outer Banks, so treacherous for coastal shipping, are a delight for fishermen—for the mingling of the cold, northern Labrador Current with the Gulf Stream, which flows within 12 miles of shore here in the summer months, brings a stunning variety of fish to the Banks.

On Ocracoke there are a number of parking areas with beach access off Highway 12, and about halfway down the island at Hammock Hills there is a well-marked self-guiding nature trail that affords an excellent opportunity to learn about Ocracoke's ecology. In less than an hour one travels from oceanside to soundside, passing from the artificial primary dunes that take the first impact of salt and wind, to the secondary dunes, which are far enough back and protected enough by the primary dunes to support thickets of yaupon holly, groundsel trees, wax myrtle, prickly ash and prickly pear cactus. Beyond the secondary dunes there is a small loblolly pine forest growing on a hillside; and past the pine forest the trail dips down to the extensive salt marsh on the island's soundside. Fringed with salt-meadow hay (in the supratidal zone) and black needlerush and salt-marsh cord grass (in the intertidal zone), the salt marsh is quieter, the waters stiller, the plant forms more diverse, the wildlife more plentiful than on the oceanfront.

Ocracoke's most celebrated wildlife are neither fish nor fowl but horse, the beloved Banker ponies that once roamed freely over the dunes. At one time there were supposedly 5,000 to 6,000 ponies on the island, but the herd was down to 150 or so by the late 1930s. The annual penning of the ponies on July 4 was a big local attraction for many years, and each year a few ponies used to be auctioned off. Today the National Park Service maintains the last few survivors of the herd—about 20 horses in all—in a pen off Highway 12 near the east end of the island.

The penning of the wild Banker ponies on Ocracoke Island. Today the small remaining herd is kept in a corral near the north end of the island. (Courtesy of the National Park Service, Cape Hatteras National-al Seashore.)

The natural world on Ocracoke and all the Outer Banks is not an easy world to know or love. What is spectacular about Ocracoke—the unbroken beaches and dunes, the narrowness and instability of the land, the pounding of the ocean surf and the lapping of the sound waters so near each other on either side of the island—hits one all at once. By the time one drives the length of the island, stops a couple of times to walk on the beach, glimpse the sound and examine the ponies, one feels one has taken it all in. Once the first impact of the spectacular wears off, Ocracoke may seem monotonous. The island lacks both the hazy tropical softness and craggy northern clarity that we commonly call beautiful. The endless-seeming dunes, the drab, flat, colorless terrain, the long straight lines of horizon and highway give the landscape the look of a desert. With no landmark to focus the attention and no variety to refresh the senses, Ocracoke can soon exhaust the visitor's store of interest. This is not to say that the island *has* no intrinsic interest. Like the desert, Ocracoke requires time and study before it reveals its secrets. The monotony is only apparent: In fact, sharply distinct ecological zones with surprisingly varied lifeforms are only yards apart. The salt marsh on one side of the island is a world apart from the ocean beach a mere half-mile away on the other side; but even the grassy flats just behind the primary dunes support plants such as broom sedge, seaside aster, wild lettuce and bayberry bushes that could not survive the full force of the ocean a few feet away. Where there is protection and enough fresh water, pockets of loblolly pines and red cedars grow. Warblers and sparrows that would never alight on the ocean beach sing among the yaupons and live oaks of the village.

Part of what is beautiful about Ocracoke Island stems from the way these zones of life exist together and separately on the same loose, sandy soil. There is beauty, too, in the drama of continual change that the elements work on the surface of the island. Anyone who has felt the wind pick up sand and salt on the Outer Banks has tasted this drama. For all their roads and houses and villages, the Outer Banks do not feel like *terra firma*. Formed and reformed by the vagaries of weather and water, these barrier islands and beaches are amphibian, transitional landforms. The sea and the land play constant, sometimes violent tug-of-war with the Outer Banks, and one has the sense that someday the sea may just win. This sensation of impermanence, of massive shifts in the earth's features taking place right beneath one's feet, dispels any lingering impression of monotony. Far from being monotonous, these links in the Outer Banks chain are in a fundamental way our most exciting, precarious, dynamic islands.

THE CORE BANKS

Area: 43 miles long; width varies from 600 feet to 1.75 miles.

Population: No permanent residents.

Location: South and west of Ocracoke Island, between the Atlantic Ocean and Core Sound.

Access: Passenger ferry from Ocracoke, North Carolina, and from Harkers Island, North Carolina; car (restricted to four-wheel drive vehicles with National Park Service permit) and passenger ferry from Atlantic, North Carolina (call 919-225-4261), and from Davis, North Carolina.

The church and houses at Portsmouth Village on the Core Banks. (Courtesy of the National Park Service, Cape Lookout National Seashore)

For the latest ferry information, contact the Cape Lookout National Seashore, P.O. Box 690, Beaufort, NC 28516; or call 919-728-2121.

Ocracoke Island may be the end of the road on North Carolina's Outer Banks, the last island you can drive down, but it is not the end of the Outer Banks. West and south of Ocracoke, the Banks complete the vast, irregular arc that sweeps out oceanward from the North Carolina mainland starting at Knotts Island and rejoins it near Morehead City. The Core Banks, the northern half of which is sometimes known as Portsmouth Island, make up the next links in the barrier island chain after Ocracoke, and they extend in a straight line for 43 miles from Portsmouth Village down to Cape Lookout. At Cape Lookout the narrow line of land takes an abrupt, almost 90° turn to the west, and the nine-mile-long Shackleford Banks, as the last link is known, point almost due west into the mainland.

Though the Core Banks and Shackleford Banks lie closer to the North Carolina mainland than far-flung Hatteras and Ocracoke Islands, they *seem* much more remote because they are uninhabited and largely untouched. Protected since 1976 by the 28,300-acre Cape Lookout National Seashore, the Core and Shackleford Banks are empty islands—East Coast barrier islands at their most pristine. Here there are no roads behind the dunes, no tourist villages standing up on stilts, no stores, motels or restaurants. In the summer months, a few people vacation in the cabins that they sold to the National Park Service and now lease back from it, either for life or 25 years. Aside from a scattering of rustic rental cabins on either side of Drum Inlet run by Park Service concessionaires, there are no overnight accommodations, although camping is permitted. Shackleford Banks, which currently has no accommodations of any type, no public ferry access, and no vehicles permitted, has been proposed as a wilderness area. Development will never encroach on these islands.

Development, however, was part of the island's past. During the 19th century, the village at the northern tip of Portsmouth Island was the second largest settlement on the Banks, after Ocracoke. Today Portsmouth is that most romantically eerie of places, a ghost town, and the eeriness is heightened all the more by its location at the end of a silent, wild barrier island. From a peak of 505 people a decade before the Civil War, Portsmouth dwindled down to a few 20th-century holdouts. The last two residents moved off the island in 1971. Since then, the National Park Service has taken over the village and restored some of the buildings, including the general store, post office, Methodist church and a number of private homes. Outside the deserted village stretches the empty island, a strange and lonely place of sand dune, beach, tidal flat and salt marsh. Portsmouth is one Eastern island that has regained its innocence.

History

The town of Portsmouth, though it died a natural death, did not have a natural birth. Unlike most towns, which grow up gradually and randomly as chance, geography and opportunity dictate, Portsmouth was decreed into existence. Before a single settler lived there, the town had a name and a plan. North Carolina's Colonial Assembly authorized the creation of Portsmouth in 1753 in order to fill the need for a port town on Ocracoke Inlet, at that time and well into the 19th century the major point of entry along the North Carolina coast. In those days, the primary channel through Ocracoke Inlet was nearer Portsmouth than Ocracoke; large seagoing vessels could enter this channel and sail up safely around the sheltered north end of the island, but the waters beyond were too shallow and liable to shoal for any but small ships to navigate. Portsmouth was created as a transshipment station, where the cargo of large ships could be unloaded onto wharves and stored in warehouses, until shallow-draft ships could collect the merchandise and carry it on to the mainland ports. It was, as David Stick notes in his history *The Outer Banks of North Carolina*, "the first and for many years the largest town on the Outer Banks."

Five commissioners were appointed to lay out 50 acres near the harbor into half-acre lots and to see to the sale of the lots at 20 shillings each. The commissioners were also in charge of a fund of £2000 to be used in the construction of a fort guarding Ocracoke Inlet. Though the Assembly passed the decree for the creation of Portsmouth in 1753, it wasn't until 1755, after the newly appointed Governor Arthur Dobbs toured the area, that work actually went forward on surveying lots, selling them off and building Fort Granville. The fort housed a small garrison of soldiers from 1758 to 1764; but with the conclusion of the French and Indian War, there was no further need to fortify the inlet and the garrison was removed. David Stick notes that "Though there is no record that a gun was ever fired from Fort Granville, and today no vestige of it remains, the fact that troops were stationed there for a time did serve as an impetus in the development of the town of Portsmouth."

Portsmouth developed slowly at first, and then more and more rapidly during the first half of the 19th century. By 1800 the town had grown beyond its original 50 acres and there were 246 residents living here. Ten years later, the population had jumped to 347 and it continued to grow for another 40 years until it reached its peak of 505 residents in 1850.

Portsmouth was built to service the maritime traffic that passed through Ocracoke Inlet, and as long as that traffic increased, Portsmouth prospered and grew. Stick notes that more than 1,400 vessels carrying two-thirds of North Carolina's exports came through the inlet in a 12-month period during 1836-37.

In the course of the 19th century, Portsmouth acquired all the institutions and amenities of settled town life, including a school as early as 1806, several taverns, a post office and Methodist church in 1840 and a federally built hospital for sailors in 1847. By that point, however, the tide had begun to turn for Portsmouth, for during the previous year a hurricane had opened two other major inlets—Hatteras Inlet and Oregon Inlet—on the Banks, and the town lost its monopoly on maritime traffic. The Civil War dealt the town another serious blow. Union soldiers took the Banks very early in the war (see Ocracoke entry), and many Portsmouth residents fled the island at this time and never returned. After the Civil War, traffic through Ocracoke Inlet virtually ceased as the channel near Portsmouth shoaled up and Hatteras Inlet became the preferred point of entry on the Outer Banks. Portsmouth went into an irreversible decline.

After the war, the town had a plant to process menhaden fish into oil and fertilizer (this business was thriving on Long Island and Shelter Island in New York state at around the same time), but this and other commercial endeavors soon failed. From 1876 to 1883 (and for a brief period in 1885) the U.S. Weather Bureau maintained a weather station at the old marine hospital in Portsmouth, and the Lifesaving Service (the forerunner of today's Coast Guard) built a station on the island in 1894. When the station closed down in 1937, the only reliable source of income on the island was gone. The 60 or so people who remained continued to graze stock on the island, but the strain of beef had become inferior since it had not been improved by crossbreeding in years, and the land had long been seriously overgrazed. Fishing was also a source of some income and, of course, food for the islanders, and a handful of summer people came for vacations and provided a bit of seasonal employment for the islanders.

But these occupations were not sufficient to sustain the community. In 1956, a century after its peak of prosperity, Portsmouth had a mere 17 residents, the youngest of whom was 59 years old. A real estate broker offered abandoned houses for sale at $495 each, but even that price was steep on an island with no economy. The school had closed in 1943, so there was nothing to keep young families on the island, mail service ended in 1949, and the store and post office shut down in 1959. With no services, no mailboat, no electricity and storms regularly sweeping over the island, Portsmouth was cut adrift from the modern world. The last two Portsmouth residents left the island in 1971, and the once busy port became a ghost town.

Portsmouth was incorporated into the Cape Lookout National Seashore in 1976, and in 1978, the 250-acre village district was listed on the National Register of Historic Places. In 1980 the Park Service organized a homecoming for the former residents of

Portsmouth, and for a day 350 people brought the place to life again. A couple of the village houses are occupied by former owners in the summer months, and from mid-May to mid-September the village ranger station is manned. Each year, about 100,000 people visit the Cape Lookout National Seashore.

Visiting Portsmouth Island

For a ghost town, Portsmouth looks surprisingly clean and bright, thanks to the restoration and preservation work done by the National Park Service. Those who come to Portsmouth Island today disembark at Haulover Landing on the Pamlico Sound side at the island's northwest corner. A rutted sandy road runs through the village, and beyond the village there is a path leading east out to the ocean beach. The island has no paved roads, and only four-wheel-drive vehicles are permitted (drivers must obtain permits from the Park Service). Mosquitoes are notoriously thick and fierce here in the summer months, and without repellent a visit to Portsmouth is pure torture. Visitors must also bring all of their own food and water.

Although Portsmouth was a planned town, its houses lie scattered here and there with no discernible pattern around the north end of the island. The Park Service maintains about 25 of the 48 village structures, and many others have fallen into ruins. From the landing, the Haulover Road takes you past the visitor's center in the Dixon/Salter house, goes by the post office, and then leads across Doctor's Creek to the Methodist church. The church, a tall, pleasing white structure with gothic windows and a tiered, shingled spire, was built in 1914 to replace an earlier Methodist church that was swept away by a storm the previous year. At present, the church and the visitor's center are the only village buildings open to the public.

Visiting the Core Banks and Shackleford Banks

A little more than a mile east of the village, past the Coast Guard Station and the old airstrip, lies the Atlantic Ocean beach, which runs for 21 miles down to Drum Inlet. Here the Portsmouth Island section of the Core Banks ends, and the lower section picks up on the other side of the inlet and runs for another 22 miles straight down to Cape Lookout, where a lighthouse has stood since around 1812. The current lighthouse, which is 150 feet high, dates from 1859, and the Park Service has recently completed restoration of the outside of the 1873 keeper's quarters. At present, Park Service concessionaires ferry visitors to points a few miles north and south of Drum Inlet and to the lighthouse area at Cape Lookout. Aside from a scattering of cabins, the beaches, dunes and flatlands are empty. The Core Banks are home to Fowler's toads, tree toads, diamondback terrapins and box turtles, and threatened loggerhead turtles nest on the beaches in the spring and early summer.

West of the Cape Lookout Lighthouse there is a small inlet, called Barden Inlet or the Drain, and on the other side of this is the nine-mile-long island known as the Shackleford Banks, situated at almost an exact right angle to the Core Banks. The Shackleford Banks was home to two well established communities in the second half of the 19th century—Wade's Hammock, located near the Beaufort Inlet, and Diamond City (it took its name from the diamond pattern on the Cape Lookout light), just across from Cape Lookout. During a severe hurricane in August of 1899, the island and the villages were flooded, and within three years all 500 residents of Diamond City had moved away, transporting their homes off the island on barges. Now the Shackleford Banks is the wildest section of the Cape Lookout Seashore, with access by private boat only; the Park Service is hoping to have the island declared a wilderness area and is managing it as wilderness until approval goes through. Because of its east-west orientation, higher dunes have formed on the Shackleford Banks—as tall as 35 feet—than on the Core Banks, and on the higher ground behind the dunes a good-sized maritime forest has grown up, a forest similar in ecology to Buxton Woods on Hatteras Island, with such species as live oak, loblolly pine and cedar. Shackleford Banks also has herds of goats, sheep, cows and horses that have gone wild. Together, the Core Banks (including Portsmouth Island) and the Shackleford Banks make up the 55 miles of coastline protected by the Cape Lookout National Seashore.

The Mysteries of Beach Preservation

Portsmouth and Ocracoke Islands are a bit like mirror images of each other: The villages lie near the tips of the islands on opposite sides of Ocracoke Inlet and beyond the villages the long, narrow landscapes of the islands unfurl like ribbons, Portsmouth unfurling south, Ocracoke north. There is, however, a significant difference in the landscapes of the two neighboring islands: On Ocracoke and the Outer Banks islands north of it, the Civilian Conservation Corps created artificial dunes during the 1930s by putting snow-fencing down behind the beach and planting beach grass and sea oats; but on Portsmouth Island and all down the Core and Shackleford Banks, the oceanfront was left in its natural state. As a result, the dune line on these islands is lower and less regular, the landscape looks flatter, and the ocean more frequently oversweeps these islands during severe storms and unusually high tides. A strong north or northeast

wind or a spring tide can cover much of the Core Banks, including the flats between Portsmouth village and the ocean, with ankle-deep water.

For many years it was thought that the lack of artificial protective dunes on the Core and Shackleford Banks and the open grazing of cattle and wild ponies on the islands were hastening beach erosion; but now that view is being contested. The livestock were finally banned by the state in the 1950s, but some think that the decades without livestock have made no difference aside from letting vegetation and beach

The dunes on all the Outer Banks from Ocracoke north to the Virginia state line were artificially created by the Civilian Conservation Corps during the 1930's.

grass grow up more thickly. The beaches look pretty much the same. Nor is it at all clear whether the Core and Shackleford Banks have fared any worse than the banks to the north that have artificial dunes. A recent article on barrier islands by Robert Dolan and Harry Lins in *Scientific American* (July 1987) points out that on the Core

Banks, where the dunes have not been altered or stabilized by man, the beaches are from 350 to 600 feet wide, whereas on Hatteras Island, where the dunes have been built up and stabilized, the beach has shrunk to 100 feet. According to Dolan and Lins, "The paradox suggests that manmade structures do not merely fail to protect beaches but actually work to destroy them." Many scientists and park rangers now feel that the best policy is to leave nature alone to build, destroy and rebuild the barrier islands as she has done for thousands of years. Barrier islands, we have learned, are meant to move—to roll over on themselves—and pinning them in place may prove as futile as resisting the wind and tide.

THE SEA ISLANDS OF
SOUTH CAROLINA AND GEORGIA

INTRODUCTION

Rich in history, vast in number, home to some of the nation's least privileged and most privileged people, and habitat of vast numbers of birds and animals, including threatened brown pelicans and loggerhead turtles, the Sea Islands of South Carolina and Georgia are among the most fascinating on the East Coast. It is estimated that there are 1,000 islands off the coasts of these two states, though when you are traveling on them or studying them on a map it's almost impossible to tell where one island leaves off and another begins. Unlike the Outer Banks of North Carolina or the Florida Keys, the Sea Islands are not cut off by expanses of open water but linked to the mainland and to each other by a vast carpet of salt marsh. Individual islands are defined by the narrow channels and creeks that snake through the cord grass and the occasional river or sound. From the air you see a network of mazes running down the continent's hem and dividing the land into interlocking tongues and whorls. In places there are five or more islands backed up between the edge of the ocean and the start of the low country mainland.

The Sea Island landscape is flat or very gradually sloping, the soil is fertile, the climate is soft and mild. Many of the Sea Islands are little more than clumps of sediment held together by cord grass; the higher islands support maritime forests of live oak, magnolia and loblolly pine. Both temperate and tropical species flourish here. Palmettos grow next to pines; deer feed near alligators; apple trees and wheat can be planted alongside oranges and sugarcane. These blessings made the Sea Islands a major agricultural district during the 18th and 19th centuries, and they are making the islands an increasingly popular vacation district today.

Change is coming fast to the Sea Islands, perhaps faster than to any island group outside of the Florida Keys. Thirty-five years ago, the Sea Islands seemed like a separate and very foreign country—a country that appeared to have more in common with Africa than the American South. The islands didn't need open water to isolate them: They were effectively isolated by history. The predominant population on the Sea Islands were the descendants of the slaves who had worked the big cotton plantations before the Civil War. When the war broke out, the white owners evacuated their plantations and the Sea Island blacks took possession of the land. From that time until quite recently, the Sea Island blacks lived in nearly total isolation from the mainland, governing themselves, dividing up the former cotton plantations into small plots for vegetables, fishing the creeks, gathering crabs and oysters out of the back waters, and passing down their stories and traditions from generation to generation. Even before the Civil War, the blacks had had little contact with white culture, for most of the plantation owners were absentee landlords who spent a good deal of the year in their town houses in Charleston, Beaufort and Savannah.

In their 200 years of isolation on the Sea Islands, the blacks developed a culture and a language quite distinct from that of the whites and even from that of blacks who lived elsewhere. Their language, called Gullah in South Carolina and Geechee in

INTRODUCTION

Georgia, is technically a creole—a dialect that fuses West African grammar with English and pidgin English vocabulary. Because it is the only creole dialect that developed in the United States, Gullah has attracted a good deal of attention from scholars, linguists and folklorists. West African influences show up not only in the language but also in such customs as head-wrapping, communal story-telling, basket-weaving and the arrangement of houses around a central, swept-earth common. And there are elements of voodoo in some of the islanders' practices and superstitions, for example, the painting of window frames blue to ward off "hants" and the placing of broken dishes and fragments of mirrors on graves.

Gullah was a product of isolation, but now that the isolation is rapidly being breached, Gullah is in danger of disappearing. Whites are once again discovering the Sea Islands, not as farmland but as vacationland. Hilton Head was the first South Carolina Sea Island to be transformed, back in the 1950s, from an enclave of blacks to an expensive resort, and in the past 15 years the pace of development has greatly accelerated on such islands as Kiawah, Seabrook, Edisto, Fripp and Dataw. A number of South Carolina Sea Island resorts, including Isle of Palms, Sullivans Island and Pawleys Island were devastated in 1989 by Hurricane Hugo.

As bridges, golf courses and expensive resort "plantations" go up, the Sea Island blacks are being pushed off the islands and absorbed into the mainstream culture. Sea Island children now learn standard English in schools where Gullah is discouraged as the language of poverty and ignorance; and adults who formerly farmed and fished now turn increasingly to service jobs in the resort areas. As land prices soar, many blacks cannot afford to pay the taxes, or cannot resist the quick profits to be made by selling their land to developers. Many have taken up again the tasks of their slave ancestors: They prepare and serve food to the white landowners, tend the golf courses and tennis courts and build the new houses. The pattern on more and more of the South Carolina Sea Islands is for the whites to own all the waterfront property and the blacks to live on the less desirable inland areas. However, even with the spread of development, a number of black communities, particularly on the inner islands with no ocean beaches, are holding on to their land and their culture. St. Helena is an inner South Carolina island that has a particularly strong black community, even though it is bridged to the mainland. One of the anchors of the St. Helena black community is the Penn Center, an educational institution, museum and community service center that grew out of the first school for Southern blacks that two Philadelphia abolitionists founded in 1862.

The disappearance of Gullah has been predicted a number of times, but still the language survives, spoken in some form by an estimated 250,000 people in the coastal regions of South Carolina, Georgia and northern Florida.

The use of the Sea Islands as vacation resorts did not originate in our time. As far back as the 18th century, Southern planters brought their families out to the coastal islands during the sultry summer months, and a number of islands were known as "Hunting Island" because planters used them as hunting grounds in the fall. After the Civil War, rich northerners began to come down to hunt and vacation on the Sea Islands, and a few extremely wealthy Yankees bought up entire islands or huge sections of islands. Bulls Island, now part of the Cape Romain National Wildlife Refuge north of Charleston; Sapelo, now owned by the state of Georgia and open to

The Sea Islands of South Carolina

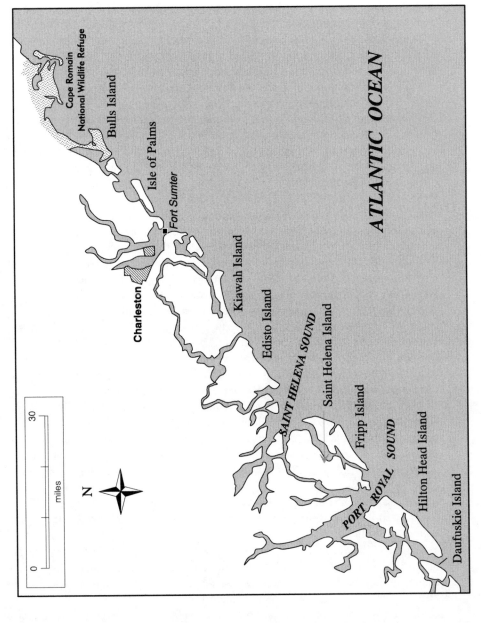

the public as a wildlife refuge and estuarine sanctuary; and Cumberland Island, the largest and southernmost Georgia island, now almost entirely National Seashore—all owe their preservation in part to the rich northern families who kept them in near pristine condition from the late 19th century into the recent past.

Together, these protected islands offer a superb opportunity for seeing the Sea Islands in their natural state. All three of these unbridged islands have extensive maritime forests of live oaks and palmettos, salt marshes on their backsides, and long sandy barrier beaches fronting the Atlantic Ocean. The Nature Conservancy also owns a number of islands off the coast of South Carolina, including Turtle Island and St. Phillips Island, but these nature preserves, unlike Bulls Island, Sapelo and Cumberland, are not served by public ferries.

The Georgia Sea Islands are far better protected from development than their counterparts in South Carolina. Only four of the Georgia islands—Tybee, St. Simons, Sea Island and Jekyll—are connected by bridge to the mainland, and several of the unbridged islands are entirely off-limits to the visiting public. Wassaw, Blackbeard and Wolf Islands are protected as federal nature reserves and may be reached only by private boat; Ossabaw, managed by the state of Georgia, is off-limits to the visiting public, as is privately owned St. Catherines Island. Among the unbridged islands, only Sapelo, owned by the state of Georgia, and Cumberland, mostly owned by the federal government, may be reached by regularly scheduled ferries open to the public. Little St. Simons is also unbridged, but it is privately owned and the public may visit only as guests of the small, rustic resort. For information about visiting this island, write Little St. Simons Island, Post Office Box 1078, St. Simons Island, Georgia 31522, or call 912-638-4404.

The bridged Georgia Sea Islands, including St. Simons, Jekyll and Sea Island, have been resorts for quite some time.

Thanks to the generosity of private owners and lobbying efforts of conservationists, Cumberland Island was saved from the resort development that is swallowing up more and more of the beachfront and forest of St. Simons and that has made Sea Island and Little St. Simons accessible only to the privileged few. Cumberland, which was declared National Seashore in 1972, is the largest of the Georgia Sea Islands and also, arguably, the most beautiful, with high sweeping dunes, herds of feral horses, stands of ancient live oaks and a pristine barrier beach. On Cumberland and Sapelo visitors can see the Georgia Sea Islands very much as they appeared when the Guale Indians had sole possession, before the coming of the French traders, the Spanish missionaries and finally the English settlers who won them and kept them.

BULLS ISLAND

Area: 5,018 acres.

Population: Refuge personnel only.

Location: 3 miles east of Moores Landing, off the coast of South Carolina.

Access: By passenger ferry from Moores Landing (contact Captain John Pryor, 803-884-0448 or the Cape Romain National Wildlife Refuge, 803-928-3368).

Visiting Bulls Island is rather like walking through a zoo in which all the animals have been set free. Animals—exotic, beautiful, flying, slithering, trilling, staring, breeding, wild animals—are *everywhere* in astonishing numbers and variety. Great flocks of snowy egrets and white ibis rise up as you approach the ponds at which they feed; alligators sun themselves on mud banks next to the nature trails; brown pelicans cruise and dive just offshore of the six-and-a-half-mile-long barrier beach on the Atlantic Ocean; songbirds fill the palmetto and live oak forest with their music; deer and raccoon hide in the forest depths. In all, there are 279 species of birds, 15 varieties of amphibians and reptiles and 19 mammal species—all on a 5,018-acre island of forest, salt marsh, fresh-water ponds, salt-water inlets, tidal creeks and sand beach 22 miles northeast of Charleston. Bulls Island, which has no residents aside from refuge personnel, no facilities aside from a toilet, picnic tables and an inclement weather shelter, and few human visitors, is like a secret Eden that the Creator finished and sealed away on the morning of the sixth day, before He had thought to make man. When you have slipped far enough inside this kingdom of the animals, you may have the unsettling feeling of being alone with—and surrounded by—the winged, clawed, beaked and scaled *other*. This is *their* world, a world that has escaped our dominion and, seemingly, our history. But for those people who love animals, and who love them best in their natural habitat, this very feeling of strangeness, of intruding on the animals in a place that belongs only to them, makes Bulls Island a wonderfully magical world.

The live oaks of this "boneyard beach" on Bulls Island were once well inland, but the rolling over of barrier island toward the mainland has exposed them to the ocean.

Bulls Island, of course, has not escaped history, and it belongs technically not to the animals but to us, the American people, for it is a part of the 34,229-acre Cape Romain National Wildlife Refuge, established in 1932 to protect waterfowl and shorebirds. Extending for 22 miles along the South Carolina coast from Bulls Island northeast to Cape Island, the refuge comprises a group of seven major islands and many smaller ones separated by mazy creeks and muddy little bays. Within its borders there are some 30,000 acres of open water, including Bull Bay. Most of the islands within the refuge are little more than humps of mud covered with grasses and shrubs—ideal for birds, but too low to the water for human habitation. All the islands with the exception of Bulls Island are wilderness areas (which means they have no facilities of any kind), and Bird Island and Marsh Island in Bull Bay are entirely off-limits to people from February 15 through September 15 when the birds are nesting. Bulls Island, which was added to the refuge in 1936, is the largest, highest and driest of the Cape Romain barrier islands, the only island that supports a forest, and the only one that is serviced by a public boat. (Captain Pryor's 36-passenger boat, which makes the three-mile crossing from Moores Landing in about half an hour, is the only passage to the island authorized by the U.S. Fish and Wildlife Service, which manages the refuge; for most of the year the boat runs on Friday, Saturday and Sunday only.)

The Cape Romain Refuge supplies a critical habitat and nesting ground for a number of threatened and endangered species. Its colony of Eastern brown pelicans is one of the largest on the East Coast, and in winter it has the largest concentration of oystercatchers anywhere. The ponds on Bulls Island provide winter homes to vast numbers of ducks and tundra swans. And a greater number of threatened Atlantic loggerhead turtles nest on the refuge beaches than on any East Coast location outside of Florida. Each year loggerheads dig between 800 and 1,200 nests on the remote Cape Island within the refuge. A refuge brochure states without exaggeration: "Cape Romain National Wildlife Refuge has become recognized as one of the most important wildlife areas on the Atlantic coast."

Visiting Bulls Island

A trip to Bulls Island begins at Moores Landing on the mainland, the site of the refuge visitor's center and the dock for the ferry. Here you can get a little preview of some of the island's wildlife. In the woods behind the visitor's center there is a short nature loop, which affords a good opportunity to get acquainted with the local songbirds. At low tide, wading and shore birds feed in the shallow waters off the public landing, and local fishermen use the pier for fishing and crabbing. As the ferry pulls away from shore, you have a sense of setting out on an expedition into deep, subtropical wilderness. The ferry to Bulls Island crosses the Intracoastal Waterway at Sewee Bay and then enters the labyrinthine channels that wind through the marshy islands of the refuge. The number and variety of birds increase as you approach Bulls Island. When I made the trip out in early April, my fellow passengers, members of a Michigan Audubon Society field trip, spotted royal terns, cormorants, kingfishers, brown pelicans and oystercatchers from the boat.

The ferry docks at the sheltered back side of the island where a vast salt marsh extends west as far as the eye can see. Unlike the barrier islands of the Outer Banks,

Bulls Island and most of the other South Carolina barrier islands are not separated from the mainland by open water but rather by salt marsh threaded by narrow muddy creeks. A giant with waterproof boots would have no trouble walking through the salt marsh from one island to the next. Within the boundaries of the Cape Romain Refuge there are 20,000 acres of salt marsh, and a single plant species—*Spartina alterniflora*, the salt marsh cord grass—dominates this immense damp prairie. Animals that live in the salt marsh include herons, egrets, clapper rails, diamondback terrapins, raccoons and otters, and the salt marsh is a nursery for many types of shellfish.

A path leads from the ferry landing into Bulls Island's high, light, rustling forest of live oak draped with silver-gray Spanish moss, magnolia, yaupon holly, cabbage palmetto, eastern red cedar and loblolly pine. The forest covers 1,475 acres on Bulls Island. A short walk takes you to a clearing where there are picnic tables, toilets, a display case of island plants and animals, and a rain shelter. There is no camping on the island and no staffed visitor's center; visitors must bring all their own food, water and insect repellent (essential during the warm months). The ferry schedule gives you seven hours to explore the 15 miles of road, the two-mile nature trail and the six miles of empty, hard-packed sand barrier beach. Unless you have come over with a group that has arranged ahead of time for a ranger-led tour, you are very much on your own on Bulls Island. Several minutes after my arrival on the island, the members of the Audubon trip had scattered and I found myself alone with the animals. Except for a few passing encounters with birders and fishermen, I remained alone during the entire day. It was an exhilarating and at times almost eerie experience.

Wildlife on the Ponds

Captain John Pryor who owns and runs the boat to the island promised there would be alligators along the two-mile interpretive trail, so this is where I headed first. The trail emerges from the woods onto a narrow strip of land that separates the Upper and Lower Summerhouse Ponds, shallow, brackish bodies of water that looked just like my mental image of where an alligator would live. An interpretive sign posted near the trail explains that alligators nest in mounds of grass and muck two feet high, that they lay 40 to 60 eggs in each mound, and that the eggs incubate for 60 to 90 days with heat generated by the decaying vegetation. I scanned the mud and muck of Lower Summerhouse Pond, and, sure enough, there was a large mother alligator (*Alligator mississippiensis*)) sunning herself near a bank of white flowers. I knew she was a mother because I saw her three babies plop into the water and disappear as I approached. With her saw-toothed tail, bumpy back that looked like a waffle-iron, tiny eyes, dark bluish-gray skin and enormous (and blessedly closed) jaws, this creature looked as if she had been resting here utterly immobile since time began. In fact, alligators can move pretty swiftly when they have a mind to; but, according to Refuge Manager George Garris, they are not dangerous to people unless people start feeding them. "We used to tell visitors that the alligators were harmless," says Garris, "but since a few alligators have recently attacked people in Florida, we have been advising a bit more caution." Alligators' preferred foods are fish and turtles, and the babies grow an inch a year on this diet for their first six years. Adult alligators range between six and 12 feet long. Garris says there are about 500 to 600 alligators on Bulls Island, "one to every acre of water."

Alligators are not the only creatures in residence on the Summerhouse Ponds. Vast numbers of snowy egrets, white ibis and great blue herons feed and nest on these bodies of water. Endangered wood storks also feed here, though they do not nest on the island. As you approach the birds, they set up their screeching cries of alarm and fly up into the trees to wait until you've passed though. There are a total of eight artificially created ponds covering 990 acres on the island—the two Summerhouse Ponds, Big Pond, Moccasin Pond, Moccasin Flats, Pools 2 and 3 and Jack's Creek Pool, which connects with Bull Harbor and serves as the island's fishing pond. All of the ponds are brackish to some extent, with the salinity levels varying according to the water table and the tides. All are thick with birds, particularly during the winter and spring. The island's waterfowl population peaks in late November or early December, when widgeons, canvasbacks, ring-necked ducks and tundra swans, among other species, winter over on the ponds.

History

Bulls Island has a photo blind next to Moccasin Pond (take Lighthouse Road east off Beach Road), and from here you can easily circle the eastern section of the island by continuing along Lighthouse Road, making a loop around Jack's Creek Pool and then returning west on Old Fort Road to the picnic area. Old Fort Road is named for the ruins of an old fort just west of the Jack's Creek inlet. The eight-sided fort was built of tabby, a kind of rough concrete made of oyster shells, lime and sand, all mixed together with salt water, that used to be a common building material in the Sea Islands. Sea Island slaves were often housed in tabby shacks, and many plantation big houses had tabby foundations. Historians disagree on the dates and purpose of the Bulls Island fort. One theory is that it was part of the network of coastal lookouts authorized by the South Carolina General Assembly in the 18th century to counter pirates and smugglers. If you imagine the area clear of trees, you can see that the fort commanded an extensive view of Bull Bay. Another theory claims that it was merely a cistern used to collect rainwater, though this doesn't explain why it is eight-sided.

The fort, or whatever it was, marks the spot where the first European settlers stopped off on their way to Charleston in 1670. A Captain Bull was aboard the ship, and the island and bay are named for him. (The island's name is given variously as Bull, Bull's and Bulls, the latter being the most common.) Bulls Island had dozens of owners over the years and probably quite a few residents. There used to be a number of houses on the island, a summerhouse on Price Creek at the west end of the island, and a lighthouse—none of them standing now. Before the Civil War, Bulls Island, like most of the other South Carolina Sea Islands, supported large farms worked by slaves. Indigo and rice were the major crops grown here. Refuge manager George Garris does not believe that cotton was grown on the island, though it was the dominant crop on most of the Sea Islands from the late 18th century until the Civil War. Bulls Island was better suited to rice because growers could impound fresh water.

During the Civil War the white owners evacuated the Sea Islands, which were particularly vulnerable to the Union navy, and after the war most of the old plantations were broken up and sold off. In the early 20th century, Bulls Island came into the hands of wealthy Northern sportsmen who used it as their private hunting reserve. The Dominick family of New York City bought the island in 1925 and built the house that still stands at the edge of the picnic clearing. Massive live oaks grow on its lawn and a wisteria bush planted as an ornamental has grown wild and draped itself over the trees of the encroaching forest. The Dominicks cleared off small areas of the forest to create open fields, turned some of the swampy flats that were used in the growing of rice and indigo into duck ponds, and hunted here. But otherwise they left the island much as they found it.

In 1936, the Dominick family sold Bulls Island to the federal government as part of the Cape Romain National Wildlife Refuge, which had been set up in 1932. Since then the island has been administered by the U.S. Fish and Wildlife Service, which is part of the Department of the Interior. The service tries to have a family live permanently on the island for maintenance and caretaking, but the isolation gets to people and they tend to move off after short stays. Each year, between 45,000 and 50,000 people visit the Cape Romain National Wildlife Refuge. But, of course, the resident and visiting herons, egrets, alligators, loggerhead turtles, swans and ducks far outnumber the people. This is only fitting. With so many of the Sea Islands going the way of resorts like Hilton Head and Kiawah, it's wonderful that the animals should have one place of their own on the beautiful South Carolina coast.

FORT SUMTER

Area: 2.5 acres.

Population: One family of National Park Service personnel.

Location: In the harbor of Charleston, South Carolina, 3 miles southeast of the city.

Access: By passenger tour boats from Charleston (call 803-722-1691). For further information contact the Fort Sumter National Monument headquarters on Sullivans Island at 803-883-3123.

The officers' quarters and the gateway at Fort Sumter on April 15, 1861, after 34 hours of bombardment by Confederate batteries stationed on the surrounding islands. The shot signaling the Rebels to open fire on Fort Sumter was the first shot of the Civil War. (Courtesy of the Fort Sumter National Monument.)

At the entrance to the harbor of Charleston, South Carolina, there is a small, manmade island around the perimeter of which rise the broken walls of a ruined fort. If one were sailing out of Charleston, one would cruise right by the flat treeless island without a second look. Unless one knew the name of the place, one might sail past the island without pausing to reflect on the terrible history that unfolded here. For on this barren, featureless island, the low stubby wall is what remains of Fort Sumter, where the first shots of the Civil War were fired and where one of the longest sieges in modern warfare took place. Today Fort Sumter is a

FORT SUMTER

National Monument and the site of a museum devoted to the history of four blood-soaked years.

The War of 1812 alerted the U.S. government to the need for a stronger coastal defense network, and Fort Sumter was undertaken as part of the defenses of Charleston harbor. As one can see on a map, a fort situated between Sullivans Island and James Island at the center of the channel that leads into the harbor would make Charleston extremely difficult to attack by sea. In the event, this was precisely the case. Work on the fort, which was named for General Thomas Sumter, the "Gamecock" of the American Revolution, was begun in 1829. Since there was no island existing on the spot, an island was constructed by piling granite blocks on top of a natural shoal. The fort was made of brick with walls five feet thick, and its plan called for an armament of 135 guns and a garrison of 650 men. However, work on Fort Sumter progressed slowly, and though the walls were in place, only 60 cannon were mounted when South Carolina seceded from the Union in December of 1860.

At the time of the secession, Union forces under the command of Major Robert Anderson held the four forts that made up Charleston's harbor defense system. Realizing that his small garrison could not defend all the forts if the South Carolina Rebel militia attacked, Anderson withdrew to Fort Sumter, the strongest and least accessible of the harbor forts. The Rebel forces immediately seized the other Charleston harbor forts. By March of 1861, Anderson knew he could not hold out on Fort Sumter much longer and he applied to Washington for relief. When the relief ships appeared off Charleston Harbor on April 12, 1861, Rebel troops under the command of General Pierre Gustave Toutant de Beauregard opened fire on Fort Sumter from the surrounding harbor forts. The first shot of the Civil War was actually a signal shot fired from Fort Johnson on James Island alerting the Confederate batteries to begin the attack on Fort Sumter. After 34 hours of ceaseless bombardment from 43 guns positioned at Fort Johnson, Fort Moultrie on Sullivans Island and batteries on Morris Island, Major Anderson surrendered and the Rebel forces took control of the badly battered Fort Sumter. The following day, President Lincoln summoned 75,000 Union troops into action and the War Between the States began in earnest.

The Confederates retained control of Fort Sumter nearly for the duration of the war, although they faced just about ceaseless bombardment by Union troops from 1863 to 1865. The Confederates held out against a squadron of Union ironclads sent down in April of 1863, and though Union firepower eventually reduced Fort Sumter to little more than a pile of rubble, the Confederate garrison stood firm. When General William Sherman's successes on land finally cut off the supply lines to Charleston, the Confederates were forced to evacuate Fort Sumter on February 17, 1865. They had endured 567 days of continuous action.

Fort Sumter was repaired after the Civil War and the federal government maintained an Army garrison here until the 1940s. In 1948, Fort Sumter was declared a National Monument and the Department of the Interior took over the small island from the Army. In 1989, Fort Sumter suffered a different sort of onslaught when an 18-foot storm surge generated by Hurricane Hugo washed over the island, inflicting damages estimated at one million dollars.

Each year, some 325,000 visitors ferry out from Charleston's City Marina to see the single tier that remains of Fort Sumter's original three-tier structure and to visit the museum. The National Park Service, which administers Fort Sumter, provides brochures that visitors can use for a self-guided walking tour through the ruins of the fort's gunrooms, officers' quarters, enlisted men's barracks, parade grounds and esplanade.

DAUFUSKIE ISLAND

Area: 5,882 acres; 5.5 miles long by 2.5 miles wide.
Population: About 100 permanent residents.
Location: Off the coast of South Carolina, 4 miles south of Hilton Head Island.
Access: By passenger ferry from Hilton Head Island (call 803-681-7335 or 803-681-8324).

Daufuskie is an apt symbol for the fate of the South Carolina Sea Islands in our time. Not too many years back, Daufuskie was a truly isolated island, a place of deep mystery and strange, dark rumors, a place few had heard of and practically no one ever visited. Though only four miles from booming Hilton Head and less than 20 miles from downtown Savannah, Georgia, Daufuskie seemed to belong to another age and another continent. Its black inhabitants, the descendants of island slaves, spoke Gullah, a creole dialect that combines a predominantly English and pidgin English vocabulary with West African grammar and intonation and that is mostly unintelligible to speakers of standard English. On the isolated Sea Islands, Gullah is more than a language—it is a separate culture. Speakers of Gullah have their own way of fishing and storytelling, praying and dressing, making crafts and arranging their houses. Daufuskie's Gullah community was among the more remote and backward on the South Carolina coast. Until quite recently, the people rode oxcarts along the deeply shaded dirt tracks that connected their shacks, their church, their school and store. Daufuskie Island seemed much more a part of timeless Africa than contemporary South Carolina. While golf balls and champagne corks popped on Hilton Head to the north and Tybee Island to the south, Daufuskie remained swaddled in its seemingly impenetrable veil of strangeness and inaccessibility. The giant of development that was stalking down the coast, squashing Sea Island after Sea Island, had stepped over Daufuskie. It seemed too odd, too black, too hard to get to for the developers to bother with.

But, as it turned out, Daufuskie was not immune—it was just on hold. Its number was called in 1980. In that year, developers moved in and began buying up land for what they termed a "low density" resort. By 1984, the developers owned all the waterfront land on the island. And they were ready to build. Today, Daufuskie's star shines brightly on the resort map. The swaddling of strangeness has been snipped away and tucked back into the dim recesses of the live oak forest. Now golf balls and champagne corks pop at Melrose and Haig's Point, two spanking new island resorts that have risen on the grounds of former plantations. One resort is a "residential country club" that members can join for a fee of $42,500; the other will ultimately contain 950 houses, mostly single-family homes, organized around a golf course and other resort facilities. *U.S. News and World Report* calls them "two of the nation's most lavish resort enclaves" and noted that plans are afoot to put in two more golf courses and a 420-slip marina. In the not too distant future there will be luxury cottages and beach homes for 8,000 leisured and monied people. Meanwhile, before the crowds descend, Daufuskie retains the dewy charm of a resort area still known only to the discerning few. *Esquire*, highlighting Daufuskie in a recent article about off-the-beaten track golf courses, described it as an island where "time yet stands still...there are no cars, no bridges, no traffic jams" and raved about its two new golf courses, one designed by Jack Nicklaus.

Despite what *Esquire* reports, time does not stand still on Daufuskie Island anymore. Seemingly overnight, Daufuskie has been rolled from the shadowy past to the refulgent, expensive future. Daufuskie has become chic.

It is still too early to tell how all this will affect the blacks and few whites who live on the island. Certainly the resorts are bringing jobs to an impoverished island where the last dependable source of income vanished in 1959 when raw sewage in the Savannah River ruined the oyster beds that islanders harvested. Already, some young people who were forced to move off the island for lack of work have come back to take jobs at the resorts. The spokesmen for the developers are the first to point out that far from destroying the island, their resorts are helping to save it by providing jobs, cash, new services. But along with these benefits have come much higher taxes on the land, and some islanders, particularly the older folks who live on fixed incomes, worry that they won't be able to afford to stay much longer. As one retired white resident put it, "I think that soon we'll all be shoved off the island, black and white alike."

It is also likely that the resorts and the changes they are bringing will eventually plow under the Gullah culture and language. A cash economy will replace the barter economy; standard English will replace Gullah as the first language; supermarket produce will replace backyard garden crops; television will replace traditional communal story-telling. Daufuskie was once an open pasture for cattle, but now the resort lands on the northern and eastern sections of the island are off-limits to the islanders, except for those who work there. In time the blacks may begin to feel like strangers on the island where their people lived as free men for 100 years and slaves for 100 years before that. Quite possibly the local community, which now numbers about 100 (about 90 blacks and 10 whites), will disperse altogether, and Daufuskie will become a resort island where help is imported from the mainland. It is strange indeed that the plantation history of the Sea Islands should repeat itself in the late 20th century. These days, however, "plantation" means not cotton, rice or indigo farm but playground for the rich. Daufuskie is but the latest casualty in a coastwide campaign.

History: The Rise and Fall of Sea Island Cotton

The first major cash crop grown on Daufuskie Island was indigo, which, along with rice, was cultivated widely in the South Carolina low country during the 18th century. (Daufuskie, like most of the Sea Islands, was not suited to the cultivation of rice because there was no easy way to impound fresh water here.) The indigo market collapsed after the American Revolution, leaving the Sea Islands with large tracts of cleared land and thousands of slaves. The white owners needed a new cash crop, and they found it in Sea Island cotton. The cultivation of this crop was to shape the lives of white owners and black slaves alike during most of the 19th century.

Sea Island cotton, a superior, long-staple strain, yields twice as much yarn per pound as short-staple cotton, and the cloth woven from the yarn is of much finer quality and greater durability. The entire Sea Island cotton crop of the antebellum South was sold abroad, where it was made into clothing for the well-to-do. Sea Island cotton was expensive, not only because it was highly prized, but also because it was much more difficult to grow. Only the Sea Islands of South Carolina and northern and central Georgia had the right climate for true Sea Island cotton: The same seeds planted inland or too far south produced coarser and inferior fiber. Sea Island cotton was also a labor-intensive crop, requiring heavy manuring, frequent hoeing, and delicate handling of the lint over a prolonged harvest period. It was, in short, a crop that could only be grown profitably by slave labor. Black slaves already outnumbered whites on the South Carolina and Georgia islands at the dawn of the Sea Island cotton era, and many more slaves were brought in as the cultivation of this demanding strain spread. Blacks have been by far the largest segment of the population on Daufuskie and on other Sea Islands during nearly all of their "white" history. In fact, for much of the year during the plantation era there were practically no whites at all aside from overseers on the island, for most of Daufuskie's white plantation owners, like those on other Sea Islands, were absentee landlords who lived primarily in their town houses in Savannah, Charleston or Beaufort.

According to island historian, Mrs. Billie Burn, before the Civil War, Daufuskie Island was divided into 12 large plantations and the entire island was "a pure white flower bed" of Sea Island cotton fields. Haig's Point and Melrose, which have been resuscitated as resorts, were two of the antebellum plantations. The Civil War swept away the cotton plantation system and effectively ended the white planters' control of the Sea Islands, including Daufuskie. The Sea Islands were particularly vulnerable to the Union's superior naval strength, and so at the outset of war, the whites evacuated their plantations, in many cases never to return. Daufuskie was evacuated during November 1861. The blacks who remained on the island continued to grow some cotton on small plots, but they also cultivated vegetables they could eat and caught shrimp, fish and crabs in the mazy little creeks that separate the islands and harvested oysters and clams off the bottoms. Some of the Daufuskie whites returned to claim their land after the war, and there was some sharecropping on the island for a time, but the blacks were not happy with this system, preferring to grow what they could on their own land. In 1916 the boll weevil put an end to what little cotton farming remained.

Daufuskie in the 20th Century

When the last white landowning family left the island in 1918, the Daufuskie blacks continued to farm their small plots of land, selling their produce at Savannah, and they also made money by cutting the island's timber. During the first half of the 20th century, a large part of the island's economy was tied to the world-renowned oysters that used to be so abundant in the region. While the young able-bodied men went out in their boats to gather the oysters from the little inlets and creeks, the older men and women shucked and bottled oysters in the island's oyster plant. Daufuskie also did a lively trade in moonshine. As Mrs. Burn writes in her entertaining cookbook *Stirrin' the Pots on Daufuskie*, "Nearly every cornstalk on the Island had a spigot...Whiskey was sold to neighboring islands, to soldiers at Ft. Screven on Tybee Island, and to people and restaurants in Savannah."

Before World War II there were 900 people on Daufuskie. But during the 1950s the raw sewage flowing down the Savannah River spoiled the local oyster fishery, and the plant closed down for good in 1959. Over 300 islanders left immediately, and those who remained had no jobs and no prospects. As neighboring Hilton Head took off on its new course as a luxury resort, Daufuskie Island died. By 1984, the year the resorts started going up, the population had fallen to around 60 people, many of them retired or school children. Those few who could work supported themselves mostly by subsistence farming and shrimping. "We were all just dying out," said Mrs. Burn. "There had to be something or the island would have died out altogether." That *something*, of course, was the resort development that has transformed the island overnight.

The first parting in Daufuskie's veil actually preceded the current building boom by some years. In 1972, the writer Pat Conroy published *The Water Is Wide*, a book about his experiences as the first white teacher at the island's two-room schoolhouse, the Mary Field Elementary School. Conroy wrote about his black students with affection and humor, but he does not disguise their appalling ignorance and backwardness. Few of his students could read or write at all, none knew the name of the U.S. president or what state their island was in. (Conroy calls Daufuskie Yamacraw, but everything else about the island is the same.) Later, the book was turned into a movie called *Conrack* starring Jon Voight. Daufuskie, briefly, was in the news. Reporters came down to have a look at the real Yamacraw and write stories about "an island forgotten by time" inhabited by people little better than savages. The islanders were none too pleased with their newfound fame.

Now that fancy resorts have opened up, the newspaper reporters are back on Daufuskie to document the impact of the modern world on the small remaining black community.

Pat Conroy wrote in *The Water Is Wide* that "Yamacraw is beautiful because man has not yet had time to destroy this beauty." Since his book was published, man has found the time, and today Daufuskie fairly buzzes with engines of destruction. For those who love islands and prize their indigenous cultures, there is something unutterably sad about this destruction, something outrageous about the intrusion of exclusive, expensive resorts on rural backwaters, something terrible about the transformation of fishermen and farmers into dishwashers and groundskeepers. Those who live on the islands, however, have more complicated feelings, feelings shaped not by wistful admiration but by immediate necessity.

What is really so awful about Daufuskie Island is that it seems doomed either way—with the resorts or without them. Until the resorts opened, Daufuskie was an island with no jobs, no economy and no hope of attaining them, an island that had lost 90% of its population in about 30 years. No matter how much the people loved the island, they could do nothing but watch it die. Now there are jobs, money, amenities, consumer goods, but in all likelihood the island community *still* has no future. The real beneficiaries of the development boom will be the whites who have bought the land, not the blacks (and few whites) who have sold it. When the developers are finished with Daufuskie Island, the blacks will have lost not only most of their land but their traditional culture as well, for the old ways of Gullah are unlikely to stand up to the new ways of America. As Patricia Jones-Jackson writes of the contemporary

The Sea Islands of Georgia

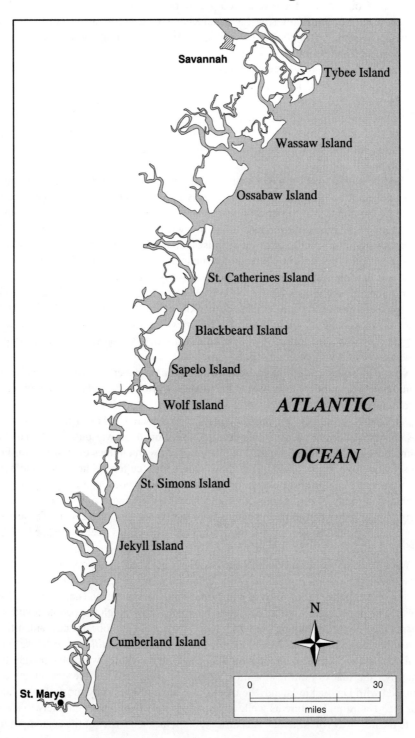

Savannah

Tybee Island

Wassaw Island

Ossabaw Island

St. Catherines Island

Blackbeard Island

Sapelo Island

Wolf Island

ATLANTIC

OCEAN

St. Simons Island

Jekyll Island

N

Cumberland Island

St. Marys

0   30

miles

plight of the Sea Island blacks in *When Roots Die: Endangered Traditions on the Sea Islands*, "Adherence to traditional ways has by and large robbed them of the ability to respond to the intrusion with equal and opposite force. The price they are paying now is one more legacy of slavery."

SAPELO ISLAND

Area: 11,000 acres.

Population: About 110 year-round residents.

Location: 6 miles off the coast of Georgia, southwest of Blackbeard Island and north of Wolf Island.

Access: By passenger ferry from Meridian, Georgia, by prior reservation only (call 912-437-6684).

Lovely Sapelo has a history of good fortune and benevolent owners. Situated at the midpoint of Georgia's Sea Islands chain—the Golden Isles or Isles of Guale as they used to be called for the Guale Indians who inhabited them—Sapelo was for nearly two centuries the private domain of a

Nannygoat Beach, Sapelo Island. This beach, like that of many Georgia barrier islands, is actually a separate island cut off from the main island by shallow water. (Buddy Sullivan; Darien, Georgia.)

succession of prominent families, all of whom loved the island and used their wealth tastefully and carefully in refashioning it. Good luck has remained with the island into the present, for the state of Georgia now owns all but 434 acres of the island and manages it as a wildlife refuge and a National Estuarine Sanctuary, leasing the south end of the island to the University of Georgia Marine Institute. The privately owned tract near the center of the island is the home of the small black community of Hog Hammock, most of whose residents are descendants of Sapelo Island slaves. For visitors to the island, the state runs the *Sapelo Queen*, a passenger ferry, several times a week, and offers full or half-day bus and walking tours. There is also camping available on the island for organized groups only (call 914-485-2251 for information).

On the trip out to Sapelo, the first thing one is struck by is the salt marsh—the vast expanse of glowing, green-gold cord grass that stretches north and south as far as the eye can see. These are "The Marshes of Glynn" that the poet Sidney Lanier (1842-1881) celebrated in his rousing poem by that name:

> The world lies east: how ample, the marsh and the sea
>   and the sky!
> A league and a league of marsh-grass, waist-high, broad
>   in the blade,

Green, and all of a height, and unflecked with a light
  or a shade,
Stretch leisurely off, in a pleasant plain,
To the terminal blue of the main...
Oh, like the greatness of God is the greatness
  within
The range of the marshes, the liberal marshes of Glynn.

These Georgia marshes, part of a vast coastal prairie that extends with a few interruptions north to New Jersey and south down to Cape Canaveral, stand out from other East Coast marshes not only for their beauty and their size, but also for the diversity of the waters that flow into them. According to scientists at the University of Georgia Marine Institute, the marshes of the Georgia Sea Islands are at the confluence of more types of salt, brackish and fresh water than any other spot on earth. These marshes are incredibly fecund, producing about three times more plant fiber than an Iowa cornfield, and providing the essential habitat for numerous shore birds including the clapper rail, common egret, whimbrel, American oystercatcher and marsh wren, as well as the nursery for shrimp, mussels, clams, oysters and other shellfish. The salt marsh surrounding Sapelo, for the most part left alone by man and buffered to the north and south by miles of undeveloped coast, is particularly rich and pristine. Here the greatness within the Marshes of Glynn reveals itself most vividly. Because of the island's remoteness from pollutants, scientists use Sapelo's water, air and soil as a control in measuring the effects of coastal development.

Sapelo is a classic southern barrier island, typical of the Atlantic islands from South Carolina to northern Florida. On the western side facing the mainland salt marsh is cut through by a maze of rivers and creeks; on the east side fronting the Atlantic Ocean there is a broad, hard-packed sand barrier beach; in between, on the higher and drier ground, grows a dense maritime forest of live oaks draped with Spanish moss and loblolly pine, the habitat of a large flock of wild turkey and a herd of white-tailed deer. The visitor to the island has a chance to see all three ecological zones—the salt marsh, the barrier beach and the maritime forest—as well as the historic houses and ruins that rose and fell in the course of Sapelo's long history.

History

The Georgia Sea Islands were among the first sections of North America to be explored, claimed and fought over by the Europeans. The French and Spanish contested each other's claims to the region in the mid-16th century, and once the French gave up, the English began to encroach from the north on the missions and *presidios* (forts) built by Spanish missionaries and soldiers. Sapelo was supposedly the site of the 16th century mission of San Jose de Zapala, the origin of the island's name. When the English forced the Spanish to abandon their holdings on the Georgia coast in 1686, the Franciscans burned down their mission buildings and cut their orange groves before vacating. The English planters started afresh in the early 18th century, and they found the land rich and fertile. Like islanders elsewhere on the East Coast, the farmers of the Georgia Sea Islands suffered the depredations of the British during the American Revolution.

Shortly after the war, the French were back on Sapelo, not as conquerors but as purchasers. A group of French aristocrats, in flight from the revolution being fought in their own country, bought the island and divided it into large estates. During the early part of the 19th century, the Marquis de Montalet and his friend the Chevalier de la Horne lived together in a Sapelo plantation house they called Le Chatelet. The slaves' name for the house—Chocolate—was quite apt, for here the Frenchmen hosted elaborate dinners prepared by Cupidon, the slave whom the Marquis initiated into to sacred mysteries of *haute cuisine*. Cupidon's feasts were the start of a long tradition of luxurious entertainment on Sapelo. The Frenchmen were apparently quite happy on their Georgia isle, though their pleasures were marred somewhat by their repeated failure to unearth truffles among the live oak roots, even with the assistance of a trained pig. The ruins of Chocolate still stand on Sapelo's north end.

Thomas Spalding, perhaps the greatest figure associated with Sapelo, purchased the south end of the island in 1802. Spalding, whose father was a well-to-do Scottish-born trader and planter on nearby St. Simons, was a man of great ability and vision who had the means of making his dreams reality. Sapelo became his private realm, and in his half-century of rule he transformed the island from near wilderness to one of the grandest plantations of the Old South. Spalding cleared off hundreds of acres of Sapelo forest for farm fields, selling the timber to shipbuilders; he designed and built his own plantation house, South End House, surrounding it with gorgeous formal gardens and furnishing it with pieces imported from Europe; he entertained lavishly and perpetually; and, in his spare time, served in the Georgia state legislature and the U.S. congress. Spalding was a gentleman farmer who took farming as seriously as he took being a gentleman. He was one of the pioneer planters of the superior long-staple cotton strain, better known as Sea Island cotton; but, unlike his fellow Sea Island planters who started growing Sea Island cotton to the exclusion of everything else, Spalding saw the dangers of a single-crop economy and advocated crop rotation and the introduction of grass for cattle grazing and sugar cane (he is still known as the father of the Georgia sugar industry). Spalding is also remembered for his kind treatment of his slaves. His headman Ben-Ali the Mohammedan (or Bul-ali as his descendants call him) was a near-legendary figure—a tall, commanding slave of mysterious French-African origin who sired a vast clan now scattered over the Georgia coast. All of the 64 residents of Sapelo's Hog Hammock community trace their ancestry back to Ben-Ali.

Thomas Spalding died in 1851, and the island passed into the hands of his heirs, but they were not to enjoy it for long. At the start of the Civil War, the white plantation owners evacuated the Georgia and South Carolina Sea

Tabby ruins of Sapelo Island's "Chocolate" plantation, built by the Marquis de Montalet in the early 19th century. (Buddy Sullivan; Darien, Georgia.)

Islands, and Sapelo fell along with the others. When the Spalding heirs regained their property after Reconstruction, they found South End House in ruins and the farm fields laid waste. They fixed up some of the smaller houses, and moved back to the island for a time, but the burden of maintaining so much land proved too much for them, and they sold off parcels as private hunting preserves.

Sapelo's next great owner, Hudson Motors magnate Howard Coffin, arrived on the scene in 1912. He bought the entire island and laid out the money to build a new mansion on the site of the old Spalding house, following some of Spalding's original plans but making the house even grander and fancier, more like a formal European villa than a Southern plantation house.

Coffin died in 1932 and the following year Richard J. Reynolds of tobacco fame and fortune took possession of the island kingdom. Reynolds kept up the Sapelo traditions of farming and entertaining, and for a time he opened the Sapelo Plantation to paying guests as a vacation resort. Starting in 1950, Reynolds donated more and more of the island to public use: First he established a boys' camp here; then in 1953, under the auspices of the Sapelo Island Research Foundation, he gave the University of Georgia's marine biology department the use of old dairy barns at the south end of the island for experiments on the island's ecology. This facility ultimately grew into today's University of Georgia Marine Institute, considered one of the world's leading centers of research into salt-marsh ecology.

Reynolds died in 1964, and in 1969 his widow sold the northern three-quarters of Sapelo to the state of Georgia. The state's Game and Fish Division of the Department of Natural Resources maintains a 8,240-acre wildlife refuge on this land, a wooded habitat for deer, wild turkey and numerous types of water fowl. In 1976 the state acquired the rest of the island with the stated goal of "preservation of the scenic and natural values of the island for the education and enjoyment of Georgia citizens." In the same year, the National Oceanic and Atmospheric Administration designated 2,800 acres of Sapelo the Duplin River National Estuarine Sanctuary. The Georgia Department of Natural Resources and the University of Georgia Marine Institute together administer the sanctuary, which protects the tidal Duplin River from its source on the island to its confluence with the waters of Doboy Sound, some six miles south. A total of 11 DNR staff members and their families now live permanently on Sapelo.

Visiting Sapelo

Unless you are a researcher or student at the Marine Institute or invited to one of their conferences, the only way to visit Sapelo is by arranging ahead of time to join one of the state-sponsored tours. On the half-day tour, offered Wednesday and Saturday

Solarium and indoor pool at South End House. (Buddy Sullivan: Darien; Georgia.)

year-round and Friday as well as from June to Labor Day, the state gives you about three hours on the island, during which time a tour guide shepherds you briskly from the *Sapelo Queen* ferry to an old school bus that bumps along the island's sandy roads. The guide narrates the island's history as the bus rumbles past the ruins of Chocolate (the plantation house of the French Marquis), the crumbling tabby shacks where the slaves lived and the grand South End House; and the visitor also learns a good deal about the island's ecology, the maritime forest in the uplands, the vast salt marsh fringing the island's backside and the barrier beach fronting the Atlantic. On the full-day tour, offered the last Tuesday of every month from April to October, the visitor has some time at the Nanny Goat barrier beach area to contemplate the island's history and beauty on his or her own. Island facilities include restrooms, water fountains and a machine selling soft drinks. Insect repellent, a must in the warm weather months (early spring to late fall), is not available on the island.

The Sapelo tour may be too speedy and too rigidly organized for some tastes, but it is informative and it guarantees that you will cover all the bases. And, of course, by moving visitors so quickly on and off the island, the state has succeeded in preserving Sapelo as a peaceful refuge for the plants and animals, and for the scientists who study them.

South End House, built by Howard Coffin on the site of Thomas Spalding's mansion in 1925. The house now serves as the headquarters for the University of Georgia Marine Institute. (Buddy Sullivan; Darien, Georgia.)

CUMBERLAND ISLAND

Area: 18,000 acres of high ground; 16.3 miles long by 3 miles wide.

Population: 20 to 30 year-round residents.

Location: The southernmost of the Georgia Sea Islands, 7 miles from St. Mary's, Georgia, south of Jekyll Island and north of Florida's Amelia Island.

Access: By passenger ferry from St. Mary's, Georgia (call the National Park Service, 912-882-4335).

The ruins of Thomas Carnegie's Dungeness, at the south end of Cumberland Island. The house, which burned down in 1959, had extensive terraces and gardens, including a stand of 500 olive trees. (Courtesy of the National Park Service, Cumberland Island National Seashore.)

The soft luxurious beauty of the tropics and the stately vigor of the temperate zone embrace on beautiful Cumberland Island, the largest and southernmost of the George Sea Islands. Dunes, some as high as 40 feet, blow off of 16 miles of white sand barrier beach. Ancient gnarled live oaks, magnolias and long-leaf pines create a vast dim forest that spreads over nearly all of the high ground on the island. Feral horses and pigs run free over the island. Alligators bask and hunt along its freshwater ponds. Loggerhead turtles (a federally protected species) nest on the barrier beaches and endangered manatees swim up into the creeks. Over 320 species of birds, including endangered wood storks, have been identified on the island and surrounding waters. An immense salt marsh, some 3,000 acres in extent, rolls out like a green and gold carpet from the mainland to the island's backside. Few Eastern islands are as richly endowed with natural splendors as Cumberland. The miracle of the island is that nearly all of this beauty is protected for public enjoyment as a National Seashore. Cumberland's riches will remain intact.

Cumberland, of noble name and illustrious ownership, has long had man's riches at its disposal to guard and protect nature's. For nearly 200 years, the island was the private domain of a number of extremely wealthy and prominent families. In the 18th and 19th centuries Cumberland supported one of the largest and most elegant plantations on the coast. After the Civil War laid waste to the plantation society of the South, Thomas Carnegie (the younger brother of Andrew) and his family acquired most of the island and used it as their vacation retreat, putting up five big houses for various branches of the family on separate estates on the island. The Carnegies and other private owners did a superb job of preserving Cumberland, and when the government acquired most of the island as National Seashore in 1972, it was in near pristine condition. The forests that had been cleared off in the plantation period for indigo and cotton fields had grown back; the beaches were empty; the wildlife abundant and healthy.

Today, the Carnegie heirs and the Candler family retain about 10% of Cumberland as private land, and one of the Carnegie homes, the Greyfield, is open to the public as an inn with nine guest bedrooms. In addition, scattered through the federal land, there are some 22 smaller private estates whose owners retain use for 25 years, 40 years or lifetime, at which point the land and houses will revert to the government. Eventually, the government plans to incorporate all of the private holdings into the Cumberland Island National Seashore.

The National Seashore lands are accessible to the public for day-use and camping. (The Park Service permits up to 300 visitors a day, including 120 campers, to use the island; reservations are accepted up to 11 months in advance.) Even as public property, Cumberland remains a princely island, generous in its proportions, exclusive in its policy toward visitors, far removed and well protected from the common world. Of all the Golden Isles of Georgia, Cumberland has the greatest glittering horde of treasure.

History

The Timucuan Indians who lived on Cumberland called it Missoe (meaning sassafras), and the Spanish, who took the island in the 16th century, called it San Pedro, for the mission the Franciscans built here. San Pedro, nearer to the Spanish stronghold of St. Augustine than the other Golden Isle missions, held out longer against the attacks of the Indians and English, but eventually the English drove the Spanish back to Florida and the island became part of the colony of Georgia that James Edward Oglethorpe founded in 1733.

A stand of ancient, gnarled live oaks on Cumberland Island. Live oaks are the dominant tree on the southern third of the island. (Courtesy of the National Park Service, Cumberland Island National Seashore.)

When he landed with his first group of settlers, Oglethorpe wisely befriended Tomochichi, one of the Creek Indian chiefs, and so smoothed the way for English control over the land. In 1734, Oglethorpe took Tomochichi and a group of Creeks to England for a state visit. The Indians were a great success with the English press and the royal family. Tomochichi's young nephew Toonahowie hit it off with William Augustus, Duke of Cumberland, the 13-year-old son of King George II, and upon the Indians' return to the New World, Toonahowie asked that the island of San Pedro be renamed Cumberland in honor of his English friend. Or so the story goes.

In the Colonial period two forts were built on the island, Fort William at the south end and St. Andrews at the north. Supposedly Oglethorpe put up a hunting lodge near Fort William, which he called Dungeness for the county seat in England's Kent. This was the first of several structures of that name to stand on the island. Cumberland changed hands several times during the period preceding the Revolution, but, although one owner advertised the land as being "fit for corn, rice, indigo, and cotton, and [containing] a quantity of live oak and pine for ship building," few of the owners cleared or farmed their holdings.

After the war, General Nathanael Greene, who had served as commander of the American Revolutionary Army in the Southern Department, bought up a good deal of Cumberland Island and planned to erect a summer home surrounded by gardens and plantation fields. Greene died in 1786 before he could realize his plans, but his family retained possession of the Dungeness Plantation and eventually built the plantation house. The grand four-story tabby structure stood on a rise formed by an old Indian shell heap; it had four chimneys and 16 fireplaces; olive trees grew around its terraces; and beyond the terraces, 12 acres of land were cleared for formal gardens. In the book *Georgia's Land of the Golden Isles*, Burnette Vanstory says that Dungeness was "the center of social life equaled by few plantations in the country" and that many of the most important military and political leaders of the day came here as guests. General Lighthorse Harry Lee, a hero of the American Revolution and the father of Robert E. Lee, was brought to the house when he took sick during a trip to the West Indies and died here in 1818. Robert E. Lee came to visit his father's grave in the Dungeness cemetery in 1829 and again, after the Civil War, in 1870. The body was removed to the Lee Chapel in Lexington, Virginia, in 1913, and the Carnegie family erected a memorial where the grave had been.

Dungeness remained in the hands of various branches of the same family until the Civil War, when the white owners here, as on nearly all the South Carolina and Georgia Sea Islands, evacuated their homes in the face of the powerful Union Navy. In 1862 Union troops removed all of the Cumberland Island slaves to Amelia Island in Florida. The owners of the Stafford Plantation, the other major plantation on Cumberland, returned after the war, though they never again farmed on a large scale; but for the family who owned Dungeness, there was nothing to return to, for the house was burned during Reconstruction.

Thomas Carnegie acquired much of the island in 1882, and he built a new Dungeness on the foundations of the old mansion. Though Carnegie died before he could enjoy his new home, his wife, Lucy, and their nine children continued to vacation at Dungeness. The Carnegies, like the family of Nathanael Greene, entertained sumptuously, employing 200 servants to run the house and maintain the grounds. Around the turn of the century, the name Dungeness appeared frequently in society pages not only for the house parties but also for the yacht that Lucy Carnegie named after her vacation house. After her husband's death, Lucy Carnegie continued buying up land on Cumberland and set to work building island homes for her children, including Greyfield (now open as the island's only inn), Plum Orchard and the Cottage. Lucy Ferguson, now in her eighties, the granddaughter of Thomas and Lucy Carnegie and one of the last major private landowners on the island, recalls mar-

Feral Horse on Cumberland Island. The 200 horses than run free on the island are the recent descendants of domesticated horses, unlike the ponies on Assateague and Ocracoke Islands, which have been wild for centuries. (Courtesy of the National Park Service, Cumberland Island National Seashore.)

velous parties at Plum Orchard, which now stands, shut up and abandoned, inside the National Seashore holdings. The Carnegies' Dungeness house burned in 1959, and today all that remains are the foundations, a few of the walls, and the garden gates and terraces, gradually being swallowed up in forest. The Dungeness lawn is one of the best places on the island to catch a glimpse of the feral horses, which come to graze here.

From Private Estate to National Seashore

In the late 1960s this princely island retreat was very nearly transformed into another Sea Island country club resort. Charles Fraser, one of the prime movers in the development of South Carolina's Hilton Head Island as a major resort, managed to buy 3,000 acres of Cumberland from the Carnegie heirs, and in 1968 he revealed his plan for Cumberland Oaks, a full-blown vacation complex complete with golf course, guest accommodations, and transportation to the mainland via aerial tramway and gondola. Conservationists came to the defense of the island, and when the government stepped in to declare Cumberland Island a National Seashore in 1972, Fraser agreed to sell his land to the National Park Service. The National Park Service opened the south end of the island to visitors in 1975. Today, about 90% of Cumberland Island is federal land.

In 1982, 8,840 acres within the National Seashore was designated the Cumberland Island Wilderness, with 11,718 acres marked as potential wilderness. In reality, the Cumberland Island Wilderness is still a "bastard wilderness" as Seashore Superintendent Ken Morgan put it, for until the leases of the private estate-holders run up, cars and all-terrain vehicles will continue to be permitted on the roads, and power lines will run to their homes. Eventually, however, the government will take over all the private estates and the area will become a true wilderness, with only hikers and horseback riders allowed. Each year, some 30,000 people make their way to Cumberland Island.

Visiting the Island

The National Park Service ferry to Cumberland Island departs from St. Mary's, on the Georgia mainland, and winds through the salt marsh and open waters for 45 minutes before arriving at the south end of the island's backside. Once on the island, the visitor is left very much on his or her own to explore the barrier beach, the dunes, the maritime forest, and the ruins of the old historic homes at the south end. There are visitor centers on the island at Sea Camp Dock and Dungeness, but the National Seashore headquarters is on the mainland at St. Mary's.

Even if you are only here for the day, you quickly lose sight of your fellow visitors as the Cumberland forest surrounds you. On the southern third of the forest, maritime live oaks are the predominant tree, many of them quite ancient, with twisted, wide-spreading branches; but as the island broadens out to the north, the live oaks occur mostly on the seaward fringe, and behind them grow hickories, long-leaf pines and loblolly pines. Willow oak, laurel oak, magnolia, red bay and holly are also common trees of the island forest. Palmetto is the predominant tree of the forest understory, and in many places the palmettos grow so thickly that they appear impenetrable. The forest is home to deer, squirrels and raccoon. The shallow brackish ponds scattered around the island support alligators, mink and otter.

Cumberland has a herd of about 200 feral horses that live all over the island; they tend to congregate on the beach during the hottest, stillest summer months, hoping, like the human visitors, for a breeze to blow the insects off them. They may also be seen in the salt marsh browsing on cord grass, on the dunes, and on the lawns of the island's historic homes. Unlike the wild ponies of Assateague and Ocracoke Islands, the Cumberland horses are recent descendants of domesticated horses, and they were interbred with mustangs, appaloosas and Tennessee walkers to improve their bloodlines. Island residents managed the horses as free-ranging livestock until 1960.

The island has 45.25 miles of trails and roads (none are paved) and 16 miles of wide barrier beach. The highest dunes, occasionally reaching 50 feet, are at the south end of the island and about three-quarters of the way north, though all the dunes are gradually eroding as sea levels rise. From April to August, loggerhead turtles dig their nests and bury their eggs along the Cumberland barrier beach. Unlike the islands of the Cape Romain National Wildlife Refuge in South Carolina (see Bulls Island entry), Cumberland Island affords a safe nesting area for loggerheads and thus no program of egg relocation has been necessary here. The major predator to loggerhead eggs on Cumberland is the ghost crab, but these little animals do not wreak the havoc that raccoons do on Cape Romain. Seashore Superintendent Ken Morgan points out that scientists have studied the Cumberland nesting loggerheads for nearly 20 years now, in which time they have come to know exactly where on the beach a loggerhead mother will nest, when she will arrive, and how many times she is likely to return in the course of the nesting season. Each year, there are some 200 loggerhead nests on the Cumberland beach.

For those interested in the history of the island, the National Park Service has established an interpretive trail—the Dungeness Trail—through the historic district at the south end. Visitors may see the ruins of Carnegie's Dungeness as well as the remains of some earlier structures. The Dungeness Trail traverses the island, passing through the maritime forest, skirting the salt marsh, and ending at the barrier beach. One former Carnegie mansion, Plum Orchard, seven and a half miles from the south end where the Park Service ferry docks, is open for occasional tours offered by park rangers.

The Park Service permits 120 campers on the island at any given time, 60 at a developed campsite where drinking water, showers and toilets are available, and 60 at three backcountry sites around the island. The backcountry sites have no facilities, and the most remote site is a 10.6-mile hike from the ferry landing. There is no food sold on the island.

Cumberland Island also offers a very different kind of experience to visitors who can afford to stay at the Greyfield Inn. This former Carnegie mansion is now run as a very low-key hotel, and the staff does all they can do to make guests feel as if they have been invited to a country house party by the family. The Greyfield has no resort facilities—no tennis or golf or poolside bar (no pool even)—but it does have Cumberland Island all around it, and, if you are so inclined, you can easily forget that most of the island is National Seashore and pretend it is an immense private estate at your disposal.

The campers on the island may feel that it's cheating to be put up in such luxury on a wilderness island, and perhaps it is. Those who immerse themselves in Cumberland's wilderness without the buffer of artificial luxury no doubt experience more immediately the luxury nature furnishes here, the softness of the subtropical climate, the brilliance of sand and sky and flowers in the intense southern light, the soothing music of crickets and tree frogs, the stirring music of horses thundering on the beach and breakers hissing up the sand. The Greyfield guests can console themselves, if they need any consolation, with the thought that they are carrying on a long tradition of high living on an island named for royalty and owned by generals of the military and captains of industry. Whether we admire the style of these wealthy former proprietors or resent their privileges, we can all thank them for keeping Cumberland Island so carefully and so beautifully for us to enjoy today.

THE ISLANDS OF FLORIDA

INTRODUCTION

Maine's license plates are branded "Vacationland," but the epithet would fit Florida just as well or better. Nowhere is the spirit of Vacationland more palpable than on the chain of islands strung out along the 350 miles of Florida's Atlantic coast. Bridges and causeways connect these islands to the mainland, giving easy access to the millions of vacationers who migrate, like the birds, when the weather turns cold up north. On Florida's eastern islands have risen such famous resort cities as Miami Beach, Palm Beach and Fort Lauderdale.

The northern Florida islands are quite similar in topography, climate and vegetation to the Georgia Sea Islands. Both temperate zone and subtropical species thrive on these fertile, low-lying barrier islands. Before the Civil War, Amelia Island and Fort George Island, near Jacksonville, supported cotton plantations. Now the Amelia Island Plantation is a posh, exclusive resort featuring year-round golf and tennis. Farther south is Anastasia Island, the barrier island that protects St. Augustine, the oldest city in the United States.

Merritt Island, about halfway down the Florida peninsula, is a large island whose northern end is protected by the Merritt Island National Wildlife Refuge. Cape Canaveral, which wraps around Merritt Island on the ocean side, is the site of the John F. Kennedy Space Center as well as the 57,000-acre Canaveral National Seashore, which includes some 25 miles of ocean beach. Merritt Island is noteworthy not only for its wildlife refuge but also for its commercial citrus groves, leased to growers by the federal government. Citrus fruits are grown extensively along much of the Indian River, actually a 125-mile-long tidal lagoon running from north of Merritt Island down to the St. Lucia Inlet south of Hutchinson Island, one of the less developed of the Florida barrier islands.

South of Cape Canaveral, the commercial sprawl begins again on Cocoa Beach and continues, punctuated by citrus groves, through Vero Beach, Palm Beach and Fort Lauderdale (all built on barrier islands), until it reaches its culmination at Miami Beach, the most intensively developed barrier island on the Atlantic coast. Miami Beach, with its apartment towers rising right at the edge of the sand, is a prime example of the havoc man wreaks when he destroys the barrier island ecology. After developers bulldozed the Miami Beach dunes early in the century, the beach began to erode rapidly. By the early 1970s the beach was practically gone, and the luxury hotels and condo towers stood at the ocean's edge. Some $67 million were laid out between 1976 and 1980 to put a new, 300-foot-wide sand beach down on the ocean shore of Miami Beach ("beach nourishment" they call it), but many scientists are sceptical about the long-term success of such projects.

South of Miami Beach, the Florida Keys begin their long sweeping arc into the Gulf of Mexico.

The Florida Keys

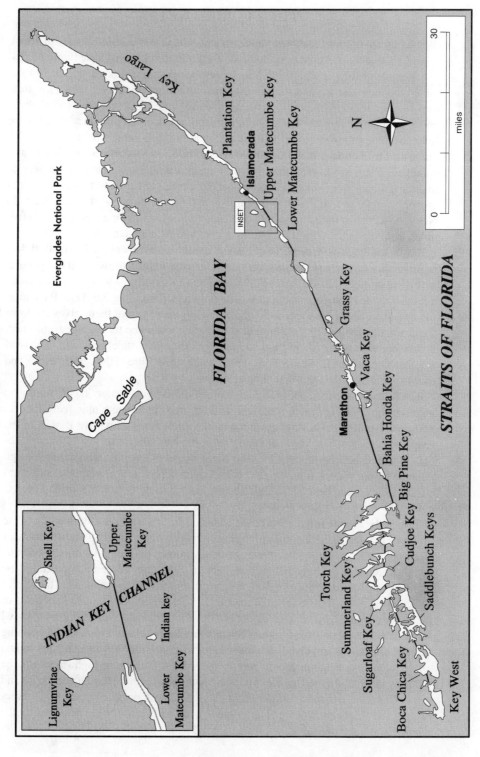

THE FLORIDA KEYS

The Eastern islands reach their southern terminus in a 180-mile-long arc of small, low-lying, thickly scattered coral and limestone outcrops known as the Florida Keys. The Keys are extravagant islands, vast in number, rich and strange in their history, fabled for their climate and their beauty, dense (and growing ever denser) in their opportunities for tourists, unique in the continental United States for the tropical plants and animals they support on land and even more spectacularly unique at sea for the living coral reef a few miles to the south that shadows their entire extent for 220 miles out to the Dry Tortugas in the Gulf of Mexico. The Keys are extravagant also in their contrasts: There are keys, entirely carved up into subdivisions and tourist service facilities, a half mile away from a key where a tropical hardwood forest has been growing slowly and undisturbed for millennia; there are keys controlled by the U.S. Navy and keys that hide hippies and drug smugglers. On Big Pine Key, less than five miles from the giant Winn Dixie supermarket and its attendant shopping center on U.S. 1, is the 2,000-acre preserve of the last small herd of key deer, the smallest deer in America, a tiny subspecies that lives (precariously) only on the Keys. If one persists in driving through the dull, scrubby, vacant Lower Keys, one winds up in Key West, a loud, crowded compact island city—the only real city on the Keys and the end of the line. And so the contrasts and jarring juxtapositions repeat themselves all down the chain: the vast, smooth expanse of shimmering water and the cramped, confined, broken horizons of the islands; ugly trailer parks shaded by stately coconut palms and smothered in riotous flowering bougainvillea; the white glare of the coralline rock and the dusty green of the trees that cling to it.

The Keys are wedged between two impressive bodies of water: To the north and west, on the Gulf of Mexico side, lies shallow (maximum depth nine feet), fecund, 850-square-mile Florida Bay, down which the thick green mangrove islands of the Everglades encroach; to the south and east of the Keys, beyond Hawk Channel, lies the coral reef; beyond the reef the Gulf Stream runs in a darker blue streak through Atlantic Ocean waters, following the island chain before it turns abruptly northward past Key Largo; and beyond the Gulf Stream, out across the Straits of Florida, is Cuba, a mere 90 miles from Key West.

That is the marine orientation of the islands. Moving landward, drawing in to the center of the islands, one comes up against a river of concrete, U.S. 1, the Overseas Highway, which has dominated and drastically altered the Keys' landscape since its completion in 1938. (Even before this, back in 1912, the railroad that preceded the highway first linked up the islands with each other and with the mainland to the north.) The highway, with its 106 miles of road and 42 bridges, binds together the bodies of the major islands like a continuous sore from which emanate ever-multiplying radial sores in the form of new subdivisions and new condo compounds, motels and shopping centers, shell shops and dive shops, bars and restaurants, marinas and gas stations and all the other incrustations that adhere to the sides of American highways. It is the highway that has plugged the Keys into the mainline of Florida tourist attractions and traps. Undersea treasure! Bottomless boats! African Queen! Flipper! Over every bridge, a new collection of signs lures you to a new collection of fun activities for the whole family. At times it's like driving around inside a pinball machine.

THE FLORIDA KEYS

The highway has brought too much of all of this tourist tackiness to the Keys. Unless one is out on the water or under it, there is no escaping the road and its intrusion upon the islands. There is the ceaseless roar of traffic, the hurried flow of new tourists, new settlers, new retirees (and the steady if quieter ebb of Conchs, Keys natives, to the mainland)—all moving along a single, mostly two-lane road, back and forth, day and night, from Key Largo to Key West. The road and what it has brought have crowded up the Keys: The islands are overbuilt, and overbuilt with much haste and little taste. Fifty years ago, the islands outside of Key West were practically deserted, and even 15 years ago they were sparsely populated, but now the Keys have a permanent population of some 63,000 people, and 70% more in the winter months.

The Keys are perhaps the most flagrant example of what happens to islands when bridges span the waters that separate them from each other and from the mainland. The surrounding water remains—but it has been transformed from perilous, intractable *element* to view. The islands still look like islands, but they no longer feel like islands. Fortunately for island lovers, nature lovers and history buffs, two keys have escaped this bondage to the highway. These are Lignumvitae Key and Indian Key, less than two miles apart, one on the bay side, the other on the ocean side of Lower Matecumbe Key. (Of course there are many hundreds of other islands unconnected to the bridged chain of keys, but these may be visited only by private boat whereas anyone can get to Lignumvitae and Indian Key by public ferry.) These two accessible, unbridged islands, each fascinating in a completely different way, are our windows on the Keys as they once were: Indian Key for the life of the early American settlers

Slash pine and saw palmetto growing along the Jack C. Watson nature trail at National Key Deer Wildlife Refuge on Big Pine Key. (Felice Nudelman)

in the 19th century and Lignumvitae for the life of the native forests and forest animals. Though they are only tiny specks of land on the long chain of islands, these unbridged keys furnish precious information and resources many times their size. Indian Key and Lignumvitae are discussed in detail in separate entries below.

Keys Geology: From Coral Reef to Limestone Island

The highway and bridges may have linked the Keys in some fundamental, inescapable way to the mainland, but these recent artificial intrusions have not altogether obliterated the mystery and strangeness of the islands. It is hard to contemplate the Keys, however idly, without wondering how they were formed, what they are made of, why they look different from the mainland and why the Upper Keys look different from the Lower Keys. Despite the overlay of highway culture, such basic questions of the land still come to mind even as one cruises comfortably between green water and blue sky. To really understand and appreciate the Keys, one needs to consider their geology. And to understand their geology, one should begin not with the land itself, but with the sea and the great coral reef that the sea sustains three to ten miles offshore of the islands.

The reef, in essence, is an intricate and interlocking series of undersea structures created by tiny tubular marine animals. John James Audubon, who visited the Keys in 1832, says in his journal that the reef "stretches along the shore like a great wall reared by an army of giants." Stony corals, coralline algae and some species of tube-dwelling worms build this wall by secreting calcium carbonate, a limy compound as hard as stone. After the corals secrete these lime deposits they die, and new corals build on top of the tiny, empty stone cups. The reef grows exceedingly slowly over thousands of years, with different coral species building their coralline pueblo cities in different shapes: balls indented with mazy passages that look like human brains, stag's horns, whips, mushrooms, fans, elkhorns. Despite its hard outer surface, the reef is extremely fragile; a single shipwreck in 1984 killed four acres of reef off Key Largo, and water pollution, fishing, siltation and the visits of more than a million divers a year are all taking their toll on the living reef.

Not only is the reef itself alive, but it is also a habitat for a fabulous variety of undersea plants and animals. Four hundred species of fish inhabit Alligator Reef near Lower Matecumbe, and a single reef may support as many as 3,000 plants and animals—not individuals but *species*. No photograph or written description can prepare one for the shapes and colors of the reef: the blazing stripes of porkfish, the flashing red of brain coral and seductive green of star coral, the shafts of light that fall through the purple sea fans, the sharp, hungry eyes of sharks and barracudas, the next tangle of color and light just beyond that beckons one to wander still farther and farther. As gorgeous as the ever-changing surface of the ocean looks to us, the living coral world under the surface is infinitely more gorgeous—bright and dim, soothing and frightening, grotesque and enchanting, and endlessly, richly surprising like our earliest memories of childhood.

Only the outer surface of the reef is living. Inside are the empty apartments of departed coral tenants. But the apartments don't remain empty forever. In time, sediments sift in and become packed together and the reef hardens and solidifies into limestone. "In this fashion," write William and Stephen Amos in *Atlantic and Gulf*

Coasts, "living organisms are directly or indirectly major geological forces, creating rocky marine habitats where formerly there were none."

When ocean levels drop or when the ocean floor is thrust upward, these underwater structures may rise into the air and become islands. This is precisely what happened on the Upper Keys from Virginia Key just south of Miami to Big Pine Key, about 30 miles northeast of Key West. These keys are old, long dead coral colonies that have fossilized into a hard, pitted white rock called Key Largo limestone. If you walk through an undeveloped area or along the shore, you will see chunks of this limestone with the intricate coralline structures still adhering to each other, the patterns still intact 100,000 years after the coral polyps made them. If you snorkel or dive through the submerged offshore reef, you will see precisely the same coralline structures in the brilliant red, green and orange-brown colors they wear when they are the living habitat not of people and cars but of even more brilliantly colored algae, fish, and the silent and swift sharks and barracudas that lurk in their recesses. The emerged reef of Key Largo limestone that composes the islands is like a ghost of the living reef that grows offshore. Or, from a different perspective, the living coral reef is a chain of underwater keys. The Keys are the only part of the continental United States where coral reefs form, because here the water temperature never drops below 64 degrees Fahrenheit.

The Lower Keys from Big Pine to Key West are also limestone, but a different type of limestone that was formed in a different fashion from the Key Largo limestone of the Upper Keys. This difference in the substrate gives these Lower Keys a different shape, a different geographical orientation and different types of vegetation from the Upper Keys. The limestone of the Lower Keys, known as oolite, is made of billions of tiny round calcium particles that look like fish eggs. During the last glacial period, when a considerable amount of the world's ocean water was locked up as ice, sea levels dropped and the fish-egg-like particles, deposited originally on the ocean floor, were exposed to the air. Over time, rain water seeped into the particles, flattened them together and glued them into the oolite that forms not only the Lower Keys but also the coastal ridge that parallels the Atlantic north from Miami. Where the Upper Keys are long, narrow islands that curve gracefully to the southwest, the lower, oolitic Keys are jagged, deeply indented land-forms turned at right angles to the long line of the Upper Keys. Where the Upper Keys were once covered with hardwood forests (a few stands remain untouched on Key Largo and Lignumvitae Key), the indigenous Lower Keys forests are pine, like the Caribbean slash pine forest surrounding the Jack C. Watson nature trail at the National Key Deer Wildlife Refuge on Big Pine Key.

History

Although the Florida Keys were among the earliest Eastern islands to be discovered by European explorers, they were among the last to support permanent white settlements. One hundred and seventy years ago not only were there no tourists, there were also few if any residents on the Keys. Even as recently as the 1930s, the Keys above Key West were largely empty islands, many of them devastated and a large portion of their small populations wiped out by the disastrous hurricane of 1935. The Keys' history is short, but very eventful.

When the Europeans first came upon these islands in the 16th century, they found the Tequesta Indians in possession. (Most popular works call them the Calusa or

Caloosa Indians, but in fact the two groups were distinct; according to *Man in the Everglades* by Charlton W. Tebeau, the Calusa occupied Florida's west coast and the less numerous Tequesta occupied the east coast and the Keys.)

The Spanish explorer Ponce de Leon discovered the Keys in the course of his 1513 expedition; he mapped the islands and named them *Los Martires*, the martyrs, because to him the land and twisted coral shores had the look of souls in torment. The word "key" is a corruption of the Spanish word "cayo" meaning little island; the Spanish called Key West Cayo Hueso, island of bones, for the piles of human bones they found there. Why the bones were there and which Indian tribe they belonged to remains a mystery, but the name stuck, although the English altered it to suit their tongue as well as the island's geographical location.

The Spanish took what they wanted from the Keys—mahogany and lignum vitae wood and in all likelihood Tequesta Indian slaves—but since the islands lacked gold to mine or good sources of fresh water and since they were plagued with "a most uncalled for number of mosquitoes" as the poet Wallace Stevens complained 400 years later, the Spanish made no settlements. Pirates also plagued the islands, using them as bases from which to prey on treasure ships sailing the Gulf Stream back to Europe. Black Caesar, who escaped from a shipwrecked slave ship and went on to plunder coastal shipping in the region, was perhaps the most notorious Keys pirate. According to one account, Black Caesar was plundering in the company of Edward Teach, otherwise known as Blackbeard, when that privateer met his end off Ocracoke on the Outer Banks (see Ocracoke entry).

It was piracy that first brought the United States Navy to the Keys, and it was the Navy's success in suppressing the pirates that led to the establishment of the city of Key West. In 1822, a Mobile businessman named John W. Simonton paid Spaniard Juan Pablo Salas $2,000 for the island of Key West, and not long afterward Commodore David Porter of the U.S. Navy sailed down to Key West with instructions to rid the Keys of piracy. Once he traded his clumsy deep-draft navy frigates for a "mosquito fleet" of shallow-draft schooners and flat-bottomed barges, Porter succeeded in chasing down the pirates to their lairs in the mangrove creeks. The end of piracy opened the way for families from South Carolina, Virginia and New England to move down to Key West; there was also a considerable influx of Tory families who had fled the American colonies for the Bahama Islands during the Revolution and who now wanted to return to the United States, albeit the nation's southernmost fringe. The descendants of these Bahamian families are the "Conchs" (pronounced "conks"), who are still so fiercely proud of their English lineage.

Wrecking and the Rise of Key West

Key West grew quickly in population and wealth. It was for some time in the 19th century the largest city in Florida and in the 1830s reputedly the wealthiest city per capita in the country (although there is no way of verifying this claim). The source of Key West's prosperity was wrecking, an endeavor that sounds remarkably like piracy but was actually perfectly respectable and legal. Wrecking worked like this: When a ship came to grief on the reef off the Keys, wreckers from Key West would intercept the ship, rescue any survivors and carry off as much cargo as they could. A system was worked out to determine what share of the salvaged goods would go to the wreckers, and Key West courts settled any disputes that arose from wrecking cases. Not only did the wreck masters and their crews profit from the system, but local merchants also made out handsomely by auctioning the cargoes that the wreckers brought back. Wrecking became so widespread that rules were written, wrecking licenses were issued and a blacklist of offenders published.

True, the wreckers did profit from the misfortunes of others, but they also risked their own lives to rescue the survivors of shipwrecks along with the shipwrecked goods. In any case, whether one views wrecking as plunder or mercy, it was wonderfully lucrative while it lasted, bringing in as much as $1,500,000 to Key West in years when seas were rough. In the decade from 1850 to 1860, approximately 500 ships—or nearly one ship per week—shipwrecked off the Keys. Key West was the wrecking capital of the south Florida seas.

One of the bridges of Henry R. Flagler's Overseas Railroad, completed to Key West in 1912. The railroad was torn up by the Labor Day hurricane of 1935 and never rebuilt; later in the 1930s, the Overseas Highway replaced it. (Courtesy of Monroe County Library.)

In the wrecking heyday of the 1830s, '40s and '50s, Key West was a place of great luxury and refinement, where homes were stocked and citizens outfitted with goods, clothes, furniture, plates, wines and silverware that would have sunk beneath the reef had the wreckers not carried them back to shore. "Everything that the commerce of the world afforded reached Key West as salvage," write Charles M. Brookfield and Oliver Griswold in *They All Called It Tropical,* an interesting collection of historical anecdotes about southern Florida. Many of the lovely Conch houses we admire today in Key West's old town were built during this period with wrecking wealth. Wrecking was not the kind of venture that could last long in an age of progress like the mid-19th century, and when the government erected a series of lighthouses along the reef in the late 1850s, the wrecking economy of Key West went into decline. (Though Key West was the wrecking center of the Keys, for a time Indian Key was the site of an important rival wrecking station. See the Indian Key entry below for the story of the island's brief prosperity under wrecker Jacob Housman.)

Wrecking got Key West started on a boom and bust cycle from which it has never really emerged. In the years since wrecking ended, several other industries have prospered and fizzled here. Key West rose to become the world's number one center of cigar manufacturing during the 1870s and '80s, and the industry provided many jobs for the city's large Cuban population until the early 1890s, when the major manufacturers moved to Tampa. Sponging was big business until the turn of the century. Green turtles were once caught off Key West, and even after they were fished out of the local waters, they were brought here for slaughter and canning—but the United States government banned the import of this endangered species in 1979. The completion of the Overseas Railroad in 1912 made the city an important trading link to Cuba, but the hurricane of 1935 destroyed the railroad and ruined not only trade but also the island's fledgling tourist industry. The '35 hurricane pretty much polished off what was left of Key West's economy. The city hit rock bottom during the Depression: It was $5 million in debt, had lost nearly all its sources of income, and had the poorest per capita population in the nation (about 80% were on welfare).

But Key West rose yet again. The military, which had pumped money and personnel into the city during the Spanish-American War and the First World War, was back for the Second World War, and again in the 1960s during the Cuban missile crisis. And of course since World War II tourism has become extremely big business here. Key West is once again a prosperous place: With tourism and the resort trade booming, real estate values are hitting their all-time highs. The city that went bankrupt during the Depression is now a gold mine for realtors, hotel owners and barkeepers.

LIGNUMVITAE KEY

Area: 280 acres.

Population: 1 (an official of the Florida Park Service).

Location: Florida Bay, .75 mile north of Indian Key Fill between Upper and Lower Matecumbe Keys.

Access: By state-run passenger boat the *Monroe* from Indian Key Fill every day except Tuesday and Wednesday. Contact Long Key State Park, 305-664-4815, for reservations.

Aerial view of Lignumvitae Key. (Courtesy of Lignumvitae Key State Botanical Site; photo: Patrick Wells.)

Lignumvitae Key is an island not only in space but in time as well. A short span of water—less than a mile—separates Lignumvitae from the Matecumbe Keys; but even more significant is the long span of years, of centuries, that separates the island from the other keys and connects it to prehistoric times. Lignumvitae is the only key that looks substantially the same today as it looked when the Spanish sailed across the Atlantic to the untouched New World in the 16th century. As Edward O. Wilson and Thomas Eisner put it in an article on the island that appeared in *Natural History* magazine (October 1968), "To enter the forest on Lignumvitae Key is to step far into the past and to come as close as we ever will to witnessing the Keys as they were before the coming of man." Here, protected first by good fortune and later by the timely intervention of conservationists, stands the last surviving, virgin tropical hardwood forest on the Keys.

From the Matecumbe Keys, Lignumvitae looks unremarkable—just another low-lying, bushy green island in a region where low, bushy green islands come in vast supply. But in fact, from the pancake-perspective of the Florida Keys, Lignumvitae is a veritable Alp, towering to 16.5 feet, which makes it the second highest point on the island chain (the highest is on nearby Windley Key). Even more significantly, the island does not rise to a single peak but is predominantly high ground. On a typical key of this size there might be five acres of high ground, with the rest mangrove swamp and sinkhole; but Lignumvitae is a kind of Keys mesa, with high ground covering 200 of its 280 acres. It is this extensive area of high ground that has allowed the hardwood forest to establish itself here.

Just as the island's profile looks unremarkable from across the water, so the island's forest with its tall spindly trees, dappled shade, uniform green canopy and dry brown forest floor seems unspectacular, even drab to the uninitiated. Lignumvitae Key has no soaring redwood grove or lushly exotic tropical rain forest. Even the strange, ancient trees that give the island its name are hard to spot, and when one does spot them they look merely stunted and wizened. The grandeur is not readily apparent, but it's here, hiding beneath the ungrand surfaces, lurking in the shadows. Luckily for the visitor to Lignumvitae, there are excellent park rangers from the Florida Park Service to reveal and explain the unique wonders of the island. The rangers lead tours along two miles of forest path, during which they point out the various plant and animal species, describe the island's ecology, and fill in the few details of its rather uneventful human history.

The state of Florida has been responsible for protecting and preserving the island since 1971, when it purchased Lignumvitae and nearby Shell Key from private owners. Visitors (up to a total of 50 a day) are welcome to tie up their private boats at the park service dock, or to come across on the park service ferry boat, the *Monroe*, which holds 24 passengers, but one may walk through the forest only on a ranger-led tour. Such restrictions have kept Lignumvitae very nearly pristine; and what the visitor loses in freedom of movement, he or she gains immeasurably in knowledge and information. After accompanying a ranger on one of these tours, one begins to appreciate just how wonderful and in its own way spectacular this precious bit of coral really is. In 1985, 5,489 people visited the island.

The Forest

Although the climate of the Florida Keys is considered tropical, the islands get too little rain and their soil is too shallow to support a true tropical rain forest. The forest on Lignumvitae, which is the climax forest of the Florida Keys, is technically known as a West Indian hardwood hammock. (A hammock is a relatively high and deep-soiled region capable of supporting forests.) Most of the plant species on the island are characteristic of dry coastal areas of the West Indies. The plants were "introduced" to the island naturally, their seeds traveling here on ocean currents, blown by winds or carried inside migrating birds.

Lignumvitae, like all the Upper Keys, is composed of an ancient fossilized coral reef that rose above sea level when glaciers locked up a considerable amount of the ocean's water. Once the coral was exposed to the air, it began to build up soil from decomposing seaweed, driftwood, and other organic matter. Eventually there was enough soil for the seeds of West Indian species to take root; over time the plants grew, shed leaves and flowers, and died, and more soil accumulated. The soil that accumulated on top of the coral was crucial for the growth of the hardwood forest, but just as crucial was the fresh water that seeped beneath the coral. Hardwood trees will not grow with their roots in saltwater, and on Lignumvitae the fresh water the trees need has gathered in what is known as a lens that rests on top of the heavier salt water that surrounds the island and penetrates its coral layers. The level of the fresh-water lens varies depending on rainfall, and it rises and falls daily with the tides, but the island of Lignumvitae is high enough above sea level always to hold sufficient fresh water to keep the forest alive. On a lower island, the salt water would push too close to the surface of the land to allow a forest to grow. So, again, it all comes back to elevation—that crucial two or three feet that makes all the difference in the zones of life on the Keys.

The island's 200 acres of hardwoods is considered a virgin forest because the trees (aside from some specimens of mahogany) have never been cut, burned or seriously damaged by hurricanes. But the forest trees do not have the majestic height or massive trunk diameter one usually associates with virgin forests. Two of the conditions necessary to grow giant trees—deep soil and reliably plentiful rainfall—are lacking here. The soil that covers the coral, though it has been accumulating for thousands of years, is nowhere more than a few inches deep; rains tend to come seasonally (late spring and summer is the Keys' rainy season) but erratically. In addition, many of the West Indian species here grow at the northern limit of their range and are further stunted by the chilly weather that does sometimes descend on the Keys. The result is a forest of thin-trunked hardwoods, often many years older than they look, that spread their shallow-growing roots out across the surface of the coral or that produce hard, knobby buttresses at ground level to support themselves. The deeper roots work their way into cracks in the coral and penetrate the fresh-water lens. The forest canopy seldom reaches higher than 65 feet here, compared with the 130 feet typical of the true tropical rain forest.

These delicate-looking hardwoods give the forest a light, lacy, fairy-tale aura. Lignumvitae looks not so much like the forest primeval as a retreat for elves and sprites. What the island trees lack in height and heft, they make up for in variety (some 44 species in all, one of the most diverse collections in any one location in North America), and oddness of name, appearance and properties.

Oddest of all is *Guaiacum sanctum*, the lignum vitae tree, which gives its name (latin for "wood of life") to the island. Just about everything relating to this tree is odd to the point of bizarreness. Its wood, the second heaviest produced by any tree (the heaviest wood of all comes from the ironwood tree, also found on the island), weighs 83 pounds per cubic foot. The wood is too heavy to float, and it is so dense with resins (which comprise one-fifth of its weight) that contact brings its oils to the surface. This dark, self-polishing, self-lubricating wood has been used on boats as marlinspikes, dead-eyes, pulleys, propeller shaft bearings (it even self-lubricates under water and has been known to outlast steel and bronze), and it continues to be used in the periscopes of nuclear submarines.

According to legend, the tree grew in the Garden of Eden and its wood was used to make the Holy Grail; Wilson and Eisner noted in their *Natural History* article that the tree's name originated in the fact that European doctors used its gum resin as a sort of cure-all, supposedly as early as 1508. Nearly miraculous in both legendary and technological application, the tree is also very beautiful. Each leaf is composed of six to eight delicate, pale green leaflets that look a bit like the foliage of the beach pea. The bark is gray and fissured; the flowers are small, dainty, true blue stars that appear at the start of the rainy season, anytime from early March to late June, and produce pointed yellow seedpods. Extremely slow growing and long-lived, the lignum vitae trees on this island have the gracefully gnarled appearance of bonsai. Because the trees here never grow very large (a 500-year-old tree will be no more than four feet across at the trunk), they were never cut. The island has the largest stand of lignum vitae trees in North America (possibly the world) and no doubt the most ancient. The oldest specimen on the island is believed to date back nearly 2,000 years.

The forest on Lignumvitae Key changes dramatically from dry to wet season. In the dry months, about half the trees shed their leaves, the forest floor is brown and crackling with the fallen leaves, the green of the living leaves is a bit blurred by dust and flowers are scarce. When the rains arrive in spring or early summer, the lignum vitae groves burst into delicate bloom, the pink Jamaica dogwood flowers open, inkwood trees produce intensely perfumed white flowers, and the tall, yellow-green-leaved mastic trees send out abundant flowers that litter the trails when they fall. In the rainy season, when all the trees leaf out, the forest is quite dark, but as the rains cease and the deciduous trees lose their leaves, the canopy opens up, the mosquitoes subside and light flickers on the dry forest floor.

Forest Animals

A number of unusual animal species inhabit the forest on Lignumvitae Key. The golden orb weaver is a giant spider that weaves webs as big as badminton nets between the trees; the females grow as big as the palm of a human hand and the thread they produce is the strongest natural fiber in the world, 30% stronger than nylon. Among the rodents are marsh rabbits, which look more like rats than rabbits, cotton mice and Key Largo wood rats, an endangered species, which was introduced here because this pristine island offers a perfectly protected habitat. A small herd of Virginia white-tail deer was introduced here for hunting purposes in 1956. There are 39 species of butterfly on the key; like the mosquitoes, they thrive here because this is the only key that is not sprayed with insecticide.

Perhaps the island's most distinguished animals are its Florida banded tree snails, *Liguus fasciatus*, distinguished because one variety of the species is found on Lignumvitae and nowhere else. Tree snails, "symbols of the primitive Keys environment" in the words of Wilson and Eisner, used to be common throughout the Keys, but unluckily their lovely shells were prized by greedy collectors who commonly set fire to the hammocks from which they gathered their specimens in order to increase their value by destroying the snails' habitat and thus limiting their numbers. Lignumvitae, which escaped this depredation, still has a rich tree population of *Liguus* tree snails, and there are five color forms found in the hardwood hammock (*L. fasciatus lignumvitae*, the variety unique to Lignumvitae, has bands of red and green on a white background). The snails are active only during the rainy season. During the dry months they climb trees, glue themselves to branches and remain there waiting for the rains to come and melt their glue, whereupon they fall to the ground and busy themselves eating lichens and fungus.

Man on the Island: From Prehistory to Preserve

The ancient forest of Lignumvitae Key and the lifeforms it harbors provide a rich, unbroken record of nature's past; the human evidence on the island is much fainter and more intermittent. When the Spanish came to the New World in the 16th century, the Keys were the territory of the Tequesta Indians (see Keys Introduction above), and a Tequesta burial mound has been identified on the south end of Lignumvitae. Radiocarbon dating of bones and charcoal have established that the mound is about 1,000 years old, far younger than the oldest lignum vitae trees on the island. According to some accounts, the Spanish occupied the island as early as the 1540s, and, using Tequesta Indians as slaves, they supposedly built a few houses and planted a grove of Seville oranges (many dismiss this early Spanish occupation as legend). The island has one strange relic that invites historical speculation: the mysterious 3,000-foot-long coral wall that runs through the center of the forest, takes a turn and abruptly stops. Wilson and Eisner state unequivocally that the wall dates from the 16th-century Spanish occupation and "was used to segregate cattle, horses, and the Indian slaves," but the rangers who lead the tours of the island insist that the mystery of the wall has never been solved. All we know for certain is that it was standing in 1873 when the island was originally surveyed. If you visit the island, the rangers will lead you past the wall, and you can take a good look at it and come to your own conclusions.

A succession of private owners bought and sold the island throughout the 19th and 20th centuries. William Bethel, a Conch, bought it for 75 cents an acre in 1881 and sold it in 1888 to Thomas A. Hine of Vineyard Haven, Martha's Vineyard, and his brother. Its most important owner was William John Matheson, a wealthy chemist and

The caretaker's house constructed by William Matheson on Lignumvitae Key. (Courtesy of Lignumvitae Key State Botanical Site; Photo: Jeanne Parks)

financier, who had the island from 1919 to 1953, during which time he built the two-story caretaker's house of coral and Dade County pine that still stands today, put in the trails that remain in use, cleared the five acres around the house and planted the ornamental trees, including oleander, sapodilla and Key lime that grace its lawn. Matheson also acquired the six cannons from Their Majesties' Ship *Winchester* that went aground on Carysfort Reef near Key Largo in 1695 and set them on his lawn. The cannons, which weigh 4,000 pounds each, make the little clearing around the house look like an armed camp, but in fact they are only garden ornaments. Another odd "ornament" in the clearing is the original gravestone of Jacob Housman, taken off Indian Key and reassembled here after vandals blew it apart looking for treasure.

Aside from putting in the house, clearing the land around it, cutting the paths, and bringing in some strange animals such as Galapagos tortoises, Angora goats and peafowl (all long gone) Matheson left the island alone and so, by a lucky stroke, did the owners who succeeded him (although one of them supposedly wanted to build a causeway hooking the island to the bridged Keys). The 1968 article by Wilson and Eisner in *Natural History*, which concludes "It would be an irreparable loss if the ecological system of Lignumvitae Key is allowed to go to ruin," brought the island to the attention of conservationists, and in March of 1971, the state of Florida purchased the island and nearby Shell Key for $1,950,000, with $200,000 contributed by the Nature Conservancy.

The "irreparable loss" was averted, and the last unspoiled key will remain just as it has been for thousands of years. In the air of Lignumvitae there lingers the pure, mysterious breath of nature, the spirit that always flees, like a wood nymph, before man's advance. For anyone who loves nature, this is the true paradise isle of the Florida Keys.

INDIAN KEY

Area: 11.5 acres.

Population: 0.

Location: The Straits of Florida, 0.5 mile south of Indian Key Fill between Upper and Lower Matecumbe Keys.

Access: By state-run passenger boat the *Monroe* from Indian Key Fill every day except Tuesday and Wednesday. (Call Long Key State Park 305-664-4815 for reservations.)

Indian Key is a tiny island with a very grand, almost operatic story. It is a story with all the classic elements—bloodshed and ambition, wealth and warfare, desire and death, pursuit and narrow escape—as well as some rather odd quirks unique to the island, including strange plants imported from Mexico and turtle kraals that figure critically in the story's climax. Indian Key flared into prominence for a brief time in the 19th century and was destroyed in the course of a night. Once destroyed, it never rose again. All that remains on the island today are the ruins and cisterns of the town that once occupied the island, the wild offspring of the plants that were cultivated here, the coral on which they grow—and the story. The story of Indian Key is a good story, and it sheds some light on the wrecking days (see Keys Introduction above), when fortunes were to be made off the Keys by salvaging the goods of ships that ran aground on the coral reef. The city of Key West rose from wrecking, and so, while it lasted, did Indian Key.

Indian Key's story is rather gruesome, and it has a fittingly gruesome prelude. Long before the Americans named the island Indian Key, the Spanish called it Matanzas, or place of slaughter. On Matanzas, the Tequesta Indians (see above) supposedly dispatched 400 French mariners who had shipwrecked in the vicinity. Whether this tale is truth or legend, it foreshadows the events that unfolded later on this same spot.

Jacob Housman and the Founding of an Island Empire

The main Indian Key story begins in 1831, when the island fell into the hands of one Jacob Housman, a wrecker, a mariner, and a would-be empire builder who chose this improbable bit of land as the site for his empire. Actually, Indian Key, minuscule as it is, is not as improbable a site for an empire as it appears. Geography explains why: The coral reef that runs the length of the Florida Keys approaches closest to the island chain at this particular link. At Key West the reef lies 10 miles offshore; at Key Largo seven miles; but the reef is only three miles south of Indian Key. In the days of sail, oceangoing ships would anchor out beyond the reef and send small rowboats in to the Keys for water and supplies before sailing north and east on the Gulf Stream. By picking up the Gulf Stream, Europe-bound ships could shorten their trips by as much as two weeks. Indian Key, being the closest to the reef and to the Gulf Stream, became the ideal stopping-off point for sailing vessels returning to Europe. By the end of the 18th century, as many as 300 ships a day were passing through the Straits of Florida. Whoever controlled the trading post on Indian Key stood to make a good deal of money by supplying ships, not to mention the money to be made by salvaging the ships that came to grief on the reef. The Indian Key store and the wrecking opportunities were the two cornerstones of Housman's empire.

How Housman happened on Indian Key is a story in itself. Unlike most of the early Keys settlers who were Bahamians or Southerners, Jacob Housman was a Yankee from a seagoing family based on Staten Island. In 1826, Housman decided he'd had enough of the life and opportunities that New York harbor offered, so he made off with his father's boat, the *William Henry,* and set sail to seek his fortune in the south. Housman got as far as Key West where, like many other mariners of the day, he wrecked the boat on the reef. Wreckers were already well-established on Key West, and Housman, after falling prey to them, went to work for them. The work suited him, and he was clearly intrigued by the considerable profits it promised, but Conch families had pretty much tied up the wrecking business in Key West and, although they let Housman work for them, they wouldn't let him succeed as a wreck master on his own. So Housman decided to look elsewhere for opportunity and that's how he lit upon Indian Key. The island already had a dry goods store and the bare bones of a hotel, but not much else to recommend it aside from its ideal location for trade and wrecking—and a complete absence of mosquitoes, ever the plague of Keys settlements (there are still no mosquitoes on Indian Key). Housman bought the store, moved to the island with his wife, and started to work putting Indian Key on the map as a wrecking station to rival Key West.

Housman prospered instantly on Indian Key. By trading not only with ocean-going ships but with neighboring Indians, he was clearing $20,000 to $30,000 a year from the store.

By the middle of the 1830s Indian Key was a busy, built-up and densely populated place, with 30 to 40 buildings and between 100 and 200 residents occupying its 11.5 acres. Housman even had soil shipped out to the island so that he could landscape the houses and the town square with tropical trees and flowers. But trouble loomed for the prosperous little paradise on Indian Key. The year 1835 marked the start of the Second Seminole War, the longest and costliest Indian war in U.S. history. Settlers fled from mainland Florida to the Keys, believing the islands to be safe, and in 1835 Indian Key was made the seat of Dade County because of its supposedly secure location. This seemed like good news for Housman and for the island, but it wasn't. With the outbreak of war, Housman lost all the Indian customers for his store, and once the island became the county seat, many residents, fearing Indian raids, moved on. Housman tried to quell these fears by paying for a private militia out of his own pocket and he fortified the island with breastworks and cannons mounted on mounds, also at considerable personal expense.

The Seminole War was bad enough for business, but in 1838 Housman suffered an even more severe setback when he salvaged a ship at anchor and auctioned off 300 bales of cotton that he had no right to touch. The case ended up in federal court in St. Augustine, Housman lost and he was fined and deprived of his wrecking license. With the profits from the store way down because of the war and with the lucrative wrecking business closed to him, Housman had very little left for him on Indian Key, and he put the island up for sale. Housman's island empire, having risen and fallen in less than a decade, was now largely worthless, and no one would buy it. But worse things were in store for Indian Key.

The Dreams and Death of Dr. Henry Perrine

The year 1838 was momentous for Indian Key not only for the decline of Housman's fortunes, but also for the arrival of the island's most distinguished resident, Dr. Henry Perrine, along with his wife and three children. Through pure ill luck, Perrine was to share in the misfortune of Indian Key, and to share with Housman the role of tragic hero. The two men, however, were heroes of a very different stamp, one brought down by overreaching, the other destroyed in large part by circumstance. Born and raised in Brooklyn, Perrine was a gifted and ambitious man, a physician, diplomat and botanist, who brought all of these skills to Indian Key during his brief residence on the island. Perrine arrived on the key by way of Campeche in Mexico's Yucatan where he served for a time as U.S. consul. In the course of this consulship, he developed a keen interest in useful tropical plants and he hit upon the idea of introducing the Mexican plant *agave sisalana*, commonly known as sisal or century plant, into commercial agriculture in the U.S. At the time, sisal was an important source of hemp used in rope production.

Perrine, drawing on his influence and political connections, obtained a grant of $175,000 from the federal government to pursue the sisal scheme, and the state of Florida agreed to give him a sizable tract of land on Cape Sable at the southwest tip of the Florida peninsula (now part of the Everglades National Park) for planting the crop. However, because of the war with the Seminoles, Cape Sable was not considered safe, so Perrine and his family chose to wait out the war on the safe haven of Indian Key. While he waited, Perrine experimented with growing potentially useful plant species, including tea, coffee, bananas and mangos here and at various nurseries on the mainland. All told, Perrine introduced 200 plant species to southern Florida while the Seminole War dragged on.

Indian Key, as it turned out, was not safe for Perrine or for anyone else. In the early morning hours of August 7, 1840, a party of over 100 Indian raiders paddled out to the island from the Matecumbes (or possibly from nearby Lignumvitae Key), set fire to the houses, looted the store and warehouse, and killed seven of the white inhabitants, including Henry Perrine. The Indian Key raid was not entirely unexpected: Housman knew that his store and warehouses made the island an attractive target and he had successfully petitioned the U.S. government to station a naval squadron on Tea Table Key, within clear sight of his island and less than a mile away. But in the event, the naval presence proved useless. Somehow the Indians learned when the squadron was going to be away, and they launched their raid accordingly.

The Indians, arriving en masse sometime after one o'clock in the morning, took the island by storm and by surprise. They moved quickly from house to house, seizing what they wanted in the way of powder, guns and supplies and setting fire to the rest. Housman's house was their first target,[*] but Housman and his wife managed to escape in their nightclothes out the back door and they ran barefoot to the shore where their boat was tied up. The family dogs pursued them barking, and Housman had to drown the animals to keep them quiet. Housman crossed in his boat to Tea Table Key, but found only three sailors there in sick bay. Meanwhile, the raid continued. When the Indians arrived at Perrine's house, the doctor, barricaded in his cupola, begged them in Spanish to stop the attack and promised in return to given medical treatment to their wounded. The Indians at first agreed and retreated from Perrine's shoreline dwelling, but they soon returned, possibly reinforced by the slaves of Charles Howe, the island postmaster who lived nearby. The attackers ascended to the cupola, killed Perrine and put his house to the torch.

Perrine's wife and three children managed to escape through the kind of amazing luck one would jeer at in a novel: Under the house, which extended out over the water, was an enclosed and hidden bathing cellar which filled and emptied with the tides, and connected to this was a turtle kraal, in which edible green turtles were penned alive until they were slaughtered. It was in this bathing cellar and turtle kraal that Ann Perrine and her children hid while Indians killed her husband, looted their house, and set it ablaze. The tide was coming in and soon the wooden boards over their heads were burning. While the two Perrine girls, Sarah and Hester, covered themselves with mud to keep from burning, the delicate and refined Ann Perrine dug out around the pilings with her bare hands. Henry Jr., a boy of nine years, squeezed through the openings his mother made, and, in one account, stole one of the Indians' boats and

---

[*] Some accounts claim that the Indians' special hatred for Housman stemmed from a proposal that he made to the U.S. government to kill or capture Indians for $200 a head. Though the government never took Housman up on the offer, it was read into the record and published in various newspapers. By this means it came to the attention of Chief Chekika of the Seminoles, who promptly decided that Housman must die and his island be destroyed.

picked up his mother and sisters just as smoke and fire forced them out of the bathing cellar. The mother and children, using their hands as oars, paddled away from the burning island and the boy stripped off his nightshirt and held it up to catch the wind in an effort to speed their escape. The U.S. Navy finally arrived on the scene at dawn, too late to save the island but in time to collect the survivors, including the Perrine family.

After the raid, the Perrines returned to Indian Key in the hopes that Henry Perrine might have somehow survived. They found his bones amid the ashes of their island home, and they buried them on Lower Matecumbe Key under a sisal tree that Dr. Perrine had planted. When Henry Jr. returned years later to claim his father's remains, he could not find the grave site, for the sisal tree had long since fallen and other sisals had grown up. The town of Perrine on the Florida mainland is named for the doctor, and his descendants lived on there until the 1930s.

The one house on Indian Key to survive the raid was that of the postmaster, Charles Howe. Howe was a Mason and the symbolic design on his Masonic apron no doubt reminded the Indians of their own religious imagery. They spared the place as holy ground, and after the raid, Howe lived in his lonely house for two more years, before abandoning the desolate island and moving on to Key West.

Key West also took back a defeated Jacob Housman, bereft of his empire, his wealth, and all he owned but his life. The Conch families that controlled wrecking on Key West were willing to let Housman resume his old trade—not as a wreck master but as one of the crew. Within six months he was dead, crushed between two boats when he slipped (or, some say, when he was pushed) while salvaging a shipwreck in heavy seas off Key West. Housman's wife refused to bury him on Key West, a city that had always shunned him, and she took the body back to Indian Key and buried it beneath a marble gravestone near the shore. But Housman was not to find peace even in the grave. The hurricane of 1935 lifted the stone and broke it; and some 15 years later, scavengers, lured to the island by rumors that Housman's treasure was buried here, possibly with him in the grave, exhumed the corpse, smashed his gravestone, and blasted chunks out of the island. No treasure was ever found, nor was Housman's corpse recovered. In 1952, the Historical Association of Southern Florida removed Housman's shattered monument from the island. A replica of the slab was set in place on Indian Key in 1976; the fragments of the original stone were brought over to nearby Lignumvitae and reassembled on the lawn in front of the Matheson house, where they can still be seen.

From Devastation to Preservation

In 1972, the state of Florida purchased the island from its private owners and turned it into a state historical site. Archaeologists excavated the ruins and, comparing what they found to records and maps from the 1830s, confirmed that this bit of coral was in fact the site of Housman's "empire." The state has since opened Indian Key to the public. Visitors may travel to the island on the Florida Park Service's 24-passenger ferry, the *Monroe*, or they may tie up their own private boats at the park service dock on the southwest side of the island. In 1985, 6,520 people visited the island. The Florida Park Service rangers conduct informative tours of the island, recounting the histories of Housman, Perrine and the Indian raid, pointing out the various trees that grow here, and describing the buildings that once stood over the piles of stone and brick. In addition, there are interpretive markers near some of the ruins and signs marking the routes of the streets that ran through the town. At the northeast end of the island there is an observation tower that affords a fine view out to the ocean and back toward the Matecumbes and tiny Tea Table Key where the Navy had been stationed back in the ill-fated year of 1840. The rangers ask that visitors not touch any of the ruins or move any of the artifacts, stone or glass fragments on the island and that they carry off all litter, including cigarette butts.

Despite the fact that the fragments uncovered on Indian Key are not much more than 150 years old, the island today is a bit reminiscent of some tiny, obscure, ancient Greek ruin on the shores of the Aegean. The bricks and stone that once housed a busy human population now crumble under the sun's heat. The old clay pipe stems and shards of pottery and glass strewn on the coral paths look as though they were last handled thousands of years ago. But the vivid narration of the park ranger guides sets the ruins squarely in their proper historical time frame. As one stands before the cisterns of the Tropical Hotel or before the bricks that mark the site of postmaster Charles Howe's house with its quarters for 30 to 40 slaves, the rangers reconstruct the life of the island in the 1830s: the activities of family life, commerce, the hotel, and of course the wrecking trade that filled these 11 acres with human noise and bustle. In the mind's eye we can imagine the town scene—the streets, the public buildings, the town square, the tropical gardens—and we can picture the flames that lit up the low Florida sky when the Indians set it all ablaze on that hot August night.

Indian Key was a bubble that had to burst sometime. If the Indians hadn't torched Housman's "empire," it would have collapsed of its own top-heaviness. If Dr. Perrine hadn't been killed, he would have moved off the key at the end of the Seminole War to the land he had been granted on Cape Sable. Housman would probably have gone bankrupt, the settlers would have moved away, the Dade County seat would have been transferred to a more convenient spot. The Tropical Hotel would have been sold, converted to a school or convent, been boarded up; the roofs of the warehouses would have collapsed; the sisals would eventually have spread over the streets and former gardens. And what the gradual wearing away of time and human events didn't take care of, the hurricane of 1935 would have finished off, for that terrible storm passed right over Indian Key, inundating the island and sweeping away many of the ruins. This was the future the island seemed destined for. But history had other intentions for Indian Key. Today, when we are far enough removed in time neither to mourn the victims of the Indian raid nor fear the same fate for ourselves, the explosion of the Indian Key bubble in a single fiery night makes a very good story.

KEY WEST

Area: 4,000 acres; 3.5 miles long by 1.5 miles wide.
Population: 28,584.
Location: The southernmost and westernmost bridged Florida Key, between Florida Bay (to the north) and the Straits of Florida (to the south).
Access: By U.S. Highway 1 from Stock Island over the Cow Key Channel Bridge.

KEY WEST

Southernmost and conch: It is difficult to spend any time in Key West without butting up against these two words. Southernmost house, southernmost motel, southernmost beach, southernmost city, Southernmost Point in the U.S.A. (90 miles to Cuba the sign states blandly). Conch chowder, Conch Train, Conch houses, Conch families, Conch Republic. Really more than words, southernmost and conch trail clouds of meaning that define a lot of what Key West is about (or would like its 1,125,000 yearly visitors to think it is about). The southernmost claim is undeniable, and though fairly insignificant in the case of a motel or a spit of asphalt and fence (which is all the fabled Southernmost Point amounts to), it does account in part for Key West's remarkable climate (the only frost-free U.S. city) and its strategic importance to the U.S. Navy and Coast Guard, importance that has waxed and waned over the years, waxing notably during the Civil War, the Spanish-American War, the Cuban Missile Crisis, the massive emigration of Cuban refugees in 1980, and the palmy days of drug-running in the 1970s, and waning in between these historic events (it's waning today).

As for conch, the word has been wrested away from those with the fairest claim to it and made to work overtime in the tourist business. Conch (pronounced *conk*, never *consh*) is first of all a marine animal, the gastropod *Strombus gigas* to be exact, which lives in large spiral shells that supposedly served as the Tritons' horn and may be used as a horn by ordinary mortals as

well. But on Key West and on the Keys in general, a Conch is a person, a native of the islands, and not just any native, but a descendant of the English families who came here from the Bahamas in the first half of the 19th century to be wreckers (see the Keys Introduction for a discussion of wreckers). Many of the Bahamian families were actually Tory refugees who had fled Georgia, the Carolinas, Virginia and New York during the Revolutionary War. Conchs tend to share a handful of family names—Curry, Pinder, Sawyer, Alberry (the spellings vary). They are fiercely proud of their heritage and can tell you without pausing to think how many generations their families go back on Key West. One Conch informed me that anyone who is not a Conch is considered and called a foreigner or a stranger, no matter how long

The Southernmost Point in the continental U.S.A.—one of Key West's major claims to fame. (Felice Nudelman)

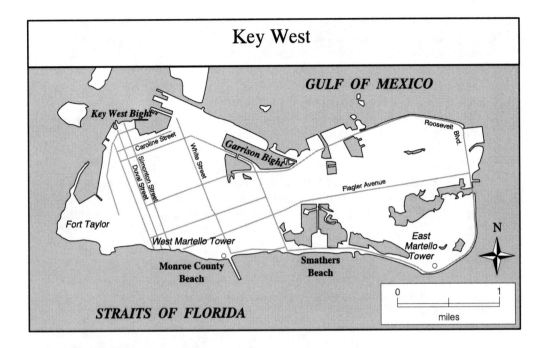

Key West

he or she has lived on the island, no matter if he or she has married into a Conch family, no matter what. You cannot become a Conch.

There are many versions of how the English Bahamians came to be called Conchs, including the fact that conch (the shellfish) was a staple of their diet (it tastes a bit like a large rubbery clam) and that they used conch shells back in the wrecking days to signal "Wreck ashore!" In any case, Conchs they became and Conchs they remain, the genuine Key West article, the old families, the locals from whom not only the name Conch but also the island itself is being dragged away on the tide of tourist development. There is definitely a Conch mystique, some of it self-created, some promoted by certain Key West writers who, though not Conchs themselves, fantasize about being Conchs through their anti-hero alter-egos. The most famous example is Henry Morgan, the hero of Hemingway's Key West novel, *To Have and Have Not*, who is a grim, tough-talking Conch fishing guide and rum-runner during the Depression, when Key West and Conchs had sunk to their low ebb. (Supposedly Morgan was based on Joe Russell of the original Sloppy Joe's, Hemingway's favorite bar; the character was played by Humphrey Bogart in the 1944 movie, which many feel is better than the book.) The heroes of Thomas McGuane's Key West novels *Ninety-Two in the Shade* and *Panama* are descendants of Henry Morgan; these latter-day Conchs have sunk to a different kind of low ebb—induced by drugs, existential angst and late-20th-century depravity. What they share with Hemingway's Conch hero is a penchant for violence, a love of the shallow, teeming, hard-to-navigate backcountry waters and a tendency to get mixed up with the wrong crowd. But Key West has always attracted wrong crowds. Key West—the Last Resort. Parties, brawls, desperation and death.

Conchs don't only exist in novels. There are still many Conch families living on the island. Some of them even live in Conch houses, those charming, gingerbread-bedecked, steep-roofed, double-porched, tightly made wooden creations of 19th-century ship carpenters that give Key West its characteristic cityscape, a style that might be described as tropical New England. But more and more these days, the Conchs are selling their homes to the highest bidder (and the bids are high, very high indeed), bidders that include the likes of Jerry Herman of Broadway musical fame and Calvin Klein of blue jeans and underwear fame. Once they've sold out, they're moving on to parts of Florida where houses are cheaper and the scene less glamorous. "Just about everything in Key West is booming…real estate prices, new boutiques, trendy restaurants," notes an article about the island in *The New York Times* (June 10, 1988). "But many longtime residents say success and big money are pushing out the little people who gave Key West its gritty cachet as a watering hole far out at sea." As the pace of tourist development grows even faster and the big money ever bigger, the Conchs and their way of life are getting squeezed ever tighter. The island, as islanders are saying all up and down the Eastern seaboard, is not what it used to be.

That's what they're saying today, but it's not the first time they've said it here, or on other Eastern islands. The poet Wallace Stevens, who came here from Hartford, Connecticut, for many winter holidays in the 1920s and '30s and whose supremely beautiful poem, "The Idea of Order at Key West," put the place for all eternity on the literary map, raved to his wife when he first set eyes on the island in 1922: "This is one of the choicest places I have ever been to …The place is a paradise—midsummer weather, the sky brilliantly clear and intensely blue, the sea blue and green beyond what you have ever seen." By 1935, Stevens had grown a little disillusioned with paradise: "Key West is no longer quite the delightful affectation it once was. Who wants to share green coconut ice cream with these strange monsters who snooze in

Key West in 1826 as drawn by Titian R. Peale. This is the earliest known representation of Key West, which was established as a white settlement four years earlier. (Courtesy of Monroe County Library.)

the porches of this once forlorn hotel" (the Casa Marina, which became even more forlorn after Stevens's time but was recently rescued, renovated and expanded by the Marriott chain). By 1940, his last year here, he sniffed, "Key West, unfortunately, is becoming rather literary and artistic."

Apparently, the "strange monsters" have been invading and desecrating paradise for a long time now. It's just possible that paradise was never quite what it seemed to be, that there has always been something a trifle bogus, a smack hollow about Key West, as if its notorious termites have long since eaten out the heart of the place and left only its gaudy, gorgeous, roaring, ever-changing shell. Setting the Conch families well off to one side, it is customary to speak of Key West with a certain conde-scension—oh that place of poseurs, of artistes, of authors. Unlike the pure, blue, chilly isles of Maine that inspire reverence in their blue-blooded devotees, or Nantucket, an island that conjures up the stern gray essence of Yankee history, Key West arouses familiar derision, even scorn, in its intimates. The Key West image is compounded of tourists, mosquitoes, fishermen, hippies, palm trees, drunken sailors, bikinis, tacky motels, aloe soaps, Key lime pie. Maybe scorn and ridicule are part of the way people love Key West. And lots of people—surely a very large percentage of those million and a quarter souls who migrate each year—really do love Key West. For all its phoniness and hollowness, Key West is very, very seductive, even for those who feel a spiritual kinship with Nantucket. It's not just the climate, though the climate (particularly in the dry season, which coincides with the northern winter) is divine. It's the tacky, tawdry spirit of the place. Key West is a bit like gossip—even if you disapprove, you can't resist it.

Sponges and conch shells for sale at the Southernmost Point. (Felice Nudelman)

An Island City

Key West does its best to live up to its image, even to live over and beyond it. Raffish, gritty, funky, exotic are the words that come to mind once you get past southernmost and conch. Urban comes to mind too after you have spent any time in Key West. Key West, unlike any place else on the Keys, is a real city with traffic and traffic lights and street life and long, straight, dusty streets and houses built close together and loads of shops and restaurants and that vibrant, sleazy, souped-up feel that seems to distinguish American cities from American towns. Key West has the reputation of being the kind of place where a sailor on shore leave can have a good old time, and that element remains deeply twisted into the fabric of civic life here.

There are bars aplenty that pump out loud rock 'n roll and buckets of giant margaritas. There are lazy back streets where little Cuban kids run around barefoot under the thatch palms and banyan trees. There are narrow little beaches where zonked out beach bums caught in an eternal return of 1969 panhandle for change and promise not to steal your camera when you come to snap the sun rising out of the silvery Atlantic. There are lovely, secret, riotous tropical gardens tucked away behind the gracious old Conch houses, many of them weathered past painting to the most delicate gray, and parrots in cages that heckle at you from verandas, and odd, shady little side-streets, no wider than driveways, like Peacon Lane, where the tour buses can't fit. There are the shrimp boats docked in the Key West Bight at the end of Grinell Street with their giant black nets, rough-looking fishermen and soft musical names. There is the nightly celebration of sunset, street performers and overpriced crafts at Old Mallory Square, where the island's tacky phoniness reaches its highest pitch.

The Key West Scene: Layers on Layers

The island city has all this—and much, much more, laid on top of the tropical funkiness, crusted over it and eating away at it. The Key West "scene" goes on simultaneously in many levels and sealed-off compartments, like movies at a multiplex movie theater. Tourist Key West is unavoidable for the visitor: the strip of big-chain motels lining the Gulf on North Roosevelt Boulevard and the old and new motels on Simonton and South Street near the little beach at the foot of Duval or, for the more extravagant, the elegant Pier House or the Reach or the restored Casa Marina; the Conch Tour Train and the Old Town Trolley that traverse the city in relentless competition, giving loads of tourists the major sights and the major facts all in one fell swoop; Duval Street, the main drag, which today is dominated by boutiques, galleries, and the loud raucous music that pours night and day out of places like Sloppy Joe's, Durty Harry's and the Bull and Whistle.

Then there is gay Key West. Tennessee Williams was supposedly the pioneer for this group, and since the 1940s when he first came to the island, lots of other homosexuals have followed him down. The gays in Key West are visible but not embattled: Though there are gay rooming houses and dance palaces, there is no gay street or gay ghetto. The gays are all over Key West and very much at home here. They own a good part of its real estate and have led the way in the restoration of the old homes that are the island city's pride and joy. Key West has been good to its gay population, and they have been good to it.

Then there is Cuban Key West. Cubans have been living on Key West as long as Conchs, and their population and influence really swelled during the cigar era (see Keys Introduction). In 1890, there were 12,000 cigar workers, most of them Cuban, making cigars in the factories that lined Truman, Whitehead, South and Simonton Streets. Parts of these streets remain strongly Cuban in their population and feel, and Spanish is spoken throughout the city. Key West today abounds in sleepy little Cuban markets, and Cuban cooking with its strong burnt coffee, pressed breads and black beans and rice is one of several influences on the complexly hybrid local cuisine.

Then there is military Key West. The Navy and the Coast Guard have a number of installations here and on Boca Chica, and between them they control most of the waterfront adjoining Old Town and a big chunk of Key West real estate. On the northwest side of Key West off Palm Avenue there is the Trumbo Point Navy Annex from which the Navy's lightning-fast hydrofoils come shooting out to perform fancy maneuvers for the tourists and intercept the occasional drug smuggler (the Coast

Guard has a detachment there too). Currently, the Navy has two squadrons stationed on Key West and Boca Chica, and the military employs a total of 3,490 people on the islands. It's in large part because of the Navy's land holdings that Key West seems so cut off from the water: You don't see the water from most of the city and aside from Old Mallory dock, you really have to hike to get to it. The Navy recently sold some 44 acres of its waterfront holdings in the Truman Annex to a Sikh convert named Pritam Singh, the former Paul LaBombard of Fitchburg, Massachusetts, who paid over $17 million for the land and plans to develop it into a $200-million "complex" of—what else?—condos, restaurants, a hotel, shops etc. The Truman Annex is also notable for containing the Little White House, the former naval commandant's quarters, where Harry Truman spend many happy winter vacations while president. Other U.S. presidents who visited Key West include Grover Cleveland, Ulysses S. Grant, Herbert Hoover, Calvin Coolidge, William Howard Taft, Franklin D. Roosevelt, Dwight D. Eisenhower and John F. Kennedy.

One thing Key West is *not* is a beach town: Yes, there are a number of beaches in and near the city. (There is one at Fort Taylor, see below; a pocket of sand and palms sometimes called the Southernmost Beach at the south end of Duval Street; Higgs Memorial Beach at the foot of White Street; and the George Smathers Beach stretched

out alongside South Roosevelt Boulevard west of the airport.) But they really don't hold a candle to the vast sandy expanses of the Atlantic barrier island beaches. However, though people rarely swim off Key West (except to snorkel or dive), fish do, and commercial and charter fishing are big business on the island, second only to tourism. The fishermen, both those in it for fun and for money, make up another facet of the Key West scene. The headquarters of fishing Key West is the Garrison Bight off Roosevelt Boulevard.

The Ernest Hemingway House on Whitehead Street. Hemingway lived here from 1931 to 1940. The house, built in 1851, is now open as a museum. (Felice Nudelman)

Key West as Literature

And let us not forget literary Key West. For a good part of the 20th century, Key West has cast its spell over a considerable number and amazing variety of American writers, from the most macho to the most refined. The island's most famous writer and the one most people associate with the place was Ernest Hemingway. Hemingway heard about the charms of the island city from John Dos Passos, who had hitchhiked here in the twenties, and he came down to see for himself and liked what he saw. In 1931 he bought one of the finest houses in town, an 1851 limestone mansion in an imposing hybrid Franco-Hispano-Colonial style (definitely *not* a Conch house) on Whitehead

Street. He installed himself, his second wife Pauline and their two sons here; sunk a lot of money into restoring the house and putting in Key West's first swimming pool; did a lot of fishing, drinking and writing (including the novels *The Green Hills of Africa*, *Death in the Afternoon*, and most of *For Whom the Bell Tolls*, the play *The Fifth Column* and the famous stories "The Snows of Kilimanjaro" and "The Short Happy Life of Francis Macomber"). Then, in 1940, he left Pauline and Key West to move to Cuba with Martha Gellhorn, whom he had first seen at the original Sloppy Joe's, his favorite Key West bar. *To Have and Have Not*, though not one of Hemingway's better novels, evokes the tough, gritty, bloody, dangerous nighttime spirit of the island.

Wallace Stevens was actually the Key West literary Columbus, discovering the place some years before Dos Passos and Hemingway did, but he was a "snow bird" winter vacationer, not a resident. The images of Key West that enter his poem are drawn from a different universe than the fishing boats and brawling bars that captured Hemingway's imagination. Though Stevens was anything but a descriptive poet, such poems as "Farewell to Florida" and "The Idea of Order at Key West" offer glimpses of how he saw and heard the island with its "oceanic nights...whisperings from the reefs" and "vivid blooms curled over the shadowless hut."

In 1936, Hemingway learned that Stevens had sneered at his work, so he did what any good Hemingway hero would do: He hunted down the poet and decked him. Stevens got up and returned fire with fire, but he broke his hand on Hemingway's jaw. All in the spirit of the place.

Tennessee Williams, the playwright of the tortured South, lived at 1431 Duncan Street from 1951 to 1983 and wrote *Night of the Iguana* and *The Rose Tattoo* here; though none of his plays is about Key West, the film version of *The Rose Tattoo* was shot here. Among the famous literary folk he entertained on the island were Gore Vidal and Truman Capote. Robert Frost was a fellow winter guest with Stevens. The poet Elizabeth Bishop lived from 1938 to 1942 in a house on White Street (number 264); today the garden is a patch of enchanting jungle on an otherwise fairly (at least for Key West) undistinguished street. Two of the prose pieces published in *Elizabeth Bishop: The Collected Prose* are set in Key West: "Gregorio Valdes" is about a Cuban painter whom she commissioned to paint her house and garden; and "Mercedes Hospital" is about a sad old Key West hospital, its eccentric nurse, Miss Mamie, and inmates. There are splashes of Key West color in many of the poems in her first collection, *Poems: North and South*, including "Jeronimo's House," "Florida," "Roosters" and "The Fish," and in "The Bight" from her second collection, *A Cold Spring*. Bishop spent some time with Hemingway and his wife, and apparently received better treatment than her fellow poet Stevens. Charles Olson rented a room in Bishop's house for a while.

Among the living Key West writers there are some who have left, including Thomas McGuane (who lived here long enough to set a couple of books in Key West and then moved on to Montana), Jim Harrison and Hunter Thompson; a few who live here year-round, including Phillip Caputo and Thomas Sanchez; and those who come down when it gets cold up north, among them Richard Wilbur, America's second poet laureate, James Merrill, John Hersey and Alison Lurie (parts of her recent book *The Truth About Lorin James* are set in Key West). Joy Williams, another Key West writer, has published an excellent guide, *The Florida Keys*, with lots of good Key West color, literary and otherwise. For those who care to stalk Key West's writers and their haunts, there is a book of photographs and brief biographies called *Key West Writers and Their Houses* by Lynn Mitsuko Kaufelt, with photos by Jeffrey Cardenas.

Key West is almost certainly the most written-about Eastern island, the island that has exhaled the heaviest haze of words. With all of these writerly sensibilities and their "rage to order words," in Stevens's phrase, buzzing over the place, Key West has been turned into literature.

Seeing the Sights

Key West history is every bit as odd and varied as its literature, and the rise and fall of the island's industries and institutions—from wrecking to sponging, from cigar making to military installations—has left its mark on the city and has provided visitors with a number of sights to see. (For a discussion of the history of Key West, see the Keys Introduction.) Some visitors come to Key West to drink pina coladas while gazing at the Gulf, to jump off boats in search of the wonders of the reef, to wear skimpy outfits and make the scene on Duval Street. But for those who come to see the city, there are a number of points of historic interest in Key West.

Fort Zachary Taylor: (entrance on Southard Street and the Truman Annex). Constructed over a 21-year period from 1845 to 1866, the fort stands on a built-up shoal to the west of the city, to which it is connected by a manmade causeway. Although Key West was sympathetic to the Confederacy, the Union held Fort Taylor for the duration of the Civil War. It was considerably remodeled during the Spanish-

The shrimping fleet at anchor off Key West. (Felice Nudelman)

American War. Excavations first undertaken in the 1960s have uncovered a treasure trove of Civil War cannons and ammunition. Fill from the dredging of the Key West channel and harbor in 1964 made the fort landlocked. A state historic site since 1976, the fort has a small museum tracing its military history and a nice (for Key West) beach fringes the surrounding 50-acre park. You can watch the sun set into the Gulf from here without the Duval Street circus to distract you.

Watlington House: (322 Duval Street). Built around 1829 by Francis Benjamin Watlington, a sea captain and wrecker born in St. Croix, the house is considered the oldest in Key West. The house was constructed of wood using mortise and tenon joinery with pegs fastening the timbers instead of nails, and the interior wall boards are laid on the horizontal, as they are in ships. This method of construction is typical of many of the early Bahamas-influenced Key West homes. In the large and lovely garden behind the house stands an outbuilding housing the kitchen and red brick oven, the last outdoor kitchen in Key West. Today the house is open to the public as the Wrecker's Museum, with displays and printed material on the history of wrecking. One-third of the house's furnishings are original.

Audubon House: (205 Whitehead). John James Audubon came to the Keys in 1832 in search of tropical birds, which he found in wonderful abundance. His search eventually took him to Key West, where he came across some interesting birds, including the species he called the Key West quail dove. Audubon's background artist used Key West as the background for the great white heron in Audubon's *Birds of America.* Although Audubon did not actually spend the night in this pretty white house

The Audubon House was built by wrecking Captain John Geiger in the 1830s. Audubon painted here during his visit to Key West in 1832. It was the first historic Conch house on the island to be restored and is now open as a museum. (Courtesy of Monroe County Library.)

that bears his name, he did supposedly paint here; in any case, it was one of the 81 houses standing in the city when he visited. The two-story house was built in the early 1830s by wrecker Captain John Geiger, noteworthy for introducing the Geiger tree (*Cordia sebestena*) from the West Indies. Geiger's house has been carefully restored as a museum and stocked with antiques and Audubon memorabilia. This was the first historic house to be restored on the island, and it set in motion the whole restoration process that has saved so many lovely old Key West dwellings.

Ernest Hemingway House: (907 Whitehead Street). For a description of the house, see above under "Key West as Literature." In addition to its literary associations, the house has some interesting objects, including a 15th-century Spanish bench, a Picasso sculpture of a cat in the master bedroom and a urinal from Sloppy Joe's that serves as a fountain for the forty-odd cats living in the garden, descendants of Hemingway's own extra-toed feline herd. Hemingway wrote amid his books and mounted animal heads in the upstairs studio of the carriage house in the garden.

Turtle Kraals: (North End of Margaret Street at Land's End Village). Green turtles, huge sea turtles prized for a bit of cartilage known as the calipee that is used to flavor soup, were penned and slaughtered here, until the U.S. government banned importation of the endangered species. The canning factory is now a restaurant called the Turtle Kraals.

Key West Houses

Perhaps the best attraction in Key West is not any of these official points of interest but the scores of old wooden Conch houses that line the streets of Key West's Old Town. Conch architecture is not a strictly defined category like Greek Revival or Beaux-Arts, but a melange of styles. As Sharon Wells writes in *Portraits: Wooden Houses of Key West*, her excellent book on Key West's Conch houses with beautiful photographs by Lawson Little, "Key West's treasury of handcrafted wooden houses comprises no simple, pure style. Rather, the collection forms an eclectic architecture that draws upon a legacy of Bahamian, New England, Creole and Victorian influences." In this mixture, we can identify certain characteristic Conch elements. The houses are

Vaulted brick archways as they appear at Fort Taylor today.

made of wood with wraparound verandas and balconies supported on slender pillars and set off by fancy hand-cut balustrades (Elizabeth Bishop described the effect as "wooden lace"); there is often scrollwork, gingerbread or some other decorative feature ornamenting the facade; the roofs are made of metal, steeply pitched and often gabled in order to maximize surface area (rain running off from the roof and collected in cisterns was the major source of Key West water for decades); windows and doors have wooden, louvered shutters to keep out the sun and let in the breezes; the houses do not have basements but sit up on piers. Some of the houses have cupolas similar to New England "widow's walks" from which wreckers scanned the reefs for ships in distress. Traditionally Conch houses were painted white with dark green trim or left to weather unpainted; light gray and Caribbean pastel colors have been applied more recently.

The pattern for Conch houses originated with the shipbuilders who immigrated to Key West from the Bahama Islands in the first half of the 19th century and adapted their shipbuilding skills and techniques to house construction. They clearly knew what they were doing. Conch houses look tall and cool, dignified but not stuffy, elegant but not severe. Even the largest and most imposing houses avoid the forbidding, aggressive posture of many American mansions. Conch houses have a gracefulness that northern Victorian houses lack; their stateliness is always leavened with a relaxed refinement, and sometimes a touch of eccentricity. They look just right in their tropical setting.

Two famous Key West houses were actually built in the Bahamas on Green Turtle Cay and then taken apart, shipped to

Delicately ornamented woodwork and two-tiered wrap-around verandas supported on slender pillars are typical of Key West's old Conch houses. The poet Elizabeth Bishop, who lived in Key West for a time, described the effect as "wooden lace." (Felice Nudelman)

Key West and reassembled here in 1847. The Bahama Houses, at 730 Eaton Street and 408 William Street, with their wide verandas, plain balustrades, and sharp clean lines show the Conch style at its purest and least adorned. Grander and more ornate Conch houses may be found along Caroline Street on the blocks between Whitehead and Duval and between Duval and Simonton; see in particular the George Carey House at 410 and the Richard Kemp House at 601 (now the Cypress House hotel). The George Patterson House at 522 Caroline shows Key West's interpretation of the Queen Anne style. (The grand Milton Curry House at 511 Caroline is not Conch at all but a copy of a Newport "cottage.") Eaton Street also has a treasure trove of Conch houses, notably the Artist House (now a guest house) at 534; the Frederick Filer House at 724; and the group of houses at 401, 405, 409 and at 511-517. Also, don't miss the John

Lowe Jr. House at 620 Southard, the Albury House at 730 Southard, the Eyebrow House at 1025 Fleming (so-called for the placement and shape of its attic windows), the gingerbread extravaganza of the Benjamin P. Baker House at 615 Elizabeth Street, and the well-maintained Gideon Lowe House (now a guest house) at 409 William Street.

The Old Island Restoration Foundation has organized a self-guided tour of distinguished Key West buildings known as the Pelican Path; you can get a copy of the Pelican Path pamphlet at the Foundation's Hospitality House on Mallory Square.

Key West is a small island and for all its tough, sexy, seedy bravado, it is also quite a small city. Small but dense and intense. It started with Conch wreckers less than 150 years ago, but in that comparatively short span of time much else has spread out over the coral, grown up between the cracks, blown or floated in from the sea, petered out or exploded, boomed and busted. Wrecking came and went. The turtling and sponging industries have left barely a trace behind. All that remains of the cigar industry is a strong Cuban culture and some old factory buildings. The Navy is not what it used to be on Key West—but as long as there is a military, there will be some sort of military presence on this southernmost outpost. The old families that put up the old Conch houses of Old Town may be moving on, but Old Town remains—a lure for newcomers, tourists, sybarites, connoisseurs and poseurs, a charming collection of carefully built fine wooden houses presiding over the daily "scene," the seasonal migrations, the changing light, the luxury trades that thrive along the side streets and main drags. It's all here, pent in by the shallow, ever-changing, reef-building tropical seas. At high noon, when the sun beats straight down, it can all seem a little glary and tired, flat and played out—irrelevant. But then evening comes again, the light softens, the flowers glow, the waters brim, and Key West turns its face to the west and sighs. All over the island, ice cubes are hardening for another brilliant sunset.

SELECTED BIBLIOGRAPHY

This is by no means a complete listing of books about the East Coast islands, but rather a selection of titles that provide more in-depth information on the islands and that will assist readers in planning island travels.

GENERAL

Amos, William H. and Amos, Stephen H., *The Audubon Society Nature Guides: Atlantic and Gulf Coasts* (New York: Alfred A. Knopf, 1985). Excellent introduction to the ecological zones of this region, their plants and animals. Exceptionally clear color photos make this useful for species identification.

Berrill, Michael and Deborah, *A Sierra Club Naturalist's Guide: The North Atlantic Coast, Cape Code to Newfoundland* (San Francisco: Sierra Club Books, 1981). A good introduction to geology, plant and animal life in the northeast coastal region. There is a chapter on the use of islands as breeding grounds for seabirds.

Farb, Peter, *Face of North America* (New York: Harper and Row, 1963). An introduction to the continent's geology for the layman.

Hoel, Michael L., *Land's Edge: A Natural History and Field Guide to Barrier Beaches from Maine to North Carolina* (Chester, Connecticut: Globe Pequot Press, 1986). A handy pocket guide for the amateur naturalist on the East Coast barrier islands.

Kaufman, Wallace and Pilkey, Orrin, *The Beaches Are Moving: The Drowning of America's Shoreline* (New York: Anchor/Doubleday, 1979). The seminal book on the contemporary plight of the barrier beaches and islands.

Leatherman, Stephen, *Barrier Island Handbook* (Amherst: NPS Cooperative Research Unit, the Environmental Institute, University of Massachusetts, 1979). A technical introduction to barrier island formation and ecology.

Leonard, Jonathan Norton, *Atlantic Beaches* (New York: Time-Life Books, 1972). Photos and concise essays on East Coast beaches; good sections on Fire Island and the Outer Banks.

Manley, Seon and Robert, *Islands: Their Lives, Legends and Lore* (Philadelphia: Chilton, 1970). Terrific island trivia and out of the way facts for island buffs.

Morison, Samuel Eliot, *The European Discovery of America: The Northern Voyages A.D. 500-1600* (New York: Oxford University Press, 1971). The classic history of the age of discovery, with information on the first exploration of a number of Eastern islands.

Morrison, H. Robert and Lee, Christine Eckstrom, *America's Atlantic Isles* (Washington D.C.: National Geographic Society, 1981). Excellent color photos and interviews with islanders on the major islands from Maine to Florida.

EASTERN ISLANDS

Ogburn, Charlton, Jr., *The Forging of Our Continent* (New York: American Heritage, 1968). A good introduction to the geology of North America, with a chapter on coastal formations and barrier islands.

Puterbaugh, Parke and Bisbort, Alan, *Life Is a Beach: A Vacationer's Guide to the East Coast* (New York: McGraw Hill, 1986). A humorous and useful guide to beaches, beach towns, beach resorts and National Seashores from Maine to Florida.

Redfern Ron, *The Making of a Continent* (New York: Times Books, 1983). Geology of North America, with a useful chapter on the Outer Banks.

Sullivan, Walter, *Landprints* (New York: Times Books, 1984). An excellent and clear introduction to the geology of the United States. With a very good chapter on barrier island formation and the formation of the Florida Keys.

Teal, John and Mildred, *Life and Death of the Salt Marsh* (Boston: Little, Brown, 1969). The classic account of the ecology and destruction of the precious East Coast salt marsh. Relevant to all East Coast barrier islands.

U.S. Department of the Interior, Bureau of Outdoor Recreation, *Islands of America* (Washington, D.C.: U.S. Government Printing Office, 1970). The first comprehensive inventory of the recreational, scenic, natural and historical features of America's islands. Includes brief discussion of island groups (by region) and listings by state of islands, with location, acreage and statistics on development.

MAINE

Caldwell, Bill, *Islands of Maine: Where America Really Began* (Portland, Maine: Guy Gannett, 1981). Popular history of Maine islands.

Conkling, Philip W., *Islands in Time: A Natural and Human History of the Islands of Maine* (Camden, Maine: Down East Books, 1981). The director of Maine's Island Institute documents the major features of Maine island geology, history and ecology. Sensitively written and full of unusual information.

Dibner, George, *Seacoast Maine* (Garden City, N.Y.: Doubleday, 1973). An attractive volume of photographs of coastal Maine, including some of the islands, with a short text on the people and places.

Eliot, Charles W., *John Gilley, Maine Farmer and Fisherman* (Boston: Beach Press, 1899). A charming and sympathetic account of the struggles of Gilley to live on Maine's Cranberry Isles from their first settlement to the advent of the summer folk, written by the president of Harvard.

Fardelmann, Charlotte, *Islands Down East: A Visitor's Guide* (Camden, Maine: Down East Books, 1984). Brief sketches of all the publicly accessible Maine islands, with information on lodging, meals, yacht moorings etc.

Jewett, Sarah Orne, *The Country of the Pointed Firs and Other Stories* (New York: Doubleday, 1956). An American classic about the people and the scenery of the Maine coast and islands; originally published in 1896.

BIBLIOGRAPHY

Kent, Rockwell, *It's Me, O Lord: The Autobiography of Rockwell Kent* (New York: Dodd, Mead, 1955). In his autobiography, the artist Rockwell Kent recounts his experiences on and impressions of Monhegan Island in the early years of the 20th century.

McLane, Charles B., *Islands of the Mid-Maine Coast: Blue Hill and Penobscot Bays* (Woolwich, Maine: Kennebec River Press, 1982). The focus is a genealogical history of the islands. Though McLane excludes all the major, publicly accessible islands, there is much useful information on them in his introductory history. Conveys a minute sense of the fabric of human life on the islands.

Pratt, Charles, *Here on the Island* (New York: Harper & Row, 1974). A beautifully written and superbly photographed account of present-day life on Isle au Haut, its people, their occupations, their history and future. One of the best evocations of the spirit and texture of daily life on the outer Maine islands.

Randall, Peter E., *All Creation and the Isles of Shoals* (Camden, Maine: Down East Books, 1980). A nice collection of photos and brief descriptions and histories of the islands.

Rich, Louise Dickinson, *The Coast of Maine* (New York: T.Y. Crowell, 1956). A popular history and appreciation of the Maine coast, with much information on the islands.

Rutledge, Lyman V., *The Isles of Shoals in Lore and Legend* (Barre, Massachusetts: Barre Publishers, 1965). A complete history of the Isles of Shoals with lots of good anecdotes about the early days, about the literary period under Celia Thaxter and about the start of the conference era.

Simpson, Dorothy, *The Maine Islands in Story and Legend* (Philadelphia: J.B. Lippincott, 1960). A good, popular history of the islands, with particular focus on colorful anecdotes.

Thaxter, Celia, *Among the Isles of Shoals* (Fort Lauderdale: Wake-Brook, 1873). A lovely prose evocation of the islands by the celebrated 19th-century poet. Thaxter's charming book about her garden on the Isles of Shoals, *An Island Garden*, with illustrations by her friend Childe Hassam, was reissued by Houghton Mifflin in 1988.

BOSTON HARBOR ISLANDS

Kales, Emily, *All About Boston Harbor Islands* (Boston: Herman, 1976). History and description of the islands.

Snow, Edward Rowe, *The Islands of Boston Harbor* (New York: Dodd, Mead, 1971). An update of Snow's 1935 book about the history and varied uses of the Boston islands.

NANTUCKET, MARTHA'S VINEYARD AND CUTTYHUNK

Allen, Everett S., *Martha's Vineyard, An Elegy* (Boston: Little, Brown, 1982). Movingly chronicles how the island has changed over the past half century, with focus on recent rampant development.

Benchley, Peter, "Life's Tempo on Nantucket," *National Geographic* (June 1970). An excellent (if a bit dated) introduction to the island today by a popular novelist.

Burroughs, Polly, *Guide to Nantucket* (Chester, Connecticut: Globe Pequot Press, 1986). Useful tourist information. The author also has a companion guide to Martha's Vineyard.

Byers, Edward, *The Nation of Nantucket: Society and Politics in an Early American Commercial Center 1660-1820* (Boston: Northeastern University Press, 1987). A fairly technical but nonetheless interesting discussion of Nantucket as a community epitomizing American liberal society.

Chamberlain, Barbara Blau, *These Fragile Outposts: A Geological Look at Cape Cod, Martha's Vineyard, and Nantucket* (New York: Doubleday, 1964). An excellent introduction to the formation of the islands and Cape and how nature continues to reshape the land.

Chamberlain, Samuel, *Nantucket: A Photographic Sketchbook* (New York: Hastings House, 1955). Elegant black and white photographs of the island town and country as they appeared 30 years ago.

Crevecoeur, Michel Guillaume St. Jean de, *Letters from an American Farmer* (Gloucester, Massachusetts: Peter Smith, 1968). The classic account of the customs, manners and institutions of various American communities in the infancy of the Republic, written in 1782 by a naturalized Frenchman and ardent lover of democracy. Contains several fascinating chapters on Nantucket, a brief section on Martha's Vineyard and a description of whaling.

Gambee, Robert, *Nantucket Island* (New York: Hastings House, 1978). Lovely, evocative black and white photos of the island, with brief but illuminating text on island history, architecture and life.

Green, Eugene and William Sachse, *Names of the Land* (Chester, Connecticut: Globe Pequot Press, 1983). A reference volume that explains the origins and meanings of a thousand place names on Cape Cod, Martha's Vineyard, Nantucket and the Elizabeth Islands.

Grossfeld, Stan, *Nantucket: The Other Season* (Chester, Connecticut: Globe Pequot Press, 1982). A photographer's collection of moody, textured black and white photos of Nantucket in the off-season, along with profiles and interviews with island residents and characters.

Hale, Anne, *Moraine to Marsh: A Field Guide to Martha's Vineyard* (Vineyard Haven, Massachusetts: Watership Gardens, 1988). A highly useful guide to the natural areas of the island. With a good introduction to the island's ecology.

BIBLIOGRAPHY

Hough, Henry Beetle, *Mostly on Martha's Vineyard* (New York: Harcourt, Brace, 1975). One of a number of books of appreciation, history, lore and reminiscence that the late editor of the *Vineyard Gazette* wrote about the island he knew and loved so well. Hough also wrote the text to *Martha's Vineyard*, a beautiful book of photographs of the island taken by Alfred Eisenstaedt (New York: Viking, 1970).

Lancaster, Clay, *The Architecture of Historic Nantucket* (New York: McGraw Hill, 1972). An excellent and thorough scholarly work describing in detail the historic houses in the town of Nantucket. Good discussion of the evolution of Nantucket's architectural styles and the town's history. Includes extensive bibliography and street-by-street listings of houses and buildings.

Lombard, Asa Cobb Paine, Jr., *Cuttyhunk: Bartholomew Gosnold's Contribution to Our Country and the Plymouth Colony* (New Bedford, Massachusetts: Reynolds-DeWalt Printing Co., 1976). A short local history of the island, with special attention to the failed Gosnold colony.

Macy, Obed, *History of Nantucket* (Boston: Hilliard Gray, 1835). The classic history of the island, written while its history was still being made.

McCalley, John W., *Nantucket Yesterday and Today* (New York: Dover, 1981). A wonderful collection of late-19th-century photos of the island set side by side with photos taken during the 1970s. A great visual history of how Nantucket has changed.

Melville, Herman, *Moby-Dick* (New York: Library of America, 1983). Melville's 1851 whaling epic contains a famous description of Nantucket Island as well as a great deal of lore and accurate information on the Nantucket whaling industry.

Plowden, David and Coffin, Patricia, *Nantucket* (New York: Viking, 1971). Brief, sensitively written text by Coffin and gorgeous color photos by Plowden capture the natural wonders of the island, the moors, wildflowers, beaches and birds.

Simon, Ann W., *No Island Is an Island: The Ordeal of Martha's Vineyard* (New York: Doubleday, 1973). An impassioned and now dated account of how development is transforming (and, in the author's opinion, spoiling) Martha's Vineyard.

Stackpole, Edouard A. and Summerfield, Melvin B., *Nantucket Doorways: Thresholds to the Past* (New York: Hastings House, 1974). A rambling, anecdotal walking tour of the town of Nantucket, full of stories about the long-gone occupants of the fine old homes. Illustrated with photographs of the doorways.

Stackpole, Edouard A. and Dreyer, Peter H. (photographer), *Nantucket in Color* (New York: Hastings House, 1973). Color photos of famous island sites with accompanying text by famous island historian, Stackpole.

Starbuck, Alexander, *History of Nantucket; County, Island, and Town* (Boston: C.E. Goodspeed, 1924). A huge and comprehensive local history by a descendent of one of the first families. Contains extensive genealogies of island residents.

Sterling, Dorothy, *The Outer Lands: A Natural History Guide to Cape Cod, Martha's Vineyard, Nantucket, Block Island and Long Island*, revised ed. (New York: W.W. Norton, 1978). A good introduction for the layman to the formation of these "outer lands" and to the plants and animals that now inhabit them. Illustrated with line drawings and color plates.

Stevens, William Oliver, *Nantucket, The Far-Away Island* (New York: Dodd, Mead, 1936). An old-fashioned, anecdotal and rather charming history of the island.

FIRE ISLAND

Johnson, Madeline C., *Fire Island 1650s-1980s* (Mountainside, N.J.: Shoreline Press, 1983). A complete history of the island.

Rabkin, Richard and Jacob, *Fire Island: The Wonders of a Barrier Beach* (Cleveland: World, 1971). A popularly written description of the zones of life on Fire Island, from ocean to salt marsh. Illustrated with colorful drawings, and suitable for older children.

SHELTER ISLAND

Duvall, Ralph G., *The History of Shelter Island: 1652-1932* (Shelter Island Heights, New York: 1952). The island's history from the Indians to 20th century, with a supplement taking the history up to 1952.

LIBERTY ISLAND AND ELLIS ISLAND

Benton, Barbara, *Ellis Island, A Pictorial History* (New York: Facts On File, 1985). A superb collection of old photographs of the island, the immigration station and the decay that ensued when the station was closed. With a brief history of the island.

Shapiro, Mary J., *How They Built the Statue of Liberty* (New York: Random House, 1985). A charmingly illustrated book for children on the building of the statue. Contains the best lists of facts and figures about Miss Liberty.

Shapiro, Mary J., *Gate to Liberty: The Story of the Statue of Liberty and Ellis Island* (New York: Vintage Books, 1986). A popular, copiously illustrated history of the statue and the immigration station.

Weisberger, Bernard A., *Statue of Liberty: The First Hundred Years* (New York: American Heritage, 1985). Full-color illustrated history of the statue, with emphasis on the artistic inspiration and the influence of the image on popular culture.

THE CHESAPEAKE

Warner, William W., *Beautiful Swimmers: Watermen, Crabs and the Chesapeake Bay* (Boston: Atlantic Monthly Press, 1976). A superbly written account of the bay and the watermen who have lived on it and worked on it for generations. With descriptions of crabbing, crab boats, traps, the life cycle of the crab etc. Contains an excellent chapter on Smith and Tangier Islands.

OUTER BANKS

Bedwell, Dorothy Byrum. *Portsmouth: Island With a Soul* (New Bern, N.C.: IES Publication, 1984). A summer resident recalls what life was like on Portsmouth before the community left the island.

Crosland, Patrick D., *The Outer Banks* (Arlington, Virginia: Interpretive Publications, 1982). A very nicely done introduction to the geology and ecology of the region, with color photos.

Olson, Sarah, *Historic Resource Study, Portsmouth Village, Cape Lookout National Seashore, North Carolina* (Washington, D.C.: United States Department of the Interior, National Park Service, 1982).

Stick, David, *The Outer Banks* (Chapel Hill: University of North Carolina Press, 1958). Though now dated, this is still the most complete history of the region. Contains a good discussion of the formation of the inlets.

SEA ISLANDS

Burn, Billie, *Stirrin' The Pots on Daufuskie* (Hilton Head, South Carolina: Impressions Printing Co., 1985). An amusing and eccentric collection of island recipes, lore and local history.

Conroy, Pat, *The Water Is Wide* (Boston: Houghton Mifflin, 1972). The bestselling novelist describes his actual experience as a teacher at the school on Daufuskie Island (disguised here as Yamacraw).

Kemble, Fanny, *Journal of a Residence on a Georgia Plantation* (New York: Alfred A. Knopf, 1961). This description of plantation life on the Georgia Sea Islands by the famous 19th-century English actress created a sensation in its day for its depictions of the brutality of slavery; first published 1863.

Jones-Jackson, Patricia, *When Roots Die: Endangered Traditions on the Sea Islands* (Athens: University of Georgia Press, 1987). An excellent discussion of the Gullah dialect and the culture of the people who speak it. Traces the parallels between the cultures of the Sea Islands and West Africa.

Price, Eugenia, *The Beloved Invader* (Philadelphia: J.B. Lippincott, 1965). An historical novel set on St. Simon's Island in the period after the Civil War. Price also set *New Moon Rising* (1969) on St. Simon's.

Rosengarten, Theodore, *Tombee: Portrait of a Cotton Planter* (New York: William Morrow, 1986). A good portrait of life on South Carolina's St. Helena Island before and immediately after the Civil War, including the history of Sea Island cotton and the rise and fall of the plantation system. Includes the journal of planter Thomas B. Chaplin, 1822-1890.

Vanstory, Burnette, *Georgia's Land of the Golden Isles* (Athens: University of Georgia Press, 1956: revised, 1981). A good history of the Georgia Sea Islands.

FLORIDA

Bishop, Elizabeth, *The Complete Poems* (New York: Farrar, Straus and Giroux, 1970). Several of the poems in the volume *North & South* draw on the poet's impressions of Key West. In addition, two of the pieces in Bishop's *The Collected Prose* (Farrar, Straus and Giroux, 1984) are set in Key West.

Brookfield, Charles M. and Griswold, Oliver, *They All Called It Tropical* (Miami: Historical Association of Souther Florida, 1985). Colorfully told historical adventures on the Everglades and Keys. Includes a chapter on the Indian Key massacre.

Federal Writers' Project of the Work Projects Administration for the State of Florida, *Florida: A Guide to the Southernmost State* (New York: Oxford University Press, 1939). Though dated, this remains an invaluable source of information for the interested traveler to Florida. Contains an excellent description of Key West.

Gantz, Charlotte Orr, *A Naturalist in Southern Florida* (Coral Gables: University of Miami Press, 1971). Keenly observed description of the beaches, roadsides and parks of southern Florida, including information on Key Biscayne and other Florida keys.

Hemingway, Ernest, *To Have and Have Not* (New York: Scribners, 1937). Hemingway's Key West novel has plenty of local color and tough-talking Conch characters.

Kaufelt, Lynn Mitsuko, *Key West Writers and Their Houses* (Sarasota, Florida: Pineapple Press, 1986). An attractive collection of photographs and brief biographies of some of the more prominent Key West writers and their island homes.

McGuane, Thomas, *Ninety-two in the Shade* (New York: Farrar, Straus and Giroux, 1973) and *Panama* (Farrar, Straus and Giroux, 1978). Both novels are set in the seedy fringes of modern-day Key West.

Merrill, James, *Late Settings* (New York: Atheneum, 1985). Contains a number of poems set in Key West, including "Clearing the Title."

Rinhart, Floyd and Marion, *Victorian Florida* (Atlanta: Peachtree, 1986). Wonderful period photographs and brief essays and descriptions of Florida in the late-19th century. With a chapter on Key West.

Stevens, Wallace, *The Collected Poems of Wallace Stevens* (New York: Alfred A. Knopf, 1972). A number of the poems in the volume *Ideas of Order* are set in the Florida Keys.

Tebeau, Charlton, W., *Man in the Everglades* (Coral Gables, Florida: University of Miami Press, 1968). A good, balanced history of the region, with some interesting information about the native peoples of the keys.

BIBLIOGRAPHY

Wells, Sharon and Lawson Little, *Portraits: Wooden Houses of Key West* (Key West: Historic Key West Preservation Board, 1982). A superb collection of photographs showing the range of styles of the island's historic homes, accompanied by a sensitive and learned text.

Williams, Joy, *The Florida Keys from Key Largo to Key West* (New York: Random House, 1987). A terrific tourist guide to the region, especially strong on Key West.

INDEX

Italic page references indicate maps.

INDEX